Tools and Techniques
for
Character Interpretation

D1256765

Tools and Techniques

for

Character Interpretation

❧

A HANDBOOK OF PSYCHOLOGY
FOR ACTORS, WRITERS, AND DIRECTORS

By Robert Blumenfeld

RARITAN VALLEY COMMUNITY COLLEGE
EVELYN S. FIELD LIBRARY

Limelight Editions

Copyright © 2006 by Robert Blumenfeld

All rights reserved. No part of this book may be reproduced in any form, without written permission, except by a newspaper or magazine reviewer who wishes to quote brief passages in connection with a review.

Published in 2006 by Limelight Editions (an imprint of Amadeus Press, LLC)
512 Newark Pompton Turnpike, Pompton Plains, New Jersey 07444, USA

Website: www.limelighteditions.com

Book design by Kristina Rolander

Printed in Canada

Library of Congress Cataloging-in-Publication Data available upon request.

ISBN 0-87910-326-4

This book is dedicated with love and gratitude to my maternal and paternal family: the Korns and the Blumenfelds, and especially to my father, Max David Blumenfeld (1911–1994), and my mother, Ruth Korn Blumenfeld.

Table of Contents

❧ PART TWO
INTERPRETING CHARACTERS:
THE PRACTICAL APPLICATIONS OF PSYCHOLOGY | 221

Foreword by Alice Spivak

*H*aving run through the gamut of plays from every century in teaching scene study these forty years and more, I have come up with some rules of thumb for character analysis. I often characterize plays written since Sophie Treadwell's *Machinal* as "post-Freudian" and all previous ones as "pre-Freudian." *Machinal* is an all but forgotten psychological drama based on a sensational real-life murder case Treadwell had covered as a journalist. It was produced on Broadway in 1928, with Clark Gable making his debut. Written in a repetitive, impressionistic style, "through the eyes" of its heroine (the murderess), this play greatly influenced the young Eugene O'Neill, who went on to write *Strange Interlude* using a "stream of consciousness" technique. Early O'Neill, Chekhov, Ibsen, Shaw, Wilde, Shakespeare, and Molière, I call pre-Freudian; Williams, Miller, Inge, Pinter, Mamet, et al., post-Freudian.

My reason for making this distinction is an important one for the actor to keep in mind while exploring the character's psyche: Freud brought about a universal awareness that is present in all post-Freudian plays, in sometimes obvious and sometimes subtle ways. Some modern playwrights, such as Arthur Miller, "spell out" their characters' problems, and some of the more poetic ones, Tennessee Williams most especially, cloak their characters, keeping them in the dark. But in all twentieth-century post-Freudian plays, the actor will discover in the subtext a good deal of intrigue and complexity, conscious and unconscious, which will eventually define his or her performance. No one can doubt the Freudian influence on the New Wave English writers, and Neil Simon's hilarious comedies all have characters with clearly recognizable psychological neuroses.

On the other hand, when exploring pre-Freudian plays, the actor must take care to hold on to a certain innocence about his or her character's motivations, for example with a playwright like Chekhov, who illuminated the human condition second only to Shakespeare. The trials and tribulations of Chekhovian characters derive from their total lack of ability to understand their own or others' motivations. It is very helpful to the actor to analyze what motivates them, but that analysis must recede into the unconscious in order for the actor to "become" the character who does not understand motivations!

A profound psychological understanding of human nature certainly can be found in plays as far back as the Greeks; yet any actress playing Antigone should not psychoanalyze her as someone with a martyr complex. Her reasons for choosing death have to be what she claims them to be or the play doesn't work. I once had a student playing Orlando in act 3, scene 2, of *As You Like It,* with the disguised Rosalind, and he was behaving very strangely. I asked him what his choices were, and he said that he naturally recognized that the "boy" he was with was really a girl, and so he felt his Orlando must know it too. Talk about the loss of innocence! Knowing but then forgetting is the actor's job in every event. However, in pre-Freudian plays of earlier times, it certainly helps actors to understand fully what psychological forces may be driving their characters, but in the end they must remain innocent of them in order to play the character. To do this, they learn to accept the text at face value, first and foremost, burying their sophisticated analyses during rehearsals. By all means analyze Hamlet's procrastination, but be sure at the same time to keep him in his Shakespearean state of self-woe and determination for revenge!

With this book, Robert Blumenfeld has done all the research into the modern science of psychology for us, which, combined with his personal experience as an actor and a coach in the theater, fills a void and goes a very long way in correcting the controversy and confusion regarding the use of Freud in both the acting classroom and play rehearsals. This book, written in a lively and readable style, helps us analyze what lies behind our own behavior and how it can be used as a source for the character in the play.

As an acting teacher and coach, I have acquired a particular aversion to the unfortunately all too common teaching approach that had its beginnings way back in the 1950s inside the Actors Studio. Grossly misinterpreting the original Stanislavsky tenets, the instructor in these types of classes uses pseudopsychoanalytic methods as a means of "opening up" acting students and "breaking down" their inhibitions. The students are often forced to "expose" themselves in front of the class in the form of "private moment" exercises and, in some cases, even appear nude! My own philosophy of teaching acting emphasizes instead a respect for my students' personal lives, treating them as "colleagues" and not as "patients."

There is no doubt that searching into one's past in order to understand how childhood events have molded one's adult behavior is a very useful step in analyzing a character in a play. Such self-analysis helps to provide substitutions, where necessary, to bring about the behavior and emotions required. However, these personal revelations should be kept private. They are not to be shared with the class as a whole. The danger in making public in class intimate details of the student's past life is twofold:

firstly, it could bring about a crisis in an especially sensitive person that the acting teacher would be ill-equipped to handle; and secondly, the Stanislavski approach actually demands secrecy!

Without secrets, the actor is never free to experiment. What caused his or her tears, for instance, has to be protected for the long run of the play, or else they will dry up—that is to say if the actor can remember what he or she used to begin with. By opening night, the substitution the actor made during rehearsals ought to have become so woven into the fabric of his or her role that the substitution itself is forgotten. There are some directors—fewer and fewer these days—who prefer an "open" approach during rehearsals and who discuss the characters, their relationships to one another, and even their motivations in front of the entire cast. But even in these cases, all personal, subjective decisions the actor makes to bring about his or her own experience should remain secret. My teacher and mentor, Uta Hagen, believed that any details of the student's private life that he or she would not reveal to a close personal friend should be censored in the class as well! This book will enable students to research their pasts to find parallels for use in character interpretation in private.

Common sense, instincts, impulses, memory, logic, recognizing one's own neuroses and/or peculiarities, sensitivity, empathy, sometimes even pity—all play a huge part in character analysis. In a pure interpretation of the Stanislavsky technique, the actor should begin the process of searching for the character in the play with an amorphous idea. By using "as if I were," the actor works to "become" a character that is not preconceived physically nor even influenced by the playwright's description, or else the performance is in danger of being just a stereotype—an intellectual idea rather than a fully realized human being. By making accessible the psychology behind behavior, Robert Blumenfeld's book inspires and aids the actor in the process of personalizing and building the character from the inside out.

Preface

❧

About This Book and
How to Use It

When I first talked with him about this book, Mel Zerman, founder and former publisher of Limelight Editions, remarked, "Theater and psychology are kissing cousins." And Dr. Gerald Perlman, a psychologist and psychotherapist whose avocation is acting and who suggested the subject of the book to me in the first place, wrote to me, "I too have thought they are kissing cousins. When I was applying to grad school after majoring in acting earlier, I would often be asked about the transitions. I had a stock answer, which was: I was going from the art of behavior to the science of behavior." This book goes in the opposite direction: it takes from the science of behavior tools and techniques that will be useful to the actor in practicing the art of behavior, to the writer in creating characters with depth, and to the director in interpreting scripts.

For the actor, these psychological tools are meant to be an addition to the actor's usual Stanislavskian kit. Many schools and approaches are surveyed in this handbook, from Freudian psychoanalysis to contemporary developments. The material presented here should prove valuable both to those who are unfamiliar with psychology and psychoanalysis and to those who are already knowledgeable.

In approaching a character interpretation as an actor or in writing characters or directing a play, you may want to take a particular school of thought and follow it through consistently: a Freudian, a Kleinian object-relations, or an existential approach using Ludwig Binswanger's questions, or perhaps a Jungian approach might be particularly interesting to you, for instance. Or you may want to be eclectic and combine approaches. For example, you might explore the application to a character of Freudian Oedipal theory and Bowlby's attachment theory together.

In part 1, you will find sections called "Questions and Considerations." These are meant to show you the practical application of the psychological principles and ideas elucidated earlier in the chapter. There are illustrative examples throughout of theatrical and cinematic characters, showing how psychological concepts and constructs apply in specific cases. Some plays—among them *Three Sisters, Uncle Vanya, Hamlet, Hedda Gabler,* and *Romeo and Juliet*—are referenced continually, so that you can view them and their characters from slightly different angles and see how different psychological points of view can be applied to them. The analyses of characters in part 2 will show you more about the practical application to both classic and contemporary plays of ideas drawn from various schools of psychology.

You will notice as you read about character types and various character classificational systems that character traits can be common to several types. It is the combination or constellation of traits that enables psychologists and psychiatrists to categorize or classify someone as belonging to a particular type, such as the ones listed and elucidated in the *Diagnostic and Statistical Manual of Mental Disorders,* Fourth Edition, Text Revision (*DSM-IV-TR*) (2000), a book that is very useful for actors, writers, and directors. It is important to note that within any classification, there are seemingly endless individual variations. And of course, in theatrical literature behavior is simplified, crystallized, and distilled, and inevitably less complex than it is in real life, enabling us to understand phenomena by isolating them so we can look at them.

A general rule, implied but not always directly presented in this book, is that the social context and the era in which a play is set are determinants of its characters' behavior, along with each character's individual development from childhood on. For instance, the kindly way in which Olga treats the old Nurse in Chekhov's *Three Sisters* as a member of the family, as opposed to the harsh, authoritarian way Natasha treats her, has to do with both individual and social psychology, and with class consciousness in the decades shortly before the Russian Revolution. The particular sensitivity of Olga, with her compassionate nature, is perhaps not at one with the era she lives in, and it heralds the birth of a new, egalitarian way of looking at the Russian world as she feels it ought to be. She sees the Nurse as a dignified, loving person, who has done everything expected of her and deserves respect in her old age. Natasha, on the other hand, is very much in tune with the general social attitudes of her time and place. She treats the old woman as if she is simply worthless and has outlived her usefulness. The Nurse, who has both dignity and a masochistic attitude of subservience, is aware of the low place she occupies in the social hierarchy, and she is hurt by Natasha's contemptuous, sadistic cruelty. In other words, the social relationships obtaining in the world that is the background to the play are reflected directly in the relationships of its characters, who are therefore responsible for the perpetuation of those attitudes. Through Olga society may begin to change, but it certainly will not through Natasha or through the Nurse, who has, in any case, already lived most of her life conforming to what was expected of her in accordance with her upbringing, just as William James points out most of us do.

Many actors like to keep notebooks about the characters they are playing. They write down their character's biography, including the history of childhood influences and the general historical and sociocultural background. Anna Freud's *developmental lines* and Winnicott's contributions to the analysis of child development, as well as the AAI (Adult Attachment Interview), should prove useful tools.

The substitution of anything from your own past that is relevant or analogous to your character's life is the most important technique when it comes to finding the character's behavior, as Lee Strasberg, Uta Hagen, Alice Spivak, and others have pointed out. You can make good use of Harry Stack Sullivan's psychiatric interview questions and the Core Conflictual Relationship Theme (CCRT), among other tools, for the purposes of exploring relationships and finding substitutions.

Every time you are called on to act a part, you have to learn acting all over again. You use the same methods, tools, and techniques, but you have to learn new circumstances and a whole new set of responses and reactions. You have to learn new behavior. I suppose psychotherapists have to learn therapy all over again every time they work with a new patient, even though the therapist will use the same methods of working with the patient and the same principles of interpretation. But every therapy is individual, just as every actor and every character is individual. New territory has to be explored each and every time. I hope you enjoy the exploration. And I hope you find this book both entertaining and useful.

Acknowledgments

I interviewed a great many people for this book, both actors and people in the field of psychology and psychoanalysis. I thank them all for their help and support.

I want to acknowledge first and foremost Gerald Perlman, Ph.D., psychologist and psychotherapist, a good friend, and—not least—a gifted actor, for suggesting that I write this book. His contribution has been invaluable, especially his vetting of parts of the manuscript and his many helpful suggestions. And I give very special thanks to Alice Spivak, with whom I studied acting many years ago. She not only wrote the foreword to this book but also had some very helpful and interesting things to say on the relationship between psychology and acting.

My greatest thanks go to my family, especially to my mother, Ruth Blumenfeld: quite an expert on films and film stars, she was able to make some very helpful suggestions for me regarding the material on films to be included in this book; to my wonderful, beloved father, Max Blumenfeld (1911–94), an admirable man who devoted much time to volunteer public service, despite his demanding job as a chemist and bacteriologist; and to my brothers Richard and Donald. I give heartfelt thanks and great appreciation to my dear cousin Marjorie Loewer, Ph.D., a professional psychologist who provided me with invaluable suggestions, and to my beloved uncle Seymour Korn for giving me many books from his late wife Dr. Shirley Korn's (1919–2004) library on psychology. She was an amazing psychologist, with whom I had a number of conversations about psychology long before I thought of writing this book, and I am deeply sorry to have lost her. Had she lived, she would have been of immense help to me on this project.

And I owe many thanks to Mel Zerman, founder and former publisher of Limelight Editions, for his always helpful advice. I give great thanks as well to my friends Ben Arthur, a writer and musician, for reading parts of the manuscript and giving me helpful criticism; Michael Mendiola, an excellent actor, for very fruitful conversations; the superb actor John Guerrasio for many helpful suggestions; and John Bloomfield, Jacob Knoll, James Hatch, Dan Truman, Peter Kingsley, and Albert S. Bennett, for their invaluable support and much useful information. Thanks also to Derek Tague for suggested reading; playwright Ian Strasvogel for excellent suggestions; Joel Markowitz, M.D., psychiatrist, for many fascinating conversations about psychology, Freud, and related issues; Paul Firestone, Ed.D., a lay Freudian psychoanalyst and wonderful playwright, for insightful discussions of Freud's ideas and for reading parts of the manuscript and giving me helpful feedback; Dr. Elfi Hendell, a professional psychotherapist and a delightful person, for helpful discussions, particularly about Heinz Kohut and his self-psychology; my dear friend Rob Bauer, a body-centered psychotherapist who practices the Rubenfeld Synergy Method, for informative, inspiring discussions; Marvin Lifschitz, Ph.D., a psychotherapist in private practice and a teacher of object-relations theory on the university level, for helpful information and for going over my chapter on Melanie Klein to make sure I got it right; the distinguished actor Morris Carnovsky (1897–1992), with whom I had many deep conversations about acting years ago at the American Shakespeare Festival in Stratford, Connecticut; my therapist, who worked with me for seven years; and that extraordinary actress and singer Kathleen Noone, who is also a psychologist and uses psychology in her work, and Catherine Wolf, a superb actress who uses psychology all the time in creating characters, with both of whom I have had very useful discussions. For allowing me to conduct revealing and insightful interviews with them, I express my heartfelt thanks to those superb actors and good friends who created roles in the original production of Moisés Kaufman's *Gross Indecency: The Three Trials of Oscar Wilde:* Bill Dawes, who played Lord Alfred Douglas; Michael Emerson, who created the part of Oscar Wilde to great critical acclaim (it was his performance that ensured our off-Broadway run); and Gregory Steinbruner, who played eighteen roles, each one a gem of characterization. I offer special thanks to Martin Moran, author and star of the moving one-person play *The Tricky Part,* for allowing me to interview him for this book.

Great thanks are due to John Cerullo, my publisher, for having faith in me and in this book. And I thank my wonderful editor, Carol Flannery, and my copyeditor, Joanna Dalin, who helped me enormously and clarified a great deal for me, enabling me to rewrite so as to make every thought and concept as clear as I could. I am very pleased to express my thanks and gratitude to the graphic designer of this book, Kristina Rolander, who has done such a beautiful job.

And, lastly, I owe an incalculable debt of gratitude to the authors of all the books listed in the bibliography. Any errors or faults are mine alone, of course.

PART ONE

§

ACTING AND PSYCHOLOGY: CHARACTER ANALYSIS FROM FREUD ONWARD

Introduction

§

The Actor's Art and Psychology: Theoretical and Practical Considerations

*T*his book rests on a fundamental premise that is common to both the science of psychology and the art of acting: it is possible to understand why people do what they do. Psychology studies the specific circumstances that lead to behavior. Acting is the art of behaving as if one were involved in a specific set of circumstances.

In *Hamlet and Oedipus* (1949), his classic psychoanalytic study of Shakespeare's masterpiece, the Welsh pioneer psychoanalyst Ernest Jones (1879–1958), close friend and biographer of Sigmund Freud, wrote of theatrical characters that "we are asked to believe that they are living persons," even though we are well aware that they are creations of the dramatist's mind. Jones was severely taken to task in some quarters for having written of Hamlet and the other characters in the play as if they were indeed real people. Yet how else can we discuss them? And if they did not give us insight into actual people, if they did not, as Hamlet says to the Players, "hold, as 'twere, the mirror up to nature," why would we want to?

The actor has to analyze the internal circumstances of a character's life. A psychologist has to analyze a patient's internal life. But of course, deductions about theatrical characters are all based on a concrete, given set of circumstances in a script where everything is laid out by the author who is telling a story. A patient in psychotherapy also has a given set of internal circumstances that are part of his or her story, but they are not so easy for the psychologist to discover, nor so concrete. And the patient may wish unconsciously to resist telling that story. But as with a play that an actor is beginning to study, the clues are there and the story will gradually be revealed.

Life is fluid. A play is a story about life frozen in place, and its life only moves within its own sphere. A play's outcome will never change, even with different interpretations by different artists who bring it to life by directing or acting it. Laertes will always kill Hamlet, and Vershinin will always leave with his regiment. Vanya and Sonya will always end the play by starting to work on the estate accounts after the Professor and Yelena have departed. And they will always depart.

Does this mean that the psychological makeup of the characters will never change? Yes and no. It will always remain as written, of course. But every actor will understand what is written in a different way, because every actor will bring an individual personality, psychological structure, and background to the interpretation of the character. The character's psychology will therefore be similar but different every time.

The most important actor's tool in bringing a character to life is imagination. But what is the imagination? For Jacques Lacan (1901–81), the enormously influential neo-Freudian psychoanalyst, the imagination is the reflection of an imagined reality similar to the reflection in a mirror, which is an image of reality. For Lacan seeing your reflection in a mirror is a turning point in self-perception.

It is startling to see yourself in a mirror for the first time; perhaps every time. What is reflected back to the viewer? An image of the self, the "I am." What does the image mean? How do we process and interpret the image? When we see ourselves reflected back to ourselves in a mirror, we see the reflection. We do not see ourselves. The reflection in the mirror shows us the otherness of ourselves for others, their otherness for us, and our own otherness for our very selves.

The world for all of us is the world of the imagination, Lacan thought. Everything in it exists in the imagination and in an imagined way. We imagine what the world is and what it is like. We imagine our place in it. And most importantly, we imagine ourselves into being. If all of this seems reminiscent of what actors do when interpreting a script, which is the reflection of an imagined reality, it is. This is exactly what actors do.

In the imagination, everything is obtainable through the power of thought. We can close our eyes and imagine that we are going to get everything we want, that our fantasies are going to be fulfilled. As long as we know we are in the realm of the imaginary, this exercise in fantasy can be fun.

But it is a huge mistake of monumental proportions to take the imaginary for the real! Are the gigantic, imposing gilded statues of horses on the Pont Alexandre III real horses? They are statues, not living flesh and blood. They are not even dead flesh and blood. They are externalizations of imaginative acts. They are imitations. They are representations. They are reflections.

Psychoanalytic schools tend to take the imaginary for the real. That is what Lacan thought. In doing so, they ignore the fact that the person in analysis is in the process of presenting to the analyst an imaginary self in which he or she is totally invested and embedded, and which he or she believes totally is his or her real self.

We are unaware that we have constructed this imaginary self. This imaginary self needs to be exploded if the analysis is to show the patient that another creative, fulfilling self can be constructed. A person is a social construction, Lacan thought.

Relations are social constructions. We act in ways others expect and want us to act, and we imagine we want to act and behave in those ways. In imagining thus, we do indeed want to act and behave in those ways. Because we think we live in the world of reality, in the world as it really is, we don't truly own those ways of behaving and acting. We might not get rid of them if we were aware that we imagined them and thus brought them into being, but we would own them, and that might enable us to keep them or discard them. We might find that happiness and inner peace consisted of things other than we thought. We might be able to reconstruct our imagination. This is, perhaps, the purpose of a Lacanian analysis: to make the person own who he or she is, because in the understanding of who we are in our imaginations lies the ability to change, to solve our problems.

Psychoanalysis and many but not all schools of contemporary psychology assume the truth of certain basic metapsychological tenets. One of them is that most mental processes and operations take place unconsciously, including most compromises effected among conflicting feelings. What is the unconscious? How do we know it? Something from the unconscious is presented to us as a discovery, but it was there all the time. This discovery, which is thus really a rediscovery, is a solution to a problem, perhaps complete, perhaps not. It is a surprise. It has closed a gap, but it can become unconscious again in a twinkling, in an instant. The unconscious exists as a gap. It is discontinuous. We imagine something. It disappears. We stop imagining it. We imagine it again.

Language constitutes the content of the unconscious. Language, into which one is born and which predates the consciousness of meaningful speech, is the eventual determining factor in how the mind perceives itself and the world. In *The Four Fundamental Concepts of Psycho-analysis* (1981), Lacan wrote his most famous phrase: "*the unconscious is structured like a language*" — an idea derived from Freud's views on language, including his underlying idea that language has healing power.

We can only talk to ourselves in language. So the nature of our language and our knowledge of our language determine the way in which we inform our unconscious and the way in which we give it form. And language can be vague and imprecise. Language is ambiguous, full of connotations, and susceptible of many meanings and interpretations.

What we *tell* ourselves is what we *imagine:* they are one and the same thing. Hamlet imagines he is Prince of Denmark. He imagines that life is the way he imagines it, and he tells himself and us, the audience, things about life. Richard the Third imagines he is King of England and that everyone is as interested in power as he is. Desdemona imagines that Othello loves her, and he imagines that she does not love him. Kulygin imagines that he is Masha's husband, and she imagines that she is not his wife. Torvald imagines that he is Nora's husband, and she imagines that she is not his wife. Hedda Gabler imagines the world is against her and that she doesn't fit in anywhere, and the world imagines it is indifferent to the fate of Hedda Gabler. Romeo and Juliet imagine they are the great loves of each other's lives. Tartuffe imagines he is a hypocrite and that nobody else perceives him as a hypocrite. Orgon imagines that Tartuffe is a wonderful man and that he, Orgon, is a great sinner. Vanya imagines that the Professor is a dishonest, unworthy person. The Professor imagines that he is a shining intellectual light, that he behaves ethically, and that nobody appreciates him. Madame Ranevskaya imagines she owns the cherry orchard. Lopahin imagines he has purchased the cherry orchard. Arkadina imagines she is a great actress. Nina imagines she is nothing. Everything they imagine is true—for them.

In contemporary American acting theory and practice, the most important technique of the imagination used in bringing a character to life is affective memory, which is a kind of reimagining. *Affective memory* means the visceral memory of emotions and feelings (emotional memory) and the memory of physical sensations—hot, cold, drunk, sick, tired, attracted to something or someone, and so forth (sense memory). Emotional and sense memories can overlap. The actor applies what seems analogous in the self to the psychological makeup of a character, thereby amalgamating reality with fiction. This process of "substitution" or, as Uta Hagen called it in *A Challenge for the Actor* (1991), *transference* is partly unconscious and intuitive. There are no necessary scientific laws for it aside from those of psychology itself. Each actor will find something new that no other actor has found or could find before and will infuse the character with new life. That is why we can enjoy watching Hamlet or Ophelia interpreted by so many different actors, and why we can discuss their interpretations.

Morris Carnovsky points out in *The Actor's Eye* (1984) that all you really have is yourself, so you have to use yourself. But as one of the "impersonating representatives" (as Jones called actors), you have to behave as if you were somebody else, whom you can't possibly be. It is always really you up there, whether you like it or not, behaving "as if" *you* are the character written by the playwright.

And we can be as involved with characters that are authors' and actors' creations as if they were indeed real people. When I watched the haunting 2003 French television miniseries *Les Thibault,* based on Roger Martin du Gard's novels about a French family and its psychic conflicts from the end of the nineteenth through the middle of the twentieth century, I was as upset and moved by the tragic fate of the characters so realistically and convincingly portrayed by the actors as if I had been watching a true story (the story itself does have a basis in historical reality). I had grown to love them, with all their faults and foibles! I felt as if my heart had been torn out of me, and for several minutes afterwards, I could not move. And yet I had been watching fiction.

Sigmund Freud felt that writers and artists had always understood the human psyche and the unconscious workings of the mind, which psychoanalysis was able to illuminate and clarify. The theater is the arena where psychic conflict is made manifest to the spectators, through the stories written by playwrights and brought to life by actors. The spectator understands unconsciously the nature of the characters' hidden motives and takes conscious pleasure in watching the story unfold, identifying in some way with the characters in it.

One of the actor's tasks is to analyze the system of repression that is present in every theatrical character. Threatening feelings, ideas, or thoughts have been eliminated from consciousness by means of certain mental mechanisms and forgotten. But they are still there somewhere in the unconscious part of the mind, stored in the memory banks, like prisoners behind bars. They may never be released, but they make their existence known in some way. Under the right circumstances, they might even be freed. The repressions tend to disappear when faced with an emotional investment in a relationship from which the character hopes for fulfillment, arousing a sympathetic identification on the part of the audience. Think of how much we identify with the love of Romeo and Juliet.

The presentation of psychic suffering in the theater or the cinema must be managed by writers, directors, and actors with a certain distance between the character and the spectator, or the suffering is too intense — too gruesome and too painful — preventing identification, except on the part of the minority who are truly sadistic or psychotic. A certain detachment must be possible in order for most spectators to look at the play objectively, so as to be able to identify with it unconsciously and enjoy it by suffering along with the characters, in a manifestation of the audience's unconscious masochism. By the end of the characters' and the audience's journey, a purging or catharsis is experienced and thus a sense of relief from emotional tension, whether the result is tears or laughter. Freud informs us in his essay "Psychopathic Characters on the Stage" (1906) that the catharsis serves to console and calm the suffering, not only of the theatrical character who experiences it, but also of the spectators, who double the character's emotions with their own responses. The theater thus has a therapeutic aspect, without actually being therapeutic in any full sense, since no permanent solution to the audience's suffering is provided. Freud is not only Freudian but also very Aristotelian in his aesthetics! This is not too surprising, given his classical education and his knowledge of the Greek and Latin languages and literature.

Among other things, psychoanalysis deals with general characterological issues. The psychological categorizations that we call character or personality types, derived from observation and data, are ideal models. Some people may have several character traits not associated with a particular type into which they might otherwise fit neatly. Freud knew this, of course, and in describing neurotic patients with disparate traits that had different sources, he said that they had a *mixed neurosis*. Nothing in psychology is that cut and dried, as Freud so often acknowledged when making prefatory remarks to some of his brilliant speculations.

Individuals have to be studied on the basis of their uniqueness. After all, as the often misinterpreted philosopher Friedrich Nietzsche (1844–1900), whose ideas intrigued Freud, wrote in "Schopenhauer as Teacher" in *Untimely Meditations* (1874): "At bottom, every man knows perfectly well that he is a unique being, only once on this earth; and by no extraordinary chance will such a marvelously picturesque piece of diversity in unity as he is, ever be put together a second time." One must add "every woman" as well, of course. Still, general character types can be very useful for the art of interpretation, with individual variations necessarily taken into account. They can suggest all kinds of things. At the very least, the actor's imagination will be aroused and expanded by studying them.

Before they can even begin to understand a character, actors must understand themselves as well as the psychological rules underlying behavior as much as possible. Talent consists partly of being able to contact, be in touch with, explore, and mobilize the different aspects of one's own personality in approaching the interpretation of literary characters who are, perforce, crystallizations and distillations of behavior, and consequently easier to analyze and understand than most real, living, complicated people. This is true whether you are dealing with a realistic, abstract, or absurdist piece; a play by William Shakespeare, Anton Chekhov, Eugene O'Neill, Ionesco, that master of psychology Terence Rattigan, Noel Coward, Arthur Miller, or Samuel Beckett. Constantin Stanislavsky's Method(s) and its derivatives and variations—such as the teachings of Sanford Meisner, Uta Hagen, Alice Spivak, Morris Carnovsky, or Michael Chekhov—are all based in psychology, especially in the area of substitution and the endowment of internal and external objects with specific properties.

Michael Chekhov's "psychological gesture" is a notable, extremely useful idea: the actor finds a gesture that seems representative of the character's emotional life and uses that gesture as a way to awaken the character sleeping within the actor's self. For instance, Uncle Vanya might try to hug himself and curl up into a fetal position. Juliet might try jumping up and looking at the stars, spreading her arms wide as she does so. Nora might look at the ground and turn away. Lady Macbeth might shake her fists and make a punching gesture. Hamlet might cover his eyes with his hand as he throws his head to one side. Feelings will inevitably be aroused, and the actor can begin to rehearse a scene within a circle of concentration and in the mood and atmosphere thus created.

All the methods of the teachers listed above offer ways to approach the psychology of characters through actual behavior, which is supposed to be reproduced and represented, not merely presented as an imitation, and certainly never illustrated or "indicated"—a dirty word in the actor's vocabulary. The actor is supposed to live through the character's life moment by moment, without anticipation and as if for the first time. Even at the 500th performance, the moment exists as if for the first time in all its own immediacy and as a result of the past that led up to it.

It is, of course, possible to imitate, indicate, and illustrate behavior without feeling emotion, at least deeply, and to make an outward show, which might even be convincing to an audience. In other words, the inner aspects of the behavior are missing. There are actors who prefer this so-called technical approach. For instance, if you are playing a shy person at a moment of embarrassment—Nora in Ibsen's *Doll's House,* Tusenbach in Chekhov's *Three Sisters,* or the young Nina in *The Seagull*—you might reproduce the sorts of physical manifestations of shyness listed in sociologist Erving Goffman's book *Interaction Ritual* (1967) in the essay "Embarrassment and Social Organization." Among these are some that amount to theatrical clichés, such as those quoted by Goffman from Mark Baldwin: "a lowering of the eyes . . . nervous fingering of the clothing or twisting of the fingers together." Goffman himself talks of subjective feelings giving rise to "dryness of the mouth, and tenseness of the muscles." But if you reproduce such behavior on a purely physical level, then you have not done the work on the character's inner life that would enable you to behave organically. Such a procedure may give rise to emotions, as Stanislavsky believed it would. And it might serve well as a Michael Chekhov psychological gesture—a way into the shyness, but not a substitute for the reality of the shyness and for knowing where it comes from. Ask yourself what we mean by the word *shy* and where shyness emanates from psychologically, especially the particular character's shyness: Tusenbach thinks he is unattractive. Nora, having been brought up to play the traditional female role of the devoted, loving, obedient wife expected in the society of her day, is afraid of the repercussions should she dare to reveal her true feelings. Nina in *The Seagull* has a bad self-image and thinks she is untalented. By exploring the character's specific inner life and by using analogous substitutions from your own life, you will go beyond mannerisms or clichés to find behavior that is real for yourself, as the character. Perhaps you might indeed come up with the standard way of portraying shyness, or perhaps you will find something new and exciting.

The standard method (with variations) used by actors to harness psychology for character interpretation can be summed up as follows: After reading the script to determine the arc of the story, the character's place in it, and the character's "through-line" or overall superobjective, the actor's first questions are usually, "Who (as a character) am I?" and "What do I want?" Two corollary, later questions are "How much do I want what I want?" and also "Why?"—which is the psychological question par excellence. And the actor asks, "How do I behave in these circumstances?" "How do I behave in a way that is real?"

The actor analyzes the character's objective or objectives (what the character wants—the character's goal or goals; a subobjective is a smaller objective on the path to achieving or accomplishing an objective) and the obstacles (what is in the character's way; the obstacle may be physical, another character, emotional, internal, etc.). The actor determines the actions to be played in going after the objective. Actions are what the character does to get what he or she wants. Internal actions are rational or irrational cognitive thought processes, including the *interior monologue,* an internal script that is a running series of thoughts in a *stream of consciousness.*

And after all of this workhorse analysis, the art of acting begins in earnest, as you decide what you can draw on from within yourself to behave as really as possible when dealing with all the internal and external circumstances. In rehearsal you will find the detailed subtextual intentions underneath the character's lines. You will find and "score" the character's personal beats in the scenes. *Beats,* or *units,* are either the beginning of a specific moment during which an action is played or a longer amount of time in which a conflict in a scene is played out. If and when an objective has been attained, or if and when it has not, there is a change of beat. When one beat comes to an end in either success or failure, another begins.

Stanislavsky came to believe that the correct action—correctly performed, based on the given circumstances in the play, and arrived at in the rehearsal process—would awaken the emotion of the character. He had previously believed almost the exact opposite—namely, that the correct emotion, when found, would lead to the correct action to be played in fulfillment of the objective.

These opposite approaches are at the heart of the disagreement between the two seminal American acting teachers: Stella Adler, who believed in the soundness of Stanislavsky's later approach (first find the correct action, then you will understand what the character feels), and Lee Strasberg, who believed in the earlier approach (first find the correct emotion, then you will understand what action the character takes and why). Both call for the use of affective memory and for imagination, but Adler's idea is to imagine the reality of the script "as if" you were imagining and living the character's life, and Strasberg's idea is to imagine the reality of the script "as if" it were your own life.

Stanislavsky was very interested in the ideas of the Russian physiologist Ivan Pavlov, whose study of reflexes won him the Nobel Prize in 1904. His most famous experiment was getting dogs to salivate when they heard a bell, even though there was no food put out for them to salivate over as there had been during the previous phase of the experiment, when the ringing of a bell meant food was provided. Stanislavsky wanted actors to respond organically on cue and to behave as the characters they were supposed to be, just as the dogs responded reflexively. In other words, the actor's reactions, timing, and actions should be automatic, after first being determined and cemented in the rehearsal process, so that the behavior appeared spontaneous and "as if" for the first time. As a result of this thinking, Stanislavsky was far less interested in the depth psychology of Freud. American schools interpreting Stanislavsky's Method, on the other hand, were far more interested in Freud than in the automatic response idea of Pavlov and his dogs.

In actuality, as the great actor and acting teacher Alice Spivak says, once rehearsal is over, actors do indeed respond organically, spontaneously, and without anticipation—if they are doing their jobs correctly. She continues by telling us that in order to play the beginning correctly, actors need to know the ending of the play and to be able to shape their character's scenes in accordance with their knowledge of the arc of the story's development. They then need to forget all of this knowledge and make a commitment to spontaneity. If the rehearsal process of forgetting has been correct, they will be able to do this and to use the inner script they have created.

In real life we all have an inner script or scripts, which consist of what we tell ourselves based on our combination of reality and fantasy in all the situations of our lives, according to the psychologist of affects, Silvan S. Tomkins. He wrote a fascinating, complicated masterpiece in four volumes called *Affect Imagery Consciousness* (1962–92) in which he says that we deal with emotions and affects in various ways as a result of those scripts. They exist in the unconscious and are driven by unconscious motivations. And they are based on introjected objects and ideas, such as the morality learned from parents and teachers. The scripts have to do with how we talk to ourselves, which has a similarity to Lacan's and Freud's ideas on the nature of language. We have scripts for the avoidance and expression of anger and for what Tomkins calls *damage repair*—meaning scripts for how we make up to ourselves and others for faults we may have committed—and we have scripts for the management and control of our emotions generally. In other words, the scripts are what we tell ourselves about our life stories. They are what characters tell themselves about their life stories.

Many actors write the "biographies" of their characters, which are similar to scripts in the sense Tomkins was talking about. But as Alice Spivak warns, "Don't 'overjustify' the behavior" based on that biography. Don't "overdetermine" the character's behavior by resorting to early childhood conditioning as a reason to behave in ways based not in the script itself but in the actor's invented life history.

Some further considerations: I have already said that a character's internal circumstances influence external behavior, but the reverse is also true. External circumstances influence internal life. They include time, place, the weather, the temperature, and the character's state of physical health. Place—that is, where one is located in space—is very important: we behave differently in a public place than if we are at home. Time is also a very specific conditioning circumstance, not only the general time of day, but also the specific moment and the myriad circumstances surrounding it. Most important of all, and inseparable from the rest, is relationship, which is the nature of the character's connection to other characters as well to mental representations of internal and external objects, and which deals with how and why the character relates to the self and to others.

Reading psychology—the word comes from Greek and means "the study of the soul"—and consulting its relevant texts can help the actor answer the first question any actor asks when approaching the study of a character: Who am I (the character)? Sigmund Freud above all is astounding, not only in the breadth and depth of his perceptions and the lucidity of his observations of who we are and how our minds work, but also for his pithy wit, his succinct style, and his extraordinary facility for setting forth his insights in an immediately comprehensible way.

Psychopathological conditions have been classified in the American Psychiatric Association's *Diagnostic and Statistical Manual of Mental Disorders,* Fourth Edition, Text Revision (*DSM-IV-TR*) and analyzed and discussed in many other books. And the psychology of nonpathological types, of the normal and mentally healthy, is well understood by now and has also been exhaustively analyzed and elucidated. The basics of mental functioning are common to both healthy and unhealthy individuals, but in the unhealthy, they have somehow ceased to function adequately to ensure the individual's well-being and the preservation of a healthy self-esteem. They have gone awry in some way or ways for reasons of self-preservation that are sometimes well understood and at other times seem obscure. Why should people think unconsciously that they have to behave in certain ways in order to preserve themselves, when, to the outside observer at least, they are only making themselves miserable, anxious, and unhappy? What do people really want, anyway? These are two of the questions that underlie not only psychology but also the drama and literature in general.

Literature can be a very useful study for actors, writers, and directors, especially the works of such authors as Henry James or Jane Austen, whose particular emphasis is on the psychology of their characters and the social psychology of their eras. Every actor, director, and writer would do well to read the masterpiece of the preeminent psychological author of the twentieth century, Marcel Proust (1871–1922). He called his multivolume novel *A la recherche du temps perdu* (Remembrance of Things Past or, more literally, In Search of Lost Time, as it is now known). The book is written mostly in the first person, and the narrator is a character in it. We are, as it were, living his life as we read; we are "I." Proust's comprehension of such psychological phenomena as the extratemporal nature of the unconscious or the manifestations of the Oedipus complex, which he may or may not have heard of by name but which he clearly understood, is brought to life for the reader in a direct, experiential way that is analogous to what happens to a theater audience. Proust can teach an actor or another writer a great deal about how people behave and how they think. He is known perhaps most importantly as a brilliant analyst of the experience of love, about which he writes in minute psychological detail. He has also given us an incredibly real portrait of the society of his time, and his characters seem so real because they each have an unconscious as well as a conscious mental life. Many analytical passages in Proust's novel seem not only Freudian but also precursive of object-relations theory (an offshoot of Freudian psychoanalysis), as well as of Lacan's neo-Freudianism. Proust apparently never read Freud, but he probably heard the "new ideas" from Vienna discussed at the dinner table by his father and brother, both of whom were physicians interested in Freud's theories.

All of which brings us in our meandering to the very door of Freud's consulting room at 19 Berggasse in Vienna's District IX. He is long gone from that grand old apartment, but his presence is as palpable as if he were about to open the door and emerge into the sitting room that is now part of the Sigmund Freud Museum, cigar in hand, a twinkle in his kindly eye . . . perhaps to flick some dust off a statuette in his famous collection of antiquities, perhaps to greet Gordon Allport, a young American on his way home in 1918 from a year of teaching in Turkey. Allport would one day be an illustrious Harvard professor and an admired, innovative psychologist in his own right.

How nice of him to come all this way just to meet the old man! And how nice of the old man, to whom he had written a rather brash letter, to consent to see him! But the young man is so nervous. Freud remains silent, just looking at him. Well, the visitor feels he has to say something. So he tells Dr. Freud about an incident that has just occurred on the tramway on his way to Freud's house. He had seen a little boy with his mother, and the child was obviously developing a phobia about dirt. He had talked incessantly about how dirty everything was. Didn't Dr. Freud find that interesting, the clear onset of a phobia? About dirt? And (the young man implied but didn't say) wasn't he astute to have noticed this? Ah, Dr. Freud is smiling!

"And was that little boy you?"

What? Why, of course not! Whatever could the good doctor mean, anyway? Young Allport was "flabbergasted" and felt, as he later said, "a bit guilty" — about what? He didn't say.

Professor Allport, none too fond of Freud's ideas as it turned out, maintained and was still rather defensively maintaining decades later that Freud had made a bad mistake and misinterpreted young Allport's "youthful ambition" and natural awe and intimidation at being in his presence. It was possible for depth psychology to be too deep! Freud was too used to dealing with sick people, and this was not a pathological case of neurotic defense mechanisms! But during a lecture at Boston University, he said that Freud had explored the deep recesses of the unconscious, stayed down there for a long time, and come up "dirtier than anyone else." So perhaps Dr. Freud had not been that wide of the mark after all. If so, young Allport was not alone. There were lots of people who thought of psychoanalysis and its founder as dirty. As far as they were concerned, Dr. Freud had dared to talk about things that nobody should even dare to think about.

Chapter One

❧

Sigmund Freud, Father of Psychoanalysis

*H*e hadn't wanted to leave Vienna. He was eighty-two years old, and he had lived there nearly all his life. And he had painful cancer of the jaw that was killing him. Traveling would be torture. But he had been badly shaken when the Nazis detained his beloved daughter Anna for a whole agonizing day. His entire diary entry for March 22, 1938: "Anna bei Gestapo." It was finally time to get out.

His home at 20 Maresfield Gardens, London, is now a museum. The peaceful, tree-lined street and lush back garden are much as they were when he spent the last year of his eventful life there. He died on September 23, 1939, three weeks after the outbreak of the Second World War. Anna Freud continued to live in the house until her own death in 1982.

In the eighty-three years he spent on this earth, Sigmund Freud achieved something that few have ever accomplished: he changed the world's mind. Quite literally. After him, nobody could ever see human beings in the same way again.

Freud was born in 1856 in an era of astonishingly rapid advances in the scientific understanding of the laws that govern the physical universe. As a young medical doctor, he studied the newest ideas in neurology and physiology. He was drawn to the philosophy of Plato, Kant, Schopenhauer, and Nietszche. He was persuaded of the truth of Charles Darwin's theory of evolution, and fascinated by the psychological theories of the physicist and physiologist Hermann Helmholtz and of Johann Herbart (Kant's successor as professor of philosophy at Königsberg), and by the work of the experimental psychologist Gustav Theodor Fechner, who had declared that it was possible to study the mind scientifically, just like other natural phenomena. The mind, he said, was like an iceberg, mostly submerged.

In 1882 Freud's fatherly colleague and friend Dr. Josef Breuer (1842–1925) confided to him the details of a strange case: A patient of Breuer's, "Anna O.," a lovely, sensitive, strait-laced young woman, had suffered since her adored father's death from loss of appetite, debilitating headaches, and a nervous cough. And she had begun to develop a "museum of symptoms," as Ernest Jones called them, including a loss of bodily sensations and occasional partial paralysis of the lower limbs and right arm. She sometimes could not remember German but conversed only in English, reading Italian or French books aloud in a spontaneous English translation. On many occasions she appeared almost catatonic—she was actually far away in daydreams that she called her "private theater." Then she began to have frightening hallucinations. And she suddenly developed two different personalities: one demure, restrained and ladylike, and the other, of which she was apparently unaware, childishly temperamental and wild. Breuer's diagnosis was that she had been stricken with hysteria.

Apart from its well-known popular definition of an uncontrolled temperamental outburst or panic reaction, the word *hysteria* designates a number of more or less severe neuroses. Hysteria was originally thought to affect only women (the word comes from *hysteron,* Greek for "uterus") and was attributed to women's overactive imaginations and a desire to be the center of attention—a dismissive, male-chauvinist attitude. But males, too, could be hysterical types. There were many Freud saw in the Viennese hospitals he visited and worked at.

At Anna O's urging, Breuer began using a *talking cure* with her, which was actually of her own devising: she put herself into a kind of hypnotic or trancelike state, during which she would talk about all the events of the day and describe the scenes of her "private theater" in vivid detail. In that state she experienced the strong emotions of her wild personality. Upon coming out of her trance after her "chimney sweeping," as she called it, she would experience a catharsis and resume her restrained, calm demeanor. This talking cure, which Breuer called a *cathartic procedure,* was a precursor of Freud's method of *free association:* the patient is asked to say whatever comes to mind, without censoring anything.

It was actually more important to Anna O. to see Breuer and to talk about herself with him than it was to deal with her illness, because she had developed what is now known as a *positive transference* (highly erotic in her case)—that is, the love she had for her father was transferred to her doctor unconsciously. The knowledge of transference phenomena was a later development in psychoanalysis. Lacking this knowledge, the perplexed Breuer had no very clear idea of how to proceed. And it did not help matters that he himself had developed a *positive countertransference*—that is, he had unconsciously developed feelings of love for his beautiful patient. In fact, he spent so much time with her and talked so much about her that his wife became jealous.

Nevertheless, the cathartic procedure continued until Anna O. had apparently been restored to health. But on the evening of the very day her symptoms had disappeared, Breuer was urgently summoned back by her agitated family, because she had complained of abdominal cramps and said she was pregnant with his baby. Of course she was not pregnant; she was in the throes of what is called a hysterical pregnancy. Horrified, Dr. Breuer gave up treating her and promptly left for Venice on a second honeymoon with his wife. Deeply embarrassed, he was later reluctant to publish the story in the book he wrote with Freud on hysteria. In fact, he left out the pseudopregnancy episode and other details, although the case still served its illustrative purposes.

After a stay in a Swiss sanatorium, Anna O. eventually recovered, and, remarkably, was able to put the "hysterical" phase of her life behind her. Her real name was Bertha Pappenheim (1860–1936), and she became a noted pioneer in social work, a well-known philanthropist, humanitarian, and feminist, leading a productive, very active life. The pseudonym was used to protect her identity, since she was still living when her story was published in Breuer and Freud's groundbreaking *Studies in Hysteria* in 1895, which described eight case histories.

Freud had been deeply moved by the suffering of Anna O. and of the hysterical people he had observed in Viennese hospitals. They had physical symptoms but nothing to account for them: how could a person with no nerve disease be paralyzed? And they seemed to be completely unaware of their own feelings. Common treatment for these unfortunates included painful shocks, straitjackets, and restraints. Their baffled doctors could not help them. There was no cure for hysteria, because nobody understood it.

But the foremost specialist of the day in the treatment of mental aberrations, Dr. Jean-Martin Charcot (1825–93), was achieving startling results in his treatment of hysterical types. Eager to learn, in 1885 Freud went to Paris to study with him. Charcot used hypnotherapy, a fairly common practice of the era, to treat patients with hysteria: he made suggestions and gave commands meant to have a healing effect while the patient was under hypnosis. In the hypnotic state, the patient could actually make such symptoms as paralysis of the legs disappear. In the ordinary waking state, the patient, having been instructed under hypnosis, was able to maintain the asymptomatic state.

Unfortunately, this cure was only temporary, which was the reason that Freud, who used hypnotherapy at first, discarded it. There were also patients whom he could not hypnotize. Most importantly, the role of the doctor was paramount, and that of the patient subordinate and lacking in the autonomy necessary to effect a real cure. Hypnotherapy did not make the patient aware of the origins of his or her symptoms. The problem had not been worked out, and the old symptoms could return or new ones take their place.

At any rate, Charcot had proved that the disorders were mental and not physical in origin, whatever the physical symptoms might be. And he had concluded that hysterical symptoms were caused by specific incidents that were so traumatic the patient had forgotten them. What sort of incidents? "C'est *toujours* la chose génitale," Freud heard him tell an assistant: It's *always* the genital thing, "toujours, toujours, toujours!"

Based on his work with Charcot and Breuer (who disapproved so strongly of Freud's budding theory of the sexual causes of neuroses that he ended their friendship and professional association) and on his own clinical observations, Freud posited that the disorders involve not simply forgetting, but actually banishing unwanted sexual feelings from the mind and converting those feelings into physical symptoms. Exactly how and why all this happens he had yet to learn, but he realized that hysterics do not know they have done this and that the symptoms had to be a sort of symbolic coded message, a clue to the source of the disturbance. *Conversion hysteria* (*conversion disorder* in current terminology) works by *dissociation:* the physical symptoms dissociate the feelings of anxiety from their source, allowing the person who has conversion hysteria to seem unaware of or indifferent to the gravity of the symptom. Freud distinguished *anxiety hysteria* from conversion hysteria: both depend on excluding sexual feelings from awareness, but in anxiety hysteria, the sufferer fails to overcome the anxiety associated with them.

At the time when Freud was beginning his studies of hysteria, psychology had no clear idea about how the mind functioned. Experimental psychology was a laboratory science, which viewed psychic processes mechanistically as electrochemical, biological phenomena. Character was considered fixed and static. The Swedish playwright August Strindberg wrote in his Preface to *Miss Julie* in 1888 that the idea of "character" was a bourgeois, middle-class attempt at categorizing people. A man was seen as a fixed automaton who had "adapted himself to a particular role in life." Freud realized that character was dynamic and resulted from dynamic physiological and mental processes. This seemingly simple idea revolutionized both the conceptual and therapeutic aspects of psychology and psychotherapy.

In their introduction to *Studies in Hysteria,* Freud and Breuer expounded an early, simple version of what was to become the theoretical basis of psychoanalytic therapy: the past must be brought into consciousness and deprived of its power to harm by talking through its effects and manifestations. But it is not enough simply to remember. You can know something intellectually and yet not know it emotionally. The patient must reexperience events with the force of their original emotional impact. "Remembering without affect almost always fails to be effective," they wrote. The past must be interpreted and integrated, which meant seeing it in a new light. Traumatic experiences would then lose their power. The patient would regain health, freedom, and functionality, and cease to "suffer from reminiscences." That, at least, was the ideal goal of *psychoanalysis*—a word that is used to mean psychoanalytic therapy, a form of treatment—and psychoanalytic theory, which elucidates the workings of the mind.

The Foundations, I: How the Mind Works

The mind is clearly a function of the brain, reacting to stimuli and giving direction and instruction to the organism as a whole. Part of the mind is conscious and aware and perceives reality. We can reason and think logically on a conscious level. We know things and we can learn. We can make plans and deal with circumstances. But conscious mental processes are like a small corner of a room illuminated by a candle, leaving the rest in darkness. Most mental processes take place unconsciously.

"The division of the psychical into what is conscious and what is unconscious is the fundamental premise of psychoanalysis," wrote Sigmund Freud in *The Ego and the Id* (1923). The boundary between consciousness and unconsciousness is fluid and dynamic, shifting and changing constantly.

One of the functions of mental processes is to harness the body's forces (energy) in order to deal with internal motivational *drives*. The drives are urges that have developed as the result of instinctual biophysiological needs. The needs, activated by bodily sensations, demand to be expressed and fulfilled. The drives impel people to act with the aim of satisfying the needs in order to relieve the tension associated with them. To put it simply, the wish to fulfill the need has a *source*, the body; an *aim*, gratification; and an *object*, an external source that supplies gratification—a useful schema for actors to keep in mind when studying objectives and obstacles. For instance, a baby wishes to be fed; lets its needs be known, by crying perhaps; and seeks the source of food (the object, the mother) until the need is met. The object and the way the infant feels about it are remembered, and the fantasy of interaction with the object is mentally revisited when necessary, the next time the infant is hungry. Once the need is satisfied, the organism returns to its previous relaxed state, which is temporary because biophysiological needs are always being renewed. Nevertheless, the organism (body and mind) wishes to maintain itself in a state of stability, to conserve its energy, and to suppress internal excitation. Freud called this the *constancy principle*.

Freud postulated that there are two basic drives, which he inferred from observable behavior. These drives exist together, not separately or in a pure state: the libido or sex drive, and the powerful aggressive drive. These two drives, found in varying degrees in the carrying out of any action, are not simply synonymous with sex or with aggression in any narrow sense, but have more broadly to do with self-preservation and seeking and obtaining pleasure, gratification, and satisfaction. In general, he concluded, the organism seeks pleasure (the relief of tension) and flees from unpleasure (the raising of tension): this is the *pleasure principle*, sometimes called the *pleasure-unpleasure principle* or the *pleasure-pain principle*. In seeking pleasure and satisfaction from external sources, the organism is confronted with the reality of the world, to which it has to adjust both externally and internally in some way: this is called the *reality principle*. Like the libidinal and aggressive drives, these two principles never work in isolation from each other, but always in tandem.

The mind has a structure that deals with tension and relief, controls the interplay of the body's forces and the expending of energy, and governs the affective organization of the drives. Freud discerned successively three hypothetical models of the mind's structure in the course of his increasing understanding of the way the mind works. Each model or construct was a natural refinement of the preceding one, amplifying and absorbing but not superseding it:

1. The system of the *unconscious*, which is a kind of dynamic mental apparatus consisting of several psychic components that flow into and out of each other,

including the sensory apparatus that receives stimuli and reacts to them, the area that stores memories and can release them to consciousness or keep them stored, and the system of *consciousness* and awareness. All of the areas of the system depend on the functioning of a hypothetical energy that could be called psychic energy.

2. The dynamic "topographical" model, consisting of the *unconscious,* the *preconscious,* and the *conscious* systems, all intimately interrelated.

3. The "structural," tripartite model, consisting of the mental agencies called the *id,* the *ego,* and the *superego,* which are areas of the unconscious that dynamically flow into each other, back and forth.

The Unconscious

In *Civilization and Its Discontents* (1930), Freud likens the unconscious to the modern city of Rome, which contains the ruins of the ancient city jumbled in and dovetailed among buildings dating from all the centuries that followed its founding—so that in walking about its streets, one has an impression of the architectural chaos of the great, complicated, layered metropolis. Much of the old city is still buried and remains to be excavated. Some of it may be found again. Much is lost irretrievably and will never be recovered. To apply this analogy to the mind, everything—including what is infantile and childish—is still there somewhere alongside what is adult.

As Freud noted, ideas are fleeting and come and go in the mind constantly, as impulses release them in the brain. Some unconscious ideas and dormant memories, as well as what we know consciously that we are temporarily unaware of or not thinking about, can easily be revisited and enter consciousness. Freud termed these ideas preconscious. They are on the edge of consciousness, just out of our awareness. "Even subtle and difficult intellectual operations" may be carried out preconsciously. Sleeping on a problem and waking up to find you know the solution is a case in point. To take a personal example, when I started to call a friend on the telephone and found myself beginning to dial my mother's number "accidentally," it was obvious that I had been thinking unconsciously of calling her and that her telephone number exists as a preconscious memory, stored somewhere physiologically in my brain.

When I was dialing my friend's phone number, I made one type of what has come to be known as a *Freudian slip,* a parapraxis that reveals a piece of the contents of the unconscious. The term is usually applied to slips of the tongue or the pen, such as the one in the following example: I was preparing a book for recording, and I came across a sentence that begins "Overhead a bird was passing," but I read it aloud surrealistically as "Overheard a bed was passing." You are free to guess the many things that might have been passing in my unconscious that gave rise to this Freudian slip. (A hint: the soundproofing in my building is very poor, and my upstairs neighbors can be very noisy on certain kinds of occasions, as they had been the previous night.)

There is constant drama going on in the unconscious, and events are played and replayed without our even being aware of the comedy or tragedy our minds have constructed. Sometimes we make slips that reveal their presence. Sometimes these dramas appear in dreams, when the controls that prevent their seeping through into consciousness are relaxed during sleep. More importantly, they emerge in our behavior.

Certain ideas and emotions have been *repressed*—that is, they have been pushed out of and excluded from consciousness and forgotten. The repression itself takes place on an unconscious level, as an idea, thought, or feeling goes through a kind of censorship process that will determine if the idea may be allowed into consciousness. If the censor (the ego; see below) decides that these ideas and emotions are not to be allowed because they provoke anxiety or pain, or are undesirable in some other way or threatening for various (unconscious) reasons, they are buried deep in the almost inaccessible recesses of the mind and held there by a dynamic force Freud called *resistance,* meaning that this force actively resists and blocks their return to awareness.

The theory of repression that Freud worked out was, he said, "the pillar on which the edifice of psychoanalysis rests." He explored its nature, the obscure and intricate processes by which something is repressed, the vicissitudes of what has been repressed, and the nature of resistance and of the multifaceted unconscious in his 1915 essays "Repression" and "The Unconscious" and in a great many other writings.

The unconscious has no sense of time and is therefore "timeless." It has no sense of its own age and is therefore "ageless"; it perceives the ages of other people, to which it attaches various kinds of importance. For everyone, events that had taken place in the past are as alive when reexperienced in the mind as if they were still actually taking place, and all the emotions experienced at the time of the event are reawakened. It is also universally true that reality and fantasy are not differentiated in the deep recesses of the unconscious: to imagine that something is real is essentially to perceive it and feel it as real, so that the body reacts as if it were in a real situation. In a way, the art of acting—that is, of projecting the self into imaginary circumstances—begins with this property of the unconscious part of the mind.

In order to explore the unconscious parts of his patients' minds, Freud developed the famous *free association* technique of psychoanalysis: the analyst asks the patient simply to say whatever comes into his or her mind, trying not to censor the thoughts to which the tongue gives utterance. When there is a pause or a stumble, this indicates resistance that prevents verbalization. Making the unconscious conscious is the beginning of the analytic and therapeutic work. The patient's dreams provide further clues as to what is really going on, and their contents can be interpreted and analyzed.

Freud was fascinated by dreams even as a child. As a boy, he wrote his own dreams down and studied them. What could they mean? Where did they come from? "We are such stuff as dreams are made on, and our little life / Is rounded with a sleep … " muses Prospero. Many in the scientific establishment of Freud's era were convinced that dreams were meaningless, merely random discharges of excess energy in the nervous system. Freud thought otherwise.

He called dreams the "royal road to the unconscious." Dreams have a manifest content—the actual dream and its story—and a latent content, which is the underlying, unconscious meaning of the story to the dreamer and which threatens to awaken the dreamer from sleep. Freud called the mental processes—including *condensation,* which gives rise to dreams and forms them from the latent content and other elements—the *dream work.* Condensation is a psychic mechanism that fuses or unites several unconscious ideas or images, and coalesces them into one image in the manifest content of the dream. The sleeper when awake cannot acknowledge the content that was latent in the dream. Why not? Because in some way, it constitutes threatening knowledge of which the dreamer prefers to remain unaware. Freud's classic book *Die Traumdeutung* (The Interpretation of Dreams, 1900), which was his favorite of all his many writings, is full of the elaborate details of the logic, symbolism, and almost surrealist landscapes of dreams, the interpretation of which is complicated and elaborate. It is also very deliberately revealing about Freud himself, based as it is in part on his exhaustive self-analysis and his own dreams. And it is important for its discussion of the unconscious in general.

He concluded that people's dreams are *wish fulfillments.* The term is a broad one. It includes several possibilities, of which any one singly, all together, or in various combinations may be elements of a particular dream. Among the possibilities are: the fulfillment of hidden sexual and other desires in the context of the fantasy world of the dream, the relief of tensions, and the finding of solutions to problems of all kinds. Dreams can be a venting mechanism for dealing with the dreamer's present-day problems as well as with past difficulties. Their manifest content may tell a coherent story or be completely jumbled and garbled, but in either case, it contains a great deal that is useful and revealing, and leads to understanding the latent meaning of the dream. Dreams are coded messages that may be either misunderstood or uncomprehended on awaking or, quite commonly, forgotten altogether—that is, repressed back into the unconscious.

The sleeper's relaxed unconscious awakens desires and feelings from somewhere deep in the inner world and attaches them to present-day problems and preoccupations. The manifest content of dreams is filled with the nocturnal surroundings of the dreamer; with bits and pieces of things that happened during waking hours; with people who have been observed, even in passing; and with remembered incidents from the past and ideas long repressed that have seeped through the barriers of the ego into the consciousness of the dream. Any of these elements may appear in symbolic and/or fragmented form.

Even recurring repetitions of traumatic experiences and other sorts of nightmares, all of which are anxiety dreams that appear to be the opposite of wish fulfillment, could actually represent disguised wish fulfillment of some kind, properly analyzed: the punishment for some transgression that would enable the dreamer to expiate his sin or crime; the representation of some terrible event in order to undo it, which is the deepest wish of the dreamer; the overcoming of some fear; or the carrying out of vengeance. The traumatic or other anxiety dream often awakens the sleeper and, since the unconscious is timeless, leaves him or her shaken and perspiring.

Freud was also inspired to study the nature of jokes, which, like dreams, may represent a key that could open a door to part of the unconscious. He wanted to know what makes people laugh. Jokes are meant to produce pleasure. But there is more to them than that. They can also act as a defense mechanism, defusing unpleasant, potentially explosive situations, for instance.

Why do we find something funny? Why do we laugh without knowing why? Some jokes arouse repressed desires, which take us by surprise. There are inoffensive and offensive jokes. What causes some people to laugh at so-called ethnic jokes, for instance? Freud loved authentic Jewish jokes all his life. He wrote and spoke beautiful, lucid German, but his mother preferred to speak Yiddish, and this was the language he must have heard in his cradle—colorful and evocative, comic and serious, and profoundly expressive. Jakob and Amalie Freud both came from the Eastern Austrian province of Galicia, home to a large, if not always thriving, Jewish community living in the midst of many ethnic groups—Poles, Ukrainians, and Russians, among others. Authentic jokes of the kind Freud heard at home come from the culture itself. Inauthentic jokes come from outside the culture, and in the case of so-called Jewish jokes, they are often anti-Semitic, just as so-called Polish jokes are insulting to Polish people. Freud thought that when people laugh at insulting, inauthentic ethnic jokes it shows that they are shocked and also that they understand the nature of the prejudice, even if they don't subscribe to it. Also, their laughter may involve a narcissistic impulse to feel superior. Something that would ordinarily cause pain causes pleasure, as the repression that restrains aggressive sadistic behavior is temporarily abrogated and then immediately reasserted after laughter, like the shutting of a cell door that was opened for an instant by a sentinel who usually keeps it closed so that the dangerous prisoner within may not escape. For a full explanation of Freud's ideas on jokes, read *Wit and Its Relations to the Unconscious* (1905).

The Id, the Ego, and the Superego

The mind cannot simply go about directing someone to fulfill desires and needs indiscriminately. As previously noted, it runs up against the reality principle, represented by physical nature and by society—other people have needs and desires, and we have to deal with them in an ethical, moral way or life becomes impossible for everyone. The mind has therefore had to develop a structure to deal with reality and insure self-preservation and survival. This structure includes mechanisms that restrain the organism out of its desire for self-preservation and a sense of obligation to the self. Among these defense mechanisms are the conscious suppression of actions, feelings, and impulses the mind considers harmful, and the unconscious repression mentioned earlier.

The roles guilt and shame play in repression are paramount. But where do guilt and shame come from? They come in the first instance from the necessity of pleasing the parent, caregiver, or authority figure, whose existence is necessary in order to fulfill the biologically helpless child's needs. Parental disapproval arouses the fear of deprivation and of the withdrawal of parental love, as well as the fear of punishment. The child feels humiliated, ashamed, and guilty for having transgressed.

Repressing the desire to which the parent was opposed and giving in to the parent ensures approval and love. The child's needs will be fulfilled. Anxiety, painful guilt, and shame are avoided.

As his ideas about the complicated, dynamic mental processes involved in repression evolved over the course of forty years, Freud formulated the tripartite structural model of the mind: the theory that the unconscious carries out its functions by means of three interrelated agencies that are in continual interaction with each other: the id, the ego, and the superego. In *The Ego and the Id*, he tells us that from the point of view of morality and instinctual control, the id "is totally non-moral," the ego "strives to be moral," and the superego "can be super-moral and then become as cruel as only the id can be."

The id is the largest area of the unconscious, much of it uncharted. It contains the biologically based hereditary instincts, drives, needs, and desires, as well as repressed thoughts and emotions swirling around them. It is irrational and knows only itself and its own desires. As the human being develops a sense of self, becomes a person, and is confronted with the reality principle, he or she also develops an ego, which is almost synonymous with self. We begin to have a sense of ourselves as separate from others and from the world. And the ego, which Freud first thought of as a differentiated part of the id and then as a structure in its own right, appears to be marked off from what is exterior to the self in quite a sharp way. The only exception to this state of the ego, says Freud in *Civilization and Its Discontents,* is when one is in love, and then "the boundary between ego and object threatens to melt away" and identification with the love object assumes supreme importance, so that the two people appear almost as one to each other. *Romeo and Juliet* provides a perfect example of this melting away of two egos.

The reality-oriented, partly conscious, partly unconscious ego is the "coherent organization of mental processes," as Freud informs us in *The Ego and the Id*. It is responsible for self-preservation. The conscious part of the ego is responsible for learning, rationality, and logical thinking. The ego learns how to fulfill the needs of the id and "controls the approaches to motility—that is, to the discharge of excitations into the external world." It is also the "seat of anxiety" when it perceives or expects an increase in unpleasure, or danger in the form of an internal or external threat. It is from the ego that repression proceeds. The ego is the part of the mind that goes to sleep at night, allowing the id some play, and it censors and alters what it allows to filter through from the id. What the ego permits to filter through takes the form of dreams, as we have seen.

The superego, which is actually part of the ego and its functions and represents internal constraints on the desires of the id, includes what we call our *conscience*—that is, what we are taught and introject from parental figures and/or other caregivers as morality and ethics. Its genesis in the Oedipal phase explains how early conflicts can continue unconsciously, since the superego has only the power to deal with the demands of the id, but not to do away with early conflicts altogether. In *New Introductory Lectures on Psycho-Analysis* (1933), Freud tells us that the child's superego is constructed from the contents of the parents' superegos, transmitted to the child, and so becomes the vehicle for tradition and the transmission of culture from generation to generation. Thus influenced by the past, "Mankind never lives entirely in the present."

The superego controls the ego and the id by means of what it has learned from reality, as well as by what it imagines or fantasizes about the parental figures. It includes what parents teach about acceptable and unacceptable behavior; even table manners and etiquette are functions overseen by the superego. It is also the storehouse of ideals and responsible for the expression of idealism. An *ego ideal* has been built up by the teaching the child absorbs. The superego wants the self to live up to the ego ideal, which is the positive image of the self as good, loving, and kind. It tells the ego, "That is not permitted," or "You can't do that now," or "You can't have that," or "That is immoral," or even, "Such behavior is counterproductive." The superego can force morality on the ego, by suppressing the aggressiveness of the id and turning it against the self.

Otto Fenichel (1897–1946), another psychoanalytic pioneer, describes the development of the superego in Chapter VI: "Later Phases of Development: The Superego" of *The Psychoanalytic Theory of Neurosis* (1945): When a child fears punishment or fears losing the parents' affection, the internal mental and emotional activities surrounding these fears continue even when the parents are not there to enforce obedience. However, "the child may pretend he feels 'bad' in situations where he actually feels 'good.'" In other words, he knows he is supposed to feel bad about doing certain things, but he actually feels good when he does them. Nevertheless, he pretends to himself that he feels bad and ashamed and guilty; even internally, he dares not contradict the parents. Later on, as an adult, the child may indeed come to disagree with the parents' moral ideas, sometimes with and sometimes without guilt feelings. But fear is not the only factor in the formation of the superego. The love and nurturing a child receives from parents is also an important factor in its genesis. Implicitly identifying with the parents, the child wants to please them out of love.

The Foundations, II:
The Stages of Psychosexual Development, the Oedipus Complex, and the Nature of Sexuality

*A*ssociated with the *libido*—the sex drive—are all those feelings of tenderness, warmth, and compassion that we call love, directed at particular external objects and also at ourselves, as well as the larger feelings of humanitarian empathy and sympathy. The original need for love is created out of the infant's *primary narcissism* (self-love) and necessitated by infantile helplessness and the long period of human immaturity. Love remains a lifelong need, involving the unconscious fantasy of returning to the primary narcissistic state, when the infant, knowing nothing beyond itself, was cared for, and all its needs were met. An important component of the mechanism of love is the projection of the ego ideal onto a love object—in other words, the unconscious idealization of that object, seeing it as endowed with the capacity to fulfill primary narcissistic needs.

In his *Three Contributions to the Theory of Sex* (1905), Freud set out the developmental psychosexual stages a child goes through on the way to adulthood. In the first through the third stages and again in the fifth, libidinal gratification is associated with a particular part of the body. The psychosexual stages are, in order:

1. The *oral,* from birth to about one-and-a-half years;
2. The *anal,* from one-and-a-half to about two-and-a-half or three years;
3. The *phallic,* from about three to about six—the latter part of this phase is when the Oedipus complex (explained below) makes its appearance;
4. The *latent,* which is the prepubescent, dormant phase, beginning at about six, after the repression of the Oedipus complex and ending with puberty;
5. The *genital* stage—distinguished from the earlier phallic stage because it is only with puberty that the capacity to experience orgasm develops.

All the early stages are there throughout life, retained in varying forms and amounts in each individual as components of adult sexuality. The demarcations between one stage and the next are amorphous and interconnected, fading into each other rather like the tones in a watercolor wash. Evolving visual, auditory, and tactile perceptions of the world, as well as issues of trust, guilt, individuation, autonomy, and initiative, also enter the picture and influence attitudes and feelings about sexuality.

How the stages develop and influence character formation depends on external factors, as well as on internal unconscious and conscious reactions. For instance, during the anal phase, the nature of toilet training, including the attitudes and behavior of the trainers and the tension and relaxation of the child, is important in helping determine future ideas about cleanliness, neatness, and orderliness. These ideas may then have an autonomous development in the unconscious so that their origin in early experiences of anality is forgotten. If the child becomes more or less fixated at a particular stage, the manifestations of that stage in adult life may be more apparent than that of the other stages, and Freud speaks of an oral, anal, or genital character, or of orality, anality, genitality, and character traits associated with those terms.

There are times when an object of desire or love has to be given up. Libidinal energy doesn't simply disappear; it must be discharged somehow. It is dealt with and discharged in the process of *sublimation*—that is, the (usually) unconscious redirecting of libidinal energy into another area of endeavor, to which the libido attaches itself. As Freud says in *The Ego and the Id,* the ego is "trying to make good the id's loss."

Libidinal energy is often redirected to work and other forms of creative activity. We owe to sublimation all works of art, architecture, literature, and music, and the great advances in medicine and science. Sublimation is a necessary concomitant of culture and often brings about advances in civilization. Since the libido does not exist in a pure state but is combined with the aggressive energy needed to attain its goals, it may have a destructive as well as a creative side, particularly when frustrated libidinal energy is coupled with aggressive sadism, displaced from its original objects, and redirected to fulfill the aims of war and imperialistic conquest, to take extreme but common examples.

Sublimation will also be necessary in resolving conflicts with the first objects towards which libidinal energy is directed: the parents or caregivers with whom the child has bonded. The aptly named *Oedipus complex* explains how children deal with the unconscious sexual urges they have directed towards those first objects of love and desire. In psychoanalysis the word *object* most often means a person, although it may also refer to an idea, event, or thing. The word *complex* is descriptive of a completely or partially unconscious constellation (that usually arises in childhood) of thoughts, feelings, interests, memories, and representations revolving around particular objects or ideas. A complex is anchored emotionally and affects attitudes and behavior.

In the ancient Greek myth, Oedipus grows up to slay his father, King Laius, not knowing who he is, and becomes king of Thebes in his place. He then marries Laius's widow, Jocasta, ignorant of the fact that she is his own mother. None of them could escape their fate, try as they might. Laius had ordered his baby son murdered in an attempt to thwart a prediction by the oracle at Delphi that his son would grow up to kill him, but Oedipus was saved and grew up far from the birthplace he did not know was his. He was led there again by inexorable circumstance, as he attempted to escape the oracle's prediction that he would kill his father and marry his mother, who, in his ignorance, he thought were his adoptive parents. When Oedipus and Jocasta discover the truth, she kills herself, and Oedipus puts out his own eyes and wanders forth in agonizing guilt, accompanied by their daughter, Antigone, who remains with him, faithful to the end.

Freud wrote on October 15, 1897, to his Berlin confidant and colleague Dr. Wilhelm Fliess (1858–1928) — with whom he corresponded for seventeen years about his self-analysis and many important psychoanalytical issues — that spectators in the theater recoil in horror and pity before this terrible story of incest and murder as Sophocles relates it in *Oedipus the King,* because the tale reawakens their deepest homicidal and infantile incestuous imaginings from the hidden recesses of the unconscious: "Everyone in the audience was once a budding Oedipus in fantasy." If you ever have to play a murderer, look no farther than these ancient, repressed childhood desires, which arise from the aggressive drive and are directed at anyone who thwarts the child's desires.

Everyone has a deep emotional investment, called a *cathexis,* in his or her mental images of the parents. These unconscious subjective images, constructed from reality and fantasy, are called *object representations.* These object representations include a schema or pattern of relationships, as well as feelings about the objects, and they constitute prototypes for the way people are perceived and dealt with in future relationships. Each of these prototypes is called an *imago.* The word means an object representation in all its aspects, and Freud writes of a maternal, paternal, and fraternal imago, because there are imagos built up not only around parents but also around siblings and perhaps other family members. Based on these prototypes, we develop cathexes throughout life with various individuals, who replace the parental figures as objects of desire. It is in connection with the parental imagos that the Oedipus complex will arise during the later part of the phallic stage.

The little boy, aware of pleasurable sensations in the genital area, wishes to share his pleasure with his mother, who nurtures and holds him and about whom he has unconscious, vague, and necessarily immature sexual fantasies. He wishes somehow to replace his father in his mother's affection. He has admired and envied his father's power and evident authority, identified with him and wishes to be like him. And he understands that his father loves his mother. Because he loves his father too, the little boy feels guilty about his intense homicidal desire to get rid of his now hated rival. He is also afraid that his jealous rivalry with his father will lead to his being rejected and punished. The punishment he fears is castration, since the genitals are the seat of pleasurable sensations and fantasies and would therefore be the scene of the expected castigation. So anxiety provoking are these fears that his masculinity is unable to withstand the shock, and he renounces his desire for his mother and consigns it to oblivion. But the desires and the *castration anxiety* remain in the unconscious, constituting a *castration complex*.

The little girl, too, is aware of pleasurable genital sensations, and she learns that males have something she does not have, a penis. The little girl is afraid she has been castrated, and she envies the male; this is called *penis envy*. Unconsciously she blames her mother, who has deprived her of a penis, so that she is now no longer complete. She begins to distance herself from her mother and to bond more with her father. And she jealously wishes to replace her mother in her father's affections. She fantasizes that he will give her a penis, or at least a baby, which will replace the penis and compensate for its loss. Because she thinks she is already punished by castration, she has a less urgent need to resolve her feelings of rivalry with her mother, although she is still afraid she will be punished in some way by her parents for her desires. She has remained ambivalently attached to her mother, so she feels guilty and ashamed because of her homicidal desire to get rid of her. And she has depreciated her mother as being castrated. All of these considerations enter into the little girl's castration complex.

Because they love their same-sex parent, with whom they identified before the Oedipal phase, children have an unconscious desire for that parent, too. This means that they also unconsciously identify with the role played by the opposite-sex parent. The boy wants Daddy to love him the way Daddy loves Mommy. The girl wants Mommy to love her the way Mommy loves Daddy. Children may experience their desires for the same-sex parent as painful and ambivalent, because they had wished to get rid of that parent. They continue to love, identify with, and have ambivalent feelings about both their parents as the Oedipus complex dissolves under the pressure of castration anxiety, which is repressed into the unconscious.

The first disappointment in love and its first failure is the inevitable and necessary deflecting of the child's libidinal interest in the parents. As Freud informs us in *Beyond the Pleasure Principle* (1920), the child's "infantile sexual life is doomed to extinction because its wishes are incompatible with reality" and because the child's stage of development is inadequate. "Loss of love and failure leave behind them a permanent injury to self-regard" and create psychic scarring.

The Oedipus complex is complicated by the parents' own conscious and unconscious attitudes and feelings about sex, which determine how they deal with their children and the attitudes and feelings they transmit to them. Parents who behave in a nurturing way help alleviate the child's distress. If they are severe or strict, children can absorb the unconscious message that their love is somehow bad, that they are undeserving or unworthy, and that love in general is therefore bad in some way. Information about sexual matters may be comfortably or uncomfortably imparted, and will influence how the children feel about sex and how they experience their own feelings. Their mental representations of their own bodies and appearances are also unconsciously influenced by how their love is dealt with. Children learn through others whether they are considered attractive or not, and feel either self-confident or insecure about their physical appearance.

After the repression of the Oedipus complex, the child enters a period of latency in which sexuality remains dormant until the onset of puberty. We seek out the love and affection of both parents, and we continue to need love, affection, and nurturing all our lives from both genders. We may act out the Oedipal conflict by treating parents and siblings in certain hostile or loving ways without even being aware of the nature or origin of our own behavior. During adolescence, the ambivalence engendered by the psychic conflicts of the Oedipus complex will unconsciously reassert itself. This is one factor in the inevitable conflicts with the parents. As the hormones physically transform the body, the child wishes to assert independence and transfers libidinal cathexes to other objects.

One of the child's early, sometimes confused desires during the phallic stage is to see adults having sex. The child also wishes to see other people's genitals and to show, or exhibit, his or her own. Incidents of children entering their parents' bedroom and seeing them in the act are often reported, and just as often, the startled child does not realize what he or she is seeing and thinks the parents are engaged in an upsetting act of violence. As the pioneer psychoanalyst, Freud's friend Marie Bonaparte (1882–1962), says in *The Life and Works of Edgar Allan Poe: A Psycho-Analytic Interpretation* (1949), the child sees the event as one of pure sadism and "the prototype of all crime." The incident—known as the *primal scene,* whether actually witnessed or a fantasy; actual events are also fantasized about—can be traumatic and is usually repressed.

The results and unconscious manifestations in adult life of the Oedipus and castration complexes are complicated and nearly incalculable. They include the following behaviors:

1. Adults who have gotten beyond the Oedipal disappointment unconsciously seek objects of love that resemble a parent. These objects may be appropriate or inappropriate, suitable or unsuitable, available or unavailable. How often have you heard the phrases, "Oh, he married his mother," or "She married her father?"

2. Others do the exact opposite, because of their *reaction formation* (a defense mechanism that turns an unwanted emotion into its opposite; see page 74) against unconscious sexual desire for a parent, and seek someone who appears not to resemble the parent, but who inevitably has some resemblance.

3. Others do not get beyond their repressed Oedipal feelings and remain unconsciously fixated on one or the other parent as an object, even to the point

where adult children continue to live with or in close proximity to their parents, behaving with them much as they did in childhood. Such people tend either to remain alone and unpartnered or to seek unavailable, inappropriate objects of affection, more or less successfully. The object may or may not be responsive.

4. Sometimes the child, displacing Oedipal desire onto an object that symbolizes it in some way, is fixated on the object, which becomes a *fetish,* remaining one in adulthood.

5. An adult may practice forms of sadomasochistic sexual behavior, so that he or she literally and physically acts out the unconscious internal reaction formation to the anticipated punishment of castration.

6. In a repetition of early Oedipal rejection, some people unconsciously seek out objects that will help them recreate and act out experiences of frustration, pain, disappointment, jealousy, rivalry, and depression. What they want consciously is to succeed in changing the way things were in the past, but they are defeated by their unconscious wish to recreate it so as to undo it. They seem incapable of ceasing to repeat the pattern that makes them unhappy. At first they will be ecstatic, as when they were infants in their parents' arms, but sooner or later, they will unconsciously ensure the breakdown of their relationships. They will then proceed to choose someone else who will help them act it all out again. Freud called this ubiquitous behavior a *repetition compulsion.*

As the child goes through puberty, he or she forms a sexual identity and plays out sexual desires directed to other objects. Here the fundamental bisexuality of human beings, which Freud said was evident in adolescents, plays a crucial role in determining how a person will live his or her sexual life, whether as a homosexual or a heterosexual.

Freud's views on homosexuality have often been misunderstood and misconstrued. To summarize his ultimate conclusions: Homosexuality is a variant form of sexual expression of which everyone is capable, since everyone is constitutionally bisexual. He explained the development of variations in sexual life as the outcome of particular ways of working through the Oedipus complex. And he felt that heterosexual development needed just as much explaining as homosexual development.

Not all of his followers or succeeding generations of analysts felt this way. Many clinicians who should have known better thought they could "cure perverts." The strenuously tortuous effort to class homosexuality as a disease (it is no longer so classified, although the effort succeeded for a time) was a betrayal of psychoanalysis, which wanted to be a humane discipline, and of Freud's original conceptions of sexuality.

But adding to the perception of his views as inconsistent is Freud's inclusion in *Three Contributions to the Theory of Sex* of homosexuality in the category of what were then called perversions. He used the word in a purely analytical sense, meaning simply a "turning away" from what most people do sexually. He did not mean it as a moralistic concept referring to a disgusting pathological sexual practice. And he was simply trying to figure out why people did what they did. In *An Autobiographical Study* (1925), he indicates his dissatisfaction with his own categorization when he writes, "homosexuality scarcely deserves the name [perversion]. It can be traced back to the bisexuality of all human beings." And in the *Three Contributions to the Theory of Sex,* he makes it clear that everyone is capable of making a same-sex object choice and, in fact, unconsciously does so.

In a reply to a worried American woman who had written to him about her son without actually saying he was homosexual, he wrote that she should not be ashamed to tell the truth, which he guessed. While being homosexual was no great advantage — homosexual activity was then a crime punishable by prison — there was basically nothing wrong with her son. It was certainly not a vice or degrading, and "cannot be classified as an illness," although he did consider that this "variation in the sexual function" was "produced by a certain arrest of sexual development." He felt that homosexuals, who are basically the same as everyone else, should be treated no differently from anyone else in society, and that persecuting homosexuality as a crime was a cruel injustice. He also told her that some of the greatest men in history were homosexuals, among them Plato, Leonardo da Vinci, and Michelangelo.

In *An Outline of Psycho-Analysis* (1940; posthumous), he describes homosexuality as "fixated to pregenital objects and aims," even though genital maturity has been attained — this is what he presumably meant by an "arrest of sexual development." Freud thought that little boys in the phallic stage are fixated on their own genitals before they are aware of female genitalia, and vice versa for little girls. But that temporal gap in knowledge can scarcely mean that boys or girls withdraw interest from their own genitalia simply because they have discovered another kind. On the contrary, it is quite clear that their interest in the genitalia of their own sex is universal and lifelong. And Freud says in "Analysis of a Phobia in a Five-Year-Old Boy" (1909) that when the male organ is autoerotically cathected, the cathexis leads directly to homosexuality.

He also believed that the usual rigid definition of "normal" sexuality as existing only for procreative purposes was incorrect, because in human beings (and in several other observable species), sexuality is a wide-ranging pleasure function, whatever the evolutionary reason for its existence. Heterosexual behavior is not simply a biological given based on the fact that there are two genders. The idea that sexually mature adults should indulge in sex in only one way is "the source of a serious injustice" towards those not so inclined, as Freud writes in *Civilization and Its Discontents.*

ABOUT NEUROSIS AND DISTURBANCES IN MENTAL FUNCTIONING

" The borderline between normal and morbid psychic conditions is … in such a state of flux that probably every one of us oversteps it many times in the course of a day," wrote Freud in "Delusions and Dreams in Jensen's *Gradiva*" (1906). The separation between mental health (which includes emotional self-control, self-regulation, a stable, secure self-image, and a general feeling of safety) and neurosis is a question of degree rather than of clear demarcation.

A *neurosis* is a nonphysiological, non-neurological disturbance in mental functioning. The term *neurotic* as a noun refers to a person who displays a behavioral pattern that indicates dysfunctionality, which in neurotics varies from mild and even benign to severe and incapacitating; as an adjective it is descriptive of such a pattern. Neurotics, who can be sensitive, caring people, are not necessarily dysfunctional in all areas and in fact generally function well in many. But they usually find it difficult to cope with certain kinds of situations or to function productively when trying to solve certain life problems.

Freud distinguished *psychoneurosis,* which results from early situations and unconscious reactions to them, from *actual neurosis,* which results from present-day situations, in particular sexual malfunctions and physical problems. These two types of neurosis could be "mixed" (with causes that have different sources) and difficult to distinguish, because actual neuroses could ultimately have psychoneurotic causes. As a result of this realization, nowadays the term *neurosis* is almost synonymous with *psychoneurosis,* and the concept of actual neurosis is less used than formerly.

Freud talked also of *neurasthenia,* a debilitating anxious condition without immediate apparent causes. Its symptoms can include exhaustion, headaches, constipation, restlessness, nervousness, feelings of anxious anticipation, trembling, breathing disturbances, cardiac disturbances, and sleep disorders such as insomnia. All of this is caused by present-day libidinal conflicts.

Neurosis results from conflict between the desires of the libido and the strictures placed on them by the aggressive drive controlling the libido. This conflict activates adaptive *defense mechanisms* against unwanted feelings, impulses, and desires that the ego feels might intrude on the neurotic's sense of well-being. This adaptation, which is an attempt to limit the expression of the drives, maintains the neurotic's equilibrium and self-image. In other words, neurosis is the result of a compromise between the desires of the id and the adverse reactions to those desires by the ego, which is then controlled by the superego that decrees what is and is not permissible. The "choice of psychoneurosis"—that is, why someone is neurotic in one way and not in another—is determined by several factors, which include among others how mature the ego is at the time of the conflict (how well it has learned to cope) and the severity of reactions to thwarted desire. This severity depends in part on the strength of the aggressive drive.

Freud, who felt he had never satisfactorily solved the problem of the choice of psychoneurosis, speculated interestingly in letters dated October 8, 15, and 16, 1895, to Wilhelm Fliess: The origin of hysteria could be traced to a prepubertal sexual experience that had shocked and frightened the child; the origin of obsessive-compulsive neurosis could be traced to "a pre-sexual [meaning prepubertal] sexual *pleasure,* which is later transformed into [self-] reproach." But he added that "my explanations are not adequate," although he felt he was on the right track.

Various types of neurosis have been defined and described. Freud used the term *transference neurosis* to mean the constellation of transferential reactions involved in the attachment of libidinal feelings to an inappropriate object, both in real life and, most particularly, in the context of the psychoanalytic process. The patient could transfer libidinal cathexes to the therapist, who was an artificial, inappropriate object, and develop a positive or negative attachment that could be highly invested and emotional in what was ultimately an inauthentic situation in which libidinal demands could not be satisfied. Freud included in the category of transference neuroses hysteria, phobic neuroses, and obsessive-compulsive neuroses (see below).

When neurosis is characterized either by overt and conscious or else by unconscious anxiety, Freud refers to *anxiety neuroses*. Actual neuroses are included in this category. Someone can be in a state of anxiety due to particular circumstances without having an anxiety neurosis. And someone with an anxiety neurosis may not always be in a state of constant or even conscious anxiety. Those neuroses such as conversion hysteria, in which the anxiety remains unconscious but is converted to symptoms, are categorized in the *DMS-IV-TR* as *conversion disorders,* not as *anxiety disorders.*

The neuroses include the histrionic, or hysterical, with the kind of symptoms Anna O. suffered from (see pages 41–42, 141–142); the traumatic, a stress-related disorder (see pages 66–68); the phobic, in which fear is displaced onto something else that is then also feared, irrationally (see pages 48, 57–59); the obsessive-compulsive, with its uncontrollable repetitions of actions or intrusive thoughts (see below and pages 48–53, 142–145); and the narcissistic, such as melancholia (see page 32).

Neurotics are typically not consciously aware of the nature of their conflicts. They frequently react and behave in what seems objectively to be an irrational way but that makes internal sense to the neurotic. Neurotic behavior allows the neurotic person to function in ways the ego permits by allowing, as a compromise, a substitute for the original impulse that has been repressed. For instance, in cases of obsessive-compulsive disorders, certain unwanted impulses have been disowned, split off, and replaced by whatever the obsessive compulsion may be. The compulsion is repeatedly acted out in order to continue warding off or avoiding the original impulse that gave rise to it. There is some satisfaction to be derived from this *compromise formation.* This satisfaction is the gain to the neurotic from the illness—a gain to which the neurotic is often attached deeply. But as Freud remarks in "Delusions and Dreams in Jensen's *Gradiva,*" "Attack and resistance are renewed after every compromise formation, which is, so to speak, never fully satisfactory." The neurotic's struggle to maintain the integrity of the compromise is continual and the inner unconscious conflict always alive. The forces of resistance and repression are constantly active, as what is repressed strains to reassert itself, and the neurotic is therefore in a state of "peculiar restlessness." Repression has failed of its purpose if it does not prevent anxiety and pain, even if the ideational content of what is repressed remains unconscious. The resort to further defenses that serve to continue the repression is necessary in order to drive anxiety away.

One of the important defense mechanisms is *denial:* a way of avoiding anxiety by repudiating the meaning or even the existence of an event or circumstance. Unconsciously the self knows that the circumstance or event really has the denied meaning. Another is *projection:* the displacement onto someone else of ideas or feelings contained in the self. These feelings, desires, or ideas are denied, but they reappear in the form of the displacement. For instance, people who are self-loathing may feel that everyone they meet has taken an immediate dislike to them. Or someone in love may see the object of affection as requiting that love, even while being rejected—"Oh, she doesn't mean it. She really loves me." Neurotics deny and project in part because they are unconsciously invested with the desire not to know the source of their problems.

In his essay "Mourning and Melancholia" (1917), Freud describes the mechanisms that melancholic, depressive people use to avoid the knowledge that they hate and want to destroy a love object after they have been rejected by that object: People in a state of *melancholia* (we would usually say *depression* nowadays) brought on by loss are deeply self-deprecating and appear deeply self-rejecting, but they seem quite unashamed of such feelings about themselves when they express them to others. And this astonishing lack of shame means that in reality—a reality hidden from themselves—they mean their unkind, destructive remarks (which appear self-destructive) to apply to someone else, namely the person who has disappointed them. Such people have reacted to their loss with unconscious rage that is seemingly boundless. They find their fury too threatening to be able to consciously acknowledge it to themselves. They are in a state of denial and have displaced their angry feelings for the other person, projecting those feelings back at themselves, even blaming themselves for the failure of their relationships. They can be characterized as having a *narcissistic neurosis* and are often unable to develop mature relationships. (The essay takes its title from Freud's comparison of the mechanisms of melancholia just described, which deal with unconscious objects; and the mechanism of mourning for the real loss of a loved one who has died, which deals with a conscious object.)

Freud thought that depression and depressive tendencies have their origin in reactions to early experiences of loss. Another factor in an adult's depressive tendencies is the unconsciously ambivalent behavior of parents, who, however good their intentions, may have been strict and appeared disapproving to the child one moment and overprotective the next. The child remained passive in the face of hostility and mixed messages because of feelings of dependence on the parents. Guilt over unconscious and conscious feelings of hostility and anger directed at them led to feelings of lack of self-worth. The tendency to depression later in life on the part of such children is increased. For more information on the subject of depression, see "Passive-Aggressive Behavior and Anger" on page 56. And for more on the ten basic defense mechanisms and their subcategories, see what Anna Freud has to say in the next chapter on pages 72–78.

One of Freud's great pioneering elucidations was his *etiology* (study of the causes) of the sexual causes of neuroses. Others before him had been aware that sex played a role in mental disorders, but they had only had a dim, confused view of the matter. The prevailing theory was that hereditary degeneracy played the preponderant role. Freud disabused the world of this notion. His innovative position was that the unconscious interferes with the search for happiness because of various internalized attitudes about what is and is not permissible with regard to sex and sexual fulfillment. Internal sexual maladjustments are manifested as inhibitions and symptoms. The infant's original helplessness and its reactions to its state of powerlessness, as well as the inevitable wounds to its narcissism, are further contributing causes, although neurosis is by no means always a necessary result of the resolution of these infantile and childhood conflicts.

The kind of specific traumatic incidents Charcot had referred to in dealing with hysteria were sometimes cases of childhood sexual abuse, incestuous or otherwise.

Freud thought at first that the origin of all neuroses could be traced to such abuse (the *seduction theory*) but discarded the idea when he realized that although he often heard stories of abuse from his patients, many, if not most of them, were fantasizing, and the incidents had not taken place in reality. He recognized at the same time that there were indeed cases of abuse, that they led to neurosis, and that they were more widespread than previously imagined. But he had to find an explanation for neuroses that were clearly not due to such incidents. He concluded that neurotic disturbances, inhibitions, and symptoms did indeed have libidinal causes but were not necessarily based on actual child abuse.

Inhibitions, which are particular behavioral restraints that mask desire (unconsciously perceived as shameful and guilt-inducing), are the result of conflicts that cause anxiety. To resolve the conflict, the thought, idea, feeling, or potential act is repressed and restrained. Inhibitions may also be induced by trauma, another possible cause of neurosis, hence the term *traumatic neurosis. Trauma* means "shock" and is a severe, almost disabling blow to the nervous system and to the psyche, which it threatens to overwhelm.

A *symptom,* which is a symbolic "return of the repressed," arises through the process of condensation (see page 20) of the conflict into a particular behavioral manifestation that may or may not be temporary—for example, a nervous tic, such as the uncontrollable blinking right eye of the lecturer in Chekhov's *On the Harmfulness of Tobacco,* which manifests itself only when he lectures; or Solyony's compulsion to douse his hands with perfume, which he does constantly in *Three Sisters.*

Despite their inhibitions and symptoms, neurotics typically function quite adequately in situations that do not involve their particular basic conflicts, have a more or less intact sense of reality except with regard to the areas where they are dysfunctional, and generally adhere to the usual social norms. But their symptoms are indicative of inner pain, anxiety, and suffering.

Neurosis, which results from repression, is not to be confused with *perversion* (a term eliminated from the professional vocabulary of psychiatry and psychology in 1987), which refers to sexual object fixations that are a manifestation of unrepressed infantile sexuality; or with the personality disorders called *psychoses,* of which there are many. In a 1924 essay, "The Loss of Reality in Neurosis and Psychosis," Freud wrote, "neurosis does not deny the existence of reality, it merely tries to ignore it; psychosis denies it and tries to substitute something else for it." Psychotic characteristics include a divorce from the real world and a completely distorted, tenuous, or almost nonexistent perception of reality. Psychotics are often severely impaired in their ability to cope with the circumstances of life in the real world. Their impairment may be intermittent or constant, temporary or permanent. These are the kinds of people who often have to be placed in institutions. Freud felt that psychosis was not responsive to psychoanalysis, the primary task of which he saw as the analysis and treatment of the neuroses, as well as the analysis of the human psyche in general. For more on the subject of psychosis, schizophrenia, and delusions, see pages 193, 212.

For an example of psychosis, see the film *A Beautiful Mind* (2001): John Nash, played by Russell Crowe, was a mathematical genius and a mildly disturbed schizophrenic. He heard hallucinatory voices in his head. In the film, the character is more disturbed than the man was in real life, and his hallucinations take visual, physical form.

Eros and Thanatos:
The Life Instinct and the Death Instinct

The horrible slaughter of World War I, in which the worst instincts of mankind were given full play, as well as his study of neuroses and of the repetition compulsion, which almost implies that some people have a "fate neurosis" and are dogged by destiny to relive the same events, led Freud to ask if there was not something beyond even the pleasure principle itself that was operative in human behavior. He was struck by the fact that the pleasure principle seemed almost inoperative in neurotics, who regularly insured that they would find themselves in unpleasurable situations and could not seem to extricate themselves from the compulsion to repeat. Perhaps there was simply an inborn instinct connected with the aggressive drive that caused people to will their own destruction unconsciously.

Freud could easily see that culture did not eradicate the sadistic, destructive instincts of mankind. Why are people so terribly cruel to each other? Why does war exist? Where does hatred come from? He thought that it had to arise out of more than simple reactions to frustration resulting from the thwarting of desire and instinctual needs. And the ability of human beings to harbor and nurture very deep resentment could not simply be explained as a turning against the self of feelings of hatred for an external object, from whom punishment might be feared.

The instincts for life, the "life force" as the Irish playwright George Bernard Shaw and others called it, Freud called *Eros,* which is the constellation of pleasure-seeking, life-affirming instincts, among them those of self-preservation and the libido. Eros was named for the Greek god of love, who was so deeply in love with the ethereally beautiful Psyche that even his mother Aphrodite, goddess of love, was jealous.

But there were questions about life that the simple existence of Eros could not explain. Some religions postulate the existence of the Devil. Freud postulated the existence of a *death instinct, death drive,* or *death impulse* (the German word *Todestrieb* can be translated all three ways), hidden and unconscious except when it showed itself in behavior—as, for instance, in sadism, which he thought might be one of its manifestations. And he was aware that his hypothesis was highly problematic. An early member of Freud's circle, the psychoanalyst Paul Federn (1871–1950), named this presumed death instinct *Thanatos,* after the Greek god of death.

Another early associate and analysand of Freud's, Heinz Hartmann (1894–1970), known as the father of ego psychology, emphasized that the ego was capable of creating a "conflict-free zone" so that a person was capable of feeling consciously at peace—as in what Freud called the *Nirvana principle,* which is the tendency and goal of Thanatos to reduce energy to zero. The organic seeks to return to the inorganic state from which it arose. Hence there is perhaps an instinct or drive that leads organic life to seek its own demise, but in its own way and in its own time. Thanatos fights the instincts of self-preservation and pleasure, which do not want even to acknowledge its existence and constantly find ways to circumvent it and limit its power. But such is the built-in biophysiological mechanism that ensures its fulfillment in the course of time that eventually it succeeds in destroying the life of the individual. For a similar explanation of how and why we are genetically programmed for death, see *Genome* (2000) by Matt Ridley.

Freud wrote that we are actually incapable of imagining our own deaths, although we all fear our own annihilation. But anxiety over death is a preoccupation of obsessional neurotics. And he thought that this anxiety, symbolized in dreams by hiding and remaining hidden and by departure, was analogous to castration anxiety—we *can* imagine the pain and terror of castration—involving the fear of suffering and pain, and anxiety over loss.

QUESTIONS AND CONSIDERATIONS: THE PRACTICAL APPLICATION OF FREUDIAN IDEAS TO CHARACTER INTERPRETATION

I) Some of Freud's Character Types

LIBIDINAL TYPES

In his essay "Libidinal Types" (1931), Freud discusses general approaches to sexuality that might fit many different character types. The libidinal types all "fall within the category of the normal" and are basically "free from neurosis," even in the case of the type he calls obsessional. In extreme form, the types may be pathological: Don Juan, the Marquis de Sade, Natasha in *Three Sisters,* and so forth. He distinguished three basic types:

1. The *erotic,* which gives in to the demands of the id with minimal interference from the superego; this type is focused on loving and needs above all to be loved, so that they are ruled by the fear of loss of love in the dependent relationships that they are often involved in;
2. The *obsessional,* which is highly controlled by the superego, so that this type has an anxious conscience and depends for a feeling of well-being on obeying the commands of the superego;
3. The *narcissistic,* based in the desires of the ego that mediates between the unruliness of the id and the strictness of the superego; this type prefers to love even without being loved in return, because they like to lead and not to feel dependent.

Freud stresses that the types do not exist in a pure state. There are mixed types: *erotic-obsessional, erotic-narcissistic,* and *narcissistic-obsessional,* for example, all of which also fall within the range of the normal and are free from neurosis. In the first mixed type, the erotic-obsessional, the superego restricts the desires of the id and maintains an extremely dependent relationship with the loved object. For Freud, the erotic-narcissistic type is "perhaps the most common of all." Its polar characteristics moderate each other, and this type is active and aggressive. In sociocultural terms, the narcissistic-obsessional type is valuable because it combines the demands of the superego with those of the ego, and this is an impetus to productive action. A combination of all three types would be ideal and harmonic, but this does not exist, according to Freud.

For writers and actors: Which Freudian libidinal type is the character you are writing or acting? Aside from physical attraction and physical type, one might say that people are unconsciously attracted to certain libidinal types. How often have you heard the phrase, "He/she is not her/his type?"

Chekhov's Vanya might be characterized as erotic-obsessional in his relationship with Yelena, because he yearns to be loved by her and he is dependent for a feeling of well-being on not being rejected. At the same time, he severely controls his behavior, as dictated by his superego. Astrov, on the other hand, is a narcissistic-obsessional type, needing to lead in love, which is why he takes the initiative in approaching Yelena. His superego leads him to be controlled in most situations. The Professor, Yelena's husband, is also a narcissistic-obsessional type, which explains in part why Yelena finds Astrov attractive: she "falls" for the same libidinal type. Yelena herself is a more purely narcissistic type without much of the erotic about her, which is why she is so indolent much of the time and so annoyed at Vanya's importunity, and why she hates feeling dependent. Sonya, in love with Astrov, is erotic-obsessional, like her uncle. This is one of the things Astrov finds unattractive about her. And Yelena finds this aspect of Vanya's personality similarly unattractive; he is really not her type.

This analysis of libidinal types is one of many places to start in approaching the network of relationships in a script, not only for actors analyzing their characters, but also for directors shaping the telling of the story. Making clear to the actors what story is being told about the relationships of the characters is, after all, one of the director's essential jobs.

Another place to start is by sifting through the information on the character's formation and deciding what is useful and what is not. Alice Spivak gives the following advice to actors: "Bring Freud into character analysis, and use it when it is playable." The actor might ask, for instance, when a desire first manifested itself, what form it took then, and how it is apparent now in the character's present behavior.

In a letter to Freud dated August 15, 1913, Ernest Jones discusses the genesis of female prostitutes' characters in general terms in connection with Bernard Shaw's play about prostitution, considered shocking at the time: *Fanny's First Play*, which Jones had just seen. In act 3, Shaw uses what was at the time a well-known London euphemism for prostitute: "daughter of a clergyman," because so many prostitutes apparently told their clients they were clergyman's daughters. Jones sees a double meaning in this euphemism, namely "a submerged longing for respectability" (a Shavian theme in the play), but also, going even deeper, an identification with the father as god, or God the Father, indicating a repressed incest fantasy, acted out as a female Don Juanism. Jones thinks contemporary prostitutes are thus "descendants of the 'sacred whores of Babylon,'" who were originally devoted to religious cults and had sacred duties, and finds the coincidence amazing. In analyzing a theatrical character who is a prostitute, this Babylonian genesis, fascinating as it is, may be useful as an image or an actor's secret, but is otherwise obviously of limited value in determining the character's psychology. On the other hand, the unconscious identification with the father and a "submerged longing for respectability," which could be a through-line or superobjective, can both be very useful. Another actor's secret could be the character's Don Juanism: wanting to have sex with as many men as she can. There will also be other characterological traits, such as orality, that will emerge when studying the script, and they will provide further specificity.

The psychosexual stages of development survive in the form of various traits that can more or less influence someone's entire character. They do not exist as single constructs, but as components. Beware of the "genetic fallacy" that would reduce character traits and behavior to their simple origins and equate their original meanings with their current ones, as if that explained everything. For instance, such behavior as kissing, or an interest in food, its preparation, and different cuisines, clearly goes well beyond an infant's elementary need to assuage hunger and the oral pleasure the infant experiences.

THE ORAL CHARACTER

The baby's first desires and experiences revolve around the necessity for food, warmth, and shelter. The somatic and libidinal energy of the infant is attached to the oral cavity. The proof that the libido centers at this stage around oral sensations is quite clear: you have only to watch babies and very small children try to put everything they can into their mouths, partly as a means of exploration and partly because of pleasurable oral feelings, and not simply because they think everything is food.

Food is associated with the relief of tension, from infancy on: a baby cries and someone feeds it, thus relieving the tension caused by hunger pangs. On the positive, joyful side, generosity can derive from orality, especially for those who love food and want to share it—to share the wealth, so to speak. "Isn't this delicious?" you might hear someone say; "You must try some!" But the frustration of oral desires during infancy can result in associating eating with tension, as opposed to the relief of tension. This negative conditioning can mean that a person will hate to eat, associate displeasure with food, and be very finicky in what he or she will eat. Speech inhibitions of various non-neurological kinds and such habits as grinding the teeth are other possible results. Other negative oral traits are greed (oral aggression), dependency (oral passivity), a deep need for nurturing, and excessive miserliness, the latter trait being associated also with anality.

As Freud points out in "The History of an Infantile Neurosis" (1918), the survival of orality is seen in the language of love: people we find attractive are "sweet," and we use such terms of endearment as "sugar," "honey," "sweetie," or "sweetie-pie." Innumerable examples from other languages could be added to the list. And people can be *oral passive*, meaning they obey the command to receive food and are submissive as adults, or *oral aggressive*, meaning that they go after the nourishment they want.

The oral character traits can be remarkably useful. Gérard Depardieu in the film *Le Placard* (The Closet, 2001) played a homophobic chief of personnel obliged to take a presumed homosexual employee to lunch in order to keep his job, or so he has been led to think. Depardieu is very uncomfortable, and as he tries to make conversation, he "stuffs his face" to stuff down his discomfort, something people often do when trying to suppress anger or other discomforting emotions. This is using food as an object in the classic Uta Hagen way.

In making his initial overtures of friendship to his colleague, he begins by discussing a subject he assumes is of mutual interest: what they are eating for lunch in the company cafeteria. Later in the film, when Depardieu wants to offer him a gift, he buys a box of chocolates. All of this is hilariously symbolic of oral sex.

In the New York premiere of Tom Stoppard's *Rough Crossing* (based on Molnar's *The Play's the Thing*), directed to hilarious effect by Steve Stettler, I played a very oral character, Gal, a man obsessed with food. The role is certainly written on one extremely simplistic and almost cartoonlike note. The play revolves around rehearsals of a new musical and takes place on board an ocean liner in one of the lounges, amply supplied with an appetizing buffet, around which I hovered, eating from time to time, always looking at the food, and occasionally putting in my oar about what was going on in the rehearsals. In another scene I entered a cabin and saw the remains of breakfast. Seating myself at the table, oblivious to the farcical chaos raging around me, I proceeded to gorge myself. "Is there any cream?" I said, while digging into some pancakes and looking for the cream for my coffee.

Harpagon in Molière's *The Miser* is a character replete with negative orality. He is excessively greedy and miserly at the same time. If you ever play this role, try using the habit of grinding your teeth as a character trait and perhaps even as a Michael Chekhov psychological gesture. Harpagon is also very anal and sadistic. Feeling unloved and rejected, he in turn withholds love and rejects people, whom he tries to control. The only thing that has never disappointed him is his money. In his obsession with money, he has become paranoid and suspects everyone of wanting to steal it from him. He goes nearly mad when he discovers his empty cashbox.

Other problems arising from the oral stage include great concern with giving and taking in relationships, and a conflict over the amount of dependence or independence a person feels comfortable with. How much can people in need of nurturing and sustenance remain comfortably alone? How much do they need to be with people? Do they behave in a needy way, as if they were hungry? George and Martha in Edward Albee's *Who's Afraid of Virginia Woolf?* talk constantly. Their drinking and their codependency and fear of abandonment imply problems with orality and disturbances in the oral phase.

THE ANAL CHARACTER

As the baby grows older and learns to control the developing sphincter muscles of the anus, libidinal pleasure begins to be associated unconsciously with the relief of tension resulting from the need to excrete. The child begins to learn mastery over his or her own body, and to feel proud and to begin to develop a positive self-image and a measure of independence when the training achieves desirable results—among them praise from the parents or other caregivers. During early toilet training, however, tension can result from the parents' nervousness and possible embarrassment. The child may be tense, and this may cause the parents discomfort, which they may not know how to deal with adequately. The child may be rebellious or passive and submissive. The diverse reactions indicate the formation of future character traits, including the harsh and punishing characteristic called *analsadistic.*

We have all heard the term *anal retentive,* which refers to the retention, as opposed to the willing release, of feces during the toilet training stage. Anal retentive people are compulsively neat and rigidly unbending. The opposite type is *anal expulsive.* The child has taken pleasure in excretion and been praised for it. Anal expulsive people may be untidy, if not downright messy; compulsively submissive to authority; and generous to a fault.

One of the traits of the anal-retentive character is the tendency to insist that everything be in a predetermined order. A room or a desk is kept neat, almost compulsively so. Plans must be rigidly adhered to and promises kept. This sort of person is almost never late for an appointment, and not merely out of the politeness Louis XVIII of France characterized as the punctuality of kings. (Not that one should be late: it is only polite to be on time.) Some people are even compulsively early, which may reflect a fear of being punished. Such behavior, whether being compulsively too late or too early, arises from the fear of disapproval that the child felt parents might display if the child did not do what he or she had to with dispatch and without sitting on the toilet forever, straining and feeling incapacitated and unable to release the feces, because the impatient, even slightly disgusted parent was present as an observer at an embarrassing moment. Unconsciously, pleasure has actually been experienced in retaining the stool.

We usually associate anality with the following unpleasant, negative character traits: crabbiness, nastiness, being hard to get along with, and being controlling and manipulative. The traits of frugality and parsimony are also associated with this character type, as are the withholding of affection for manipulative reasons and stubbornness or obstinacy — the inability to "let go." On the more positive side, a person may be persistent where persistence counts and may really get a job done that needs doing. But there is also frequently an element of sadomasochism in such characters, again unconsciously associated with the fear of punishment during toilet training.

As a result of tension and frustration during the oral and, especially, the anal phase, the child may begin to develop an unconscious hatred of the parental figures, who are seen in the child's mind as the cause of the frustration. Ambivalent feelings develop. The beginning of a desire for independence, as well as willfulness and rage, are further results. All of this will complicate the later Oedipal phase.

Anal characters are usually comic and laughable in films and plays. The series of hotel clerks played by Franklin Pangborn are prissy in the extreme. He is very ordered in his gestures, compulsively neat, and slightly fey, in that closeted, stereotyped way gay people were so often mockingly portrayed in early cinema. Another example of the type is the prim, repressed and prudish spinster played by tight-lipped Margaret Hamilton in *My Little Chickadee* (1940). Again, Harpagon in Molière's *The Miser* is very anal, as well as very oral: he takes in money as a baby takes in food, and does not want to release it but to retain it. Shylock in Shakespeare's *The Merchant of Venice* has anal-retentive traits and so does his nemesis, Antonio, whose unconscious fantasies revolving around both Shylock and Bassanio are analsadistic.

Phrases and words using the component *tight* to depict character are tellingly descriptive of anal retentiveness or negative oral problems. Some examples: tight-lipped, tight-fisted, tightwad, tight-assed, and just plain tight.

Malvolio in *Twelfth Night* has anal-retentive traits, and he is also negatively oral in a way similar to Harpagon. The emphasis in Shakespeare, however, is not on Malvolio's parsimony or miserliness but rather on his need to control other people. And he has other unenviable character traits, such as his anal-retentive sadomasochism, which emerges in his fawning servility to those he thinks are superior and a nasty dismissiveness to those he thinks beneath him, as if he is defecating all over them. He is a histrionic personality type with a hysterical side to his reactions, as in the scenes when he confronts the late-night revelers or, later, finds the letter supposedly written by Olivia.

When I was playing the part in the journeyman production at the American Shakespeare Festival in Stratford, Connecticut, I asked Morris Carnovsky for some advice — he had played the role at the Globe Theater in San Diego, California. In an instant he became Malvolio: he wrinkled his face up, and he looked just like a prune. I laughed, for Mr. Carnovsky was very funny. And then he said in his mellifluous voice, "Remember: to Malvolio, everybody smells slightly." This even includes Olivia, of whom he is enamored, or rather by whom he is besotted. I adopted Carnovsky's excellent advice, which further suggested the anal side of Malvolio because of the unpleasant smell of excrement associated with his attitude that everyone needs to take a bath. You will not find the idea that to Malvolio everyone smells slightly expressed directly in Shakespeare's play, but it is implied in Malvolio's words, and I thought it was brilliant of Morris Carnovsky to have thought of it. He was a great teacher as well as a great actor.

THE GENITAL CHARACTER

The growing maturity of biophysiological development does not mean the maturity of the psychological ability to deal with sexuality. That comes as the child grows accustomed to sexual sensations and discovers what is pleasurable and desirable. Even immature desire and its external actualization in autoerotism do not yet mean that an adolescent is comfortable or capable of dealing with the manifestations of his or her own sexuality, which require psychological adjustment and self-acceptance.

When, as a result of puberty, the genital area — which has also long been the seat of urethral eroticism as the child took pleasure in urinating — inevitably and naturally comes to predominate as the seat of pleasure, after the phallic and latent phases, Freud speaks of *genital primacy*. This refers to post-pubescent adult sexuality. The romantic relationships portrayed in nearly every film and play show people in this physically mature phase of development. Two of the genital character traits are the ability to be assertive — although aggressive desires are sometimes accompanied by shyness, sometimes by self-confidence — and taking pleasure in lovemaking. People in this phase have an increasing ability to sublimate and create art or do research in science, or simply to throw themselves into work. In the film *Frida* (2002), Alfred Molina plays the Mexican artist Diego Rivera, who throws himself with fervor into painting, politics, and lovemaking. Selma Hayek plays Frida Kahlo, the activist and artist who falls in love with him. Their passionate affair is portrayed with all its ups and downs, and is illustrative of the mature genital phase of development and its aggressive drive for sexual fulfillment.

The mature genital character is not to be confused with the *phallic* character, who remains unconsciously fixated on the phallus, and whose aggression and desire for power and domination are uppermost. In fact, Rivera in the film may be more phallic than genital. See Reich on the phallic-narcissistic character, page 145.

THE HYSTERICAL OR HISTRIONIC CHARACTER

Hysteria and the theater have an intimate relationship in some ways. Histrionic personality types — the term *histrionic* often replaces the term *hysteric* nowadays — have to be the center of attention: "Look at me!" Of the many symptoms of this series of disorders, one of the most striking is the vivid histrionic daydream that takes the patient away from present reality to a world of fantasy and wish fulfillment, as in the case of Anna O. So real are these imaginings that the hysteric really appears to be living them, yet they are not hallucinations or psychotic delusions: all the time, the seemingly far away daydreamer knows where present reality is located and can be recalled to it in an instant — exactly like an actor performing in a play.

Hysterics have an intense level of anxiety and may go from crisis to crisis in their lives, overwhelmed by too much excitement, which they have trouble dealing with. And they have extremely high unconscious levels of guilt and shame over sexual matters. Sometimes they put on an act, behaving seductively and teasingly, and then, when someone responds to their blandishments by making a sexual approach, they react as if they are completely unaware of their own behavior: "What do you mean? Just who do you think I am? How dare you behave like that with me?" may be the startled and startling response as they reject their would-be seducers. They actually are unaware, because they have been able to split off threatening sexual feelings and affects from their behavior, so that they prevent themselves from *feeling* sexual, even though their behavior would seem to indicate that they do.

The basis of this behavior harks back to the way they behaved as children when they were overstimulated and confused by a sexualized relationship with an adult figure, often a parent who behaved seductively with them and may even have actually abused them. The histrionic's adult behavior reproduces the behavior of the adult figure they were involved with and is thus a kind of coded message about what happened to them in childhood. The memory of these things has been split off from consciousness but reappears in their behavior. And their seeming incomprehension and reaction as adults is the same as when they were children and were powerless to resist their seducer. But as adults, they can and do resist.

Characteristic of the hysterical or histrionic personality is the sort of immature childish behavior that consists of the self-centered seeking of attention, as previously noted. In fact, they are quite unhappy and uncomfortable, and feel unappreciated unless they are the center of attention. Such people often carry out every action with a generally seductive air. Out of their jealousy and need to be the cynosure of all eyes, hysterical types will do anything to get attention, including threatening suicide or feigning illness, of which they may even develop the symptoms. In describing people and situations, they tend to exaggerate: "That was the most delicious meal I ever ate in my life!" "Oh, he/she's the most wonderful person in the world!" In other words, from the point of view of cognitive psychology, hysterics are incapable of clear thinking. They cannot think through their problems with any lucidity or understand logically what is happening. The hysterical personality deals not in facts but in general impressions. If you ask why that person is so wonderful, they find it difficult to give you details or reasons. They respond quickly but superficially to situations, and their focus of attention may shift just as quickly, because they are incapable of intense, prolonged concentration, and they lack curiosity. They tend to avoid knowledge and shy away in particular from sexual knowledge. Fantasy and nostalgia are their stock in trade: the Prince Charming who will rescue the damsel in distress is a favorite idea. Malvolio's view of Olivia is very much this sort of hysterical reaction when he finds the forged letter in which she presumably and cryptically reveals her love for him. Internally, they feel like small, helpless children, needing rescue. And they may even develop the counterphobic desire to rescue others. They can be warm and loving but passive people, overdoing displays of affection to counter their anxiety.

British and French farce would not exist without hysterical types. Basil Fawlty, played by John Cleese in the television series *Fawlty Towers,* is hilariously hysterical and endlessly histrionic. For more about him and about the hysterical type from Wilhelm Reich's point of view, see pages 141–142. Mrs. Bennett in Jane Austen's often-filmed *Pride and Prejudice* is another hysteric, especially as played, for example, by Mary Boland in the 1940 film. So is Mrs. Jerry Cruncher, who is always "flopping" in Dickens's *A Tale of Two Cities,* another novel that has been adapted numerous times for the stage and screen. In *Hamlet,* Ophelia, in her madness, displays symptoms of the hysterical personality. So does Natasha in Chekhov's *Three Sisters* and Madame Popova in *The Boor.* And both Lomov and Natalia in *The Marriage Proposal* are hysterics. Mrs. Malaprop in Sheridan's *The Rivals* is another hysterical personality. Blanche in Tennessee Williams's *A Streetcar Named Desire* is histrionic in her reactions and retreats into hysterical fantasies. Even when doing something as simple as offering someone a glass of lemonade, she is seductive and wants to be adored. No wonder Stanley misunderstands the messages she broadcasts and responds to them in the worst way. And we must not forget Lady Macbeth in her "sleepwalking" scene: "Out, out, damned spot." A blank stare, very useful in playing Lady Macbeth, is one of the major signs of a sleepwalking disorder. Out of her guilt and fear, she has developed into a hysteric—gone mad, as the Elizabethans put it—one of the most striking in theatrical literature.

One of the lessons to be learned from a study of the histrionic character is how vital it is for actors, writers, and directors creating and interpreting characters to understand as much of any character's unconscious as possible. Internal obstacles can interfere with seeking an objective as much as external obstacles, if not more so. In a nice feat of psychological legerdemain, an actor must be conscious of what the character is unconscious of.

II) Topics

The Death Wish and Suicide: The idea of a *death wish* is not the same thing as Thanatos, with which it is often confused. There really is such a phenomenon as a death wish, whereas Thanatos is a hypothetical concept. The death wish exists as a syndrome in which someone is continually putting him or herself in harm's way, or as a wish at a particular time and place and in particular circumstances. But it is a popular, not a technical, term.

Usually when people say "I wish I were dead," they don't really mean it. What they really wish is that they could immediately solve whatever problem is causing them pain. Clearly, there are times when someone might genuinely wish to die and will choose suicide. Some people do this out of a futile desire for revenge because they have been rejected in love or for any number of other reasons — "I'll show you! You'll be sorry when I'm gone!" In "Mourning and Melancholia," Freud writes that suicide is a form of self-punishment in which inadmissible homicidal desires are turned against the self. This is the case with Treplev in *The Seagull* and with Ivanov, whose despair and pessimism seem general. Some kill themselves out of a wish to escape disgrace and punishment. There are those who want to protest injustice — this is suicide in a heroic but futile vein, such as that of Szmul Zygielbojm, a Polish Jew in exile in London who killed himself to dramatize in as extreme and shocking a way as possible his pain at the Nazi murder of Jews, against which he wanted to galvanize the indifferent, apathetic world into action. Not least important among the reasons for suicide is the desire to end the terrible suffering and pain of an incurable illness. Then there are people who are so deeply ashamed of themselves that they want to avoid the look of others, whose gaze of reproach they cannot bear: The deeply painful film *L'adversaire* (2002) is based on a true story. Daniel Auteuil plays the murderer of his entire family with uncanny reality. He is desperate to avoid the hatred and misery of facing the consequences of his acts.

Characters with a death wish abound in Shakespeare. Macbeth clearly has a death wish near the end of the play, but perhaps unconsciously from the beginning. So do Antony and Cleopatra, who face defeat and punishment. Othello wishes to die and kills himself after the revelation of his fatal errors. Romeo and Juliet wish to die because they think they have lost each other to death. All these characters feel they have lost everything that makes their lives worth living and that it would be pointless to continue.

Denial and Projection in *Hamlet* and *Rebecca*: The defense mechanisms of denial and projection described on pages 31–32 are the stuff of drama and melodrama in films and plays, particularly where neurotic or paranoid characters are involved.

Because he feels guilty for having murdered his brother ("My offense is rank"), the paranoid Claudius is sure his nephew Hamlet wants to murder him. But actually it is Claudius who wants to murder Hamlet. He is projecting his own desire onto his nephew. He is right about Hamlet's wish, but he doesn't actually know that: Claudius just thinks Hamlet should want to murder him, because he suspects that Hamlet is aware of his uncle's crime. In this way Claudius justifies getting rid of Hamlet. Like Iago, Claudius "for mere suspicion in that kind/ Will do as if for surety."

Gertrude exists in a state of denial. Has she chosen not to know that her husband murdered his brother, Gertrude's first husband and the father of her son? She does not wish to understand Hamlet's melancholy and denies that it is too important—just a passing phase. He will be fine once he gets over his father's death; he's just upset temporarily. In fact most of the characters in the play deny at some point or other what they know to be true and do not wish to acknowledge.

Alfred Hitchcock's *Rebecca* (1940), based on Daphne du Maurier's novel, is a very different kind of story, but similar psychological mechanisms drive it, although it takes place centuries later than the story of Hamlet—some psychological phenomena are universal, as Freud thought.

Out of her fears and insecurities, the unnamed heroine played so appealingly by Joan Fontaine projects onto Rebecca, her husband's dead first wife, all the marvelous qualities she feels she doesn't have. In fact, Rebecca had none of those qualities, and they actually belong to the character played by Joan Fontaine, who doesn't realize how innocent, sweet, and loving she actually is. Her unconscious thought process—her *inner monologue*—might run something like this:

> I am not a worthy, deserving person, really, even though some people seem to think I am and even though I would like to be, and I have to compensate for not deserving the happiness that has come my way by being almost overly nice, so that people will not see what I am really like. My former employer thinks I am just a conniving, opportunistic social climber. She said so when she found I was going to marry Max. Perhaps she was right, although I wouldn't like to think so. And I really love and admire Max! But why did he want to marry me? I am completely unworthy as a person and certainly unworthy of him. I cannot compare to Rebecca, who was obviously the epitome of sophistication and brilliance, and whom he must almost have worshipped. I have no idea how to handle myself in my new situation. I am out of my depth and out of my class, and this proves my unworthiness. Even the housekeeper, Mrs. Danvers, would be more worthy than I am to occupy my present position.

Along with her unfavorable comparison of herself to Rebecca, she has convinced herself that her new husband, the suave aristocrat Max de Winter (Laurence Olivier), adored Rebecca, whom he has refused to discuss, when in reality the opposite was the case. Max and his beautiful wife—who was cold, viciously nasty, and unfaithful to him—ultimately couldn't stand each other. He ended up hating her, so that he can hardly bear to talk about her. Max is in a state of denial when it comes to the unfortunate effect his refusal to talk about his past life is having on his new wife, convincing her unintentionally that he almost regrets having married her and that Rebecca was the only person he really loved.

The malevolent housekeeper, Mrs. Danvers (Judith Anderson), who loved, idolized, and adored Rebecca, and disapproves tacitly of Max—whom she unconsciously hates and who in her mind was unworthy of Rebecca—behaves with steely, judgmental coldness towards Max de Winter's new wife, treating her with the utmost disdain covered over with minimal, servile politeness. Realizing that Max's new wife is insecure, feels unworthy, and is unused to the social circles in which she now moves, Mrs. Danvers does everything she can to reinforce the unfortunate new wife's invidious comparison of herself to Rebecca. Mrs. Danvers actually feels the deepest contempt for herself, unconsciously—which does not, of course, excuse her behavior—and is in a state of denial when it comes to her own self-loathing. And she has kept everything as it was when Rebecca was alive, in order to preserve her memory of her as intact as possible, almost as if she wishes to deny that Rebecca is indeed no more. She has projected an idealized image of herself onto Rebecca, the person Mrs. Danvers unconsciously wishes to be.

These mechanisms are at the heart of many stories. Examine any script for examples, and when you are playing a part, ask yourself in what ways your character is in as state of denial and how projection enters into the story.

Doing Plays and Films Set in Freud's Era: Should you play a man or woman from the late nineteenth-/early twentieth-century periods (or from any other period, for that matter) or should you direct a play or film set in that era, you will have to do research not only on the way people carried themselves because of how they dressed, and how that physically conditioned their movements or gestures (men's stiff, attached shirt collars; women's long skirts), as well as on what was considered proper dress (women were expected to wear hats and gloves; men wore hats and gloves as well), but also on the attitudes towards sex typical of a particular period. Too often, this latter research is neglected, resulting in far too contemporary a feeling and a consequent curious lack of reality, as we in the audience perceive too little a gap between a long-ago era and our own time. Despite the commonality of human emotions and psychology that spans eras, we expect to see some different behavior, as opposed to being simply "taken back" in time with the help of decors and costumes.

In his essay "Some General Remarks on Hysterical Attacks" (1908), Freud described a hysterical woman's possible sexual fantasy, involving her reading on a park bench while lifting her skirt slightly to reveal her foot. This shows us not only how differently women dressed in the late nineteenth and early twentieth centuries but also how different the sociocultural environment and sexual attitudes of early twentieth-century Hapsburg Vienna were from our own. Clearly, what was considered sexually titillating has changed for us.

Another example of this difference, this time from theatrical literature: in *A Doll's House,* Nora provocatively shows Dr. Rank some new silk stockings, which is the occasion of a conversation that is veiled but was considered when the play was first produced to be shockingly sexy. Nowadays she might show him some lacy silk underwear, and the conversation would be much more direct.

In *Psychoanalysis and Anthropology* (1950), the Hungarian-born American founder of psychoanalytical anthropology, Géza Róheim (1891–1953), who grew up in Budapest and was familiar with life in Vienna (he knew Freud), says that Howard Lindsay and Russell Crouse's Broadway play *Life with Father* "represents society or the family ... in [turn-of-the-century] Vienna as much as in New York." Michael Curtiz's 1947 film with William Powell and Irene Dunne is readily available on video or DVD.

Reading Marcel Proust's *In Search of Lost Time,* set in France (and Venice) in the same era, can prove equally instructive. The novel is a vivid portrait of French society in the late nineteenth and early twentieth centuries, with its hierarchy and social customs and manners, its way of dressing, and its cultural and class attitudes.

In every era there are manifestations of psychological universals that seem typical of the age. The sociocultural manifestations of primary narcissism, sadomasochism, and sexual repression in the era in which Freud lived and worked, for instance, included a repressed, prim, tight-lipped social context of patriarchal, nationalist male chauvinism and imperialism. Europe saw itself as the center of the world and the arbiter of civilization. The idea that there are races, meaning particular human groups perceived as different from each other and with whom are associated an ensemble of psychological and physical characteristics, had become the basis of thinking about human biophysiology. Race was considered an important key to individual psychology, although, obviously, the idea tends to obscure the psychology of the individual. And the idea of superior civilized and inferior primitive races that arose with the concept was not only ethnocentric but also poisonous in its effects.

The idea of race had been around for centuries but was only "scientifically" studied and crystallized by the nineteenth-century scientific and academic establishment. With twentieth-century advances in the study of genetics, the concept that there are different races has been shown to be erroneous. All human beings share the vast majority of genes, and only a tiny percentage accounts for such superficial differences as skin color or eye shape. In other words, race is a sociocultural and political construction, and not a valid scientific, biological truth. But racism pervaded scientific and popular thinking for more than a century and a half to noxious and tragic effect, and it still infects the minds of the ignorant and the sociopathic.

Freud believed that individual psychology was more important than characteristics associated with a particular group for understanding people, although the sociocultural effects of belonging to a particular group have to be considered in their effect on individual cases. He wrote in *Group Psychology and the Analysis of the Ego* (1921) that so-called group characteristics were irrelevant when dealing with individual psychology. After all, as a Jew, he knew from firsthand experience that characteristics associated with a particular group are based not on scientific observation but on misperceptions and prejudices. Freud's struggles with anti-Semitism and its effects on him certainly influenced his views of the world and its irrationality. The ubiquitous anti-Semitism of Freud's Europe is also an important background factor in plays and films set in his era. Of course—this is so obvious it hardly needs to be said—there were many non-Jews who accepted Jews as basically no different from themselves, and many Jews and non-Jews befriended each other. There were many loves and marriages between the two groups, so the situation is not all black and white by any means, and one must learn to perceive the many shades of gray in the complicated history of the epoch.

Imperialism in the late nineteenth and early twentieth centuries is another factor one must take into account in plays and films set in this era, particularly with regard to the attitude of the colonizers that they were superior and the colonized inferior. This form of ethnocentric racist prejudice did untold damage to the psyches of the colonized. If you ever play any characters in films or plays about historical or contemporary colonizers, such a point of view will inform the attitudes of the characters you play. If you play one of the colonized, you may be playing a character who has absorbed something of the image held of the colonized by the arrogant, self-important colonizers as primitive and uncivilized, which becomes that character's self-image. Some of the colonized began to feel inferior and powerless and to behave in a servile manner, allowing exploitation. But there were those who refused to accept the negative stereotype at all and eventually rebelled at what was being done to them. The image and status of inferiority were foisted on the exploited by force of arms, and the assumptions of superiority led the narcissistic colonizers to behave as if everything they took and did was taken and done by right and entitlement, often buttressed by their religion—"God is on our side."

The kind of thinking described above will inform your character's inner life. Whether you are playing a Jew or a non-Jew; a European, an American, or a non-European; one of the colonizers or one of the colonized, the pervasive racist thinking of the era (such attitudes still exist, as we know), including the acceptance in some quarters of the concept that the Jews are a race, will imbue the consciousness of the character you are interpreting with a perception of differences. Your character will either accept or reject racist attitudes. This is true even if there is no text that expresses the character's views on race and ethnicity. The automatic feeling of comfort and even superiority experienced unthinkingly by the ruling majority, even those who reject racism, and the discomfort felt by the excluded minority are facts of life that directly impact character and relationships.

Some questions for the actor: What does your character think about race? Is he or she consciously racist, in the prejudicial sense? Does he or she believe that there are different races? Does the character believe these differences are superficial and literally skin deep, or psychologically indicative of a person's character? Does the character believe in the concept that some groups are "primitive" and "uncivilized" and that if they are, this makes them inferior? Does the character believe that so-called higher civilization is found only in a European context?

Dreams: Characters in plays have their own dreams. What does your character dream? And what is the nature of those dreams? What does your character wish to tell him or herself through the dreams? What wishes are fulfilled? What does a nightmare represent to your character? As an actor, you must make the answers up, unless the author has informed you specifically, as in Hitchcock's *Spellbound,* where a specific dream is of supreme importance. You can set your imagination dreaming about the character. See where it leads you.

Another actor's question: What has your character repressed from waking consciousness that appears latent in a dream? Why? Was there something that required repression because it might destroy the character's self-image as a good, moral person?

If you are a director, you might want to discuss these things with the actor, in order to clarify aspects of the story you are telling. You might lead actors in improvisations revolving around their dreams. This will help in exploring objectives and obstacles as well as actions. An excellent book, worth consulting for its many productive exercises, among other things, is Janet Sonnenberg's *Dreamwork for Actors* (2003).

If you are a writer, you might want to consider what the characters dream and why. And actors, writers, and directors would do well to read Freud's book *The Interpretation of Dreams*, discussed briefly on page 20. This book deals with much more than just dreams and goes deeply into unconscious motivations generally.

Hypochondriasis: *Hypochondriasis* is a syndrome revolving around the idea that one is ill, in spite of overwhelming evidence to the contrary. It is a form of phobic behavior and results from a morbid fear of illness and, ultimately, a fear of death. The hypochondriac surrounds him or herself with medications and nostrums, and consults doctors regularly, sometimes going from physician to physician and taking test after test until the desired answer — "Oh, yes, you are dreadfully ill" — is obtained. And the imaginary invalid pampers and coddles him or herself in order to take care of the imaginary illness, which amounts to a mania or a fixation. The illness cannot be diagnosed, but its psychological causes are to be found in a feeling of being abandoned and unloved. Marie Bonaparte characterizes hypochondriasis as "narcissistic regression," and indeed, the narcissistic need for attention of the kind one got from parents when one was ill as a child is paramount. Controlling the people with whom the hypochondriac is surrounded is the underlying desire of someone who, on a conscious level, says he or she is not in control but in the grip of a serious malady.

The most famous example of the type in theatrical literature is the title character in Molière's *The Imaginary Invalid*. Argan, the hypochondriac, is a domestic tyrant and uses his illness to try to control his family. He is hysterically funny to the audience but not to his family, and is taken advantage of by the medical profession, which is mercilessly mocked by Molière. He makes much of the fact that there are quack doctors who cater to such individuals and will do anything for money. Tante Léonie in Marcel Proust's *Swann's Way* is an imaginary invalid who will hardly leave her bed. Proust's description of her would be helpful to anyone who has to play a hypochondriac or to the people who deal with such a neurotic.

Neurotic Symptoms: Solyony and Kulygin in Chekhov's *Three Sisters*, Nyoukhin in *On the Harmfulness of Tobacco*: Neurotic symptoms that symbolize internal conflict are of great use in interpreting characters. The actor and director are free to invent them, even if they are not supplied by the author. Some playwrights, however, are very purposeful and specific in describing neurotic symptoms — Chekhov, for instance.

Lomov, the suitor in *The Marriage Proposal*, is a mass of neurotic symptoms. He is in a state of anxiety. And he is so incredibly nervous that we sympathize with him, but at the same time we find him almost unbearably funny; see page 268.

In the course of his career, Freud returned again and again to the problem of anxiety, its origins and its meaning. He distinguished anxiety from fear: Fear has a specific, definite object, while anxiety tends to be generalized, even though it is brought about in specific circumstances. Anxiety is generated when a person feels incapable of controlling a particular situation or of attaining a certain goal. And it is always loaded with the unconscious possibility of depression---that is, someone who is anxious is prone to sinking into depression in the context of the predicament that gave rise to the anxiety. The object of anxiety is vague---the desire for approval, for instance. But what does that mean? And what form would the desired approval take? People afflicted with anxiety only see the worst possible outcome (and not the best) that might result from their situation. In their nervous anticipation and subjectivity, they are immediately thrown---or, more accurately, unconsciously throw themselves---into a completely passive state. Their extreme passivity is then paradoxically the most active part of them. At the same time, they experience internal disorientation that prevents them from seeing the external, objective reality of the moment. However, Freud thought that anxiety was not necessarily always neurotic, although all neurotics had anxiety as one of their symptoms.

The formation of neurotic symptoms is described on page 33. Understanding their origins makes it very easy to play a part and give it depth. The symptoms will naturally fall into place without the necessity to act them technically. In any case, where such symptoms exist, understanding the reasons behind their formation is essential to character interpretation. To recapitulate, the symptoms are coded messages revealing and masking the problem at the same time. They represent a compromise that enables the person to obtain some sort of unconscious satisfaction of the original desire that gave rise to the symptom, but in a distorted way. The question for actors is: What was the original desire and how do the symptoms provide relief from the tension it engendered, satisfying the desire in some way? To put it another way, Freud asked what the sufferer had gained from the illness. What has the character gained?

Whenever we see him, Solyony is in the act of dousing his hands with perfume and rubbing them together. This obsessive-compulsive behavior is a neurotic symptom. His self-loathing takes the form of feeling that he stinks. Chekhov does not tell us where Solyony's symptom originates, but the actor playing the part can guess: repressive, uncomfortable early toilet training led to an obsession with cleanliness and unpleasant excremental smells that have to be compensated for. And repressed sexual feelings, which may include homosexual attractions, are viewed as filthy. Solyony has to get rid of his dirtiness by constantly cleaning his hands, which have offended no doubt by autoerotic stimulation involving such fantasies. And to Solyony, who projects his self-loathing, everybody actually smells bad, even Irina. His desire to be accepted by her is a pose and a lie he tells himself, born of jealousy, because she prefers Tusenbach to him. (In reality, she is not in love with Tusenbach but agrees to marry him for a number of reasons.) A typical paranoiac (see page 54), Solyony is unconsciously attracted to Tusenbach, but this is so deeply inadmissible and threatening that he displaces his desire and unconsciously imagines Tusenbach sleeping with Irina. Solyony overcompensates for his inadmissible desire by being nasty and sadistic with Tusenbach, instead of just leaving him alone. It is this behavior that is a clue to his attraction to Tusenbach. He seeks him out constantly and is then horrible to him. Killing Tusenbach will symbolically kill Solyony's unacceptable unconscious wish.

In any case, Irina won't accept Solyony if he smells bad. His use of perfume will deflect all unpleasantness, he tells himself, and everyone will find the beautiful smell attractive, but he feels dirty all the time anyway. The neurotic compromise of washing his hands and dousing them with perfume as compensation for masturbation and its attendant fantasies (and to get rid of the dirtiness associated with excrement) serves to enable him to continue his autoerotic activities once he is "clean": "Clean yourself up, and you can do it all over again," says the ego.

Solyony's other symptoms include his almost uncontrollable desire to sneer at and belittle everyone else—and to quote Lermontov, the romantic Russian poet and novelist whom he unconsciously misinterprets to bolster his own pretense at heroism and manliness, because Solyony feels less than manly. When aroused, repelled, or disapproving, he can be fierce and even terrifying, as he is with Natasha when he talks about cooking her baby, a macabre joke she finds horrible. A typical defense mechanism of his is isolation (see page 74), so that he can say and do the most awful things without affect and without guilt.

In short, Solyony suffers from the psychoneurosis known as an obsessive-compulsive disorder, the genesis of which is in the distant past. He appears sometimes to understand the nature of his compulsions and obsessions, but never their origin. He is uncomfortable with his understanding and tries to neutralize his anxiety by ingratiating himself with the people around him, who, however, find his behavior so strange that they are repelled almost more than they are when he is at his most neurotic. They don't know what he might do next. He appears capable of anything, and he is frightening. They therefore reject him, causing him even more anxiety and exacerbating his paranoia.

Kulygin, on the other hand, can be said to be suffering from an actual neurosis, brought on by his wife Masha's love for the attractive army officer Vershinin, who reminds her of her father in some ways, as does Kulygin. Kulygin continually denies that anything is wrong and insists he is contented, because he is in a state of denial and emotional stasis that prevents him from taking action. In any case, what action could he take? He cannot bear to admit that his wife no longer loves and admires him, but hates him.

Kulygin's actual neurosis can be distinguished from his deeper, lifelong psychoneurosis. One of the symptoms of his psychoneurosis is his masochistic inability to assert himself about what really means something to him. Instead, unconsciously afraid of being punished should he assert his desires, he displaces his disappointment and upset onto something trivial. It seems more important that a clock is seven minutes fast than that his wife might betray him. He does not have a full-blown obsessive-compulsive disorder, but he does have a compulsive side, evidenced by his obsession with time (symbolized in the play by the many references to clocks that either malfunction or are broken). Things must be done at the right time. He is also occasionally phobic, as we can see from his joke about thirteen being unlucky. He makes a joke of it, but he is serious. Such a rational man as Kulygin is in his own eyes should not be superstitious, and Kulygin is ashamed to have to admit to himself that he is.

In *On the Harmfulness of Tobacco,* the nervous lecturer Ivan Ivanovich Nyoukhin, who will become increasingly distraught as the lecture continues, begins suddenly to blink his right eye. He becomes very conscious of this nervous tic and brings it to the attention of the audience in the unlikely event that they had not already noticed it. He probably wants to arouse their sympathy. "Yes, I know. When I lecture, my right eye blinks, but pay no attention. ... It began to blink on ... the day my fourth daughter ... was born." What a wealth of psychological material Chekhov has put into this one brief statement! The twitch is first of all a product of his nervousness, which he feels as almost incapacitating, and we know he resorts to alcohol to help calm his nerves. It is a hysterical symptom of his anxiety neurosis and helps him avoid the anxiety aroused by his repressed thoughts. Nyoukhin, in typical hysterical fashion, appears far less anxious about the symptom itself: "pay no attention."

What is the source of his inner conflicts? For one thing, Nyoukhin's neurotic symptom has been engendered by his conflict over having another girl, when he probably wanted a son. But simply having another child to support in his economically deprived circumstances has brought on an anxiety attack as well as the blinking. As he continues his talk, the blinking gets worse, and he reveals the further conflicts behind his nervous tic: his misery in his marriage and his disappointment in the way has whole life has gone, which he finds it almost unbearable to acknowledge. In the end it is all too much for him, and he tells us everything. And the blinking stops!

It is as if Nyoukhin had been saying, "What the eye does not see, the mind does not know." He blinks away what he does not want to see or notice. One of those things is the mockery of his wife and daughters, the jokes at his expense. Perhaps the audience will find him ridiculous and make fun of him, just as his wife and daughters do. He certainly almost ensures that they will, by the sort of masochistic, pathetic manner in which he presents himself and the outright silliness of some of his ridiculous remarks. He just blinks all that away. An actor can make all of this nervous twitching very real simply by concentrating on its sources in the rich inner life of the character. For more on this play, see page 269.

Obsessive-Compulsive Personality Disorder: In various writings from 1907 through 1909, Freud described obsessive-compulsive behavior as involving anal character traits, such as the ones described above: obstinacy, parsimony, and an excessive concern for orderliness among them. In general, obsessive-compulsive people are anal retentive—they just can't let go of their obsession, at least not without the greatest effort. Freud explains in his essay "Repression" that in obsessional neurosis, withdrawal of the libido, which is the usual aim of repression, is accomplished. But the repression is basically unsuccessful in providing a solution to the psychic conflict. It has only succeeded in substituting things that provokes anxiety—an obsession with something and/or a compulsion to repeat certain actions and/or to think certain unwanted intrusive thoughts—for the anxiety aroused by the original impulses.

David Shapiro points out in *Dynamics of Character* (2000) that those who are compulsively conscientious have substituted their compulsion for the rational-cognitive ability to judge reality. In fact, they do not judge reality at all. Rather, their compulsive conscientiousness is "an *alternative* to a judgment of reality." This has acute characterological and behavioral consequences, and implies among other things an inability to be flexible in relationships. Such people construct their world and dismiss anything from it that is not absolutely consonant with their view of the world as they wish it to be. The world revolves around the fulfillment of their compulsions and obsessions. This does not imply psychosis, because obsessive-compulsives are in touch with reality, but they ignore the parts of it that do not fit in with their scheme.

Many people have obsessions that are temporary and situational, and that they may find compels them to carry out some task. This does not mean that they are obsessive-compulsive neurotics. People can be conscientious without being compulsive. Or they can be obsessive-compulsive neurotics and at the same time be highly productive, hardworking individuals able to live their lives relatively well adjusted to society. They are not as sick as those at the lower end of the scale (who can hardly think straight) and may even be perceived as normal but a little odd and not to be crossed.

The *Diagnostic and Statistical Manual of Mental Disorders (DSM-IV-TR)* makes a distinction between obsessive-compulsive disorder and obsessive-compulsive personality disorder, which have a number of characteristics in common: People with an obsessive-compulsive disorder, as opposed to those with an obsessive-compulsive personality disorder, often realize at some point that their "obsessions or compulsions are excessive or unreasonable," although some have little or no insight into themselves. Even those who do are nevertheless preoccupied obsessively with certain thoughts, feelings, or ideas that cause them anxiety and that they experience as inappropriate without quite knowing why. They attempt to suppress and neutralize their feelings, unlike those people with an obsessive-compulsive personality disorder. Solyony, described above, is an example of this type. In *Hedda Gabler,* Tesman is obsessed with his scholarly work to such a point that he has to be forced to marry Hedda, whom he then virtually ignores, even on their honeymoon. Hedda herself is obsessed with her own unhappiness and narcissistically self-absorbed.

People with an obsessive-compulsive personality disorder are often "excessively devoted to work to the exclusion of leisure activities and friendships," as the authors of the *DSM-IV-TR* inform us. They also list overconscientiousness and inflexibility with regard to moral values and ethics, and these traits are "not accounted for by religious or cultural identification." Such people are also incapable of throwing anything away, and they are almost incapable of delegating tasks. In general, they are tense, stubborn, and rigid, which has a great deal to do with the nature of their toilet training and their anal character traits, as described by Freud. Finding spontaneity threatening, they narrow their experiences by imposing acceptable limits. In other words, obsessive-compulsives are deeply defended against anything that might intrude on the self-imposed system of order that structures their lives and prevents anxiety, even small amounts of which they find intolerable. They see life and the world as confusing and the order they put into their lives as a necessity. They live under self-imposed pressure. In extreme cases, their superegos react harshly against them at the slightest breach of their ego-ideal system. See also the analysis of the type in the chapter on Wilhelm Reich, page 142. In *Character Analysis* (1933), he characterized obsessive-compulsives as "living machines," and there is indeed an automatism and a machinelike quality to their behavior.

There are, of course, many obsessions and compulsions: some people are preoccupied with food, or with alcohol or drugs if they are compulsive substance abusers, or with their personal appearance. But the basic rigidity and highly defended personality are common hallmarks of the type. See also the section on addiction on page 179.

The Oedipus Complex: Whether you are writing, directing, or acting a character, some of the most important questions you can ask are: What are the ramifications of the Oedipus complex in the character's life? How does the character act out the unconscious, repressed early Oedipal conflicts in adult life? What is the adult child's present relationship with his or her parents? In what way is it the same as it was in childhood? Whom does the adult choose as someone with whom to establish a relationship, and why? Has he married someone who resembles his mother? He may feel his spouse is the opposite of his mother, but is she? Has she married someone who resembles her father? She may feel her spouse is the opposite of her father, but is he? In gay relationships, the same questions apply: Which parent does the partner resemble, and why has he or she been chosen? Does the character have a repetition compulsion?

In Eugene O'Neill's *Long Day's Journey into Night,* the Oedipus complex echoes through the life of the play's characters. Edmund has to try very hard to understand what he has been through and what the family relationships are all about. And he has to learn how to deal with both his parents and to seek his own independence. His older brother, Jamie, clearly has problems dealing with his own unconscious Oedipal jealousy of the affection and worried tender solicitude their mother has for Edmund. He also feels his father doesn't love him. And the father is indeed particularly hard on his older son, disapproving of him and berating him in very sarcastic terms. He hates the ne'er-do-well and drunk he thinks his older son has become. Both brothers feel misunderstood by their father and, to some extent, excluded from his affection, even though they know he loves them. James, the famous actor, with his narcissism and his stinginess, has a conflict between his unconscious jealousy of his younger son and his love for his wife, as well as the necessity to assert — sometimes rather futilely — his patriarchal authority with both his wife and his children. His jealousy of Edmund is one of the reasons he does not want to spend the money to get him proper medical care. Another is his negative oral aggressivity, his parsimony. His unconscious fear is that if he spends all his money on doctors, he will not have enough to eat.

Oedipal ramifications in Jamie's character are also apparent in the sequel, *Moon for the Misbegotten,* in which Jamie is the principal male character. Both parents and his brother are now dead, and Jamie has returned home bearing his mother's coffin. His isolation neurosis is Oedipally based; see page 74.

Tennessee Williams's *Suddenly Last Summer* shows us an unresolved Oedipus complex that leads to mayhem and murder. Joseph L. Mankeiwicz's 1959 film with Katherine Hepburn as the far-too-doting mother and Elizabeth Taylor as a psychiatric patient is strange and disturbing. In *Summer and Smoke,* which was first a play and then a film, directed in 1962 by Peter Glenville, Geraldine Page repeats her stage performance as Alma, a neurotic spinster in a small Mississippi town. In a constant state of denial, she has to deal with her kleptomaniac, mildly psychotic mother (Una Merkel). Alma, who is a hysteric/histrionic personality and has never gotten over her Oedipal feelings, is hopelessly in love with a young doctor, played by Laurence Harvey.

Paranoia: Everyone is capable of harboring suspicions that are irrational. And as Freud tells us in *Civilization and Its Discontents,* everyone "behaves in some respect like a paranoiac, corrects some aspect of the world which is unbearable to him by the construction of a wish, and introduces this delusion into reality." A question for actors: How has the character you are interpreting done this?

Paranoia runs the gamut from paranoid feelings to the paranoid personality disorder to delusional disorders and the paranoid type of schizophrenia. The authors of the *DSM-IV-TR* point out that this disorder does not necessarily occur only in connection with such psychotic disorders as schizophrenia or as the result of a medical condition. In other words, it can occur as an aspect of neurosis. In the psychotic varieties, as Patricia McWilliams puts it in *Psychoanalytic Diagnosis,* the paranoiac is "confused about where thoughts leave off and actions begin."

Freud theorized that paranoia resulted from repressed homosexual tendencies due to an unsatisfactory resolution of Oedipal conflicts with the same-sex parent. The paranoiac finds these tendencies completely unacceptable. As part of the defense mechanism involved in their repression, the paranoiac develops a submissive, if not entirely passive, relationship with that parent. But the passive homosexual overtones of the relationship threaten to seep through the defenses. So menacing are they to the ego's sense of well-being that the process of repression takes the course of turning love for the parent into hate. This arouses such deep guilt that the hate for that parent is then intellectually justified on the grounds that it is actually the parent who hates the child. The parent, of course, may be completely innocent of such a charge and completely unaware of what is going on.

There are other factors that may form part of the genesis of paranoia, including such feelings as lack of self-worth and powerlessness. In overcompensation for such unconscious constructs, the paranoiac does not usually have access to feelings of shame. A particular physical manifestation, noted in clinical studies, is a downward left eye movement when the paranoiac feels challenged.

Some of the important traits in the listing of the elements of paranoid personality disorder in the *Diagnostic and Statistical Manual of Mental Disorders* (*DSM-IV-TR*) are that paranoids harbor the suspicion, not based on evidence, that someone is out to deceive and harm them; that they are "preoccupied with unjustified doubts about the loyalty or trustworthiness" of the people in their lives and suspicious about the fidelity of their partners; that they are afraid to confide in other people because they think the information might be used against them in some way; and that they bear grudges and never forget real or fancied injuries. They often feel attacked when no attack was intended. Frequently, other people do not even understand why the paranoiac feels attacked.

Another characteristic of paranoiacs is their constant seeking of clues that will affirm the correctness of their suspicions, to which they are wedded. Any piece of evidence that would deny that they are right is either ignored or, if it cannot be ignored, interpreted so that it can fit into their system. They experience anything unexpected as extremely upsetting, because, like obsessive-compulsives, they require their world to be in order, systematized so that they can understand it. In extreme psychotic cases, they view the world as full of clues that will justify their paranoia. Paranoiacs exist with a high level of tension and a distrust of any kind of spontaneity, which immediately arouses their suspicions. Since they always feel threatened, they narrow their lives as much as possible to the tried-and-true routines they have worked out, once again much like obsessive-compulsives.

The film *Above Suspicion* (1995), in which Christopher Reeve and Joe Mantegna portray adversaries, shows us a disabled policeman whose suspicions concerning a love affair between his wife and his brother are justified, and he admits to killing them in self defense. But Joe Mantegna, who plays a detective investigating the case, suspects that Reeve really planned the murder, and he tries to prove it. At certain points in the film, Mantegna is led to believe that he is just being paranoid.

Paranoia may be induced by guilt over crimes or misdeeds the paranoiac has committed. Macbeth, feeling that murder will out, grows increasingly paranoid, and that is why he has Banquo murdered. But full of self-pity, he hardly feels guilty about his crimes: "I am in blood / Stepp'd in so far, that should I wade no more, / Returning were as tedious as go o'er." So all those horrible murders were merely tedious. As for Lady Macbeth, she was paranoid to begin with. The repressed tendencies underlying her paranoia are shown in her complex about masculinity: "Unsex me here. … Stop up the access and passage to remorse, / That no compunctious visitings of nature shake my fell purpose … " The image in those lines is clearly sexual: the "passage" is the vagina, and the "visitings of nature," not to be allowed, are the penis, quite aside from the surface meaning of the lines regarding remorse. Instead of the paranoiac's usual imperviousness to guilt, her foul misdeeds weigh unconsciously upon her psyche, and she descends into hysteria; see page 41.

Iago is a genuine paranoiac in the classic mold. Freud's analysis about unacceptable repressed homosexual feelings at the root of paranoia applies very well to this man who destroys so many lives, including his own; see pages 240–244.

Strindberg's 1887 play *The Father* furnishes us with a more modern example of paranoia. How do we know who the father of a child really is? The cavalry officer Captain Adolf wonders about that. Only the mother knows for sure, and Adolf's wife, Laura, holds that question over her husband's head, torturing him and controlling and manipulating his suspicions to her own ends. Did she have an affair or not? Is Bertha really their daughter, or is someone else her father? She refuses to enlighten her husband on the subject. Strindberg is nothing if not misogynistic!

Paranoia is an essential component of the phobic neurosis of prejudice, which in its extreme form, such as that taken by the Nazis, the apartheid supporters in South

are times when fears are rational, such as when one is assaulted by muggers and threatened with a knife or a gun, but such fear is clearly different from an irrational phobia.

A phobia is a compromise formation, involving a repression of sexual or aggressive situations the ego perceives as threatening and undesirable. The repression results in the displacement of the fear aroused by the conflict onto an external object or situation. Whatever is then feared produces anxiety and is usually avoided. Freud considered the repression involved in phobias "radically unsuccessful," since in maintaining avoidance and fleeing from the upsetting cause of the repression, with the objective of diminishing pain and eliminating anxiety, one idea was simply replaced by another, but anxiety and pain were still not avoided.

Sometimes people with a particular phobia will resort to superstitious behavior and magical thinking to ward off bad luck, as in the well-known theatrical superstition about its being unlucky to quote from Shakespeare's *Macbeth* (referred to obliquely as the "Scottish play") within the precincts of a theater. In one version of magical, superstitious behavior, those who inadvertently cite the Bard's most unlucky play must leave the room, turn around three times, and ask permission to reenter.

Among the most commonly known phobias are acrophobia (fear of heights— whether open, exposed, or viewed from what is objectively a safe vantage point, such as behind a barrier—often accompanied by sweating, vertigo, or dizziness), claustrophobia (fear of closed places and of being enclosed or trapped in confined spaces), agoraphobia (fear of open spaces or of going out into public places, resulting in reclusiveness and, in extreme cases, in personal neglect), aviatophobia (fear of flying), and xenophobia (fear of foreigners or strangers). Hypochondriasis is also a form of phobic behavior.

Some people have a social phobia, or a social anxiety disorder, which is activated when the person is in social situations, particularly among strangers in unfamiliar surroundings. People with this disorder fear that they will act in such a way as to bring humiliation and shame upon themselves. They feel anxious and perhaps, in severe cases, may have a panic attack. Any actor can understand the feelings involved, because the experience of stage fright is close to this disorder. People who have phobias and who are phobic characters experience such symptoms as sweating, nausea, dizziness, feelings of faintness, the inability to move, temporary paralysis, breathing difficulties, and an accelerated heartbeat in the presence of the things they fear, even when those fears are completely irrational.

For Freud, phobic neurosis represents the cathexis of particular objects to which underlying psychic conflicts attach themselves because they symbolize aspects of the situation that provoked anxiety and represent the unconsciously felt danger. For instance, in zoophobia (fear of animals), an instinctual libidinal impulse directed towards the father (or possibly, another authority figure), accompanied by a fear of him, is repressed. The father or authority figure ceases to be an object of libidinal interest as the impulse disappears from consciousness. But quantitatively, energy is still invested in the situation, and anxiety is the result. In a substitute formation, the fear is displaced and projected onto some animal, whether a domestic pet or an animal in a zoo, or some wild beast—"The result is a fear of a wolf, instead of a claim for love from the father," writes Freud in "Repression." Someone who is zoophobic may shrink back on perceiving the animal or animals of which he or she is afraid, even if the animal is caged in a zoo, and begin to perspire profusely and feel faint. There are other factors to be taken into account as well: unconsciously, there may be an aggressive desire to take revenge against the authority figure who has frustrated the libidinal desire and a fear of doing so.

Some people develop *counterphobias*—that is, they seek out the object of their fear in order to overcome it. People who have acrophobia may take up mountain climbing, someone afraid of dogs may acquire one as a pet, and so forth.

Religion: Freud makes clear in his essay "Obsessive Actions and Religious Practices" (1907) that he thought there was an equivalence between obsessional neurotic symptoms and religious rituals and practices. In *An Autobiographical Study* (1935), he says that these rituals are a precipitate of primeval experience from the dawn of history. Both neurotic symptoms and religious rites have the same function and serve the same purpose—namely, to ward off guilt, particularly guilt about sex, by the defense mechanism of displacement; and to protect the individual from threatening knowledge, such as that of humanity's mortality, by means of denial. For Freud, religion, whose doctrines are illusions that can be neither proved nor refuted, is a reflection of unconscious conflicts in the psyche. Freud saw religion as a "universal obsessional neurosis," while an individual obsessional neurosis was a kind of private religion with its own rituals and practices.

He analyzed several causes for religious belief. He thought that the more someone controls his or her aggressiveness, the more it is turned against the person's own ego, because of the building of an *ego ideal.* In requiring a person to live up to that ideal, writes Freud in *The Ego and the Id,* the superego can be "super-moral and then become as cruel as only the id can be." Furthermore, "even ordinary normal morality has a harshly restraining, cruelly prohibiting quality. It is from this, indeed, that the conception arises of a higher being who deals out punishment inexorably."

Freud also thought that religion and religious sentiment arose from the infant's looking on parents as if they were all powerful. This feeling was accompanied perhaps by the "oceanic feeling" of limitless beneficence descending from the cosmos, which the French author Romain Rolland described to him in a letter of December 5, 1927, detailing his reactions to Freud's *The Future of an Illusion.* Rolland talked about the oceanic feeling of being in touch with limitless eternity. He also felt that there was a mystical energy source that conferred inestimable benefits. Freud felt that these feelings, which he said he was incapable of experiencing himself but believed others did indeed experience, arose from the infant's undifferentiated view of everything as a limitless extension of the self, for whom the parental caregiver supplies whatever is necessary to fulfill the baby's needs and with whom the infant's ego merges in a feeling of narcissistic omnipotence, until that feeling disappears due to the inevitable separation from the parent in later developmental stages.

In seeking an explanation for the universe and for humanity's limitations, and in trying to overcome the dread and fear connected with the presentiment of death, humanity has convinced itself that there must be a loving yet possibly punishing god (modeled unconsciously on parental figures), who requires appeasement so that punishment may be warded off and immortality assured in some form or other—whether by a life after life or by reincarnation. So the existence of God is an illusion based on wishful thinking. The illusion is later justified and "proved" on philosophical grounds.

For more on the Freudian view of religion, see *Civilization and Its Discontents, Totem and Taboo* (1913), and *Moses and Monotheism* (1939), the latter a very interesting bit of speculation indeed, full of historical truth as well as some intriguing if far-fetched analysis; and Freud's correspondence with the Swiss Protestant pastor, pedagogue, and psychoanalyst Oskar Pfister (1873–1956), one of Freud's early supporters. After Freud published *The Future of an Illusion,* Pfister wrote a long article called "The Illusion of a Future" in rebuttal. But he remained Freud's cordially esteemed friend and always affirmed his belief in psychoanalysis.

When you create or play a religious character, you must decide the true basis of that person's beliefs. The reasons that people believe in religions are many and varied, from faith based on true philosophical conviction to more or less unthinking ingrained acceptance of what they were taught in childhood, the overwhelming need to believe in something other than the reality they see around them in this "vale of tears" in which they suffer, or the murderous fanaticism of psychopathic and dangerous people who absolutely and fiercely require everyone to believe what they consider the truth. The latter two types of belief imply an underlying disbelief that has to be defended against.

Tartuffe in Molière's play is well known to theater audiences as an opportunistic hypocrite who does not really believe in the principles he preaches. His name has become a byword for religious hypocrisy. Orgon in the same play is a perfect example of Freud's idea of the equivalence of obsessional neurosis and religion. He is obsessed with Tartuffe as well as with religion, and he really is a believer. Eventually his faith in Tartuffe, although not in religion, is destroyed when Tartuffe attempts to seduce Orgon's wife.

For a story about the hypocrisy and fakery of evangelists, see the 1960 film *Elmer Gantry,* based on a novel by Sinclair Lewis that is even more denunciatory (some would say inflammatory) than the film adaptation. Burt Lancaster plays the title role of a con man and reprobate who bilks willing suckers, of whom, as the famous saying has it, one is born every minute. For a tale of religious fanaticism taken to psychopathic extremes, see *The Passion of Darkly Noon* (1995), with an extraordinary performance by Brendan Fraser as a deeply disturbed young man.

The title character of Martin Luther in John Osborne's play *Luther* finds the fount of his belief and of his straining protests and demands for reform in his problems with constipation and its relief. This is perhaps ahistorical, but as far as the character in the play is concerned, one can quite imagine his problems with early toilet training and his protests against his severe, strict, unforgiving parents. The character of Luther in the play is certainly a complicated individual, extremely troubled and sadomasochistic. In real life he projected many of his sadistic fantasies onto Jews, whom he viewed as the purely evil spawn of Satan, and especially onto the Catholic Church, which he denounced and excoriated on moral grounds. He also defamed and demonized the

Church's hierarchy. Luther raged and fulminated, and he found many followers who were not as fanatic he was but who shared his belief in the necessity of reform in the Church.

Here is an incident I put in my actor's memory banks for future reference: An individual with a rather odd expression in his eyes approached me as I was waiting at a bus stop one Sunday morning. "Have you been to church today? Are you born again?" he asked me. "No," I said. "Well, you better be, or you're goin' straight to Hell!" He proceeded to expostulate with me and told me of the deep anger he had felt towards both his parents, because he was severely physically abused as a child. Since he had found Christ, he had been able miraculously to forgive them completely and to pray for their salvation. From the manner in which his whole being appeared highly animated and emotionally charged when he went on and on about how often and how severely his father had beaten him while his mother stood by and encouraged her husband, it was apparent to me that the deep rage and fury he felt towards his parents was by no means gone and that he had not forgiven them at all. He was clearly in a state of denial. While he continued to harangue me, I made a mental note that if I were ever to play such a character, he was a perfect model. And boy was I glad when that bus came along!

Sexuality and Love: For actors: There are always, always, always sexual feelings, repressed or not, towards all the other characters. Sexuality and feelings about sex that may be partly or wholly conscious, or completely unconscious, always condition all the relationships. Mostly these feelings are subtextual, just as they would be below the surface in real life. It does not matter whether you are playing a waitress who appears for two minutes in a scene in a diner or the leading role. Every character has a full life, and that includes sexual feelings and relationships. These questions are also considerations for writers when creating characters on the page or for directors helping actors in rehearsal.

Even if the role is a minor one of two lines, you can deduce the nature of the character's sexual attitudes, defenses, and repressions from the given behavior and words in the script. The major-domo whose simple function it is to announce the arrival of the guests at a grand royal ball has a self-image and a sexual life, although his lines may consist only of the names of characters. The Princesse de Guermantes' usher in Proust's *Sodom and Gomorrah,* having had a sexual encounter with an anonymous gentleman whom he had wished to see again, is called on several days later to announce him on his entrance to a soirée and thus learns his name. He makes the announcement in a proud tone of voice, flushed with pleasure at the remembrance of his experience.

One of Marcel Proust's points of view, shared by Freud, is that sexual orientation and gender make no difference in how people experience love and desire or in how they behave when they are in love. This is a good lesson for any actor who has to play a character whose adult sexuality is different from his or her own.

Some essential questions for actors: Is your character secure or insecure, repressed or comfortable with his or her own sexual feelings and behavior? Is your character ashamed about sex, feeling it is somehow "dirty?" What sexual feelings does the character have towards the other characters? Does your character feel attractive or unattractive? Which Freudian libidinal type is your character (see page 35)? What does your character know, feel, or think about the sexuality and sexual attitudes of the other characters? What does your character feel about the sexuality and sexual orientation of others, whether different from or the same as the character's? How does this feeling influence the way he or she behaves in the context of a relationship? How does the character behave in approaching the establishment of a new, desired relationship?

For writers: All of the above questions are applicable when you are creating a character. How much do you want the character to know or be aware of? How much do you want the other characters to know about the character in question? How do you want to let the audience know these things about the character? Do you want to reveal these aspects gradually? Do they form core elements of the story you are telling?

For Freud, the words *eroticism, sexual attraction,* and *love* are almost interchangeable, because love is a combination of tenderness and sensuality. As Freud tells us in his 1914 paper "On Narcissism: An Introduction," the libido has cathected the ego, and part of this cathexis "is later yielded up to objects." Sexual desire is thus a manifestation of narcissism, since the ego cathexis "persists and is related to object cathexes much as the body of an amoeba is related to the pseudopodia which it puts out." We find narcissism in others charming and their narcissistic inaccessibility attractive. And we want them to be not self-involved but involved with us, because of our own narcissism!

Among the characteristics of love are an exclusive, almost compulsive attachment to the love object and absolute, credulous obedience to the dictates of the heart. In this reliving of the infantile narcissistic attitude towards the mother, the love object is often overestimated. Judgment and logic are weakened with regard to the object, which is treated almost fetishistically and also loved with constancy. Yet there is always in addition an element of ambivalence in any love, as there was in the early relationships on which the adult relationships are unconsciously modeled.

Why do people choose one person rather than another to fall in love with? There are many variables in the reasons for the choice of a love object, just as there are many diverse destinies once the choice is made. In "On Narcissism: An Introduction," Freud distinguished two possible types of unconscious choices, susceptible of endless variations. They are models that reflect the earliest libidinal cathexes: first, the narcissistic, autoerotic cathexis of the individual by him or herself; and second, the cathexis of the mother or other caregiver as an object of love.

The first type is called a *narcissistic* object choice. Some people seek and choose someone who represents something that was once part of them, or else someone who resembles them as they are, once were, or wish to be. The second type of choice is called *anaclitic,* meaning someone a person can lean on. People transfer childhood relationships to an object that they feel may enable them to recreate and reexperience dependent parental relationships, in which they were fed and nurtured. They seek either "the woman who tends" or "the man who protects." Not being necessarily mutually exclusive, the choices may exist in combination and often do.

Perhaps Yelena in *Uncle Vanya* chose to marry the Professor for unconscious narcissistic reasons. But Vanya has fallen in love with her for anaclitic reasons: ideally, he wants her to take care of him, as his fantasizing in his act 2 monologue shows, even though he says he wants to take care of her. But all his actions show us otherwise. Astrov is attracted to Yelena for narcissistic reasons. He is disappointed when he realizes how bored she is by his passion for ecology. Freud's libidinal types show why and how relationships with the object choices may be acted out in specific ways.

In Terence Rattigan's *The Browning Version,* made into a classic film in 1951, Sir Michael Redgrave plays Andrew Crocker-Harris, a classics teacher about to retire from a prestigious English public school for boys. Jean Kent plays his beautiful but bitter and sadistic wife. She has certainly married him for narcissistic as well as anaclitic reasons. He was handsome as a young man, and she thought he had wonderful prospects. She felt he would give her prestige and validation in her own eyes, just as narcissistic parents live vicariously through their children's achievements. She would be the admired wife of a highly respected man of position, and he would take care of her. For him, a shy, confused man when it comes to sex, the primary reasons for marrying her were anaclitic, and he was dazzled especially by her show of interest in him. The marriage has turned out badly, of course, and he is deeply hurt. She is bitterly disappointed and disillusioned with her husband. Since he has not advanced in his career, she views him as a failure, which is indeed how he sees himself, but for different reasons. He feels he has betrayed his trust over the many years he has been teaching and let down the boys to whom he should have communicated a sense of his love for the Greek and Latin classics, as well as a sense of humanity. They think of him as strict, harsh, and even terrifying, because in his shyness and insecurity, he has indeed appeared that way. Although he has indulged in sarcastic jibes to his students, he is really a person of touching awkwardness and sincerity; a dedicated, passionate, vulnerable, and unappreciated man with whom we empathize. Having realized how his students feel, he is deeply upset. He finds it difficult to express his emotions, and when he does, we are deeply moved. Sir Michael Redgrave's poignant, riveting performance is one of his greatest. The 1994 remake with Albert Finney is quite good, but the earlier version is somehow much more involving.

Romeo and Juliet have made essentially narcissistic object choices of each other: neither one wishes to recreate the anaclitic, dependent relationship with their parents. But there is an anaclitic aspect to their choice of each other nevertheless, because each wants to be loved and nurtured by the other unconditionally, just as when they were babies. Each wants to be everything for the other, and each wants the other to want that.

For actors, it should be easy to see what the choice was in the way the relationship is played out in the script.

The Therapy Session: If You Play an Analyst or Analysand: If you write, direct, or play a character who is in therapy or a psychotherapist, psychoanalyst, or psychiatrist, the following information about what happens in psychoanalytic therapy sessions and how they work should prove essential.

As Freud says in "Delusion and Dream in Wilhelm Jensen's *Gradiva*": "Every psychoanalytic treatment is an attempt to free repressed love, which has formed a miserable compromise outlet in a symptom." The question before us now is how the treatment—the cure through love, as Freud characterized psychoanalytic therapy—works. The information below describes a fairly typical course of analysis.

After an initial evaluation or assessment session at which the patient and the analyst agree on such basics as fees and appointment times, and the therapist explains what analysis is all about and how long treatment might be expected to last, the therapeutic sessions begin in earnest. For a seriocomic look at the assessment session, see *The Scout* (1994), in which Diane Wiest evaluates Brendan Fraser under the watchful and wary eye of Albert Brooks. Fraser has been signed by the Yankees and is required to undergo a psychiatric examination.

Analysts have various ways of conducting therapy sessions. The patient may sit in a chair facing the analyst or lie on a couch with the analyst slightly behind or to the side of the couch. The latter method helps prevent the patient from being distracted in any way from his or her own thoughts. The analyst usually takes notes during every session, which lasts forty-five or fifty minutes.

In the first session, the analyst explains the *fundamental rule* of psychoanalytic therapy, which is that the patient should *free associate*—that is, talk without censoring him or herself and say whatever comes to mind, while the analyst listens and does not plant suggestions in the analysand's mind by interpreting the material offered. The analyst refrains from giving too much instruction to the patient so as to allow the patient to feel free to say whatever he or she wishes. The analyst remains neutral, impartial, and nonparticipatory, and simply listens to the material presented by the patient. While listening in a fluid way, the analyst allows him or herself to associate his or her own thoughts freely as they occur during the course of listening to the patient, and to pay what Freud called "evenly suspended" attention to the material being presented. The analyst must abstain from gratifying the patient's desires for emotional satisfaction, approval, and so forth. The patient's needs, desires, and longing must be allowed to persist, so that they may become clear and can be worked on. Also, the analyst does not reveal personal information to the analysand but remains a neutral person, whom, eventually, the analysand will flesh out in what is called the *transference,* meaning a projection onto the analyst of unresolved emotions—positive or negative—and libidinal feelings. The analysand will cast both him or herself and the analyst in certain roles, unconsciously recreating earlier life situations, usually childhood relationships with the parents.

At a point when the patient stops talking, pauses, or hesitates, which might even be just before starting to talk, the therapist knows there is an unconscious (it may be preconscious and just on the point of reaching consciousness) resistance to talking about some topic of concern to the patient, whatever it may be. The patient is deflecting some threatening feeling by changing the subject to one more neutral and less emotionally charged. The therapist may simply take notes for a time, and then at a certain point, when the patient has stopped or hesitated several times, encourage the patient to talk about why he or she has stopped, again without asking suggestive questions that would interfere with the analysis. But the therapist may eventually suggest a "conscious anticipatory image" (as Freud calls it in "Analysis of a Phobia in a Five-Year Old Boy") that will put the patient "in a position to recognize and to grasp the unconscious material." Ultimately the cause of the resistance will be revealed. Once the unconscious is made conscious, the patient's inner equilibrium will be disturbed as thoughts begin to surface that the patient would prefer not to know about. The patient will continue to resist, and the resistances will take other forms. Freud realized quite early that attacking symptoms directly was counterproductive and could even be harmful. So resistance therapy has to be slow and painstaking.

In analyzing the patient's transference of positive or negative feelings onto the analyst, the therapist may find him or herself reacting emotionally to the analysand and transferring positive or negative emotions onto the patient: this is called a *countertransference*. At first Freud thought that transference and countertransference were obstacles to analysis. The countertransference was contrary to the basic scientific idea of a neutral, detached, uninvolved, and unaffected observer. But he realized that, on the contrary, they were useful projections that could themselves be analyzed and used in the patient's treatment. For instance, in what role had the analyst unconsciously been cast by the analysand, and how did the analyst fit into that role and actually play it unconsciously? Why did the analyst feel love, hate, indifference, or boredom? Analyzing this could yield fruitful results in understanding the analysand.

Once a person has had insight into the origin of a behavior pattern or a problem, whether in therapy or through self-analysis, the analytical work on overcoming resistances continues with working through the material. The insight is the starting point in dealing with patterns of behavior that one wishes to change. Working through the resistances afterwards is crucial. The therapist at various points in the analysis will be empathic, encouraging and supportive, or else confrontational, as necessary. Analysts may elaborate on their interpretations or make them brief clarifications.

People need time (some need more time than others, for instance in the case of traumatic neuroses), as Freud pointed out, to become more conversant with their resistances and to overcome them, so as to alter their perception of objects and change the aims of the drives. Only in that way can change in someone be effective and produce the desired results of new behavior patterns, freedom, and autonomy.

At some point in the analysis, both the therapist and the patient will feel that it is time to terminate the treatment. The patient will have learned to deal with anger, come to grips with the past, grown significantly, and developed a more positive self-image and self-confidence. The therapist will feel that he or she has done all that can be done for the moment and will feel satisfied to have led the patient to self-knowledge and functionality.

In a startling departure from the therapeutic method described above, the neo-Freudian therapist Jacques Lacan instituted his famous controversial *short sessions:* He would rudely, abruptly, and seemingly arbitrarily terminate a therapy session. The length of the session varied, and he might interrupt it at any time. Why did he do this? He had many reasons and, no doubt, gauged carefully the moment of his terminating the session. Perhaps he wanted to reawaken the trauma of separation — the inevitable, necessary separation of children from their parents — in the most disconcerting way possible, at a point where the patient's resistance to unconscious knowledge was all too apparent in the patient's discourse, almost as if Lacan's message was, "You want to talk nonsense and skirt around the issue? I don't have time!" Certainly, he wanted to shake up the patient and the patient's expectations of what should happen in a therapeutic situation, as well as the patient's expectations in general, and to disturb his or her imaginary ideas of what is certain and dependable, including the patient's idea that the therapist will listen to him or her for about an hour and help the patient by analysis. Also, to upset and disturb the idea of what time means, in particular, and the way one works in and with time, calculating how much time one has to get through what one wants to say. Also, to teach the patient the meaning of frustration and the patient's own, individual reactions to frustration, and to disturb and stir up the patient's defense mechanisms.

In another, earlier departure from standard psychoanalytic practice that was a direct contravention of standard therapeutic techniques of detachment and objectivity, the pioneer Hungarian psychoanalyst Sándor Ferenczi (1873–1933), Freud's one-time amanuensis, tried to develop a psychotherapy based on a more equal relationship between analyst and analysand. He would even have the analysand analyze the therapist when Ferenczi deemed it appropriate and helpful. This created a great scandal in the psychoanalytic community and accentuated the split between him and Freud, although Ferenczi, deeply upset, never broke with Freud the way Jung and Adler had.

For more on the way therapy sessions work, consult Dr. Glen O. Gabbard's *Long-Term Psychodynamic Psychotherapy: A Basic Text* (2004) and *The Art and Science of Brief Psychotherapies: A Practitioner's Guide* (2004) by Drs. Dewan, Steenbarger, and Greenberg, as well as Anthony Bateman and Jeremy Holmes's *Introduction to Psychoanalysis: Contemporary Theory and Practice* (1995).

Traumatic Neurosis: A *traumatic neurosis* is a stress-related actual neurosis that develops as the result of a traumatic shock. If the reaction to the shock is of brief duration and not overwhelming in the long run, its influence may not be overly severe and may even disappear altogether without leaving permanent consequences and giving rise to a traumatic neurosis. But a traumatic shock may be unusually severe and devastating, and so powerful as to cause post-traumatic stress syndrome (PTSS) to develop. There is a breakdown in psychic functioning as the stimulus of the shock overwhelms the psyche, and the trauma may have devastating long-lasting consequences. Stricken with panic, the person feels completely helpless, and there is usually a breakdown in the autonomic nervous system that accompanies the loss of psychic equilibrium. It is so intense and unbearable that it must be urgently repressed deep into the unconscious and forgotten. Although the mind has adjusted to the trauma by repressing it, the traumatic event emerges in some way as symptoms, indicating neurosis. The person's behavior is neurotic because, driven by the unconscious, that behavior is not in accord with present reality, and he or she behaves as if still involved in the past event and as if it still threatened to be overwhelming and needed to be defended against. The reactions to present happenings are frequently inappropriate.

The symptoms of this type of neurosis include severe, general anxiety, which may come and go and vary in its intensity; suspiciousness and lack of trust, sometimes amounting to paranoia; general withdrawal from society, even when surrounded by people; and recurrent nightmares and occasional waking flashbacks of the traumatic experiences. The flashbacks and images can be unexpected and unpredictable as to both duration and intensity.

Traumatic neurosis may be the result of surviving such natural catastrophes as earthquakes or hurricanes, during which someone was continually menaced with a life-threatening situation; such man-made disasters as shipwrecks, automobile, or other accidents, which are so terrifying as to cause more than a situational stress reaction; or criminal attacks or such terrible, life-threatening experiences as being on a battlefield (see "war neurosis," page 218); or those of concentration camp inmates (many of whom were the sole survivors of entire families) who managed to live through World War II or people who witnessed and survived the massacres in the former Yugoslavia or Rwanda or the Armenian genocide of 1915–23. However marked they may have been by their terrible, unforgettable experiences, not all survivors or even a majority of them develop traumatic neuroses. For those who do, through therapy or simply working things out personally, these neuroses can be more or less successfully overcome.

The title character played by Rod Steiger in Sidney Lumet's *The Pawnbroker* (1965) suffers from classic traumatic neurosis. A Jewish Holocaust survivor, he periodically and for brief instants relives moments and sees images of the concentration camp experiences that haunt him and are preconscious except when they suddenly and unexpectedly intrude themselves, unwanted, into his consciousness. In a brilliant touch that only the cinema could provide, these intrusions are shown as actual split-second images flashed on the screen or as somewhat longer flashbacks. He also has what is known as "survivor guilt," which is the irrational feeling that somehow his survival is due to the fact that others died because he lived, and that he is therefore responsible for their deaths in some way.

For more information on the psychological reactions and responses of those who lived through the horrors, read Primo Levi's *Survival in Auschwitz* (1987) and *The Drowned and the Saved* (1988). And see the very disturbing film *I Love You, I Love You Not* (1996), with Jeanne Moreau, admirable and moving as a Holocaust survivor who was able to begin a new life without that gnawing anxiety and nightmarish lack of trust in everyone around her that betokens a personality disorder. Despite or perhaps because of the horrors she went through and the lifelong memories that have left inevitable psychic scars and deep sadness, she is truly loving, understanding, and compassionate. In a story of survival against all odds, Adrien Brody's sterling, Academy Award–winning performance, based on the memoirs of Władysław Szpilman in Roman Polanski's *The Pianist* (2002) is unforgettable. So is Louis Malle's heartbreaking film *Au revoir les enfants* (1987), based on incidents from his childhood in occupied France. What happened at the religious school where he was a student in 1944 stayed with him and haunted him all his life: three Jewish students who had been hidden there under assumed names by priests were taken away by the Gestapo, along with the school principal, named Fr. Jean in the movie, and killed. It took more than forty years until he was finally able to come to grips with his experiences enough to be able to make the film.

FREE ASSOCIATION:
AN EXERCISE FOR ACTORS, WRITERS, AND DIRECTORS

*D*o this exercise after having read a script and familiarized yourself with the place in the story and the through-line of a character you are preparing or the entire script you are directing. If you are a writer, you may find this exercise useful in helping you to create not only characters but also an entire story, play, or film.

Place a pad of paper and a pencil handy, sit down in a comfortable position, and begin to let your imagination roam around the character. Write down whatever comes into your mind (visualizations, words, etc.). When you find your mind drifting towards something that seems irrelevant in the context of the exercise, notice exactly what you were thinking when you began to drift. What was the resistance to the process that made you not want to continue with it? Did you feel tense or uncomfortable in some way? What thoughts were awakened regarding yourself or the character? Were those thoughts about the character in some way reminiscent of conflicts within yourself? The answer(s) may provide a clue to relevant substitutions. Continue to write everything down. When you stop the exercise, put the paper aside. After a lapse of time that may be as long or as short as you wish, read what you have written.

In concluding this chapter, I wish to recommend two films about Freud. The first is the German television film *Young Dr. Freud* (1976), about Freud's early life and discoveries, available with optional subtitles on DVD from Kino Video. Karlheinz Hackl plays Freud. The film is beautifully acted, and the script is a very good exposition of his career as a young physician, his studies with Charcot, his relationship with Dr. Breuer and the treatment of Anna O., his dealing with anti-Semitism, and the skepticism that greeted his theories. His relationship with his parents is empathetically depicted. His mother called him *mein goldener Sigi*—my golden Sigi. He remained close to her all his life. And his father, using Yiddish words that add spice to his German, says in the film that Sigi had more *saykhel* (common sense, intelligence) in his *tukhos* (behind) than most people have in their entire heads.

The second was made for French television and is called *Princesse Marie* (2003). At the time of this writing, it is only available on DVD in Zone 2 format. Catherine Deneuve plays the fascinating and wonderful Princess George of Greece and Denmark, née Princess Marie Bonaparte, a great grandniece of Napoleon's. Princess Marie was instrumental in establishing psychoanalysis in France, which she unselfishly used her fortune to do, and she wrote a number of pioneering books, including a riveting psychoanalytical study of the life and works of Edgar Allan Poe. Fascinated by psychoanalysis and deeply troubled in her personal life, she had gone to Vienna to be analyzed by Freud himself. Freud is played sensitively and insightfully by Heinz

Bennent, who gives the character the great dignity, compassion, and charm Freud reputedly had in real life; without those qualities, he would never have been able to attract so many followers and adherents. As a result of her analysis, Marie Bonaparte became a psychoanalyst herself. She was not only Freud's ardent admirer and great friend but was also instrumental in making him leave Vienna for London after the Nazi takeover in 1938. The princess pulled every string she could, eventually securing the intervention of President Franklin Roosevelt on Freud's behalf, through United States Ambassador to France William Bullitt, another great admirer of Freud and his collaborator on a psychoanalytic study of President Woodrow Wilson. With the vitally important help of Ernest Jones, she got Freud and members of his immediate family and household, as well as his personal physician Dr. Max Schur (1897–1969; a psychoanalyst himself and Freud's second major biographer after Jones) and Schur's wife, safe to England. Unfortunately, although she made strenuous efforts on their behalf, she was not able to save Freud's four elderly sisters, who were all murdered. (His fifth sister had already left Vienna for America.) In France, despite splits in the psychoanalytic movement there, Princess Marie is still highly and deservedly revered.

Chapter Two

§

Mothers of Psychoanalysis: Anna Freud, Sigmund's "Antigone"; Helene Deutsch, "Freud's Darling"; Karen Horney and the Neurotic Personality

Anna Freud, Sigmund's "Antigone"

She was the youngest, the baby of the family. As a child she had felt lonely and alienated. Papa was always so busy. To get his attention, she would do naughty things. He called her a little devil sometimes and wagged his finger at her, but he smiled too. Her greatest rival for his affections was psychoanalysis. Identifying with him and with it, she was the only one of his six children to become a psychoanalyst herself. And her relationship with Sigmund was one of intense mutual love and devotion.

Anna did her training analysis with her father, and this was something of a scandal in the psychoanalytic community. One is not supposed to analyze anyone who is a family member or intimate—although early psychoanalysts often did, sometimes with disastrous results. Analyze those you are close to and you will lose them, was Freud's dictum. He broke his own rules, but both father and daughter seemed quite satisfied with the results.

Anna Freud (1895–1982) became a pioneer child psychoanalyst and had a distinguished career in both England and America. She was tireless in her work on behalf of children's welfare, founding clinics, hospitals, and institutions. A great and indefatigable champion of her father's work, she wrote, lectured, taught, and participated in innumerable conferences.

Although constantly involved in public work, she remained intensely private. She never married or had children of her own. But she had a satisfying, deeply committed partnership with the psychoanalyst Dorothy Tiffany Burlingham (1891–1979), an upper-class New Yorker with whom she lived and worked for fifty years and whose children she helped raise. Whether or not they had a sexual relationship is not known.

Questions and Considerations

Defense Mechanisms: Two of Anna Freud's most useful contributions to psychoanalysis—certainly useful as well for the purposes of actors and writers—were her emphasis on the importance of *ego psychology* (the study and analysis of the reality-oriented functions of the ego as well as the ego's role in personality development) and her categorization of ten major defense mechanisms, along with several that are subcategories or variations. She discusses all of them in a clear, easily comprehensible way in *The Ego and the Mechanisms of Defense* (1936), a book which she presented to her father on the occasion of his eightieth birthday.

The defense mechanisms, which are unconscious self-preservative adaptations to internal situations, can exist alone or in combination. As Otto Fenichel points out in *The Psychoanalytic Theory of Neurosis,* "there are no sharp lines of demarcation between the various forms of defense mechanisms." They are all related to each other, and they can be organized into a more or less inflexible defense system. But they are never perfect. They represent compromises with desires unconsciously perceived as inadmissible and disturbing. In some form or other, frequently disguised so as to be almost unrecognizable, the desires will reassert themselves in some way. Defense mechanisms may be either normal, healthy, mature functions of the ego—as are certain suppressions, repressions, and sublimation (number 10 on the list below) or the appropriate use of humor to lighten heavy situations—or pathological, as in the others on this list. Maturity and mental health do not necessarily preclude the use of some immature and even pathological defense mechanisms, which may be temporary adjustments to specific situations:

1. **Repression:** *Repression* is "motivated forgetting"—that is, forgetting something for a particular reason. Such forgetting is immediate and involuntary. It is the sine qua non of all defense mechanisms, and together with its subcategory denial, it precedes all the others.

   Denial represses awareness of an external threat to the ego by negating the idea of the threat. Is your character in a state of denial? What is the threat to the character's ego? What would be the result of the threat if it were to be realized?

   Madame Popova in Chekhov's *The Boor* denies how much she hated the husband for whom she is supposedly in mourning. This hatred is eventually revealed as she falls in love with Smirnov, the male chauvinist who has come to collect the debt her husband owed him. Her husband treated her brutally, and here she is falling in love with another macho brute, because of her masochistic repetition complex. She is disdainful of Smirnov's brutishness, while all the while she is sexually attracted to him.

   Kulygin in *Three Sisters* denies his wife's feelings for Vershinin and goes around telling everyone how much she loves him, Kulygin. But this may be for public consumption and not because he really believes it, much as he tries to convince himself. However, he avoids acknowledging the truth about the more important issue of his failed marriage, about which he is in a state of denial.

Julius Caesar refuses to acknowledge the depth of hatred Cassius obviously feels for him, even though he is clearly mistrustful of the man with the "lean and hungry look." But he denies that Cassius's venomous glances in his direction mean anything in particular beyond envy.

In Eugene O'Neill's *Long Day's Journey into Night,* James Tyrone tries to deny the knowledge that his wife, Mary, has gone back to her addiction. His son Jamie sets him straight, earning not gratitude but opprobrium for baldly stating the truth his father would prefer not to hear. In his illness, the younger son, Edmund, scarcely notices his mother's return to morphine addiction at first. And Mary pretends to deny even to herself that she has broken her promise and descended back into the depths, but the pretense cannot last long. She knows consciously what she is doing, although she denies the meaning of her acts at first. Her indignant outrage at being accused is a denial to herself as well as to the others. Eventually she will just give in to her addiction.

2. **Regression:** *Regression* is a retreat by the ego to an earlier developmental stage. Someone regresses to a more comfortable state of being than the present stressful situation in which the ego finds itself.

To avoid the misery of the present situation, the shy Laura in Tennessee Williams's *The Glass Menagerie* withdrew from life a long time before the play began, partly because she is ashamed of her limp, and in her involvement with her collection of glass animals has regressed to the prepubescent latency period of psychosexual development, to a time in her childhood during which she was at least oblivious of the awfulness of the family's situation.

Sigmund Freud once said to Anna, regarding the way children are brought up, "We supply them with a map of the Italian lakes and then send them off to the North Pole." That remark would seem to apply to Laura's mother, the formerly wealthy Southern belle Amanda Wingfield, who unwittingly behaves destructively out of her anxiety, although her desire is only to be constructive and to help her children. But Amanda, too, lives as much as possible in a state of regressive, narcissistic denial, which she works diligently and arduously to maintain in the teeth of the facts, so that her "map of the Italian lakes" is uppermost, as if she were still there, and she is entirely unconscious that she has sent her children "off to the North Pole."

Relating the story to the audience in retrospect, her son, Laura's brother Tom, has had to work hard to overcome the psychological handicap under which he labors. He was more in touch with reality and planned eventually to escape from the miserable oppressive situation at home in a way his unrealistic, unhappy mother—and certainly his sister, who, as Tom says, "lives in a world of her own"—could not do.

Amanda's hysterical, pathetic desire to present her almost literally unmarriageable daughter to a "gentleman caller" only leads to further unhappiness, as it was bound to do. Amanda dresses up and behaves flirtatiously like the Southern belle she once was, even to the point of using a fan and talking as if she were sitting on the porch of an antebellum plantation mansion. The gentleman caller cannot help but be surprised.

He is subsequently dismayed and put off by the young girl he knew vaguely in high school, when she was already shy and withdrawn. He himself has not succeeded in life as he had hoped to do, but he remains out there in the world nevertheless and goes to night school. He fancies himself a bit of a philosopher and psychologist, and glibly tells Laura that her problem is that she has an inferiority complex and that other people never really noticed her physical defect, magnified many times in her imagination. He encourages her to overcome it. Unfortunately, she mistakes his attentions as showing a far greater interest than they do and is deeply disappointed when he explains that he cannot call again because he is in love and engaged to be married. He had not realized the situation when he accepted Tom's invitation. Tom himself did not know of his friend's engagement, which had not yet been announced. Laura, of course, reverts to her regressive defense. See the 1950 film with Gertrude Lawrence as Amanda; Jane Wyman as Laura; Arthur Kennedy as the down-to-earth dreamer, Tom; and Kirk Douglas as the gentleman caller.

In order to avoid confronting the unhappiness of her present dependence and poverty, Blanche Dubois in Williams's *A Streetcar Named Desire* regresses to a pleasant adolescent fantasy when she was admired and courted. She also avoids thinking about her past actions and what she has actually done with her life and allowed herself to become. She wants to believe she is still the attractive, gorgeous young belle of the ball, a lady deserving of respect and courtesy. She denies the reality of her present life and regresses to a past that, although possibly imaginary in itself, represents and contains an acceptable reality.

3. **Reaction Formation, or Believing the Opposite:** A *reaction formation* involves turning feelings that the ego finds unacceptable into their opposite, repressing the unwanted emotions and denying that they exist. Such reaction formations typically occur very early in childhood character development.

"Believing the opposite" is a typical defense mechanism seen in action in innumerable gangster films. When subordinates deal with their brutal bosses, they ward off the consequences of the anger they feel at the bosses by being obsequious and giving in at every juncture where there is potential conflict. They have turned the terror at potentially being killed into respectful awe. At any rate, they act as if they respect the bosses.

In *Three Sisters*, Kulygin actually hates Masha for her betrayal of him with Vershinin. He cannot acknowledge this hatred to himself. His denial is a kind of reaction formation, and he consciously believes what the unconscious knows to be a lie. Believing the opposite is a form of denial.

4. **Isolation:** In this compromise formation, the ego remains conscious of an impulse or a desire it finds unacceptable and removes emotional affect from it, isolating it from feeling. As Anna Freud states, the ego "simply removes the instinctual impulses from their context, while retaining them in consciousness" so they can do no harm to the ego. In other words, the desires are isolated from affects one would ordinarily associate with them. Such impulses can then be acted on, and the person feels he or she will not be punished and has done nothing wrong because he or she has not felt anything. Intellectual justification

for feelings that ordinarily would make a person feel guilty further isolates the unwanted impulse or desire. The tension set up between the id and the ego is resolved: "Yes, I know this desire exists, but it doesn't mean anything, and I have no feeling about it. It exists by itself, isolated from the rest of my feelings. I can do what I like about it. To some people my desire may seem immoral, but it really isn't." We all sometimes isolate unwanted threatening feelings of which we remain conscious.

This defense, which is typical of obsessional neurosis and of obsessive-compulsive people, usually results in the conflict being resolved by the person "giving in" to the compulsion, even if that results in destruction. The superego would appear not to function strongly in such types, whose only desire is for their own satisfaction. A sense of morals and of consideration for other people is almost nonexistent.

The existence of homicidal feelings in serial killers and other sociopaths is an extreme example of this defense mechanism, one of many in the complicated psychic structure of such people. But it is this particular formation that enables the serial killer to actually commit murder under feelings of compulsion to do so. The character of the hit man in so many gangster films depends in part on the active and unconscious isolation of feelings that would engender guilt. Iago and Richard the Third are prime examples of characters in whom this defense mechanism operates to particularly horrific effect.

In the case of Lady Macbeth, the isolation mechanism is what enables her to be an accessory to murder. But her guilt breaks through her defenses. She reacts by developing anxiety hysteria in the classical Freudian meaning of the term. Her sleep disorder is a further debilitating result of the breakout of her guilt. Knowledge of the defense mechanism of isolation and how it works should make it easy for any actress to get inside the role, so that the "sleepwalking" scene, for instance, should almost play itself, particularly once the analogous substitutions or transferences from the actress's own life are in place.

Solyony isolates his cold-blooded homicidal impulses towards Tusenbach in *Three Sisters* and justifies them intellectually. For more on his symptoms and behavior, see pages 48–50.

Isolation is sometimes seen in people dealing with guilt over sexual feelings. The ego is forced to admit they exist but may deflect the affect from them by isolating them. Otto Fenichel informs us in *The Psychoanalytic Theory of Neurosis* that as a result of repressed Oedipal feelings, some men, for instance, cannot enjoy sex with a person for whom they have tender feelings of love but only with someone with whom they have no emotional connection. Sigmund Freud put it succinctly in *Introductory Lectures in Psychoanalysis* (1916): "Where they love they do not desire, and where they desire they cannot love." Such people may be compulsively promiscuous and/or may frequent prostitutes. These men acknowledge their sexual feelings but remove the affect from them, indulging only in the exciting physical and not the emotional side of sex.

In *Long Day's Journey into Night* and *Moon for the Misbegotten,* the elder brother, Jamie's, self-destructive addiction to alcohol is made possible by the isolation of impulses that allow him to go on drinking binges and his frequenting of low-life characters without allowing guilt to intrude. He has been warned about his habits and severely criticized by his father, against whom he rebels by continuing to indulge in them. And he has been able to isolate any affect connected with them. His isolation neurosis also explains the incident with the woman on the same train that is carrying his mother's coffin to her final resting place. His maudlin unhappiness is compounded by his self-loathing, misogyny, belligerence, and masochism, as well as by his romantic posturing, a result of his identification with his actor father, a classicist of the old school.

5. **Undoing:** This behavior is also characteristic of obsessive-compulsive disorders. *Undoing* involves "magic," "magical thinking," and rituals, such as séances and religious rituals meant to defend against unacceptable ideas, feelings, and the damage done by already completed actions. It is typical of neurotic thinking that ideas are considered to have real power to bring about external events, such as communication with a dead loved one, simply because one wishes to communicate.

    In the film *Séance on a Wet Afternoon* (1964), Richard Attenborough, the timid husband of "medium" Kim Stanley, is powerless to help his deeply ill wife, who is involved in magical thinking and undoing. The believers who flock to her séances are also deeply troubled.

    Compulsive phobic behavior is also based on magical thinking or undoing: those who are terrified of bad luck brought on by spilling salt will toss some salt over their shoulder. Within the precincts of a theater, those thoughtless enough to quote from the Bard's "Scottish play" must perform certain rituals in order to undo the potential harm caused by their blunder.

    See also "parapsychology" on page 205 and "phobia" on page 57.

6. **Projection and Its Subcategories Altruistic Surrender, or Sacrifice, and Displacement:** *Projection* is a kind of denial. It takes the form of the displacement of feelings, emotions, attitudes, unacceptable wishes, or particular ideas or qualities onto an external object to whom those feelings or attitudes are attributed. These feelings can then be viewed as *ego-alien*—that is, as not part of the self.

    In *altruistic surrender* or *sacrifice*, someone's narcissistic needs are satisfied by fulfilling another person's needs. This may involve masochistic attachment to the other person.

    Displacement involves rerouting aggressive desires. They are acted out with someone who is not actually guilty of anything but who is an available, unthreatening target. For instance, a sibling who is angry with a parent or teacher might take out that anger on another sibling, who is guilty of nothing. The original object of an angry reaction is too powerful or too threatening in some way. The anger against this object is therefore repressed but reappears as displacement. Its expression has simply been unconsciously postponed. It seethes in the unconscious and must find an outlet somehow. The angry person has repressed the reaction so far as to deceive the self as to its real nature, which enables its expression to well up from the unconscious and to be directed against another object.

See below under "Reversal": Vanya's reactions leading to the climax of the third act involve not only reversal but also displacement of the kind just described. Vanya is a master at bottling up his emotions, particularly his rage, and at postponing their expression.

7. **Introjection; Identification with Its Variation, "Identification with the Aggressor":** *Introjection* is the symbolic ingestion or absorption of an object. By means of introjection, or internalization, *identification* may be achieved.

In its positive form, introjection and identification involve accepting as true and believing in ideas and principles that one has absorbed from an admired person: from certain political thinkers, politicians, teachers, or religious figures, for instance. In childhood, one introjects parental objects and their teachings. One identifies with the parent and often tries to behave like the admired mother or father.

In its negative form, "identification with the aggressor" — as in the "Stockholm Syndrome," where hostages identify with their captors and even justify their own kidnapping — a person may identify with a feared aggressor, justifying the aggressor's attitudes and behavior. This kind of magical thinking and "undoing" serves to help avoid expected harm and ward off terror. But it doesn't always work successfully. The terror simply remains repressed and will emerge in some way, often unexpectedly. A hostage may appear to be getting along perfectly well with a captor, and when the captor leaves the room, the hostage may suddenly have the urge to vomit, for instance.

An abused child may consciously come to think that the parent's abuse is justified and the punishment deserved. When the child grows up, he or she may even suppress or repress the knowledge of the abuse and talk admiringly of his or her childhood. See Alice Miller's books, listed in the bibliography, for a discussion of this common phenomenon.

In the startling, original film *The Crying Game* (1992), about hostage taking in Northern Ireland, Stephen Rea plays a member of the IRA. He takes a British soldier hostage, gets to know him, and befriends him. The soldier begins to identify with the man who has captured him.

8. **Turning-Against-Self, or Self-as-Object or -Target:** Related to the defense mechanism of identification with the aggressor is the idea of turning against the self. A person may be deeply angry at someone but turns the anger inward against the self, for a variety of reasons, among which is the menacing nature of the other person at whom the anger ought to be directed. In punishing the self, the person unconsciously wards off a worse punishment. This masochistic reaction involves guilt and shame, and results in depression and feelings of lack of self-worth and inadequacy. Uncle Vanya frequently turns against himself.

A variety of turning against the self is *asceticism*. This reaction involves giving up or renouncing the fulfillment of needs, thus warding off punishment. The message is, "You see how good I am? I am sacrificing the fulfillment of my needs, so you don't have to punish me. I am punishing myself." This defense is often seen in adolescents, who do not know how to deal with their emerging sexuality and feel threatened by it, so that they give up acting on their desires out of guilt.

9. **Reversal:** *Reversal* is very similar to reaction formation, of which it may even be seen as a variety. Someone turns active impulses into passive reactions. This reversal wards off expected punishment or unpleasantness for feelings the ego considers menacing and destructive. A sadistic impulse may be turned into a masochistic one, for instance, or vice versa. In fact, this defense mechanism is typical of sadomasochistic personalities, who alternate between provocative sadistic behavior and self-punishing masochistic reactions.

When he sees Yelena embracing Astrov, with whom she has fallen in love, Vanya realizes for the first time that Yelena does not love her husband, the Professor. Vanya had thought that one of the principle reasons for her lack of response to his amorous overtures was, in part, that she did love her husband and was faithful to him. His realization causes him to go into a state of shock and induces a sort of semiparalysis of the emotions, leaving him temporarily speechless and throwing him into an immediate depression. He has automatically and unconsciously reversed his impulses of rage, anger, frustration, and love, turning them into passivity. Finally, later on, he blurts out, "I saw you!" He also displaces his rage at Astrov and Yelena onto the Professor, who is a ready target and who has also caused offence, but of a different kind, by proposing that the family sell the estate that Vanya has worked so hard to preserve. Vanya has difficulties in his relations with the Professor anyway because of his jealousy, which has helped change his view of the Professor from a positive to a negative one. But the explosion of his rage at the end of act 3 is partly a displacement of his feelings about Yelena and his supposed best friend, Astrov.

10. **Sublimation:** For more on sublimation and Sigmund Freud's analysis of it, see pages 24–25. When a person *sublimates,* he or she turns an emotion or libidinal impulse into a productive, socially acceptable behavior. Pain and punishment are warded off. The person's ego finds the new impulse a satisfactory substitute for what was originally desired and substitutes the reward of receiving praise and applause for the satisfaction hoped for by the fulfillment of the original desire. Sublimation, like humor, can be a healthy, mature reaction to frustration: instead of falling apart or becoming depressed, a person gets involved in productive activities for which he or she may even receive great affection and adulation.

Developmental Lines: Anna Freud took a major and original step forward in the understanding and clarification of how character is generated by tracing what she called *developmental lines* in *Normality and Pathology in Childhood: Assessments of Development* (1965). The lines show perfectly normal, healthy, non-neurotic development and "ego mastery" of internal reality and external circumstances. They can show pathological development as well when there are interferences in the process for whatever reasons. The lines develop in connection with each other and are not separate and discreet, but each one can still be traced on its own and will yield fruitful analytical results.

We have already seen one of these kinds of developmental lines, her father's stages of psychosexual development, which Anna also describes in her book: the libidinal line goes from oral through anal, phallic, and latent to genital and includes seemingly endless variations. Another line of development that Anna Freud mentions is traced in the next chapter on Melanie Klein's object-relations theory: the *object-relations line,* on which the infant proceeds from the part-object to a realization of the existence of the whole object and from the paranoiac to the depressive position. Anna Freud's lines of development are:

1. (This is the line she uses as a prototype for all the others.) The line "from dependency to emotional self-reliance and adult object relationships": from the egoless, symbiotic, dependent relationship with the mother leading eventually to separation from the maternal figure and to individuation. The line goes from the symbiotic stage to the stage of *object constancy,* in which a "positive inner image of the object" is maintained, regardless of whether the relation to it is satisfactory or not at any given moment; from the ambivalent, pre-Oedipal analsadistic stage to the Oedipal, object-centered stage; and finally, to the latent, preadolescent, and adolescent stages;
2. (These next three lines are intimately tied together.) The line from being fed as an infant to feeding oneself;
3. The line from having excretory functions attended to by caregivers to learning to control bowel and bladder;
4. The line from inability to the development of the ability to manage bodily functions and necessities in a responsible, self-reliant way, paying attention to hygiene, nutrition, and so forth;
5. The line leading "from egocentricity to companionship": from primary narcissism and autoeroticism to the realization of the other as a separate sentient being and love of others and the desire for companionship;
6. The line that leads "from the body to the toy and from play to work": from children's autoerotic play with objects such as toys and other children; and from play to hobbies, which are halfway between play and work, to real work.

How the child handles and is taught to handle the line of physical development, which is part of all the other lines, will determine feelings about the body and will impact on feelings about self-confidence and sexuality. The line proceeds from infant movement through early and later childhood, from physical inability through to mobility and independence and even to grace and athleticism.

Add sensory development to all this, and a line leading from early, simple defense mechanisms such as projection and denial to more sophisticated, complicated developments such as sublimation and intellectualization, along with the development of linguistic and other cognitive abilities, and you have a pretty complete general picture of how children develop into adults. See also the section on Piaget's developmental theories on page 190.

As a writer creating a character or an actor tracing your character's biography, you might want to ask how the character developed along any or each of the lines. The physical development of a dancer or an athlete will obviously be different from the development of a sedentary scholar, for instance. For the habits people develop, see what William James has to say on page 152.

The Uses of Frustration and Anxiety: In *Normality and Pathology in Childhood,* Anna Freud proposed a "metapsychological profile of the child" for the use of psychotherapists in evaluating their child patients. She presented an actual draft of this diagnostic profile, and there are two questions in it that might prove useful in helping actors with character interpretation. Aside from asking general questions about development based on genetic and environmental factors, as well as questions about the child's conflicts and the economy of the child's energy and drives, she asks the analyst to evaluate the child's tolerance for frustration and the child's attitude to anxiety. With regard to theatrical characters, these questions concern how invested the character is in pursuing objectives and how easily the character might be deflected from his or her goals.

If not attaining an objective provokes heavy anxiety, for instance, the character may work that much harder or else abandon the objective altogether. Romeo's anxiety over his love for Juliet motivates him to pursue her even more forcefully. Macbeth, on the other hand, is so anxious about the impending murder of Duncan that he almost abandons the objective of killing the king and wants to leave everything to his wife. But he commits the murder nonetheless.

If tolerance of frustration is low, the character may either react temperamentally and perhaps even violently or else behave in a way that avoids frustration altogether. For instance, Vanya's frustrating pursuit of Yelena eventually leads him to lose his temper and, in a bout of temporary insanity, to displace his feelings of rage at Yelena and to attempt to shoot the Professor, although he has the Professor's own attitudes and behavior as a plausible pretext as well.

How much does Hamlet tolerate frustration, and why? What is his attitude towards his own anxiety? He seems to have an almost endless tolerance for frustration and anxiety.

HELENE DEUTSCH, "FREUD'S DARLING":
THE PSYCHOLOGY OF THE FEMININE AND FREUDIAN THEORY

She had fallen in love with Freud almost immediately upon meeting him. She decided to go into analysis with him. And he was very attracted to her. She was a beautiful young woman. During one session, she had been talking about her difficulties in finding a wet nurse, because her young son had developed problems, such as bed wetting, after the departure of a previous nurse, fired by Deutsch for taking over too much of a mothering role and excluding Deutsch herself. Hearing some vague snoring sounds, she turned around and discovered . . . that he had fallen asleep!

Was Freud simply bored? He generally concentrated during their analytic sessions on the difficulties she had had because of her early identification with her father, and on her problems during a love affair with a friend of her father's — all of that seemed to interest him greatly — and neglected her difficulties with her mother, who was terribly abusive, and Deutsch's own problems with being a mother herself. In fact, Freud was not bored: he was simply having his own difficulties wrestling with his feelings for his beautiful analysand. And he had just had a very "Freudian" reaction to the talk about motherhood coming from someone with whom he was a bit in love. A friend of Deutsch called her "Freud's darling."

Helene Deutsch (1884–1982) was one of the first women to become a psychoanalyst. It is interesting to note that the profession of psychoanalysis enabled women to advance rapidly to the top of the professional ladder, where other professions were often closed to them at the time. That is not to say that male chauvinism never came into play, both then and in our own time, but in Freud's era, there was perhaps less of it than in other professions. Freud wanted women to be treated with absolute equality. Although often excoriated by feminists for his perceived male chauvinism, he was an egalitarian where women were concerned, and he never intended his ideas on the psychosexual development of women to imply that women were not completely equal to men. He felt that women should be men's equals in social terms, as they were in every other way. And no woman was ever turned away from the study and practice of psychoanalysis because of her gender. It is worth noting that Freud thought women analysts superior to men in some ways, notably in that during the very important transference stage of an analysis, they could arouse in the analysands the same emotions they had had towards their mothers, which men could not do, at least not as easily.

Deutsch left analysis with Freud and resumed it later with one of his early followers in Berlin, the prolific writer and lecturer Dr. Karl Abraham (1877–1955), who analyzed her twice; he was also Melanie Klein's analyst, as well as Karen Horney's. Helene Deutsch became the first director of the Vienna Psychoanalytic Training Institute and made major contributions to the understanding of women's psychology, amplifying and extending Freud's ideas, with many of which she agreed. (Other pioneer women psychoanalysts, however, took issue with some of his theories on feminine psychology.) But she left her life in Vienna behind when she and her husband, Felix Deutsch, emigrated from Europe to America during the Nazi era. She lived and worked in Cambridge, Massachusetts, until her death at the age of ninety-eight.

Having been indifferent at first to the subject of feminine psychology, she developed a consuming interest in it. She attributed this to her own narcissism and her feeling that psychoanalysis had concentrated almost all of its efforts on dealing with men. She felt psychoanalysis was very father-centered, even though Freud talked about the role of mothers. The difficulties of women in dealing with menstruation, defloration, pregnancy, motherhood, and the menopause had been neglected — or analyzed as being identified with early, unconscious fears of castration and so dismissed from the necessity of further analysis. But Deutsch said the difficulties were due instead to a conflict between narcissism (love of the self) and the desire to be a good, nurturing mother and love others. The violence of the body acting upon itself in ways that women could not control but had to deal with was the instrument of this conflict. The little girl's fears of her first period were due to the lack of control involved and the confusion it engendered. These were lived through again unconsciously every time a woman had her period.

Both Freud and Deutsch saw the most important development in feminine psychology and sensibility as the maternal feeling of wanting to nurture others and the desire for motherhood. This feeling involved self-sacrifice, as the ego gave up its narcissistic desires in favor of serving the needs of others. According to Freud and Deutsch, the development of women therefore usually included a masochistic side, sometimes in conflict with a more sadistic desire to attain to the masculine position of greater freedom, in social terms; this included the idea of the little girl's penis envy, which Deutsch though was an accurate conception (see page 26). Deutsch and Freud both felt that this conflict could explain a great deal about good and bad mothering.

In a reply to a letter from her husband (who was teaching in St. Louis while she remained in Boston to work), in which he had said he didn't need her to act like a mother to him ("the mother has been overcome"), she said that a man needs his mother from his birth until his death—whether he hates or loves her; fears her or blesses her; flees her, because of confusion or the necessity to be free; or seeks her in another woman.

The major question to be answered was whether or not a woman's psychology is different from a man's. Obviously, women are constructed biologically differently from men. A woman's mature biophysical sexual cycle is longer than a man's and includes conception, parturition, and lactation, while a man's cycle essentially ends with orgasmic release. Do those biophysical differences mean that there are also intrinsic psychological differences between the genders? Freud and Deutsch thought not.

For Sigmund Freud, everyone is basically the same, whatever their gender or background. That is, we all go through the same stages of psychosexual development and we all function in much the same way psychologically. We all have an id, an ego, and a superego, and the mind operates by the same means for all of us. We all have the same instincts and drives. There is one libido for all of us, not one for women and another for men. This idea includes the existence of basic constitutional bisexuality. And all human beings function physiologically in the same basic way, despite hormonal gender differences. Despite the chauvinist cliché, women are not more emotional than men, and men are just as emotional as women.

But it was obvious nevertheless that women and men were assigned different societal roles that were differentiated as children developed. One could therefore trace certain developments in feminine psychology (such as the desire for motherhood) that tended to differentiate men and women psychologically.

The perception of the roles assigned to men and women because of gender has changed in our day, as women have become more liberated. This does not mean that there is not continuing inequality with the concomitant necessity to continue the fight for equal rights. In performing roles in plays and films, it is important to keep the era and the social roles in mind and to put behavior and attitudes into their historical context.

Deutsch thought that whatever the era, girls in the Oedipal stage often perceive their mothers as passive. Therefore, they seek love and approval in a passive-aggressive, almost shamefaced way, which boys, with their phallic confidence and aggression, do not feel they have to do. This was perhaps largely true in Freud's day, when the societal role played by men called for their being the aggressor in sexual matters, while women were supposed to wait for men to ask them. This is changing, but it is also true today in certain cultures and milieus and is inculcated from an early age.

In Britain, where psychoanalysis took hold very early, some analysts disagreed with Freud's basic premise of a universal, biologically based psychology for both genders that differentiates with the onset of different stages of psychosexual development. Some analysts proposed that there was indeed a basic, biologically based difference between masculine and feminine psychology. In both schools of thought, however, the woman was seen as having a mothering instinct, as being nurturing in a way that a man could not be. Winnicott and later Bowlby and others concentrated on the mother's role in children's development, as opposed to the Freudian emphasis on the role of the father.

Questions and Considerations

The Psychology of Gender: From the actor's, writer's, or director's point of view, all characters need the same basic approach, which would tend to support Freud's original idea of a basic universal psychology for both genders. An actor breaking down and analyzing a character will use much the same method, no matter what the character's gender or sexual orientation. You still have to know what the character's objectives and actions are, and why and how they are pursued. You have to explore the character's development from childhood on and to decide what the character's attitudes or positions are regarding his or her sexuality. How does the female character feel about being a woman? Is she comfortable with the social status that has been conferred upon her, depending on the time and place in which the play is set? How does she feel about pregnancy? How does she feel about abortion? How does she feel about becoming a mother? How does she feel about being a mother if she is one? Is she a good mother or a bad one?

Madame Arkadina, the narcissistic actress in Anton Chekhov's *The Seagull*, is among the bad mothers in theatrical literature. Although a famous, revered, and much applauded actress, Madame Arkadina resents not being a man and being able to have the kind of freedom and power men in society have; hence, in part, her disapproving attitude towards her son, on whom she unconsciously takes out her feelings of frustration. And the drug addict Mary Tyrone in Eugene O'Neill's *Long Day's Journey into Night* is a loving if ineffectual mother, unable to cope with her younger son's illness, which she uses as an excuse to go back to morphine. Lady Bracknell in Oscar Wilde's *The Importance of Being Earnest* is not a bad mother but is hidebound by Victorian convention and the customs of the upper-class sphere in which she circulates and to whose snobbish principles she subscribes, all in her daughter Gwendolyn's interests. Good mothers include Mrs. Darling in James Barrie's

Peter Pan and Edward the Fourth's widowed Queen in Shakespeare's *Richard the Third*. Jane Darwell won an Academy Award for her moving portrayal of the quintessential earthy mother figure Ma Joad in John Ford's 1940 film of John Steinbeck's *The Grapes of Wrath*. How do these women feel about their social status? How do they feel about being women and about womanhood?

Karen Horney on Feminine Psychology and on Neuroses

Karen Horney (1885–1952) was another great pioneer psychoanalyst, educated at a church school in Hamburg and at the medical school in Berlin. She trained in psychoanalysis with Karl Abraham, who treated her for depression.

Her father, who had had four children by a previous marriage, was a Norwegian ship captain who took his daughter on sea voyages. Her mother, the daughter of an architect, was Dutch. The two met in the German seaport of Bremen, where they married. Karen grew up in Hamburg in a home that was divided by quarrels. She sided with her mother, whom she adored. At the age of thirteen, she decided to become a doctor and was soon fascinated by the new Freudian approach to psychology. Deeply opposed to the Nazis, Karen Horney immigrated before World War II to Great Britain and eventually to the United States.

She accepted Freud's ideas on the structure and nature of the mind, but she rejected what she saw as Freud's phallocentric view of human sexuality in favor of her own interpretations of feminine psychology. She thought that Freud's idea of penis envy as fundamental in creating the girl's future feminine identity derived from "masculine narcissism." Based on her clinical experience, she also felt that little boys had a fear and dread of the female genitalia that was even more important for future development than penis envy. But she believed that little girls could indeed experience penis envy at certain early developmental stages and that girls are brought up from their earliest years to have a sense of inferiority regarding their own gender. The social inequality of the genders was a primary focus of her work.

Eventually, Horney retreated from Freud's ideas on childhood sexuality as instrumental in character formation. Influenced by Adler, she emphasized instead societal interactions with the child, including first of all the way in which parents nurture their children. Good nurturing was of primary importance in character development and in the consequent growth of human beings as socially adjusted members of a culture. Bad nurturing led to the development of troubled people in need of therapeutic help. Horney saw neurosis as dependent not simply on the way the ego dealt with instincts and needs but rather on the way it dealt with those parental and social factors that influenced the ego and superego. And she explored the roots and genesis of neurosis in social interactions.

Like Freud and Deutsch, Horney saw femininity as based around the instinct for mothering. And she was the first to discuss men's envy of the ability to bear children, *womb envy,* which was often a suppressed desire. Georg Groddeck in *The Book of the It* (1923) had also recognized the truth of this assertion and believed it to be universally true that men envied women this capacity.

Horney also saw that little girls did often envy boys their penises, not for the reason Freud elucidated—namely, that they wanted to have one—but rather because it gave boys advantages, such as being able to urinate while standing. On the contrary, women were happy to have vaginas. But during the Oedipal phase, little girls knew that the father was too large to penetrate them and consequently had mostly unconscious fantasies of being genitally wounded, which was their punishment for their desire to replace the mother in the father's love. This was the equivalent of the male castration complex. These fantasies—as well as identification with the mother, with whom a nurturing post-Oedipal relationship was reestablished—were the bases of feminine psychology. Later personality development depended on those bases and on the innate, constitutional bisexuality of all human beings as elucidated by Freud.

Questions and Considerations

Neurotic Lifestyles: Among Horney's many contributions to psychoanalysis, one of the most useful for actors, directors, and writers is the categorization of neurotic lifestyles. Horney also refers to *character neurosis,* meaning impairment in functionality of the entire personality. The term is similar in meaning to *personality disorder.*

A psychiatrist acquaintance says that when he first started practicing psychoanalysis, he used Horney's theories—"she is very seductive"—but he found they really didn't work, whereas Freudian principles produced the desired healing results. He feels that the categories actually "defend against deeper understanding." Nevertheless, they may be of some practical value in interpreting scripts. There are three basic categories:

1. **Shallow Living:** A person indulges in a great many activities and thus avoids deep thinking on any subject. Such people don't want to know about themselves and are full of inhibitions. In extreme cases, they are obsessive and compulsive.

    The butler played by Anthony Hopkins in the Merchant/Ivory film *Remains of the Day* (1993) is able to ignore his employer's fascism. He throws himself into attending to the numerous tasks involving domestic arrangements, in which he involves himself emotionally as well as physically, precisely in order to avoid thinking, because on some level, he knows exactly what is going on. Indeed, his shortcomings are pointed out to him in no uncertain terms by the character of the housekeeper played by Emma Thompson. She is particularly shocked when he fires two maids on his employer's orders simply because they are Jewish.

    Some of the servants in Robert Altman's *Gosford Park* (2001) live in a shallow way. So does the character of the pampered, spoiled aristocrat played by Maggie Smith. The character's knowledge of the trivial and inconsequential details of life seems nearly limitless, as she educates her new servant in them. In her narcissism, self-involvement, and narrow-mindedness, she seems to think of nothing beyond the banal. What to wear at the hunt or the evening party assumes great importance for her, as does what other people are wearing, and she judges people by how well or poorly they dress. She would never dream of talking about personal, intimate subjects to anyone—not even, probably, to herself. For the actor playing such a part, avoidance of deep thinking thus becomes an actor's objective, albeit a negative one. To the actor's question, "What do you want?" the answer is, "I want to put on the right dress for the occasion." This answer defines an immediate objective or subobjective, but the real objective is, "I want to avoid thinking deeply about myself and everything that is going on around me. What I think and feel is my business and nobody else's. I refuse to allow people to judge me."

Such limited people can only feel safe within the narrow purview in which they have chosen to live, which avoids the necessity of confronting the chaotic conditions of life by circumscribing which of those conditions will be allowed to have any influence or importance. They concentrate on conditions that can be easily dealt with, such as the choice of clothing for the day. If anything in their narrow world goes awry, the person may go a bit berserk and lose his or her temper, indulging in tantrums, so much has importance been attached to trivialities that are actually a sublimation of repressed, unsatisfied sexual desire. For such characters, Uta Hagen's advice in *Respect for Acting* (1973) on the use of external objects (props) assumes almost more importance than it does for characters who deal with aspects of their lives other than the immediately material.

2. **Persistent Resignation:** Persistent neurotic resignation is characterized by inertia. People whose unconscious attitude is defeatist are incapable of taking action and don't know why. Such resignation actually serves to withdraw someone from a conflict, while at the same time appearing to be a conscious engagement with it. But this engagement only takes the form of thinking or ruminating about it, not of taking action. Such a person typically assumes a pessimistic attitude towards particular circumstances and perhaps towards life in general. Boredom, stagnation, and ennui are typical manifestations of persistent resignation.

Yelena in *Uncle Vanya* is trapped in her unhappy marriage but feels morally bound to honor her commitment to her difficult, demanding husband. Unconsciously, she feels she deserves no better than she has gotten, so she resigns herself to doing her duty and will not admit to anyone that she feels unhappy. Finally, in the late-night scene with her stepdaughter Sonya, she reveals the truth, although not the whole truth.

Horney contrasts this form of resignation with what she calls *dynamic resignation,* which is a conscious, realistic attempt to deal with an untenable situation by seeking ways out. In certain military situations, for instance, when an army is surrounded and does not wish to surrender although outnumbered, it will fight to the last man. Such people refuse to admit defeat, even if their situation seems temporarily unfavorable.

Matt Damon as Ethan Bourne deals with dangerous situations with endless ingenuity in *The Bourne Identity* (2002) and *The Bourne Supremacy* (2004). This is an example of dynamic resignation, because he knows he has no choice but to cope with situations he doesn't want to be in.

3. **Rebelliousness:** This is actually a form of persistent neurotic resignation, because no action is taken. Instead, the rebellious person, repressing the knowledge that nothing is actually being done, appears to be engaged in action. Rebelliousness can either be directed to the external world, towards those who frustrate demands, or internally towards the self, in the forms of self-hatred or self-loathing. But the point is that no real action is taken towards solving the problem that has theoretically caused the rebellious behavior and resentment. This is not like the behavior of real revolutionaries who want to change society and may organize themselves in order to do so, whether by peaceful or by violent means. Rather, this behavior is unproductive and only creates internal conflict. Passive-aggressive behavior is one of the manifestations of fruitless rebelliousness. Such people can be masochistic and profoundly unhappy. They find it very difficult to assert themselves and to go after what they want in life.

Many Chekhovian characters, among them Ivanov and Vanya, embody this lifestyle. They talk a good game but do nothing. Hamlet is another example of a person whose rebelliousness remains internal for most of the play.

Ways of Being: Horney also distinguished several basic ways of being, such as the directions in which people move in relation to others in their lives:

1. **Compliant:** Such people *move towards* others, trying to create a comfortable atmosphere of friendship. If they are neurotic, they do so in a clinging way, craving love, tenderness, and affection. They appear to be compliant, but one dare not cross or contradict them, lest one arouse their wrath. Such people typically need approval and have to be taken care of. If you have ever met anyone who could be characterized as "high maintenance," this is the type that moves towards others not in order to give but in order to take whatever they feel is missing in their lives. Dealing with people who appear to be compliant but are actually demanding can be very draining.

2. **Detached:** These types tend to *move away* from people and claim to desire freedom. This can give them a sense of integrity and serenity. They need to prove they are self-sufficient, but they often are the opposite. Their detachment masks a deep-seated fear of relationships. On the other hand, in people with a healthy self-image, detachment and moving away can represent a healthy rejection of conditions that would represent stagnation and decay, or that would prevent a person's self-realization.

3. **Aggressive:** These people *move against* others, because they feel they live in a competitive society and must make their way and secure the fulfillment of their needs, sometimes by force in extreme cases. They assert their power, and

they can be very dangerous. They feel that others are hostile and inimical and must be made to comply with their demands, because only then can they have a sense of security. As an extreme case, the psychopath/sociopath constantly moves against others.

In healthy people, these directions can be conscious and controlled, but they are unconscious defensive mechanisms in neurotics. Horney considered a combination of all three attitudes absolutely necessary to the complete development of human beings. This required a certain intelligent and intuitive approach to living, and flexibility in adjusting to situations. The neurotic lacks such flexibility, and this is one of the problems of the neurotic: the inability to perceive the appropriateness of action by taking any of the three directions, as circumstances might require.

The foregoing information about directions has directly to do with the classic Stanislavskian idea of objectives and actions. Is one of these directions dominant in a character? Are they combined, depending on circumstances? How does the character you are writing or acting combine these three directions?

Depending on whom he is dealing with and how he feels about that person, Hamlet tends to move towards, away from, or against that person—sometimes all three, depending on the situation. For instance, in act 2, scene 2, where Polonius tries to sound Hamlet out, the young prince appears to be friendly enough, despite his suspicions as to Polonius's motives (moving towards), but is eventually very insulting and sarcastic (moving against) and finally dismissive, so that Polonius leaves the scene (moving away from; at this point they move away from each other). Polonius has moved towards Hamlet, then away from him—moving against him in the mildest way, as he attempts to make him talk so that Polonius can decide if Hamlet is insane or shamming. For each direction there is a change of beat, representing the end of the attempt to attain one goal and the beginning of an attempt to attain the next goal. The directions the characters move in counterbalance each other's directions. As one moves towards, the other may first move towards then move away from the other one, particularly as they perceive each other's objectives to be in conflict.

Is your character living in resignation, persistent or dynamic—resigned to having to solve a problem and either taking real action to solve it or not? Is your character devoted to shallow living, thus avoiding self-knowledge and conflict, surrounded by triviality and banality? Is your character rebellious and, if so, against what? Does the rebelliousness take the form of actual resignation or of real action?

Chapter Three

Melanie Klein and Object-Relations Theory in Great Britain and the United States

KLEIN'S PSYCHOANALYTIC THEORIES AND THE BEGINNINGS OF THE OBJECT-RELATIONS SCHOOL

*S*he had wanted to become a doctor, which was something of a novelty for a woman in turn-of-the-century Vienna. Instead she had married her second cousin, Arthur Klein, a highly successful chemical engineer, when she was only seventeen. Her brother and mother doted on him, but the marriage was not a great success, and she felt trapped. Because of his job, they moved to Budapest in 1909. There Melanie Klein met Sándor Ferenczi, with whom she went into analysis, because for a long time she had been subject to periodic bouts of depression. He encouraged her interest in becoming a psychoanalyst herself and especially in pursuing the field of child psychology, for which he felt she had a particular aptitude. She was soon treating children at his Budapest Clinic. His faith in her was not misplaced, for she became an outstanding child psychoanalyst.

When at the close of the First World War the family had to separate for economic reasons, Klein left her daughter, Melitta, who later became an analyst herself, with her in-laws. She placed her son Hans in a boarding school. He felt she had abandoned him. He never forgave her. In order to work, she went to Berlin. And she took her other son, Erich, whom she was analyzing, with her. There she continued her own analysis, this time with Karl Abraham, who supported her in her work in treating children, became a close friend, and even sang her praises to Freud. In 1923 the family was reunited in Berlin. But after their brief, unhappy reunion, she finally worked up the courage to leave Arthur.

Eleven years later, she lived through what no mother should ever have to experience: in 1934 Hans died in an accident during a mountain-climbing expedition. Melitta was convinced that her brother had committed suicide. Melanie was too miserable even to go to his funeral in Budapest. This devastating loss was an ineradicable source of guilt, depression, and nightmares. She threw herself into her work.

Aside from her contributions to the understanding of child psychology and the treatment of child patients, Melanie Klein (1882–1960) is known principally for her innovations in the area of *object-relations theory.* Her work had an enormous influence on her own and the next generations of psychoanalysts.

The underlying idea of object-relations theory is a simple one: we are always in some relationship to objects. The word *object* most often means a person, although it also means a place, thing, or any external or internal matter for contemplation. It may also refer to the self: the self as internal object, meaning the self objectified, externalized, and held up to the light, so to speak, so that we can examine it. Both conscious and unconscious self-images are objects.

We have a mental representation of an object, and it is actually to this image that we are attached; this is called an *object representation.* An *object choice* is the selection of another person whose image becomes an object representation, sometimes for libidinal reasons, as when we "fall in love." In other words, we have introjected and cathected the object, and our attachment to it is based on our representation of it. The question is whether our representation is a real and accurate perception or only the result of projecting our own feelings, needs, and desires onto the object. In fact, it is a combination of the two.

We introject and cathect objects from infancy on. And we transfer feelings of love and/or hate that we felt for the first objects of our love — parents or caregivers — onto those new objects. As Klein says in her essay "The Origins of Transference" (1951), "In some form or other transference operates throughout life and influences all human relations." So far, so Freudian.

Klein accepted Freud's ideas about sexuality, feminine psychology, and the penis envy of the little girl, as well as his concepts of the id, the ego, and the superego, and his analysis of the nature of the unconscious. But she departed radically from Freud's idea about the superego: she felt it developed not as a result of the dissolution of the Oedipus complex and the identification with the parents but concomitantly with the Oedipus complex as it was in progress. And she placed the inception and end of the complex at much earlier ages than Freud did: it began at about the end of the first or the beginning of the second year and reached its peak at about age three, which is when Freud thought it *began.*

The "severe" superego, with its strictures and morality, was difficult if not impossible to change — *immutable* was Klein's word. Although initiated by reactions to the parents, the superego and the ego-ideal actually arose from the child's circumstantial necessity to control natural sadistic impulses during the oral phase and to deal with early experiences of anxiety. *Imagos* — object representations — of the parents are formed in the child's mind, but they are separate images around which the child's desires revolve and have little to do with the formation of the superego. Freud thought all of this "completely impossible" and a total contradiction of "all my postulates," as he wrote to Ernest Jones on May 31, 1927.

On the other hand, Klein was one of the few analysts to take Freud's idea of Thanatos, the death instinct, as more than mythological and symbolic. Freud's speculations were actual facts, as far as she was concerned. Klein thought that the self had to defend against deep-seated anxieties brought about by the death instinct, from infancy on. The anxious self gave rise to paranoid fantasies, provoking further anxiety.

She used a metaphor to explain the origins of inner conflict: the "good breast" versus the "bad breast." The *good breast* is the mother providing nourishment. When the infant is hungry and the breast is desired but is not immediately there to gratify the infant's desire, it becomes the *bad breast,* and feelings of hate born of frustration and narcissism emerge. The infant oscillates between feelings of love for the good breast and feelings of hate for the bad breast. And the infant exists in a world that it is no position to understand, much as a psychotic exists in a world of delusion. In fact, the infant's state of mind is psychotic in some ways. The infant fantasizes in a way that sees no difference between its fantasies and reality, similar to the way in which psychotics hallucinate. This schizoid-paranoid thinking remains on an unconscious level and can be reasserted in adulthood.

The infant feels such fantasies viscerally and forms vivid mental images. Without knowing what its bodily sensations mean, the infant feels threatened and attacked when it experiences frustrations and discomfort brought about by hunger or other bodily functions that it has no idea how to interpret. In addition, as Klein says in "The Origins of Transference," the resulting "destructive impulses against the object [the bad breast] stir up fear of retaliation." And the infant, who wants to feel secure, is also invested in having the "good" object be a protective one. At the same time, there is an important development: the primitive destructive feeling of envy, based in a strong aggressive drive, is born. This is an alternative to gratitude over the good things the good breast has provided. Arising from the intolerable frustration over wanting to greedily possess the good breast and failing to do so, the infant feels it wants to spoil and destroy the frustrating object, because it envies the object's power and independence. The infant does not want to have to depend on the object and would rather destroy the object than feel helplessly bound to it. It is only with time and the growth of perception that the infant will learn to adjust to reality and overcome fear.

The good and bad breasts are conceived of as objects of attention and attachment, but the breast is called a *part-object,* because the infant does not see the whole object, the mother, to whom the part-object belongs. In fact, the infant typically sees no boundary between itself and the external world; there is only one, whole object for the infant—it and the world are one. As Klein wrote in "Notes on Some Schizoid Mechanisms" (1946), "With the introjection of the complete object [the mother] in about the second quarter of the first year marked steps in integration are made. This implies important changes in the relation to objects. The loved and hated aspects of the mother are no longer felt to be so widely separated, and the result is an increased fear of loss, states akin to mourning and a strong feeling of guilt, because the aggressive impulses are felt to be directed against the loved object."

Concomitant with this feeling is the libidinal attitude of the infant, characterized by the Scottish object-relations theorist W. R. D. Fairbairn in his essay "Schizoid Factors in the Personality" (1940) as "one in which the aspect of *'taking'* predominates over that of 'giving.' " Furthermore, the infant cathects what is taken in as an object. And there is a concentration on the dichotomy between feelings of emptiness and feelings of fullness, as when a baby is hungry in contrast to when its hunger is satisfied.

These attitudes may be carried over into adolescent and adult life, particularly because during the Oedipal phase, the child has unconsciously absorbed the idea that his or her love is "bad." An adult who has never felt satisfied as a child may be needy and unable to give. Such an adult can only take and will feel perpetually empty emotionally, with the need to feel filled from an external source — namely, the loved object. When such people do give, it is only with the objective of taking — an objective of which they may be entirely unconscious. If the nature of their behavior is pointed out to them, it will come as a shock. They will feel hurt, aggrieved, and deeply disappointed, as they did when they were children and felt unfulfilled and miserable.

When the infant projects its own feelings onto an object, it automatically feels that the object feels the same way as the infant does. This is called *projective identification*. Satisfaction and deprivation are both internalized, and with deprivation, a sense of danger and loss. But the infant cannot bear deprivation or danger and in order to feel comfortable, splits off the introjected object, just as adults split off parts of their egos by repressing uncomfortable, threatening emotions. An infant is incapable of harboring two contradictory emotions — feeling safe and feeling in danger, for instance — at the same time. The negative feeling is therefore split off or discarded, and the infant focuses on warding it off. The infant then externalizes the split-off feeling in the form of physical reactions, such as crying or temper tantrums, meant to get rid of the unpleasurable emotions.

Klein thought in terms of *positions* people unconsciously adopted. These positions were stances they took as attitudes towards themselves and the world. They derived from the infantile id. She distinguished two such positions:

1. **The Paranoiac Position:** This arises from the fear of one's own death. It is the earliest position taken, and it is inborn and therefore a normal phase, through which the infant, unable to distinguish reality, passes. The infant fears that someone or something from without will cause annihilation. In adults, this position is defended against by the mechanism of denial and the feeling of omnipotence — "Nothing can happen to me."

2. **The Depressive Position:** This arises later. The infant has discovered that the good and bad breasts are one and the same. This gives rise to guilt over the desire to destroy it, and the infant feels that there must be some kind of reparation. The infant is afraid that the bad internal objects in the ego will destroy the loved object from within. As Klein informs us in "The Origins of Transference," "The infant's aggressive impulses and desires towards the bad breast (mother) are now felt to be a danger to the good breast (mother) as well." This fear turns into depression. In adults this position is overcome by devaluing and disparaging the introjected object, thus removing its power.

The depressive position is developmentally positive: in adulthood someone can see good and bad in the same person. In other words, the ability to tolerate ambivalence is an important developmental achievement. To see things in terms of black and white is less evolved and indicates that someone has not gone beyond paranoid-schizoid thinking.

Children unconsciously split off from the paranoiac and depressive positions in what Klein calls a "flight to the good." They alternate between paying attention to the self as a loved object, worthy of preservation, and to external loved objects, particularly the parents, and wanting to preserve them. But they feel guilty because of the hatred engendered in the bad-breast phase of oscillation. Guilt drives love, according to Klein. Experiences provide an oscillation throughout life between love and hate, envy and gratitude, based on the early reaction formations represented by the good and bad breasts. Klein sees this oscillation as a central experience. People are discontinuously mentally healthy and unhealthy, going back and forth between the two as experiences are integrated into the ego. Because of this, depressive anxiety is a constant oscillating feature of the psyche and of human existence generally.

Questions and Considerations

Objects: In *Respect for Acting*, Uta Hagen uses the word *object* in much the same way as it is used in psychology. She emphasizes the necessity of making external and internal objects, whether animate or inanimate, specific and personal to the character. The actor endows the objects with properties and individuality, basing the endowment on substitutions of analogous objects from his or her own life. The actor's feeling about them is thus infused into the life of the character. This is true of both inanimate objects and people with whom the character has a relationship. You, the character, know all about that cup from which you drink your coffee every morning, just as you, the actor, know all about your own personal coffee cup. Someone with whom you, the character, are in a relationship exists not only in the external world of the play but also as a mental representation endowed with your character's projections, needs, and desires, just as with relationships in real life.

It was interesting that in the off-Broadway production of Nicholas Wright's *Mrs. Klein*, Uta Hagen played the person whose principle focus in her theoretical psychoanalytic writings was on objects. The play, which concerns among other things her problematic relationship with Melitta, who in real life resented her mother's interference in her marriage, is worth reading for the information it provides about her as a personality, as well as for seeing how a writer creates the character of a psychoanalyst.

Morris Carnovsky's interpretation of Stanislavskian method as set forth in *The Actor's Eye* is also reminiscent of the Kleinian concentration on objects and our mental representations of them. Carnovsky tells us that the actor must concentrate on three things: the self (who one is as a character, with all the psychological complexity that implies), the action to be played, and the object. The object may be another person one concentrates on or an objective.

An object may be mentally represented in whole or in part. We may visualize a part of a person — their face, their hand, and the like — or the person as a whole, with an awareness of the person as a sentient, feeling human being with his or her own mental constructs and emotional life. Objects can be accepted or rejected, and Klein talks of the phenomenon of *object constancy*, which is the ability to remain faithful to an introjected object, such as a person one is in love with or a beloved parent.

For actors: If the character you are in a relationship with is the object of your own character's love and desire, how do you represent or visualize this object mentally? Do you see the object as a whole or in part? Are there times when you concentrate on the whole object and other times when you concentrate on a part-object connected with it? Does your character accept or reject the object? Visualization of part-objects (they can stand in for whole objects) can be quite helpful for actors and writers, because they provide a focus and a point of concentration: perhaps someone's general expression or eyes or mouth makes you love that person. Without worrying about the character, you might find something about the other actor that attracts you to him or her as a person and use that to give reality to the relationship. That would be your actor's secret part-object, which even your acting partner need not know about. What objects — part or whole — regarding the story as a whole and the individual characters in it immediately come to your mind?

For writers: Lincoln-green clothing, bows and arrows, Sherwood Forest, the hunting horn, the King's deer: to anyone who knows the story of Robin Hood, these objects — Freudian phallic symbols as they are — immediately suggest the story. Tell anyone the following objects: a trail of breadcrumbs in the woods, a gingerbread house, two lost children, and if they know "Hansel and Gretel," they can immediately tell you the entire story. Long hair and a tower are objects that tell the story of Rapunzel at once. And you can reconstruct the entire story from those two objects alone. These kinds of salient details stick in readers' minds and help make a whole story memorable. The same thing is true in creating the characters in it: select a few outstanding internal and external objects and you will begin to create a memorable character, as Shakespeare was able to do so many times. Who can forget Falstaff's fatness and lechery, Hamlet's cloak of "inky black" and his melancholy, Juliet's innocent purity, or Romeo's ardor?

As a writer, you might want to describe one or two physical aspects or character traits to stand for the whole object or to make them stand out in a theatrical character. In Chekhov's hilarious farce *The Boor*, Smirnov, who has come to collect a debt owed by Madame Popova's lately deceased husband, falls in love with her and dares to tell her as much. She rejects him, but at the end of the play — being highly libidinous — falls into his arms. She refuses to pay him, claiming her husband never owed the money, and he most ungallantly challenges her to a duel, but she doesn't know how to handle a pistol (an obvious phallic symbol), and he teaches her how to aim and fire a gun, demonstrating by holding and guiding her arm. Her arm becomes a part-object for Smirnov, as do her eyes: "Those eyes! Those eyes!" he says at one point, in an aside to the audience. Actors can use the part-objects supplied by playwrights to great comic effect.

In Molière's *The Miser,* Harpagon's cash box, which should be a part-object, seems to become a whole object for him. He treats it is as if it were a beloved child. It contains his fortune and is all-important to him. The actor playing the part with this in mind could use the substitution of a beloved person to represent the cash box. Caressing it tenderly even after he has been robbed, Harpagon might croon and coo to it as if it were a baby. Another possible substitution for Harpagon's cash box: the little treasure chest represents mother and the good and bad breasts. When its contents are stolen, panic sets in and arouses the kind of separation anxiety the infant feels when it has to separate from Mommy. Where did she go? Will I ever see her again? What will happen to me? She gives me food, and now that she is gone, I will starve!

Love: For Klein, love is driven by guilt and ambivalence. On the one hand, we desire to preserve the love object and to keep it from harm from both external objects and the demands of our own id, to enjoy being with it and taking care of it. On the other, we desire to possess it as ours and even to ingest it in some way, in an unconscious, cannibalistic primitive identification with food as the earliest source of libidinal pleasure. These destructive, possessive desires induce feelings of guilt and shame. Tenderness toward the love object is one of the results of these emotions. If, on the other hand, our love is unrequited, we feel rage toward the object that has thwarted our desires, and the more primitive emotions of the id are allowed by the superego to seep through the ego defenses.

For actors: How does your character exemplify Klein's point of view about the constant oscillation between love and hate, and between depressive anxiety and feelings of comfort? How does the character oscillate in specific relationships with other characters?

As a writer: How can you create this oscillation in a character?

We feel sad over the impending loss of an object, because that is always a possibility, so we exist in a state of uncertainty.

For actors: Where do you hope the relationship will lead? What do you want and expect from it? What do you want and expect to happen? And what actually does happen? Are your desires thwarted or fulfilled? How do you feel in either case? How do you react? How do you behave? What do you do? What actions do you take?

The various emotions of Romeo and Juliet include not only pleasure and deep attachment but also anxiety and a sense of impending loss and doom. In the course of their story as it develops, you can trace the arc from desire, accompanied by fear and anxiety; to achievement, accompanied by deep sexual and sensual pleasure and tender love; to loss, as Romeo is forced to leave Verona; and to the ultimate tragedy of their double suicide when they feel the loss of the whole object, which represents everything to them that is meaningful and desirable in life. The predominance of Thanatos over Eros is the culmination of the play, and the loss felt by the survivors is overwhelmingly sad and horrible.

The film *Mystic River* (2003) is an intense story about love and loss. The terrifying experience of the three children at the beginning of the film and the later ramifications manifested in the adult lives of all three, even though only one of them was abducted and abused (Tim Robbins's character), show how individual conditioning, both psychological and sociocultural, are of the utmost importance in together determining character development. The kidnappers and the car remain in the unconscious, sometimes coming into consciousness—as objects, both in part and as a whole, in the form of particular recurring pictures. And the haunting image of the kidnapped boy peering through the back window of the car that is taking him away remains a disturbing object memory and representation in the audience's mind as well as in the minds of the characters throughout the film.

As an adult, the Tim Robbins character remains confused, upset, and under the sway of his early traumatic shock. One of the boys (Sean Penn) becomes a criminal; the third (Kevin Bacon) becomes a police detective. The spouses and children of these three are in problematic relationships with them, in which Klein's ideas on the ambivalence and uncertainty of love can be clearly seen in various manifestations.

THE DEVELOPMENT OF OBJECT-RELATIONS THEORY, ATTACHMENT THEORY, AND SELF-PSYCHOLOGY

*A*fter the death of Karl Abraham in 1925, Klein felt unappreciated by her colleagues in Berlin. A successful lecture tour in England aroused interest in her ideas, and she immigrated to London in 1926 with Erich and Melitta. She was already well established in Great Britain by the time the Freuds arrived there. Ernest Jones had been much taken with her and had even had her analyze his wife and children. His support for Klein was the occasion of some coolness in his relations with the Freuds, although ultimately they remained the closest of friends.

Klein had long felt a rivalry with Anna Freud on theoretical grounds, thereby earning Sigmund's further distrust, especially since, as we have seen, he already had disagreements with her interpretation of psychoanalytic theory. Klein and Anna Freud were at odds about how to treat children therapeutically, and Sigmund predictably supported his daughter, with whose innovative ideas he agreed completely.

At Klein's death, Anna Freud expressed her regret at the loss of her great debating partner, whom she mourned, and decried the idea that they had disagreed out of personal animosity. In fact, in *Normality and Pathology in Childhood*, in connection with her developmental lines, she gives Klein full credit for those aspects of object-relations theory, such as the use of whole and part-objects by the child, that she found to be true on both theoretical and practical grounds.

Klein's techniques involved *play therapy*, in which the child's actions served some of the same purposes as free association did in adult analysis, revealing parts of the unconscious. But otherwise, based on her theory of the development of the superego, she used classic psychoanalytic interpretative techniques, much as she did when working with adults. Anna Freud was opposed completely to Klein's theoretical analysis of the child's immutable superego and to what she considered her unprovable ideas about the infant's preverbal object relations, the depressive position, and so on. And she had learned through her work with children that they had not yet developed stable egos, let alone superegos, so that the usual techniques that had been developed by her father when working with adults were not effective in treating children. She felt that a child's analyst had also to assume the role of an educator. Even after a period of nonanalytic preparation for analysis, the therapist could and should deal more directly with children, without offering the child early interpretations of his or her play actions as Klein did, but not remaining aloof as the analyst traditionally did with adults when following the classic rule of abstinence. And the analyst should maintain contact and communication with the child's parents. Klein felt nonanalytic preparation and constant contact with the parents was unnecessary and interfered with the analytic process.

Many British psychoanalysts were fascinated by Melanie Klein's ideas on object relations, and she had many followers, who extended, expanded, and amplified her work. Throughout the Second World War, the British Psychoanalytic Society was the scene of impassioned debates on the subject of child analysis and object-relations theory. There was a deep split in the psychoanalytic community between orthodox Freudians and advocates of the Kleinian reworking of Freud.

Among the major British object-relations theorists are, first and foremost, D. W. Winnicott (1896–1971), W. R. D. Fairbairn (1889–1965), and John Bowlby (1907–90), whose emphasis was on attachment theory and who left psychoanalysis. Margaret Mahler (1897–1985), who concentrated, like Anna Freud, on ego psychology, must be added to the list of important contributors to object-relations theory. So must Edith Jacobson (1897–1978). Both were refugees from Europe and worked in the United States.

Mahler laid great emphasis on the paramount importance for healthy development of the holding stage in infancy, described below under Winnicott's contributions, and stressed the importance of not being overprotective. She explored infancy and early childhood in depth, and worked with autistic children.

Jacobson in *The Self and the Object World* (1964) added to the Freudian theory of the instincts, slightly changing it in the process: She sees the libidinal and aggressive drives as potentials that are modified with experiences of pleasure and unpleasure "under the influence of autoerotic and of beginning functional activities." The unconscious contains "memory traces of pleasurable and unpleasurable sensations" that will help shape the child's development. One of her important concepts is that we all have a desire to merge and fuse with another person. Fantasies of merger and fusion take place throughout life and can be very gratifying and pleasurable: this is similar to Freud's ideas of the melting away of ego boundaries when people are in love. In early developmental stages, merger fantasies can be a hindrance to the process of individuation, but later they constitute an important element in relationships and are one of the reasons for the experience of pleasure during sexual relations.

Heinz Kohut (1923–1981), who had also immigrated to America, practiced *self-psychology*, an offshoot of the object-relations school; see below. Ivan Boszormenyi-

Nagy, another immigrant to the United States, made some important contributions to our understanding of the self with his *contextual therapy,* which focuses on personal development in the context of family relationships. For his idea on *destructive entitlement,* which is very useful for actors, directors, and writers, see below.

W. R. D. Fairbairn lived in Edinburgh, isolated from his colleagues in the south of Britain, and maintained a sense of independence, all the while remaining an important and influential contributor to psychoanalytic thought. In a departure from Freudian theory, he felt that psychoanalysis should concern itself more with the current or past events in any relationship than with the theoretical adjustment to erotogenic zones that implies that the autoerotism of the child is an explanation for the genesis of personality, although he did not discard the child's sexuality as a theoretically generative factor. He believed that in analyzing the parent/child relationship, primacy should be given to the actual events that led to the development of personality. The individual's personal, narcissistic internal development was less important than interaction with the environment, which was a primary factor in the development of character. In other words, Fairbairn concentrated more on Freud's reality principle than on the pleasure principle. He maintained that the infant has an ego from birth and seeks objects from the beginning because of the inborn need to obtain sustenance and nurturing from external sources. Disagreeing with Klein, he felt that the infant first sees the mother as a whole object and then the breast as a part-object. Thumb sucking is a substitute for that object, when it is unavailable to the infant. Because its relationship with the object is unsatisfactory at a certain moment, the infant attempts to supply its own needs autoerotically. This is not because the mouth is an erotogenic zone providing libidinal pleasure, as in the basic Freudian model, but because the desired object is unobtainable. He proposed that the early phases should be called the breast, the feces, and the genital, rather than the oral, anal, and phallic, because that would provide the basis of a true object-relations theory of development.

Fairbairn also thought that Freud's ideas about the libido needed to be modified: in particular, he felt that the libido did not simply seek out pleasure, although that was usually the desired result of its search for a sexual object, at least on the conscious and preconscious levels. He thought that the libido sought objects, period. Because of the introjection of unpleasurable object-seeking episodes during the Oedipal phase and perhaps even earlier, the libido sought the same objects again later in life, without knowing why, because the id had cathected them and demanded that the ego find them again. The person does not seek sexual gratification and relief from tension per se, as a means of pleasure, but seeks an object with which the libido is familiar. Fairbairn felt that the very nature of the libido was to adhere to something and that the infant at birth is programmed to adhere to the outside world, which will fulfill its needs in whatever way the parents are able to do, taking into account their own problems in dealing with themselves, which will affect their interactions with their child and the nature of their parenting. If the parents provide pleasure, the child will learn to seek pleasure, which is the most desirable, productive form of interacting with other people. But if the painful situations attach themselves to the libido—which they so often do, as evidenced by the ubiquity of the repetition compulsion—the child will have learned to seek out counterproductive, unpleasurable situations.

Fairbairn's idea constitutes a very interesting explanation of the repetition compulsion, but it is hardly a complete explanation. And it does not nullify Freud's idea that the libido seeks pleasure: we can still say that it seeks pleasure but that it is confused as to what constitutes pleasure.

Donald W. Winnicott, a specialist in pediatrics who decided to become a psychoanalyst, had a Kleinian analysis and was later supervised by Melanie Klein herself. He branched off on his own, but his version of object-relations theory is very Kleinian in both its origins and its orientation. However, there are a number of ways in which his ideas differ from Kleinian theory.

Winnicott distinguishes the *true self* from the *false self*—this notion is similar to the existential idea of authenticity versus inauthenticity. The true self emerges if the infant is allowed to express itself and if it has "good enough care," but if the parents feel threatened in some way, the infant feels obliged to comply with their demands and builds an externally acceptable false self in order to obtain the parents' approval, keeping the true self with its desires hidden. This can lead to problems later on, in adolescence and adulthood. The false self is a narcissistic, self-protected, defended construction associated with the *subjective object,* which is the object onto which subjective desires and needs are projected, forming a false object representation largely separated from reality. The object is not seen as an independent entity existing in its own right for itself.

The true self is associated with the *objective object,* perceived more realistically as separate from the self and distinct in having its own desires and needs: "the object as an external phenomenon, not as a projective entity," as Winnicott says in his classic essay "The Use of an Object and Relating through Identifications" (1968). The essay's main topic is the move away from narcissistic "self-containment and relating to subjective objects" towards the "realm of object usage." Winnicott thinks that the baby feels in its frustration and rage that it can destroy the "bad" object. There is joy in the infant's discovery that the object does not retaliate but can accept the rage and hatred directed at it. The object has survived! Therefore, the object really exists independent of the infant, and this is the beginning of consciousness of the existence of others. The destruction of the object has helped to create "a world of shared reality."

Destruction, or at least the desire to destroy, is thus paradoxically equated with creation. The subject that has internally destroyed the object perceives that the object has value and has survived the destruction without wreaking retribution. This causes the subject to experience feelings of love for the object, which it has the power to use in that "world of shared reality" and which can relate back and nourish the subject. In other words, in order to continue along the path of development, the child must eventually move away from the introjection and subjectivity of dealing with objects to the realization of the autonomy and otherness of objects: "projective mechanisms assist in the act of *noticing what is there,* but they are not *the reason why the object is there.*" This is a great step forward.

Among Winnicott's major contributions concerning the development of children are:

1. The three overlapping stages of infant and child development:
   - The "holding" stage at which the infant needs to be held and is incapable of independent movement away from the mother. This is a very important aspect of health, since the child needs physical contact and the security it brings;
   - Mother and child living together and adjusting to each other, as the child begins to develop physically, mentally and emotionally, without yet feeling its independence;
   - Child and both parents living together and learning to know each other.
2. The nature of parental care and the importance and influence of the environment. Winnicott describes the following kinds of "care": good-enough care in a good-enough environment, which ensures healthy development; average expectable environment and average care—the usual, with its conflicts and ups and downs, much of them brought about unconsciously; the facilitating environment with more than good enough care.
3. The relation of infants to objects, such as a toy or a blanket; such relations are an early realization of the fact that the infant's early perceptions of the world as simply an extension of the infant need to be adjusted to reality. Winnicott calls these *transitional objects,* because they facilitate the move from subjective objects to objective objects. They teach perception, and they lessen the pain of the necessary physical separation of mother and child. Children can become very attached to these transitional objects, and the attitudes of possessiveness they develop can carry over unconsciously into the relation with objects in later life.

Influenced by Fairbairn's and Winnicott's theories, John Bowlby branched off from object relations to devote himself to *attachment theory.* For actors and writers, the important principle to be extracted from his incredibly researched, exhaustive study of attachment is the idea that the nature of the attachment of the infant to the mother determines behavior in future relationships.

Basing his approach on the observation of infants and on biological studies of various species, Bowlby concluded that there are a number of inborn behaviors that serve to secure the infant's attachment to the caregiver, usually the mother, who is the most important figure in the infant's life. These behaviors are part of an organizational system that is biophysiological in origin and specific to each species; he also studied the attachment patterns of other primates. The behavioral system is the result of evolutionary development—Bowlby was a Darwinian. Some of these inborn, instinctual behaviors are crying, smiling, approaching by lifting the arms, following, clinging, and so forth. The infant receives feedback when it behaves in certain ways; *imprints* the image of the mother figure, which is differentiated from other members of the species; and begins to learn what behaviors are effective or ineffective in assuring that needs are met. Both heredity and the environment are important in determining character development. Disturbed patterns of attachment give rise to problems both in childhood and in adulthood. Bowlby attempted to unite biology and psychoanalysis in a complicated, balanced approach to understanding human behavior.

Questions and Considerations

Bowlby on Attachment: Bowlby's distinguishes three basic types of attachment:

1. **Secure:** Someone who forms secure attachments in adulthood has had a loving childhood and was well cared for by a good mother. Characteristics of a secure person include willingness to learn from others, a feeling of comfort with and acceptance of other people, trust, and independence. Secure people tend to be undemanding and are not dependent on other people.

2. **Anxious/Avoidant:** A person who has been abused or neglected in early childhood and has had minimal physical contact with the mother figure develops into an insecure adult who can be hostile, distant, angry, and independent, and less interested in other people than in his or her surroundings.

3. **Anxious/Ambivalent (Resistant):** Someone who has had an unresponsive, neglecting mother who may have her own psychological problems will be full of anxiety and fear, mistrustful of others, always wary, and unable to form lasting attachments. Such people may be clinging and demanding. At the same time, they are resentful, immature, and manipulative. They feel betrayed—a feeling they do not usually dare to express, unless it be in the form of temperamental outbursts.

In 1988 the American attachment theorist Martha Welch modified the categories somewhat, as follows:

1. **Secure:** Very much as in Bowlby's analysis. She adds that people who can form attachments with which they feel secure are confident, self-reliant, and generally of a cheerful disposition. They are not easily ruffled, have good self-esteem, and often have a good sense of humor.

2. **Resistant:** Resistant attachment is formed by people who tend to cling and simultaneously to avoid an inner feeling of attachment. They are impulsive, passive, defeatist, negative in their approach to life. They tend to develop codependent relationships.

3. **Avoidant:** Very much as in Bowlby's analysis. People whose attachments are avoidant are actively hostile, bullying, complaining, and unable to make commitments. They tend to be addictive personalities, attaching themselves to drugs or alcohol and avoiding real, satisfying contact with other people. They are quick to anger and to blame others. They avoid accepting responsibility.

4. **Disorganized:** This is often a combination of characteristics of the other three types. Depression and inhibitions are common. These people alternate between

trust and lack of confidence that the attachment is real, and believing that the other person really means the love he or she expresses.

For actors: You might explore any relationship from the point of view of its type of attachment. The details and specifics of the attachment will give depth to the way the relationship is played out and will help in analyzing the objectives and obstacles involved. What a character wants and why can be determined by his or her style of attachment.

Rimbaud and Verlaine in Christopher Hampton's *Total Eclipse* are attached to each other in an anxious/ambivalent way, involving guilt and shame, despite their iconoclastic principles of complete freedom and their denunciation of bourgeois culture and morality, especially Rimbaud's. Rimbaud had an unfeeling, disapproving, exceptionally harsh mother, who was also a religious fanatic. His father deserted the family. What he wants from Verlaine is the unconditional love he never got from his parents. Verlaine wants adoration and love from Rimbaud. They alternately cling to and drive each other away. At the same time, they are both immature and manipulative. Each one feels betrayed by the other. Theirs is a relationship based on insecurity.

Even the manner in which people say hello and goodbye, whether the person they are talking to is a love object or simply a clerk in a store, is very much the manner in which they said hello or goodbye to the first object of affection, usually the mother. A vestige of the same emotional affect is present. There is always unconscious separation anxiety that comes into play when someone says farewell. How is this played out in the character's manner? Is he or she abrupt or does he or she linger on the doorstep, so to speak? Does the person saying farewell appear to need reassurance, or will that person be all right on his or her own? The manner of saying farewell wards off the separation anxiety that was first manifested when the baby's mother was not easy to locate, having perhaps left the room. Usually, the actor is so completely unconscious of this that the automatic way he or she has of saying goodbye simply becomes the character's way. But look a little deeper into the character's particular manner of expressing unconscious separation anxiety, and you may find a different way of expressing it. Romeo and Juliet's farewell scene is a true expression of separation anxiety. Indeed, they have no idea if they will ever see each other again.

Personality Assessment: Kelly's Role Construct Repertory Test and the Adult Attachment Interview: There has been a proliferation in the last seventy years or so of psychological evaluation and diagnostic tests. Among them are the 1931 Bernreuter Personality Inventory, one of the first tests; the Minnesota Multiphasic Personality Inventory, a three-hour true/false test designed to facilitate psychological assessment; the 16 Personality Factor Questionnaire, with similar assessment capabilities; and the Adult Attachment Interview. For another contemporary approach to psychological assessment, see the Core Conflictual Relationship Theme (CCRT) on page 169.

The American psychologist George A. Kelly (1905–67), who developed what he called the *personal construct theory,* did not believe in the unconscious, the ego, emotions, motivations, or cognition, among other things. He felt that people anticipate the future based on their experience of the past. In trying to understand themselves and others and to control their world, they build *personal constructs,* which are conceptions and ideas about who they and other people are, and about their relationships to others and to themselves. These personal constructs are hypotheses that may turn out to be accurate in their predictions or not, and may be revised if necessary (*constructive alternativism*) or become fixed as basic ideas. They are then incorporated into the personality.

In order to understand someone, you have to understand how he or she understands his or her personal constructs. To that end, Kelly devised the Role Construct Repertory Test (REP test), a personality-assessment test in the form of an elaborate questionnaire. The person taking the test fills in fifteen blanks listing family members, teachers, friends, partners, coworkers, and the person he or she considers the most intelligent, the most successful, and the most interesting. The second part of the test determines what sort of construct each of the listed people belongs to. The constructs are poles that are either emergent ("I have a real relationship with someone") or implicit — that is, it might be possible that it would be emergent in the future ("I have no real relationship with that person"). The people listed are compared and contrasted, and can then be seen in various categories as, for instance, accepting or rejecting, emotionally predictable or unpredictable, nervous or easygoing, and feeling inferior or self-confident, dynamic or weak, and contented or unhappy. People taking the test will then begin to understand how they see themselves and others, how they behave towards those other people, and the roles those people play in their lives. An actor or a writer could use this idea to list the contrasting feelings about the other characters in a play and the roles they might play for him or her, and to decide how important each of the other characters is. You might list all the characters and then write next to them several adjectives that describe their salient characteristic (happy or unhappy, etc.) and several that describe the nature of their relationship with you (accepting or rejecting, for instance). Think of how you behave in response, and you might help clarify ways of playing actions, as well as understanding why you deal with the other character the way you do.

Based on the ideas of Bowlby and their further elucidation by the noted American psychologist and attachment theorist who worked closely with him, Mary Ainsworth (1913–99), the Adult Attachment Interview (AAI) is a series of probing questions formulated in 1991 by Ainsworth's former student Mary Main. It can be used for surveys and for working with patients. The AAI was also recommended by the Anna Freud Institute, which is devoted to child psychology and children's welfare, as a test for determining the fitness of prospective adoptive parents.

The suggested questions elicit the interviewees' recollections about their relationships with their parents and other people they were emotionally attached to during childhood. The interview is scored partly on the interviewees' ability to give a coherent account of the experiences and their meaning, and based on a scale determining whether the parents and other important people were perceived as loving, rejecting, neglecting, involving, or generally applying pressure to the child. A second set of scales evaluates the interviewees' state of mind as to coherence, the tendency to idealize or to denigrate, anger, fear of loss, idealization, and the ability to recall events. The interviewees are subsequently classified as belonging to the one of the following categories: *autonomous-free, dismissive-detached, preoccupied-enmeshed* or *incoherent.*

The AAI consists of eighteen basic questions or instructions, and the interviewer asks further questions in order to explore the responses to each of the eighteen. The questions are a useful tool for writers creating characters and for actors exploring characters' biographies. You might try as an exercise or for any current project taking well-known theatrical characters and giving their answers to the questions. Here is a slightly modified version of the questionnaire:

1. Describe your early family situation. (Where were you born? Where did you live? What was the environment like? Did you move around or stay in one place?)
2. Describe your early relationship with each of your parents from as far back as you can remember.
3. Choose five adjectives that describe your childhood relationship with your mother. (Why did you choose each of those adjectives?)
4. Choose five adjectives that describe your childhood relationship with your father. (Why did you choose each of those adjectives?)
5. To which parent did you feel closest? (Why? Why didn't you feel as close to the other parent?)
6. When you were upset as a child, what would you do? (Describe specific incidents.)
7. What is the first time you remember being separated from your parents? (How did you respond? How did they respond? Are there any other separations that stand out in your mind? What were your reactions?)
8. Did you ever feel rejected as a young child? (If so, how did you react? What did you do?)
9. Did your parents ever threaten you in any way? (Did they discipline you? How? Did they threaten you in a joking way? If so, how did you feel? How did you react? What did you do?)
10. How did these experiences with your parents affect your adult personality? (Do you feel that any early experiences prevented you from developing healthy responses? Did some experiences set you back in your development?)
11. Why do you think your parents behaved as they did during your childhood? (How well do you know and understand your parents as individuals?)
12. Were there any other adults with whom you were close as a child? (Were any other adults especially important to you?)
13. Did a parent or other loved one die while you were a child? (What was your reaction? How did you behave? What did you do?)
14. How has your relationship with your parents changed over the course of your life? (How is it different now that you are an adult?)
15. What is your relationship with your parents like now?
16. If you are a parent, how do you feel when you separate from your child?
17. What kind of future do you envision for your child?

18. Is there something you feel you learned above all from your childhood experiences? (What would you hope your child might learn from his or her experiences of having you as parent?)

The categories mentioned above (autonomous, dismissive, preoccupied, and incoherent) have to do with the way an adult has integrated childhood experiences. Psychotherapy would ideally enable people to move from the three categories that indicate difficulty in talking about their childhoods to the autonomous-free category:

1. **Autonomous-Free:** Such people value their relationships and their attachments but remain objective and independent with regard to them. They feel free to explore their own thoughts and feelings and are relatively comfortable talking about them. They are less repressed and more aware of their childhood experiences than either the dismissing or the preoccupied group.

2. **Dismissive-Detached:** Such people limit the depth of their adult relationships and their experience of attachment. They dismiss the knowledge of their parents' possible imperfections and of any negative effects their parents may have had on them, which they cannot acknowledge. They are not in touch with their anger. The category also applies to those who contemptuously dismiss their parents and cannot acknowledge any positive effects they might have had.

3. **Preoccupied-Enmeshed:** These people are subjective and confused about their childhood relationships, and they are preoccupied with trying to understand and come to grips with them. They tend to be passive and to generalize, and they are deeply fearful, angry, unhappy, and conflicted. They find it difficult to move beyond their preoccupation with their parents and are dominated by past affects connected with them. And they have a hard time acknowledging, let alone understanding, their difficulties in both their childhood and adult relationship with their parents.

4. **Incoherent:** These people have gaps in their memories of their childhood and frequently pause and stumble when answering questions. Typically, they have suffered childhood trauma such as abuse. They are very angry and conflicted and find it difficult to acknowledge the abuse they have suffered, let alone to talk about it in a coherent way.

For actors: To which category does your character belong? What are the reasons for the character's fitting into a certain category? Those reasons will be found through an exploration of the character's state of mental health.

The categories can overlap: Vanya might be described as preoccupied and dismissive with regard to his relationship with his mother. This is subtextually apparent in the few exchanges he has with her. Unconsciously he thinks about her more than the audience will ever know. Hamlet is dismissive of his mother in some ways but preoccupied with her and with his father. The two sons in the Tyrone family in *Long Day's Journey into Night* are also an example of preoccupation and dismissiveness: Jamie and Edmund are preoccupied with both their parents, and Jamie is dismissive of both of them, while Edmund is on the way to being in the autonomous-free category.

The incoherent category is found in films dealing directly with abuse. In Martin Moran's *The Tricky Part,* on the other hand, the author/actor is autonomous-free in being able to talk coherently about what happened to him and trying to go beyond it. He remains preoccupied-enmeshed on some level, but this does not prevent his talking freely about his preoccupation. In the course of the play, he relives the incoherence that resulted from his childhood trauma.

Heinz Kohut and Self-Psychology: The term *self-psychology* is associated with the work of Heinz Kohut. Originally from Vienna, Kohut, who had close ties with Anna Freud in London, taught psychoanalysis at the Chicago Institute for Psychoanalysis and began as an orthodox Freudian. He felt that his theories remained on an "unbroken continuum" with classical psychoanalysis, but he began to rethink the Freudian concept of primary narcissism. The primary narcissism of the self-directed libido evolves into object narcissism — that is, the ego directs the attention of the libido to objects in order to satisfy needs, those objects being in the first instance the parents or caregivers. The infant self begins to develop as a function of how it perceives and experiences the parents or caregivers.

Primary narcissism is a component of object narcissism. The emotional investment in the object includes the narcissistic desire to possess and control the object. Frustration of primary narcissistic striving for satisfaction is in part what causes the pain of the Oedipal situation. That frustration also causes the repression of the Oedipal feelings so that rejection will not damage the ego. The component of primary narcissism contained in the transference onto a cathected object will apply to adult transferences as well as to childhood transferences. In other words, the object unconsciously cathected by the self becomes a *self-object,* invested with the narcissism of the self, as if the object had no autonomy or self of its own and existed in order to provide satisfaction to the cathecting self. Other self-objects succeed the parental self-objects during all of one's lifetime.

Among other things, narcissism accounts for the fact that people need to feel and be right. The common phrases "Oh, he always has to be right" or "She can't stand to be contradicted" are examples of this persistence in both the person being talked about and the person making the remark, indicating that the speaker feels miffed, judgmental, and slighted in some measure. The speaker feels that his or her own narcissism has been impinged upon in some way.

Kohut perceived that there is an extension or projection of all of these repressed narcissistic feelings into the existentialist dilemma of the painfully isolated, alienated self in a meaningless world. Humanity is not simply full of guilt and shame over forbidden wishes but objectively involved in a meaningless existence to which it has had to give meaning.

Eric Erickson (1902–94) had similar ideas about the importance of psychosocial development and *ego identity* as a central factor in personality development and healthy functioning. The ego continually learns from its surroundings and in adolescence wants to develop a sense of who the person is, what his or her role in society is to be, and who he or she will be as a person. There may be crises of identity at various stages of a person's life, similar to the existential crisis in Kohut's idea of the alienated self.

Kohut thought that healthy narcissism, as opposed to overestimating oneself, was important in the development of personality and added richness to relationships, rather than interfering with them. A good dose of healthy self-respect, self-esteem, and self-love was an important part of the good self-image of any personality and ensured healthy relationships and functionality, as opposed to the sickness of narcissism that put the self above everyone. This latter sort of self-love derived not from being loved too much as one was growing up but from the early experience of neglect or insufficient love. The self becomes vulnerable to splitting and fragmentation. Sexuality may be used to try to reunite the fragmented self and to supply it with something it lacks.

For actors: What kind of love has your character received? Was your character able to receive love? If so, of what nature was this love? Did it smother the character and kill with kindness, or was it nurturing and supportive? What does your character expect and need in relationships with the other characters? How good is your character's self-image? Is the character's narcissism overweening or healthy? Does the character feel insecure, so that there is a paramount need to control and manipulate others?

Boszormenyi-Nagy on Destructive Entitlement: An important and often overlooked aspect of family relationships and the nature of attachment they imply is the unconscious narcissistic sense or attitude of entitlement, and of outright ownership of parents and children by each other, which can be very destructive to both. The desire for freedom as children grow up and want to be independent is naturally countered by obligations to the family, so that freedom and obligation have to be balanced. Freedom and obligation are not, however, necessarily mutually exclusive, although they may impinge on each other. As Fairbairn points out in his essay "A Revised Psychopathology of the Psychoses and Psychoneuroses" (1941), in cases of disturbed individuals, there is a deep desire to renounce infantile dependence and a simultaneous desperate longing to continue it. In a further demonstration of ambivalence, the attitude of destructive entitlement enables a person to destroy what he or she loves. Aggression and the desire for power are in opposition to the libidinal desire to love and to be loved.

As Ivan Boszormenyi-Nagy (born 1920) — the creator in the 1950s of *contextual therapy*, which concentrates on intergenerational relationships — indicates in an interview in the March/April 1993 issue of the magazine *Psychology Today*, the idea of destructive entitlement has to do not only with the psychological aspect but also with the moral dimension of behavior. People behave as if they have the moral right to ownership. But behaving and feeling entitled does not mean that one actually is entitled.

Particularly where there is a sense of entitlement and ownership on the part of parents who control their children, independence is inevitably trampled on. The peremptory tone in which such parents speak to their children will be mirrored unconsciously in the way those children speak to their parents. Both the children and the adults feel entitled to say and do what they wish because they own each other, and if one owns another person, that person must obey the owner's wishes. When there is disobedience, there is a sense of justice and loyalty denied.

The family context determines how the children will relate to and speak with others outside the family circle. The behavior of entitlement will be reproduced in other intimate relationships. Children who have suffered at the hands of their parents feel unconsciously entitled to revenge and may act this destructive sense of entitlement out in the arena of their other relationships.

The psychopathic, narcissistically disordered Richard the Third has a strong sense of entitlement. He is also extremely destructive and brooks no contradiction.

In *Hamlet,* Gertrude feels entitled to order her son around, but he will not obey, despite his line, "I shall in all my best obey you, mother." She in turn feels frustrated and angry with him. Hamlet feels he is entitled to more love and consideration than he is getting from Gertrude, and the lack of the response he desires from her is not only disappointing but makes him unconsciously deeply angry. They both feel betrayed and destroyed.

Lord and Lady Macbeth are perfect embodiments of destructive entitlement at its worst. They feel entitled to commit murder! The consequences of their acts are social upheaval, destruction, and war.

Torvald feels entitled to control Nora in *A Doll's House.* She feels he is destroying her and finally has the courage to leave him.

The Professor in *Uncle Vanya* feels entitled to more consideration than he thinks he is getting, so he behaves dictatorially and sadistically, especially to his long-suffering wife, who displays a certain amount of masochism in her responses. Vanya feels entitled to tell his mother to shut up and doesn't even think twice about it, so automatic and deep is his sense of entitlement and ownership. Sonya, on the other hand, doesn't feel quite so securely entitled to tell her uncle that he is being boring. Unable to stand any more and a bit ashamed for her beloved uncle because of the way he carried on, she does so somewhat timidly and reticently.

In *The Seagull,* Madame Arkadina behaves in destructive ways with her son, partly out of a sense of rivalry with him and partly because she feels she owns him and is superior to him and entitled to do what she wants with him. She treats her lover, the poet Trigorin, in a similar way.

In *Three Sisters,* Natasha feels a sense of ownership of the whole family once she has married Andrei; you could not have a clearer example of destructive entitlement than is seen in her character. Appearing at first eager to be accepted, knowing Andrei's sisters look down on her, she hides her sadism behind a mask of sweetness and shyness. Since she is engaged to their brother, the sisters feel entitled to be critical of her, and she is upset at what she takes as their meanness. They criticize her taste in dress, which is symbolic for them of her general vulgarity. In fact they are being rather mean, but their attitude turns out to be justified by later events. They knew whom they were dealing with, even if their brother did not.

Once Natasha is a member of the family, she treats the sisters with disdain, masked as politeness—a good example of the playing of opposites—and behaves as if she were entitled to make them obey her. She feels she is entitled to have an affair with Protopopov behind her husband's back, because she has lost respect and love for Andrei now that she has him where she wants him, under her thumb, just as Lady Macbeth has contempt for her weak-willed husband. Natasha feels entitled to do anything she wants. But Andrei is no Macbeth, merely a man who is weak and has lost his ambitions. He was made so much of by his sisters that he felt entitled to be made much of by the world, which remained unresponsive, as perhaps his father the general had been to him.

Natasha owns their baby, of course; the child scarcely belongs to his father Andrei, even though it is he who takes the responsibility of caring for the infant and wheels him about in his pram. And Natasha feels she can be insulting and contemptuous of the old Nurse, whom she considers more or less a nonperson, deserving of no consideration despite her long years of service. Natasha has no sense of justice, only one of needy and destructive entitlement. It is axiomatic and obvious that underlying her behavior is deep insecurity. Less obvious is that her insecurity includes the unconscious phobic attitude that she may lose everything and be out in the cold.

Rimbaud and Verlaine in *Total Eclipse* seem also to have a sense of destructive entitlement with each other. They even go so far as to act it out physically. Rimbaud stabs Verlaine in the hand, and Verlaine tries to shoot Rimbaud. This is certainly taking things to extremes, but then they are extreme people who live with a sense of hungry desire. They want to experience everything to the full: pain and euphoria, despair and ecstasy.

Edward Barrett in *The Barretts of Wimpole Street* and Dr. Sloper in *The Heiress* are two further embodiments of unconscious destructive entitlement. They feel they own their daughters and exact strict obedience from them.

We have an object lesson in how terrible destructive entitlement can be in the upsetting but ultimately optimistic film *This Boy's Life* (1993), based on a real story. A young boy (Leonardo DiCaprio) and his mother (Ellen Barkin) are severely physically abused by her irresponsible, demanding sociopathic husband (Robert De Niro). When they finally escape from the brutal treatment and run away, the audience cheers. This film is an example of what Freud meant when he said there has to be a certain distance between the spectator and the violence in order for us to be able to identify with the characters. That distance is created here by our empathy for the mother and son and by De Niro as well because of his complete understanding of his character's psychology. He plays this unhappy, self-pitying, sadomasochistic monster with depth and compassion. By contrast, the sociopathic serial killer played so brilliantly by Charlize Theron in another film based on a true story, *Monster* (2003), failed to arouse sympathy from the start because she is so narcissistic, nasty, and unpleasant. The brutality and sadism of the murders she feels entitled to commit, which would be hard to take in any case, are completely nauseating. The rage and violence are unmitigated by any sense of guilt, remorse, or feelings of pity on the part of the character.

The questions for actors to ask are: Why, with whom, and in what ways does my character feel a sense of entitlement and ownership? How is this manifested in ways that are destructive to the person toward whom this sense of entitlement is directed? How does this attitude show lack of respect for the other person and his or her needs? What do I feel I deserve, and why do I feel that way? Who owes me what, in my opinion? Do I consciously behave in an ethical, moral way in my relationships?

Chapter Four

❦

The Rebellious Crown Prince: Carl Gustav Jung and Analytical Psychology

PROLOGUE: THE CONFLICT BETWEEN JUNG AND FREUD

*C*rash! There was a loud report from the old bookcase. The two men jumped up, startled, afraid the bookcase would topple over onto them. They had been sitting for a long time in Freud's study arguing about parapsychology. Jung took such things very seriously indeed. To the unmystical Freud, parapsychology was nonsense. Jung was getting more and more upset. Freud's irritation with his young colleague was growing more apparent by the minute.

In *Memories, Dreams, Reflections* (1963), Jung described this 1909 visit, only his second to Freud in Vienna. He had suddenly felt a red-hot glow "as if my diaphragm were made of iron" just before the "loud report." Jung maintained that this noise was a perfect example of a "so-called catalytic exteriorization phenomenon": his stomach pains had been the catalyst for the "loud report" from the bookcase. Freud was obviously astonished. "Oh, come," he exclaimed. "That is sheer bosh." It was an old bookcase. The heat in the room had caused the dried boards to shrink. Jung predicted there would be a second loud noise, and there was. He insisted on his spiritual, metaphysical interpretation, and Freud "stared aghast at me." Jung left. Freud wrote to him and said that his idea was "wholly implausible." They never discussed the incident again.

Ah, "when they were jung and easily freudened," wrote James Joyce in *Finnegan's Wake*. Joyce's punning phrase is just about as neat a summary of the early part of the relationship between Freud and Jung as you could find. Jung, who was never *easily* Freudened, could not bear to remain so for long in any case.

Carl Gustav Jung (1875–1961) was the son of a Swiss Protestant pastor and grew up in a very religious atmosphere. While preparing for his qualifying exams as a medical doctor in Basel, Jung came across a textbook of psychiatry, and it was a revelation to him. Fascinated by mental aberrations, he became a psychiatrist and secured a job at the famous Burghölzli Clinic. Presided over by the august Eugen Bleuler, the clinic was the foremost of its day in treating psychoses. In the early 1900s, Jung treated patients for what he called *psychic conflicts* or *lesions*, in part by a *word association test*, proposing to them a list of key words, to which they had to respond. When they were silent or stumbled in some way, he had found a small inroad into their unconscious. This was obviously akin to Freud's *free association* method.

In 1903 Jung reread Freud's *The Interpretation of Dreams*, which had not previously impressed him, and was startled to notice a similarity between his and Freud's ideas. He also immediately felt a rivalry with Freud. This was to be exacerbated in their later conflicts, although Jung at first suppressed his feelings. Instead of publishing the results of his work, as he had intended to do, without referring to Freud, he decided to speak on Freud's behalf and defended him on at least two public occasions at psychological conferences. He also sent Freud a copy of his book, *Psychology of Dementia Praecox* [the old term for schizophrenia] (1907), and Freud, quite impressed, suggested they meet.

Jung was handsome, charming, and erudite, and Freud was immediately attracted to his warmth and liveliness. So rapidly and astonishingly did their relationship develop into one of almost filial closeness that Freud soon considered Jung his brilliant crown prince, heir apparent to the psychoanalytic movement. Freud was more than happy to have someone who was not Jewish in that position. Almost all of Freud's early followers and the members of his inner circle were, in fact, Jewish, and psychoanalysis was already under attack from some quarters as a "Jewish" science without universal applications. Freud had Jung named president of the International Psychoanalytic Association, but he and Jung nevertheless found themselves increasingly at odds.

The definitive break came in 1913 on the eve of World War I. The year before, Jung had published the second part of his book *Transformations and Symbols of the Libido* (revised in 1952 and renamed *Symbols of Transformation*). It contained ideas that Freud found anathema. The disappointment on both sides was bitter, and Jung left psychoanalysis to found his own school, which he called *analytical psychology.*

Among other things, Freud could not accept Jung's spiritualism or certain quasi-mystical ideas such as *synchronicity.* In the Jungian view, synchronicity is the acausal but meaningful connection between ego consciousness and the external environment. The two connected events are nearly simultaneous, one of them external and observable, the other internal and psychological. For example, you think of a friend you haven't seen in a long time, and you arrive home to find a letter from that friend. There are other kinds of synchronicity: you think of something that is actually occurring far away, even though you can have no knowledge of the event—this is called *remote viewing;* you see a future event that then takes place as predicted—this is known as *precognition.* To Freud this was preposterous.

But the most important reason for the split was that Jung rejected the centrality of sexuality in the development of personality and in the human psyche, even though he saw it as playing an important role, particularly "as an essential—though not the sole—expression of psychic wholeness" and as an expression of the "dark side of the God-image." Nor could he abide the idea of the Oedipus complex, which he preferred to call the *incest complex,* as a prime determinant in character development. For Jung, incest had spiritual significance as a symbol but only rarely signified a "personal complication." Even the idea of childhood sexuality, which Jung accepted, was not to be viewed as developmentally central. On those reefs the ship of their friendship foundered. Freud wrote to Ernest Jones on October 22, 1927 that Jung, in promulgating his theories, had made analysis "unreal and impersonal."

Jung's jealousy of Freud, which exacerbated his "unconscious" anti-Semitism, was another major factor in the breakup. It is beyond the scope of this book to go extensively into the vexed question of Jung's collaboration with the Nazis, which left a permanent stain on his reputation that even his Jewish followers have difficulty explaining away. To summarize briefly: At first he detested the Nazis, and then he yielded to their blandishments. He thought Hitler was a pathological liar but also a *thaumaturge* or medicine-man archetype who had tapped into the "collective unconscious" of the Germans. And Jung simply couldn't resist the honor of being made the de facto grand panjandrum of the German psychological establishment and having his analytical psychology viewed as sacrosanct.

From a Jungian point of view, Jung's *shadow*—his dark side—asserted itself during that period of history. In 1945 he said to Rabbi Leo Baeck, albeit in private, that his egregiously stupid 1934 article "The State of Psychotherapy Today," in which he talks about the so-called differences between "German" and "Jewish" psychology, was nonsense and that he had "slipped up." It is worth remembering that during the Nazi darkness, he was helpful to many individual Jews, among them some of his fellow analysts. He even sent Freud money to help him leave Vienna, but Freud refused to take the present.

The school Jung founded is still a major force in the world of psychology. He was a man of wide-ranging intellectual and cultural interests, which was one of the things that Freud found so attractive about him. Jung's interest in what archaeology revealed about ancient life, as well as in mythology and in religion and the part they play in human consciousness and culture and the way they serve as background to personal character, adds a fascinating, necessary dimension to our understanding of humanity. In fact, Freud shared his interest in these things, but he did not empathize with Jung's giving credence to astrology, paranormal phenomena, sorcery, the occult, or alchemy.

Jung was much enamored of ancient Chinese philosophy—including Confucianism, Taoism, and Buddhism—and of the writings of various other cultures. He traveled extensively. India and Africa, North America and Europe—all impressed and fascinated him. He was enchanted by all the cultural and spiritual phenomena he came across. People who are religious often admire Jung, in part because he validates their feelings and beliefs about religion. He took such feelings very seriously indeed, having grown up with them. He maintained that there was a deep layer of the unconscious that was, in fact, spiritual.

Many of Jung's ideas are Freudian derivatives. As Jung himself admitted, "Without Freud's psychoanalysis, I wouldn't have had a clue." Nevertheless, the major Jungian concepts represent a radical departure from Freudian thinking. Most importantly, Jung believed that the religious and cultural ideas transmitted by preceding generations to each new generation arise from a *collective unconscious,* which he defined as "all psychic contents that belong not to one individual but to many, i.e., to a society, a people, or to mankind in general" and further as "mythological associations, the motifs and images that can spring up anew anytime anywhere," as they do in folk tales and fairy stories, for instance, in all cultures. The existence of the symbols Freud had analyzed in dreams was an instance of the contents of the collective unconscious, and Jung felt that Freud had not adequately dealt with this collective aspect of dream symbols. Jung also felt that dreams were communications of various kinds, rather than simply attempts to represent wish fulfillments. Jung's writings about dreams present a vast, comprehensive, and complicated view of their contents and symbols.

For Jung the individual conscious and unconscious are imbued with and derive from the collective unconscious. People need to learn to understand this collective and spiritual unconscious and how it shapes who they are. It begins for them as something obscure and only dimly perceived. Therefore they have to undergo education both at home, where they learn from their parents, and in educational institutions.

In dealing with mythological and cultural symbols, on which he was quite an expert, some of what he says in *Jung on Film,* videotaped interviews conducted by the American psychologist Dr. Richard I. Evans in 1957, reveals a great deal about the differences between his thinking and Freud's. He tells us about a case in which a young woman claimed to have a snake in her abdomen—not a real snake, she said, but that was how she felt. Jung tells us about the snake being an ancient Hindu symbol and a worldwide cultural symbol, but does not mention what the snake symbolizes. In Jung's account of the treatment, foretold by his intuitive patient as lasting only ten sessions (which it did, in the manner of any self-fulfilling prophecy), the subject of sex is nonexistent. Jung calls the young woman's fantasy a "collective fantasy" and says that people are looking for an archetypal experience, and that it will give the individual who finds such an experience a sense of liberation. All of this is obviously as far away from Freudian thinking as it is possible to get.

The Major Concepts of Analytical Psychology

*H*ere is a summary of the major Jungian concepts and ideas. Such terms as *unconscious* differ from Freudian usage even where the words are the same, and Jung's concepts alter Freud's in certain of their emphases and meanings, even where they derive from his ideas. For instance, for Jung the ego is a wholly conscious area of the self and not part of an unconscious structural system as it is for Freud, for whom the ego is partly conscious, partly unconscious, and partly preconscious:

1. Jung says that psychology is an aspect of matter, because we are all made up of matter, and that the psyche is the internal world, including consciousness and the unconscious. The unconscious consists of two areas: a) the relatively superficial *personal unconscious,* which is the repository of ideas, emotions,

and various complexes, among them the incest complex, sexuality, repressed emotions, and conscience; and b) the shared collective unconscious common to all of humanity. The collective unconscious contains the deepest primal instincts and universals of personality; it is the repository of the *archetypes*. The divide between the two aspects of the unconscious is fluid.

2. In Jung's view, babies are not born tabula rasa but filled a priori with categories they have inherited and which represent the wisdom of eons of human existence. Man is completely different from animals, says Jung, and is born with certain universal archetypes, which are behavioral models linked to the instincts. Jung first thought of them as "primordial images," such as those of masculine or feminine behavior. They cut across cultural lines and have existed since the dawn of civilization. Archetypes are the result of repeated experiences such as war and giving birth that have left their imprint on the nervous system. The latent archetypes await activation in the appropriate circumstances. You can also think of them as psychosomatic images, because they will have physical as well as mental effects when activated. They are transmitted by adults who (perhaps unconsciously) teach children the archetypes and bring them out, and they will be more fully developed through experience.

Jung sees the child as being born with a complicated character but without a psychology of his or her own, despite the inborn imaging system of archetypes that will develop later, because children exist in the mental atmosphere of their parents and are influenced by and imbued with their parents' psychology, which they express in childish ways.

The infant inherits proclivities that find their natural development and flowering during the process of *individuation*—Jung's term for the lifelong process of becoming an individual or person, absorbing what is necessary from the archetypes and actualizing the potential they contain in order to differentiate a particular person from his or her cultural surroundings. The process of individuation enables the person to be a participant in the culture from which he or she comes.

The archetypes include: the Child-God, such as Christ born in the manger or the Dalai Lama; the Mother, including various female relatives who can take on the role of nurturing woman; the Trickster, or Magician, who has magic powers and can be half animal, half human; the Hero and its shadow opposite, the Demon, a villainous opponent; the Wotan, or Father, archetype—the all-powerful god; the Venus archetype (think of the Hollywood screen goddesses); the Bacchus archetype—sensual, lustful, given to pleasure; and the Eternal Child archetype—think of Peter Pan; the Wise Old Man, or sage teacher; and other, more complicated primordial images, such as that of dual birth. The Self is an important archetype. The archetypes also include such behavioral models as the saints of the Catholic Church and the saints and saintly personalities of other religions, with other mythologies and legends providing other behavioral model archetypes. The gods and goddesses of mythology are all archetypal aspects of the human psyche. Much of Jung's thinking is based on stories that cut across cultural lines. It includes such phenomena as the myth of the Great Flood, common to several cultures, and the findings of cultural anthropology.

For a fuller picture see *The Archetypes and the Collective Unconscious* (1959), and consult Edith Hamilton as well as other books on mythology.

3. There is a shadow archetype within all of us, which is the "dark side" of our personalities and the opposite of the positive self-image we cultivate. It constitutes the side of ourselves that we would prefer not to recognize, such as tendencies to sadism and rage. Every archetype has its shadow, or opposite: the Prince of Darkness and the Prince of Light, for instance.

4. The idea of the *persona,* the individuated personality, includes the idea of a self-image, which may be idealized. The persona is our presentation of the image of ourselves to the world, our social mask, ourselves as we wish the world to perceive us. The word has taken on a common meaning of the surface manifestations of personality. One can have the persona of a gender (a masculine or feminine persona), of a developmental stage (the persona of a teenager or of an old man or woman), or of a profession (the persona of a teacher, lawyer, or doctor). Too close an identification with the persona leads to problems and malfunctioning, and even to dysfunctionality that may have to be dealt with psychotherapeutically.

5. Another key idea in analytical psychology is the *imago.* The imago is subjective, unconscious, and prototypical, and is not only an image or visual representation of an object (person) but also includes the feelings someone has about the object. The imago may be the result of fantasy and wishful thinking located in the personal unconscious, as well as of archetypical images from the collective unconscious. Everyone develops positive and negative imagoes—sometimes revolving around the same person, such as a parent—indicating ambivalence in one's feelings about that person. Somehow the contradictions must be resolved into a whole imago, at least ideally, although one or the other pole may assert itself at various times, particularly when conflict arises. Complexes are built of imagoes.

6. The *anima* and the *animus,* which are archetypal patterns of masculinity and femininity, exist in varying degrees in everyone. "Either sex is inhabited by the opposite sex up to a point," writes Jung in *The Archetypes and the Collective Unconscious,* and the feminine aspect of a man, his anima, is usually unconscious for him, as is the masculine aspect of a woman, her animus, for her. The anima and the animus are sometimes conscious, sometimes not. The animus is usually stronger as a self-image in men and the anima usually stronger in women. Falling in love comes about because one has an internalized archetypal image of the ideal man or woman. As Jung informs us in the 1985 documentary *Matter of Heart* (Kino Video DVD), the archetype can seize a person, who may see someone that resembles his or her inner image and fall in love. But it may turn out to be a dreadful mistake. A man seeks a woman who resembles his archetypal anima, and a woman seeks a man who reflects

her archetypal animus, and the result may not be what they desire; or it may, on the contrary, be a perfect relationship.

Character consists of two basic attitudes (extraversion, introversion) and four primary functions (thinking, feeling, sensation, and intuition), described in the section below.

QUESTIONS AND CONSIDERATIONS:
THE PRACTICAL APPLICATIONS OF JUNG'S IDEAS ON
CHARACTER AND CHARACTER TYPOLOGY

*J*ung's most practical ideas for actors include the persona and the imago. Both are useful ways of looking at character from the point of view of how we wish others to perceive us and how we perceive them. His ideas on character typology can be useful as well. Two words he used in describing people have passed into everyone's vocabulary: they are *extraversion* and *introversion,* both of which are attitudes to the world. Both extraversion and introversion are possibilities that may be brought out in anyone in varying degrees under the influence of the environment and, importantly, "the given fact of the psyche as it is born," including its combination of genes.

The two attitude-types have striking differences. Introverts are generally afraid of the world and extraverts are not. At the same time, neither the introvert nor the extravert realizes that both types hold the world within the self. Jung informs us that the introvert "is always intent on withdrawing libido from the object." For Jung the concept of libido is much broader than it is for Freud or the object-relations theorists, and means life force or energy, akin to the Freudian idea of Eros. On the other hand, the extravert "has a positive relation to the object," for whom it may become, in fact, overly important as he or she concentrates his or her energies on it. Introverts are withdrawn, shy, and reserved, sometimes to the point of inscrutability. But extraverts are approachable, friendly, and sociable, even jovial and outgoing.

The type or category to which a person belongs is the decisive factor in her or his judgment and outlook on life. Extraversion and introversion represent adaptations to life and are therefore subject to modification. For extraverts a direct relation to objects and external circumstance is more important than their subjective views. Although introverts perceive the external, the important factors for them are their subjective impressions. Thus, each type assimilates the perception of the external differently. But Jung also said that personality types ultimately are simple orientation points that help us understand people, and that such terms as extraversion or introversion are only for that purpose. They only represent some aspects of a personality, which has many more complicated sides to it.

Jung talks not only of the two *attitude-types* but also of four *function-types.* The primary functions are: thinking and feeling, which are both rational functions because they involve the dominance of the reasoning and judging faculties; and sensation and intuition, which Jung considered irrational functions. He meant that they are beyond or outside the rational and based on "the sheer intensity of perception" without judgmental selectivity. Feeling might appear to an outside observer to be an irrational function, but from the feeling person's internal point of view, it is object oriented and involves selectivity and judgment.

He distinguished between what he called *primary* and *secondary,* or *auxiliary,* functions. A function is primary when it dominates, perhaps only part of the time, and becomes secondary when it accompanies a primary function. Primary and secondary functions could complement each other or be antagonistic to each other. They are found in various combinations.

Any one of the four functions may be uppermost in any individual at a given time, and they are usually paired. For instance, thinking (primary) might include intuition (secondary), and exclude feeling; and feeling (primary), which would exclude thinking, might include sensation (secondary). If intuition is primary, perhaps it includes feeling as a secondary or auxiliary function. If sensation is a primary function, perhaps it includes either intuition or feeling as a secondary function, and so forth and so on.

Added to these ideas is Jung's concept that everyone has an ability to transcend adversity and find inner harmony — the *transcendent function* — by harmonizing all aspects of the self: the appropriate archetypes, the anima and the animus, introversion and extraversion, the primary functions. For optimal health, there needs to be a balance among all the animating forces of the personality.

Actors, directors, and writers interested in the Jungian approach to characters should consult his *Psychological Types* (1921) for more detailed information.

He warned that the types were not rigid, fixed, or inflexible, and that not everyone fit into these categories in an easy, simple, classifiable way. People were a mixture of types, and of introversion and extraversion, and had all the functions in varying degrees. The classification of anyone as being of a particular type arose from the fact that certain of those traits were dominant over the others. Their shadow sides had also to be taken into account. In his model of character typology, Jung distinguished the following eight personality or basic psychological types:

1. **The Extraverted Thinking Type (Rational):** Like some thinking introverts, this type appears repressed and lacking in feeling, arrogant and cold. They think they understand the world and can control it, and they expect everyone else to go along with their ideas. Some scientists, academics, and researchers, particularly those who like to communicate their ideas to the public and involve themselves in animated discussions, may belong to this type. They enjoy holding forth on the topics that interest them.

   Astrov in *Uncle Vanya* appears to be rather cold and a bit arrogant, although his pain at the death of the patient who died while Astrov was ministering to him humanizes him and makes him sympathetic in our eyes. And when he gets going on his favorite subject, ecology, it is hard to stop him.

   Many of George Bernard Shaw's intellectual characters — such as Professor Higgins and Eliza Doolittle, who is not an intellectual, in *Pygmalion* — also fit into this category. The fact that they are the same type may explain why they are at loggerheads with each other, as their thoughts clash.

2. **The Extraverted Feeling Type (Rational):** Such people are known as "flighty," and their emotions change with circumstances. They don't even know why, nor do they care to analyze their feelings. They are reactive and responsive, and may be very emotional and given to moods that vary from elation to depression, as in a bipolar disorder. Emotional actors can be found in this category. Relationships with others can be short-lived and tempestuous, or at least quite intense. Feeling extraverts appear to enjoy life and to be the "life of the party," but they may descend into the depths of despair as easily as they rise to the heights of elation.

   Basil Fawlty and some other hysterical or histrionic personality types are extraverted feeling types.

   Madame Arkadina in *The Seagull* is in this category. She can be extravagantly emotional, loving one moment and hating the next. She is moody, reactive, and passionate. She needs to be the center of attention, and she finds her son's desire to be a playwright threatening and feels he is competitive and wants to usurp her place in the spotlight.

   Miss Julie in Strindberg's play also belongs in this classification. She is flighty and moody. Her feelings are intense and tempestuous.

3. **The Extraverted Sensation Type (Irrational):** These people are the practical types who get things done, from construction to all kinds of engineering to business. They are realistic and often quite hardheaded. They don't think much about life or the world, but they accept things as they are and they function in life as it is, without trying to change it. They may also enjoy thrill seeking, such as bungee jumping or car, motorcycle, or horse racing. They can be reckless or careful, depending on their mood or on circumstances. And this type is to be found among addicts and obsessive-compulsives. They live for the experience of physical sensation, as opposed to feeling. They can sometimes be dangerous to themselves and/or others.

   Judge Brack in *Hedda Gabler* is an example of this type: he loves the thrill of illicit sex and his attempted seduction of Hedda could prove dangerous. He is realistic and hardheaded. Rather than thinking about life or his own actions, he simply indulges himself in fulfilling his desires.

4. **The Extraverted Intuitive Type (Irrational):** Thomas Alva Edison, Galileo, Andrew Carnegie, and other great visionary inventors and entrepreneurs were extraverted intuitives. People of this type may or may not stick with something once they have found it. They are often incapable of sustained interest and flit about from project to project. Producers can be like this, and this is a good quality, because it means they are always creative and looking for the next project. In the theater or in the world of film, they will see a project through to its conclusion and immediately go on to the next one.

   The title character in George Bernard Shaw's *Major Barbara* fits into this category. She is active and energetic. And she intuitively fights for justice and morality. The play pits her against her father, Andrew Undershaft, the international arms manufacturer and dealer, who is very much the same type as his daughter. Both of them stick tenaciously to their points of view.

5. **The Introverted Thinking Type (Rational):** Those who appear cold and aloof, such as certain academics or writers, may be primarily of this type. Such people seem lacking in affect and distant from others. Their emotions appear to be controlled, and they seem more interested in ideas than in people.

Further possible qualities of this psychological type are arrogance and a tendency to be unconsciously insulting to others. But such people may also be tenderhearted, even if they appear standoffish. They may, in fact, simply be shy. They withdraw into the more comfortable inner world of their thoughts because of this shyness, which is, in part, fear of the external world.

The introverted thinker may ignore others to the point of being inconsiderate, as Tesman does in Ibsen's *Hedda Gabler*. Although he does not intentionally neglect Hedda, she feels that his neglect is due to the fact that he doesn't really love her as he says he does.

E. Housman in *The Invention of Love* is in this category, but he also has a very large feeling and a large sensation component, and it is these latter traits that allow him to express himself in poetry. Otherwise, he is always trying to figure things out, and he uses his thinking side in his work as the greatest classics scholar of his age.

6. **The Introverted Feeling Type (Rational):** This type appears withdrawn from the world and hides feelings. Artists, composers, and writers, whose intense emotional life finds expression not in their lives but in their art, are often the introverted feeling type. They are prone to sudden outbursts and emotional tempests — as, for instance, Beethoven notoriously was.

Among many other artists and poets in theatrical literature, Rimbaud and Verlaine in *Total Eclipse* are both this type, although their extraversion asserts itself quite prominently as well, particularly when they are in public together. The Brownings in *The Barretts of Wimpole Street* and Emily Dickinson in *The Belle of Amherst* can all be categorized as the introverted feeling type.

7. **The Introverted Sensation Type (Irrational):** The greatest interest people of this type have is in their own psychic life and sensations, which may be stormy indeed, but you would never know it, because the persona they present to the world is one of calm placidity and self-control. They discount their feelings about the sensations they experience as well as thoughts they may have. And they often have great difficulty communicating, even though many of this type become artists of various kinds. They tend to dwell on the irrational aspects of existence, particularly their own existence.

In *Hedda Gabler,* the poet Lövborg's inner life is so stormy that he ends up committing suicide. Hedda herself is the introverted sensation type, but with strong feeling and intuition functions as well. In both their cases, they are prey to their shadow sides, and this is their undoing.

Chekhov's version of a Russian Hamlet, Ivanov, is another example of this type. Ivanov is tortured and self-involved but appears quite placid and self-controlled. He lives by sensation and finds his feelings confusing and conflicted. Ivanov has no idea how to communicate his love or his feelings generally. He muses and ruminates, but makes no rational judgments about his sensations or feelings. And he ends up by committing suicide.

Hamlet is largely an introvert, but otherwise hard to categorize because of his constant alternation of the four functions.

8. **The Introverted Intuitive Type (Irrational):** The prophets of the Bible, mystics and visionaries of all kinds, and cranks and crackpots are to be found among the introverted intuitives. They withdraw from the world into their own psyches and a world of images—and sometimes, in extreme cases, of hallucinatory, primordial feelings, which they have great difficulty in communicating. They are impractical, but if they are artists or writers, they may come up with the most striking, original conceptions and intuitions.

Such characters as the seer Tiresias in Sophocles's *Oedipus the King* and the Trojan prophetess Cassandra in plays about the Trojan War are the introverted intuitive type.

How do these types develop? How are a person's preferences determined? Heredity plays a role, and there are innate qualities of personality that help determine future choices. They are seen very early in a child's life. A child may have tendencies that are quite different from his or her parents and may develop into a completely different—indeed, an opposite—type. Parenting and education may modify these inborn tendencies, since there is often a pressure to conform. Children frequently rebel when under such pressure and assert themselves as they develop into their own type of personality. For Jung, the parent owes respect to the child's type and has a duty to nurture and foster it and help the child develop along his or her own lines, without imposing strictures that might lead to disturbances in the psychic functioning and to neurosis or, in extreme cases, even to psychosis.

For the actor: To which character type does your character predominantly belong? What is the balance of the anima and the animus in your character? Does your character represent a particular archetype, and if so, how is this manifested in external behavior? How has the character individuated the archetype? What other archetypes have come into play in the course of your character's individuation process? How well does your character balance all the different aspects of his or her personality and relationships (the transcendent function)? What is the background of the particular collective unconscious from which the character comes? How does this manifest itself behaviorally? Avoid stereotypes and clichés in answering this question, as Jung warned. What are the cultural and spiritual aspects of the character's individual participation in the collective unconscious; in other words, how has the character individuated the self and become the person he or she is, while remaining part of the culture from which he or she comes or rebelling against that culture? Think, for instance, of the ways the characters in *Fiddler on the Roof* have reacted to the situations in which they find themselves. What is the character's persona—that is, the character's presentation of the self to the world? What are the imagoes the character holds of the other characters and of the people who may not be in the play, such as mother or father, but of whom the character nevertheless necessarily has an imago?

For a Jungian approach to *Hamlet,* see page 249.

Chapter Five

§

Two Outstanding Pioneers: Georg Groddeck and *The Book of the It*; Alfred Adler and Individual Psychology

*T*he kindly, humorous doctor who had thought Germany needed a strong leader had been quickly disillusioned and harshly criticized the new regime. He had actually written to Hitler to try to persuade him to change his policies! Invited to lecture by the Swiss Psychoanalytical Society, he went just in time to prevent his arrest by the Gestapo, although he had had a heart attack two weeks before. It would be his last lecture. And the Nazis would burn his books, of course, along with those of Proust, Freud, and many others.

Much interested in Christian mysticism, Georg Walther Groddeck (1866–1934) began his professional life as a littérateur, only later becoming a medical doctor. He presided over a sanatorium, where he was known as "The Healer of Baden-Baden," and devised therapies for psychosomatic ailments. In fact, he was the great pioneer in the field of psychosomatic medicine — he saw the term itself as simplistic.

Groddeck was a man whom Freud admired and who fully returned his admiration, so much so that despite his originality, he was self-effacing enough to have been thought of as an orthodox follower of Freud. But by 1911, when he discovered Freud's work, he had already been exploring the human psyche since 1895 along lines similar to Freud's, if not exactly the same, but without publishing his findings. The simultaneity of some of their ideas accounts in part for the great empathy they had for each other, and Groddeck accepted wholeheartedly such Freudian concepts as the Oedipus complex, transference and resistance, and repression. And Freud in turn not only took the word *Es* (*id* — literally, *it*) from Groddeck, giving him full credit, but was also deeply impressed with Groddeck's revelatory and insightful classic, *The Book of the It* (*Das Buch vom Es*). Among other things, he felt that Groddeck had really made important points regarding the general, essential passivity of the ego and the feeling we have all had of being "'lived' by unknown and uncontrollable forces."

Groddeck sees the id in somewhat different terms than Freud, which is why the term *It* is used in English in discussing his concepts: the It is the ensemble of characteristics, both unconscious and conscious, that make up that elusive, sometimes ephemeral entity we call the self, or the personality, and it is fundamentally what the French call *insaissisable* (ungraspable). The analyst can only work with parts of the It, in its polar relationship with the ego, but can never truly understand or grasp it or even see it as a whole. Nobody is in a position to fully understand him or herself, let alone, of course, other people. We see everything as through a glass darkly. Groddeck famously said that we do not live, but rather we are lived, by the It. Every object and person either attracts or repels us, directed by the It that is living us, and we often don't know why we experience these things, but the repulsion and/or attraction, which often exist side by side with regard to the same object or person, are the result of transference.

I recommend *The Book of the It* to any actor, writer, or director: written in the form of an epistolary novel in which the first-person narrator, Patrik Troll, is writing to a young lady at her request in order to enlighten her about psychology, it is chock full of fascinating, useful analyses and ideas. We don't see her letters, but Patrik's often begin as replies to something she obviously wrote in hers. The form he chose enabled Groddeck to range widely over many areas and subjects, and at one point, he informs his correspondent that his ideas are all based on those of a certain Viennese doctor named Freud.

Groddeck was never actually a psychoanalyst, but he did attend a great many psychoanalytic congresses. Despite his adherence to Freud's ideas, Groddeck called himself a "wild analyst" and was sometimes so considered by the more strait-laced members of the psychoanalytic establishment, because of his whimsicality and some of his well-nigh unprovable assertions, such as the statement that all illnesses are psychosomatic in origin. What Freud felt he lacked in scientific rigor, Groddeck made up for with his spirit of joy and his sense of humor and compassion. He can be outrageous and sometimes wrongheaded and deliberately bizarre, even disturbingly right wing in earlier writings (which he later regretted), but he is never less than thought provoking.

Questions and Considerations

Transference: Groddeck talks about the phenomenon of transference, not simply in terms of an analysand's unconscious transference of feelings of love or hate for parents onto the analyst, but also in broader terms. As psychoanalytic theorists from Freud to Klein and others have also pointed out, transference occurs all the time, as we shift our feelings of love for previously cathected objects onto different people, who often resemble in many ways of which we are not even conscious those earlier objects of affection. A simple physical resemblance may provide a clue to account for the transference. A particular way of reacting to situations, a general resemblance of character or manner of behaving, or even a way of walking or sitting in a particular position reminiscent of the way mother, father, sister, or brother sat may be the reason for the object choice. Unconsciously directed by the It, the transference may be a manifestation of the repetition compulsion, as someone continues to choose similar objects time after time.

Vanya loves Yelena partly because she resembles his beloved dead sister. The Professor's first wife was that very same person, Vanya's sister, and he may have married Yelena for her resemblance to his dead wife—a choice based on an earlier imago of his mother or sister. Sonya loves Astrov because there are certain aspects of his personality that remind her of her father, the Professor—namely, his tendency to didacticism and perhaps even his way of sitting or standing. Yelena has fallen in love with Astrov because he resembles in some ways a younger version of her aging husband. These transferences are part of the reason that both Sonya and Yelena have been attracted to the same man, although there are clearly many other factors. A director who wished to emphasize the transferences might direct the actors to move in the same way sometimes, or to sit in the same posture or use similar gestures.

In *Three Sisters,* Masha falls in love with the army officer Vershinin partly because in his bearing and appearance as well as his gentleness, he resembles her dead father, the General. She married Kulygin because he, too, in some ways resembled her father. She also married him because in the provincial backwater in which they live, the schoolteacher who quotes Latin sayings is one of the few people whom she could at least pretend is cultivated and refined, as her father was. Masha has been disillusioned and disenchanted, however, well before the arrival of Vershinin and his regiment.

Ambivalence: One of Groddeck's most interesting elucidations concerns the fundamental, biologically based ambivalence in all human beings. Incidentally, the science of psychoanalysis owes the use of the term *ambivalence* to the Swiss psychiatrist best known for his study of schizophrenia, Dr. Eugen Bleuler (1857–1939), Jung's boss at the Burghölzli clinic. Freud said, with his usual dry wit, that it was not a matter of chance that his friend Bleuler was the one to have come up with this concept.

The word *ambivalence* means the simultaneous existence of seemingly contradictory or mutually exclusive feelings, such as love and hate or anger and desire. The terms *ambivalence* and *ambiguity* mean very similar things, but ambivalence is unconscious and ambiguity is conscious—one might say that it is ambivalence made conscious.

For Groddeck, all our lives we unconsciously remain children, even while we are also adults. Fundamentally unconsciously bisexual, we are therefore both homosexual and heterosexual. And we are always a man/woman and/or a woman/man. Human sexuality is basically ambivalent, even though we think it is not and that we have a particular sexual identity. The following dictum expounded by Groddeck is always applicable to theatrical characters: Love and hate exist together, and are found side by side. For actors, writers, and directors, exploration of the ambivalence and ambiguities in characters deepens any characterization and gives it rounded, specific reality.

Ambiguous feelings may exist with regard to particular circumstances. And one can be ambivalent about another person or sometimes about oneself, when, for instance, self-love and self-loathing exist intertwined in the unconscious. In *The Book of the It,* Groddeck gives us a perfect if controversial example of ambivalence that many would find off-putting when he talks about *mother love* and *mother hate.* A mother's love for her child runs very deep, but she also hates the child. How many times have you seen mothers bored, annoyed, or angry with their children? One minute they love them; the next they can't stand them. And they are saddled with them for life. How could a mother not feel ambivalent in such circumstances? She adores her child, who is her flesh and blood and whom she carried, and she resents her commitment and lifelong duty. She remembers the pain of giving birth. But maternal love and nurturing are much stronger than any feelings of hate, which often remain deeply unconscious. For a seriocomic look at all this, see Albert Brooks's delightful film *Mother* (1996), with the ever fresh and wonderfully sweet Debbie Reynolds as his and Rob Morrow's mother (the theme of sibling rivalry is also deftly and comically handled). In Chekhov's plays, Vanya's relationship with his mother is full of ambivalence, as is Constantine's relationship with Madame Arkadina.

In general, you can ask yourself: Does my character have ambiguous and ambivalent feelings towards another character? How does Masha really feel about Kulygin? She resents his continued existence, since she loves Vershinin, but she knows he is basically a good-hearted person, even if he is priggish, arrogant, and pedantic. Yet she loves him, too, and remains with him in part because she feels she has no choice—this is ambiguity. But in her unconscious there is also ambivalence: she regrets having married him at all. They have perhaps ceased to have a sexual relationship long before the play begins. There is a stormy drama going on in Masha's unconscious, with thoughts of homicide and passionate love intermingled.

There are ambivalent feelings in every relationship. And Freud tells us that every love is ambivalent, like every violent passion. Groddeck tells us that if you have ever imagined the death of someone you love, you will realize if you search inside yourself that behind such imagining is the implicit, tacit wish for that person's death, because that person has inevitably, unavoidably disappointed you in some way. The fact that you were able to imagine someone's death at all is proof that you did at some point wish it, at least as far as Groddeck is concerned.

And there is ambivalence in every person as an individual. Inside every person with problems is the solution to those problems. Everyone who has some kind of mental or emotional dysfunction or disorder also has the capacity for health. In exploring ill, dysfunctional characters, the actor should ask in what ways they are healthy and functional. People are complicated, whole beings, and they can have illusions and misperceptions along with sanity and accuracy. They are weak in some ways and strong in others. They can collapse one minute and bounce resiliently back the next. The same person can experience inertia and initiative. In short, we are capable of the whole gamut of emotions and reactions. Sometimes we are healthy and sometimes we are not. In what way is this true of the character you are in the process of creating? How does your character hate and love the self at the same time? How does your character love and hate another person? As a corollary one might ask the important question: When you are in love with someone, how do you try to overcome that moment of hatred?

How does Romeo love Juliet, and how does he hate her? How does Juliet love Romeo, and how does she hate him? What do they dislike about each other, even though they adore each other? How does this hatred manifest itself at any given moment? Would the marriage of Romeo and Juliet even work out? She may love him, but what about the rest of the family? Could she love them? Could they love her? He may love her, but what about the rest of her family? Could he love them or they him? They would each naturally side with their own family in the ancient quarrel. This is how they might love and hate each other at the same time.

Incidentally, speaking of ambivalence, it is worth remembering that *Romeo and Juliet,* like all of Shakespeare's plays was originally performed by an all-male cast, since women were not permitted on the stage. When Romeo wished he "was a glove upon that hand," Juliet's cheek that he dreamed of kissing so tenderly was actually the cheek of another male actor. The change in thinking that allowed women to be actresses is portrayed in *Stage Beauty* (2004), a study in ambivalence, among other things. In a television interview about the film, Billy Crudup, who plays a male actor known for his portrayals of women in the era when real women were just beginning to be allowed to act, expressed his opinion on the uses of psychological theory in acting. He said that real people are so complicated that an actor should approach characters, too, by taking account of their psychological complexity.

There are few more overtly ambivalent characters in theatrical literature than the noble, high-minded Brutus in *Julius Caesar,* the only conspirator to have acted out of principle and not, like the others, out of envy. Filled with ambivalent feelings about Caesar, Brutus is at "war with himself" over the moral dilemma of assassinating the would-be tyrant, and this fills him with pain, but he accedes to what he conceives to be the higher good and becomes a prime conspirator, filled with ambivalence even after the deed is done.

Hamlet can be seen as a play about ambivalence. All the characters in it are embodiments of ambivalence, from Hamlet himself, who is ambivalence personified, to Polonius and the other courtiers. Even the Gravedigger, who appears so cheerful as he plies his grisly trade, wards off fear and avoids thinking of death, which terrifies him.

Iago is ambivalent about what he is doing, which we can infer because of his constant implausible justifications, meant for himself as well as for the audience in whom he confides in that wonderful Elizabethan convention, the soliloquy. And Othello has ambivalent and ambiguous feelings of love and jealousy for Desdemona, who has her ambiguous feelings about Othello, particularly once he begins treating her badly.

King Lear is certainly ambivalent about his daughters, who are equally ambivalent about him. Goneril and Regan once loved him, and the banished Cordelia continues to love the father who has misunderstood her so profoundly. Indeed, she cannot even admit that what he has done to her is hateful, but goes away in sadness and continues to keep watch over her father from afar.

Shylock feels ambiguous about lending money to the anti-Semite Antonio, but he does so nonetheless. Antonio feels ambivalent about taking it.

In short, wherever you turn in theatrical literature, you find ambivalence and ambiguity.

Two Exercises Based on Groddeck's Ideas

The Thoughts of the Unborn Child: Groddeck asks the question, "Have you ever tried to get inside the thoughts of an unborn child? Try it once. Make yourself very, very tiny and creep back into the womb from which you issued." He adds that this is not as crazy as it may sound, because our main, unconscious desire is to return to the peace of the womb, to close the gap that separates us from the mother. Close your eyes and relax. Have a pad of paper and pencil handy, and write down the thoughts as they occur to you. You can do this as a general exercise or as one involving a specific character. Take yourself back in time in your mind, and try to feel the sensations of being at peace and completely self-involved. Give yourself over to this and see where the exercise takes you.

How Do You Say "I Love You?": In *The Book of the It,* there is a very interesting observation about the great actor Joseph Kainz's playing of Romeo: Groddeck noticed that he always pronounced the word *love* on a high, "strangely boyish tone." And he goes on to say that everyone pronounces the word love on a higher pitch. This is so because the word alone automatically and unconsciously awakens the deep, first, never-ending love, with its upward strivings: that of a child for its mother, no matter what the vicissitudes and developments of that love. As Groddeck says, "No man can easily cast off this mother-being; right to the grave she rocks him in her arms." So if you have difficulty playing a love scene, just think of what Groddeck wrote. All you have to do is to say the words "I love you" as sincerely as you can — an example of the Stanislavskian idea of playing the action, in this case the verbal action, as correctly as you can, and of Michael Chekhov's psychological gesture, a verbal one in this instance. You will find yourself flooded with all the emotions you could wish, aroused by those simple, profound words. As an exercise, close your eyes and say the word *love* to yourself. See what feelings and thoughts the very word awakens within you. Write down your observations.

ALFRED ADLER'S IDEAS ON BIRTH ORDER AND THE INFERIORITY COMPLEX

*A*lfred Adler (1870-1937) studied with Freud in Vienna. Like Jung, he split acrimoniously with Freud over the psychoanalytic emphasis on sexuality and founded his own therapeutic school, which he called *individual psychology.* They remained bitterly divided for the rest of their lives. The second of six children, perhaps Adler was jealous — as he was all his life of his older brother, whose name was also Sigmund!

For Adler, the aggressive instincts and the drive for power and dominance, the striving for perfection, and compensation for feelings of physical and psychological inferiority were all more important than the libido in determining the course of a person's characterological development. Adler distinguished four basic personality types, all of which were based on the idea that neurosis arises from a deficiency in social orientation. But personality types were a fiction, he thought, and a convenient way of looking at social phenomena. Everyone ultimately had to be understood on an individual basis, and it was certainly possible to give people the courage to change an unhealthy, neurotic, asocial personality to a healthy, socially productive one — Adler's main therapeutic goal.

1. The *ruling* or *ruling-dominant* type, whose aggressive interests and desire for power as compensation for feelings of inferiority are uppermost;

2. The *leaning* or *leaning-getting* type, who depend on others' support to supply their emotional and physical needs — this type is involved in taking something from others rather than being able to give;

3. The *avoiding* type, who prefers to remain apart from all social interaction — at its extreme, this type descends into psychosis;

4. The *socially useful* type — the mark of such a healthy, adjusted personality is *Gemeinschaftsgefühl*, or fellow-feeling, and the desire to support, nurture, and foster others, which was in the "social interest" (a phrase that Adler preferred as a translation of the German word).

It was not that Adler discounted sex as an important factor in personality. However, he thought Freud's emphasis not only overdone but also class based. Adler had worked with members of the laboring class, and he thought socioeconomic factors very important indeed in determining psychosocial development. Freud had been analyzing members of the bourgeoisie, and as far as the politically progressive Adler was concerned, this had led his former mentor to a somewhat limited, distorted view of psychology.

Freud, of course, disagreed emphatically — even though he, too, took sociopolitical factors into account — but he thought class made no difference in the genesis of character formation. A baby doesn't know what social class it belongs to. The baby only knows if needs are met and whether it is frustrated or contented, fed or hungry. And the baby's needs and desires for love from parents or other caregivers are the same, no matter what social class the baby is from. Later on, socioeconomic factors become more important in character development. It is also clear that whether the child comes from an abusive background — physically, psychologically, or both — does not depend on social class.

Adler's emphasis on factors other than libidinal was a contribution to the understanding of psychology and an expansion of its theoretical and practical parameters. Some of his ideas were to find an echo in the thinking of Karen Horney, Harry Stack Sullivan, and Erich Fromm, and in the humanistic psychology of the American Abraham Maslow (1908–70), for whom the ideas of self-actualization and dominance in human relationships were central factors in personality development. Maslow thought that internal confidence was the prime factor in developing a *dominance-feeling,* an idea Adler might well have agreed with, although he might have had his doubts about Maslow's emphasis on the essential goodness of humanity.

On the other hand, he would doubtless also have agreed with Maslow's categorization of human needs, many of which are unconscious. Maslow attempted to unite Freudian and Adlerian theories, as well as several other schools of thought, in his ideas on human motivation, as set forth in *Motivation and Personality* (1954). He says the human being's primary motivation is to gratify needs, which he categorizes in hierarchical order as follows:

1. Basic biophysiological needs come first (hunger, warmth, shelter, sleep, etc.);
2. Safety needs come next (security, continued good health);
3. The need for love, affection, and belonging are then extremely important; as is
4. The need for self-esteem; and finally
5. The need for self-actualization, which is individuation and self-realization.

The needs for knowledge, understanding, and aesthetic satisfaction are concomitant with these other needs.

For Adler, birth order is crucial in determining character development, partly because of the sibling rivalries it engenders and also in giving rise to what Freud called the *brother complex*—that is, a complex regarding relationships with one's siblings in general. The simple triad of mother, father, and child becomes a quartet, a quintet, or whatever number are in the family, creating sibling rivalry and inevitable conflict, covered over and controlled by the parents as much as they can, using whatever methods are at their disposal. Included in how well they can control the situation, if they indeed attempt to do so, is their own level or amount of consciousness and self-awareness.

Being the eldest child carries the advantage of not having to share the parents' love at first and the disadvantage of the parents having to learn how to be a parent. Upon the arrival of a second child, the first-born may experience narcissistic rage at being replaced. Possible developments may include a competitive drive to assert the self, a rebellious streak, or an authoritarian meanness that seeks to control other people. Conversely, the child may become a centered, compassionate adult who feels empathy with others. The first child may achieve much but often has a tendency to solitariness in adulthood.

The second child in a family has the advantage of the parent's experience with the first child and may be much loved and pampered. On the other hand, the second child may be at the greatest disadvantage of all if there is a third sibling. The second-born sees him or herself replaced in the parent's affections by the arrival of the baby of the family and feels less respected than the older sibling. The reaction may be one of narcissistic fury, resulting in severe personality problems and a superiority complex later on; one of sad, sullen depressive withdrawal, resulting in inferiority feelings and reactions to them; or one of becoming a deeply caring, compassionate person out of narcissistic sympathy with one's own suffering. The middle child in a family of three tends to be competitive, particularly with the younger sibling.

The youngest child is often one to whom the greatest affection and coddling are shown or, conversely, if the parents are tired and worn out from dealing with their other children, the one to whom the greatest severity is shown. The last child may feel neglected and develop personality problems later on. The youngest child in a family may develop feelings of inferiority, having been surpassed by elder siblings, and may become very competitive in compensation.

Being a twin or an only child has its own set of influences, as has gender. If the father is a male chauvinist, his daughters will have problems with feelings of inferiority, as he displays preferential treatment for his son, on whom he may dote in a very different way than he dotes on his daughters. There are obviously many variations on these themes.

Questions and Considerations

Birth Order: Where does your character fit into the family? How has gender influenced the way your parents treated you as you were growing up, particularly in relation to your siblings? How many siblings are there in the family, and in what order were you born into the family? How did you feel about your parents and about your siblings growing up? What was the birth order of your parents, of your grandparents? How did this influence the way in which your grandparents treated and dealt with your parents and how they treated you?

David Storey's *In Celebration* is about the sibling rivalry of three sons who return home to the coal-mining town in the north of England where they grew up to celebrate their parents' fortieth wedding anniversary. Lindsay Anderson directed both the play at the Royal Court in London and the 1975 film, with the sons played by Alan Bates, James Bolam, and Brian Cox. The three sons are at loggerheads and alternately get along with and bait each other. There are issues revolving around a fourth brother who died when he was a teenager working in the mine. An important question for the brothers, as it is in many families, is whom did their parents prefer, and why?

Chekhov treated the subject of birth order with great insight in *Three Sisters,* which deals with a family of four siblings and the spouses of two of them. How differently each sibling has developed and the nature of their relationships with each other and with their dead parents are important underlying themes.

The Inferiority Complex: There is no doubt that jockeying for power plays an important part in socioeconomic contexts. It is supremely important in such institutions as schools, offices, and other workplaces: law courts, military and naval institutions, or royal courts, for instance. Feelings of inferiority and superiority play their part as well in the fight for equality in all areas of civil rights, and for economic parity and justice in the fight for workers' rights.

Adler thought that women, born into a society that overvalues men and gives them power, felt inferior and compensated for this feeling with a *masculine protest,* to which they adjusted either by pursuing careers and asserting their superiority and aggressiveness or by surrendering to their situation and retreating from it, obeying social strictures and restrictions and playing the subordinate roles assigned to them, whether at home or at work.

Adler's idea of the part played by feelings of physical, or *organ,* inferiority is also extremely important. Physical handicaps and the compensations for them may be developments in adulthood, such as the paralysis of Ron Kovic, the Vietnam vet who protested the war, played by Tom Cruise in *Born on the Fourth of July* (1989). Or they may be something the character has had to live with all his or her life, as in *My Left Foot* (1989), a poignant and hilarious film based on Christy Brown's autobiography. Daniel Day-Lewis gave an Academy Award–winning performance as Brown, an Irish writer and artist born with cerebral palsy. He refused to let his condition get the better of him and remained a feisty, witty iconoclast.

Jockeying for power is raw and graphic in such plays as David Mamet's *Glengarry Glen Ross* and Shakespeare's history plays. The part played by aggressive drives for power in the attempt by men to dominate women forms the background and core story of George Bernard Shaw's *Man and Superman.* Films and plays set in racist or colonialist societies or involving revolutionary struggles—such as the many films showing events in the American, French, or Russian Revolutions, or the innumerable films about World Wars I and II—also obviously deal with power struggles. For a satiric look at one-upmanship, class rivalry, hierarchical structure, and animosity between generals and the soldiers they command, see the side-splittingly funny *Black Adder Goes Forth,* which takes place on the Western Front in 1917; it is available from BBC Video.

From an Adlerian point of view, aggressive drives and feelings of superiority and inferiority are the psychological and sociological background to struggles in all societies. They are a very important factor in Claude Berri's *Germinal* (1993), adapted from Emile Zola's 1884 novel set in coal-mining country, about the struggles of the rural working class to rise above the squalor and poverty in which they are forced to exist. An actor exploring family relationships might also look to Adler's analyses of power struggles, because even within the family, viewed as a microcosm of society as a whole, one can find people who are power hungry or even power mad.

The idea of the struggle for power is useful in interpreting the spine of a role in Shakespeare, Ibsen, Shaw, and Chekhov; in such plays as Eugene O'Neill's very Freudian *Mourning Becomes Electra;* and even in Oscar Wilde's satire of social class in *The Importance of Being Ernest,* which is a deadly serious play for all its hilarious light comedy. Lillian Hellman's *The Little Foxes* provides another example of the struggle for power within a family threatened with economic ruin and consumed by greed. Roger Martin du Gard's epic series of novels about the Thibault family also shows how the struggle for power pervades all social classes, including the upper-bourgeois Thibault family itself. There is an excellent 2003 French television miniseries, *Les Thibault,* loosely adapted from the novels, superbly acted in general, and with particularly notable performances by Jean Yanne as the family patriarch and Malik Zidi as his rebellious younger son, Jacques. Incidentally, this is one of the few examples on film where the adult Jacques physically resembles the same character as a boy; the match is perfect.

Willy Loman (low man — on the totem pole) in Arthur Miller's *Death of a Salesman* is a victim of the power structure. His own aggressive will to power is frustrated. Loman is also the victim of his own massive inferiority complex. He is always comparing himself unfavorably to others. His inability to rise above circumstances and to go beyond his self-imposed limits haunts him and leads to his destruction. Adler's concept of the inferiority complex is also useful in preparing such roles as Monsieur Jourdan in Molière's *Bourgeois Gentilhomme* or Orgon in *Tartuffe*. And the idea of the superiority complex has its place in the study of such characters as Sir Joseph Porter in Gilbert and Sullivan's *H.M.S. Pinafore.* The masking of the opposites from consciousness means that the person who feels inferior actually feels superior to everyone underneath it all, and the person who claims superiority feels inferior and masks those feelings with bravado and pompous posturing, as Sir Joseph does. Such people are always playing games of one-upmanship and take every opportunity to insult and put down others, pouncing on the least error or possible mistake somebody else makes.

In act I of *H.M.S. Pinafore,* Sir Joseph admonishes Captain Corcoran not to insult British sailors. The captain says, "I am the last person to insult a British sailor, Sir Joseph." The cutting, quick reply comes out like a shot: "You are the last person who did, Captain Corcoran." The sometimes inane, completely unqualified First Lord of the Admiralty gets seasick even when a ship is riding at anchor in the harbor, but lords it over everyone else nonetheless. The captain, on the other hand, is "never, never sick at sea" — well, hardly ever. He likes to think he treats his crew as if they were his equals, until a lowly sailor falls in love with his daughter. At that point, his superiority complex emerges in all its fury.

Such obnoxious behavior as that indulged in by the sneering Sir Joseph, whose song "When I was a lad" reveals his humble origins and social-climbing snobbery, makes real-life people with a superiority complex highly disliked, however much their behavior may mask pathetic feelings of inadequacy. You may laugh at such types in the theater, but in everyday dealings with them, you may experience extreme annoyance and worse.

Conversely, the often cringing, passive-aggressive behavior of people with an inferiority complex makes them into living doormats. They secretly resent the people who take advantage of them and secretly feel superior to them. In fact, their unconscious objectives in behaving passive-aggressively as they do are to assent their hidden feelings of superiority and comtempt, and not to have to run the dangerous risks entailed in taking action. The person who is much put upon and always picked on feels the deepest contempt for his or her tormentors but seldom dares to express it openly.

Chapter Six

§

Wilhelm Reich and Character Analysis

*F*reud had refused to analyze him and he was disappointed. But it was against policy for Freud to analyze the members of his inner circle, and he hoped the brilliant medical student who had come to Vienna from the eastern Austrian province of Galicia and eagerly introduced himself to Freud understood. He had become one of Freud's favorite students, and Freud had high hopes for him. That was why he had invited him to become a member of his circle and why he was so pleased when the young man, who had rapidly become expert in psychoanalytic technique, assumed the demanding post of Director of Training at the Psychoanalytic Institute of Vienna. Unfortunately, Freud himself was soon to be disappointed.

Wilhelm Reich (1892–1957) published *Character Analysis* in 1933. This penetrating, insightful book outlines technique concisely and amplifies Freud's ideas about the formation and nature of character. Reich concentrates on the way in which the body economizes energy, particularly libidinal energy, and how that economy allows the flow of life-sustaining energy or else impedes the healthy functioning of the organism. He views behavior and character formation in terms of their functions, which means that they serve particular purposes for the individual. And he emphasizes the ubiquitous harm done throughout the millennia by the damming up of libidinal energy.

But at the same time, Reich was developing his theory that the incapacity to experience full, satisfying orgasmic release is the cause and not the result of neurosis. This is a total departure from the Freudian view, which is the exact opposite of Reich's. In his view, human happiness and functionality depend on freely functioning, liberated sexual energy. This is a second disagreement with Freud, for whom civilization involves the sociocultural necessity of sublimation and the channeling of sexual energy into productive activities. Freud, too, of course, recognized the need for sexual freedom and for a sane approach to sexuality and an end to the repression of natural sexual functioning. Like Freud, Reich was excoriated for such views. In the 1960s, the publicizing and popularizing of his ideas among intellectuals was partly responsible for the so-called sexual revolution. In fact, *The Sexual Revolution* (1945), is the title of one of his most important books.

Reich's third major departure from Freudian theory virtually did away with it altogether: For Reich the cause of neurosis is not found in childhood or in the reaction formations resulting from the Oedipus complex, but in present-day societal constraints on sexuality—in other words, in society's antisexual attitudes. Psychic conflict arises from the obligations imposed by society. Freud's idea of actual neurosis is thus paramount in Reich's thinking, while the ideas of psychoneurosis, infantile sexuality, and the unconscious causes of internal conflicts lose their importance.

Horrified by the rise of fascism and the brutal treatment of Austrian workers by the police during demonstrations for workers' rights, Reich became a Marxist. He tried unsuccessfully to find a theoretical and practical way of combining Marxism and psychoanalysis. He believed that the capitalist system depended on the repression of sexuality and sexual freedom, and that a Marxist system would eliminate repression and restore full functionality. Reich tried to educate Communists in psychoanalysis and psychoanalysts in Marxism. Both groups ultimately rejected him and he them, which left him feeling betrayed. And his fascination with what he considered a groundbreaking discovery increased: he believed he had found the basic life energy, which he called *orgone energy.* He characterized it as universal and primordial. Others characterized it as a psychotic delusion. What followed was very sad.

He fled the Nazis to Denmark and then to Norway, where he experimented with his discovery. Remaining one step ahead of the Nazis, he gained refuge in 1939 in the United States. Safely ensconced in his laboratory on his estate—Orgonon, in Rangeley, Maine—Reich devoted himself to further orgone experiments. And he invented, patented and constructed "orgone boxes" to trap and accumulate it. You could sit inside the boxes and feel them tingle as the orgone energy penetrated your body. He advertised and sold them, claiming they could cure everything from the common cold to cancer. And he was sincerely convinced that this really was the case. He was not out to enrich himself. In fact, Reich used the profits he made for further orgone research.

But this was all too much for the Food and Drug Administration, who had never even been applied to for approval of the medical use of orgone boxes and who considered Reich a quack and a charlatan. In February 1954, the FDA filed a restraining order against the Wilhelm Reich Foundation and against Reich himself, prohibiting him from shipping orgone energy accumulator boxes and the literature he had published about the orgone in interstate commerce. Reich responded by filing a motion contending that the government had no jurisdiction over his scientific research. The government filed an injunction ordering the destruction of the orgone boxes and all literature published by Reich's Orgone Institute Press. Eventually they would chop up most of the boxes and burn the literature, destroying Reich's entire library in their overzealousness. But before that, a lengthy legal process ensued, and Reich lost. He was put on trial for violating the injunction and convicted.

Distraught and despairing, Reich was led away to begin serving his two-year sentence. He could hardly believe this was happening. He had always had a streak of paranoia, and his imprisonment drove his psychosis over the edge. In Lewisburg Penitentiary, high on a Pennsylvania hill in the midst of bucolic splendor, miserable and humiliated, he descended further into delusion, maintaining that Eisenhower had sent the planes he heard flying overhead to protect him. In 1957 he died in his cell of a heart attack. What a terrible and tragic ending to a life devoted to the relief of human suffering!

At the time of his death, Reich had long been looked on as a fraud or a madman by the scientific establishment. His controversial idea about the existence of orgone energy had found no takers. Einstein, who actually met and briefly corresponded with him, wrote that all Reich's data could be explained by already observed and observable physical phenomena, so that it was not necessary to postulate another form of energy.

His many books have been republished, and they make fascinating reading, but one sometimes has to sift through them to separate the wheat of analysis from the chaff of orgone theory, unless one subscribes to it. There is a museum devoted to his memory on his former estate in Rangeley. And there are several magazines, such as the *Journal of Orgonomy*, that publish new findings and older articles by Reich and his followers and adherents, of which he has many. Reichian therapy, which includes the physical as well as the psychoanalytical, is still widely practiced, and there are institutions such as the American College of Orgonomy devoted to teaching it and to propagating Reich's ideas.

THE EMOTIONAL PLAGUE

One of Reich's most important concepts is that we all suffer from *emotional plague,* which can be seen in reactions of hatred, anger, and almost uncontrolled rage on an individual level, and in war and conquest. He conceived of the emotional plague as something biophysically based, inherited and passed on from generation to generation for millennia. But the inheritance of the plague is not genetic: it is sociocultural and cuts across all cultural lines to infect every individual in every social class, and it exists in every part of the world throughout the human community. The plague is due to repressed, unfulfilled orgasmic strivings, because human beings were taught to be terrified of sex very early in history. When libidinal urges are frustrated, the aggressive drive is activated, and the more those urges are unsatisfied, the worse is the increase in angry, sadistic impulses to destroy. For Reich this is one of the causes of the rise of fascism and Nazism, as he explains in *The Mass Psychology of Fascism* (1933).

The plague's results are devastating: murder, lynching, mob violence, rape, child molestation, and the pillage and looting that accompany war are only some of them.

Serial killers are severely plague-ridden individuals, and the plague explains the genesis of their sociopathy. For Reich, the plague concept goes a long way towards explaining the existence of evil in this world, and towards answering the questions about evil and the irrational self-destructive and destructive tendencies of human beings that so disturbed Freud. Although Reich thought the emotional plague challenged and even nullified Freud's idea of the death instinct, it may actually be seen as a manifestation of it.

Reich stressed that the entire process of passing the plague down from generation to generation is unconscious. Nobody escapes the ravages of the emotional plague except the very few who are able to realize what it is and thus learn how to overcome it. Full sexual satisfaction is one means, but that arouses the plague-filled hatred of the majority, who will then persecute those who have found and who advocate such satisfaction, which the majority cannot tolerate or begin to handle in a rational way.

Plague reactions are very hard to control once they are aroused and unleashed. They tend to take over the organism until the plague tensions are relieved in some way, hopefully before harm is done. This is more possible on an individual than on a societal basis: once war is unleashed, for example, it is nearly impossible to control the processes until they come to a kind of natural ending. Reich advised that when you experience an attack of rage coming on, the best thing to do is to go off by yourself for a time until it naturally subsides, which it will. If you do this you will not cause harm to others.

Character Armoring

Reich believed that character is a formation arising from the infant's earliest attempts to master instinctual conflicts. Hereditary factors and cognitive processes play little if any part in forming character, which arises out of reactions to the constraints of the environment. Character binds libidinal energy somatically. It is a general stabilizing defense. And it allows a flow of energy to and from the outside world in necessary economical amounts. With growth into adulthood, the character formation loses its original function of mastering a specific instinctual conflict, but it remains, nonetheless, as a general formation.

Reich thought that repressed ideas and feelings are not only stored somewhere in the brain as memories but that they also exist elsewhere in the body as well; that repressed feelings are anchored physically in the musculature. The muscles are held or tensed in certain ways that have become habitual and unconscious, so that the person is no longer aware of the tension. If you have ever had a massage, you may remember the massage therapist saying something like, "Your shoulders are tense today," or "You have tension in your upper back." Often you will not even have been aware of the tension, until it is pointed out to you. At other times, you may be aware, and you might say, "I have a lot of tension in my lower back. Could you work on that, please?" But this tension may be temporary, whereas in the case of character formation, the unconscious binding of energy in the body takes on a permanence that is difficult to alter, particularly since the person is unaware of the binding.

Once Reich had observed that muscular holding anchored emotional conflicts and tensions and that the holding was unconscious, he realized that this binding was the result of what had once been a conscious reaction. One of the aims of Reichian therapy is therefore to make the patient conscious of the muscular armoring in his or her body, so that the bound tensions can be released and health restored to the organism. Importantly, psychosomatic illnesses are one possible result of the unconscious armoring.

Among the reactions that people physically armor themselves against because they produce anxiety, sometimes very severe, are anger and rage. When something happens to trigger the release of the armoring, emotional-plague reactions can be released, but not relieved until they naturally spend themselves, exhausting the organism and triggering the sleep hormone.

Reich also observed that the body was divided into segments. He called the segments the body's *armor* and spoke of *character armoring*. Different character formations resulted in part from a different muscular anchoring. He distinguished five basic segments and two subdivisions, making seven segments in all, which, as Reich said, "*comprise those organ and muscle groups that are in functional contact with each other*" [Reich's italics]. The next-following segment is not affected by the activity of the one contiguous with it, except for the arms and legs, which act in connection to the segment to which they are attached. The armoring is never lengthwise along the body but always "*transverse to the torso*":

1. The ocular segment, above the mouth. The muscles of the eyes and the forehead are contracted and held almost immobilized, accounting for an empty expression and a rigid, masklike demeanor. Fear and terror, as well as the ability to cry as a way of releasing tension, are anchored partly in this segment.

2. The oral segment, from the mouth, chin, and throat down to the top of the chest. The jaw may be tightly held, with the muscles around the mouth taut and the teeth clenched. Or conversely, the jaw may be unnaturally slack. A smile or a sneer may be an unconscious, habitual expression when the muscles around the mouth are tightly held and tense. Or there may be an unconscious expression of sadness, with the mouth muscles turned down; or of cruelty, indicating a sadomasochistic attitude. The jaw may be thrust forward or held farther back. Anger and the ability to cry or otherwise express emotions are bound in the gag reflex, which, when activated, can release all sorts of emotions.

3. The cervical or neck segment, which is a subdivision of the oral segment. It includes the tongue. Anger and crying are defended against in this subdivision, as they are in the higher subdivision. The important gag reflex, when activated, allows the release of tension stored in the oral segment and also farther down in the stomach.

4. The chest or thoracic segment, down to the diaphragm and including the arms. It can also be subdivided into upper and lower segments. It contains the lungs and the heart. Deep anxiety and rage, as well as longing and desire, are bound in the chronically tensed muscles of the chest. The thoracic binding of the

muscles results in shallow breathing, respiratory problems, high blood pressure, and so forth, as the person restrains and holds back deep feeling, trying to be self-controlled and to overcome deep rage and "intolerable longing." Another result is awkwardness of arm movements, although the arms are relatively free to carry out necessary tasks.

5. The diaphragmatic segment. There is no spontaneous diaphragmatic pulsation when this segment is armored. Stomach problems and lack of feeling in this segment are further results of the armoring. Fear of being attacked is bound in this segment, as it is in the lower subdivision.

6. The abdominal segment, a subdivision of the diaphragmatic segment, includes the lower abdominal muscles and the stomach.

7. The pelvic segment, including the genital and anal areas and the legs. The armoring of this segment, the unconscious holding of anal and other muscles in the area, perhaps due in part to toilet training experiences, arises from the terror of sex and prevents full orgasmic release. For Reich armoring of the pelvic segment is an almost universal condition, accounting for much of humanity's misery, and Reich talks of *pelvic anxiety* and *pelvic rage.*

Reich also distinguished three basic layers of armoring:

1. The surface or social layer, which includes the manner and posture that a person presents to the world and, often consciously, to him or herself.

2. The middle layer, where the repressed emotions and unconscious desires, often the opposite of the expressed surface emotions (the body's subtext, if you like) are located. The emotions of anger and fear that have resulted from repression are found here, as well as guilt and shame, with their deep emotional investment. There may also be emotionless or affectless layers that defend against going deeper and experiencing repressed emotions.

3. The deepest, unconscious layer, where health and the emotional and physical fulfillment that is its result reside. It is rational and has the ability to regulate the self. The goal of Reichian therapy is to release it from its irrational binding and armoring so that the health with which the organism started life can be restored.

The usefulness for actors of analyzing a character's armoring as it affects gait and carriage, among other manifestations of character, will be apparent in the next section in the descriptions of character types and the ways in which their bodies are armored or, in other words, the way in which the muscles are held or tensed. The armoring may provide a way into the character's inner world, giving the actor a clue as to the psychological gesture so prized as an acting technique by Michael Chekhov. And analyzing the layering of the armor is useful for subtext and for playing opposites, so that, for instance, a person may be enraged and yet smiling.

For actors, directors, and writers, Reich is one of the most helpful psychologists to read and study, because he is not only insightful but also very clear in describing the character traits that would be helpful in writing and interpreting characters, and because of his insistence on describing the whole construct of character types, including their appearance, physicality, and armoring. He distinguished a number of character types along Freudian lines, together with both their physical and psychological constructs. The structure of character is such that layers of affect and defense against feeling—those defense mechanisms described by Sigmund Freud, Anna Freud, Otto Fenichel and others—are inevitable components of character structure.

QUESTIONS AND CONSIDERATIONS: THE PRACTICAL APPLICATION OF REICHIAN IDEAS TO CHARACTER INTERPRETATION

Some Character Types

THE HYSTERICAL CHARACTER

Hysterical types are "nervous, agile, apprehensive" people. They are also *histrionic*—that is, much given to putting on an act. The appearance and manner of the hysterical type, as described by Reich, include a seductive, coquettish manner in women and a soft-spoken overpoliteness in men. Before he loses his temper, Basil Fawlty, the intense, temperamental hotel owner played by John Cleese in the television series *Fawlty Towers,* frequently has this quality, when he fawns snobbishly over guests he mistakenly thinks are of a high social class. He can lose his cool at the drop of a hat, or at least at the drop of a moose head he is trying to fasten to a wall.

In general, the hysterical type is soft in facial expression and does not move quickly or jerkily, but proceeds smoothly when in the intensively passive state that precedes or follows a hysterical outburst. In any state, the hysteric's movements are agile and flexible, which is great for playing characters in farces by Chekhov or Molière and all the others. The armoring is pretty loose and fluid.

As a sexual goal appears to be on the point of being reached, apprehensiveness asserts itself, because the hysterical character always "suffers from direct sexual tension" and tends to view everything unconsciously as having sexual overtones and connotations. This view accounts for inappropriate, embarrassed outbursts of giggles, for which the hysteric cannot account: "What's so funny?" "I don't know . . . " Viewing everything as having sexual undercurrents is a great thing to have as an actor's secret.

Sexual strivings are unusually strong and usually unsatisfied, because they are deeply feared. The armoring is more flexible than in other types, as feelings and emotions flit from area to area of the body. Another quality frequently found in hysterics is ticklishness, which represents a displacement of sexual feelings.

Hysterical characters are less prone to sublimation than other types. Instead, they roll their sexual thoughts around and around in their minds, unconsciously or consciously, so that they have no time or inclination for intellectual pursuits and no time for the reflection that would result in understanding themselves. This is because, so Reich informs us, the sexual energies are not discharged in sexual activity but rather in reactions of anxiety, fear, or apprehensiveness.

The fluttery, flustered matriarch in *My Man Godfrey* (1936) played by Alice Brady, and so many other women given to fainting fits in the screwball comedies of the era, are hysterical characters. The maiden aunt wooed by Tracy Tupman in Dickens's *Pickwick Papers*, as well as Mrs. Bardell, are two more examples: see the 1954 British film, where these parts are played to hugely comic effect.

THE COMPULSIVE CHARACTER

Compulsive types are "predominantly inhibited, self-controlled, and depressive." Their facial expressions are usually heavy and gloomy, as is their overall carriage and gait, as if they were weighed down by care. And their armoring is heavy and tense, the muscles tightly held and controlled.

In keeping with his idea that character formations serve certain functions, Reich maintained that the compulsive character served the function of a "defense against stimuli, and the maintenance of psychic equilibrium." Stimuli of all kinds are threatening to the compulsive character. To ward them off, the compulsive is often obsessed by particular circumstances, such as a task that must be performed in the short term; or may have a more general lifelong obsession, such as a passion for collecting things. This behavior serves to avoid thinking. Among the compulsive character traits are:

1. A "*pedantic concern for orderliness,*" which is perhaps the most typical, well-known compulsive trait; it can take any number of forms. Everything in a compulsive person's life has to follow a prearranged program or schedule, and any deviation from the plan immediately throws the compulsive person into a state of anxiety, sometimes very severe. Such people find it very difficult to adapt to circumstances or to anything unforeseen. Certain academics and scientists are among these types. And generally speaking, they want what they want when they want it.

2. Compulsive people often indulge in "*circumstantial, ruminative thinking,*" which, however, often leads them nowhere but around and around in circles. They do not solve problems — except for those of immediate, pressing concern — or seek to change situations for the better, but seek rather to preserve situations and circumstances as they are, particularly where their emotional equilibrium is concerned. In other words, they are basically very conservative in their approach to life. This does not mean they are necessarily right wing in their politics; they may be compulsively left wing. But whatever they feel and think, they always feel compelled to continue on the same path they started out on. Such people think about the trivial and banal as thoroughly as they do about the more important aspects of their lives. Everything has to be thought through, but often to very little purpose. However, such people will not let go until they have performed specific tasks, which brings them relief from tension. Solving a scientific research problem or a mechanical problem with an engine,

for instance, brings them great, if temporary, satisfaction, but they are usually, although not always, incapable of thinking more widely. The insignificant is as important to them as the far-reaching and creative; in fact, they are seldom creative.

3. The compulsive is highly defended against feeling, and except for the occasional flare-up of rage—with which they are unconsciously filled, and which makes the compulsive extremely anxious and has to be repressed immediately—feelings are flat and shallow. Ideas have no affect connected to them, so that the idea of being in love, for instance, is not deeply felt. Rather, circumstantial, ruminative thinking regarding the love object is indulged in, so that the compulsive may fit the object and any feelings it arouses into his or her mental system.

4. Underlying their compulsions are great feelings of guilt, which they defend themselves against by two means: throwing themselves into situations, such as doing a job until it is done, even if it is killing them; and, because of unconscious reaction formations of hatred, lashing out at anyone who stands in the way of their fulfilling their compulsions, even by such simple means as asking a question that requires them to stop and think for a moment in the middle of performing some task. After lashing out, they feel guilty all over again and are sometimes momentarily paralyzed before resuming their task, which absolutely must be completed, come hell or high water.

5. Compulsives are also filled with underlying, unconscious doubt and self-doubt. They do not trust others or themselves, as if their motto were, "If you want something done well, do it yourself." They appear decisive but are actually indecisive, because they are ambivalent, hence the ruminative thinking described above. If something does not fit into their categorical system, it can cause them to become very nervous and unpredictable.

6. They belong to the anal type, particularly the anal retentive, described by Freud. Their compulsions result from extremely strict toilet training, which engendered extreme self-control.

7. In keeping with their analsadistic impulses, compulsives are often very avaricious and thrifty, like Harpagon in Molière's *The Miser*. Their hostile, aggressive impulses are gratified in their exaggerated orderliness, which, in relation to what they demand of others, often takes the form of wanting to control and manipulate them. An extreme but hilariously comic example is the character of Bob, played by Bill Murray, in the film *What About Bob?* (1991).

8. They have repressed all knowledge of their analsadistic side, which hides something they have repressed even farther into the unconscious, and that is a striving for genital satisfaction, which they cannot acknowledge because of their fear of punishment.

THE IMPULSIVE CHARACTER

In some ways, the impulsive character is the same as the compulsive character, but in other important ways it is the exact opposite. For instance, anal-retentive compulsive characters are often overly clean and neat, and cannot function in a disorderly environment, whereas impulsive characters are often anal-expulsive slobs who simply don't care about neatness. On the other hand, compulsives can also be selectively neat: they must have a clean place, but they don't care about brushing their teeth or their personal appearance, or vice versa. Impulsives, too, may behave in such a way as to maintain a neat environment, which they periodically clutter up and then clean. All of these behaviors go back to the anal phase and the excretion of feces, which was felt as pleasurable, whereas the whole process of toilet training and learning to control excretion was extremely unpleasurable for the compulsive.

The following character traits form the basis of the impulsive type:

1. They are ambivalent and don't know what they should do or what is expected of them, so they will do anything on impulse, such as the famous phenomena of "impulse buying" or compulsive gambling, where compulsive and impulsive behavior are combined.

2. The superego introjection of moral principles and ethical standards is very weak, and impulsive people often have no conscience and lack consideration for others. In some cases, kleptomania is an aspect of their personalities. They simply take what they see when they see it, if they want it, or even if they don't really care. Impulsive characters are embodiments of the Mad Hatter's remark in Lewis Carroll's *Alice's Adventures in Wonderland:* "You might just as well say that 'I see what I eat' is the same thing as 'I eat what I see!'" Urges are simply given into, even if they are altogether immoral. This can be very dangerous when coupled with psychopathy. There are no guilt feelings connected with sadistic impulses or actions, as there are with overly conscientious compulsive people, who feel terribly guilty if they haven't fulfilled their appointed task and done it absolutely right. For impulsive people, there *are* no necessary appointed tasks.

3. The relation between ego and superego is ambivalent and factitious — that is, it depends on circumstances. For instance, if a kleptomaniac feels he or she may be caught, he or she may not indulge in gratifying the whim to steal. From the impulsive's point of view, the important thing is not to get caught cheating, stealing, or lying.

The ordinary, nonpsychopathic impulsive is not a dangerous person but may be terribly annoying to the people in her or his immediate environment. There is a lack of self-control and the willingness to give in to any desire that breaks through the relatively loose armoring, as muscles that lose their tension then immediately resume it. Their behavior may have the charm of spontaneity, or it may lead to disastrous consequences. Impulsive people are imbued with a kind of primitive narcissism, which may be life affirming for them but obnoxious to others. Their tenuous moral principle is something like, "Life is short, you only live once, so do what you want!"

Woody Allen and his cohorts in the hilarious *Small Time Crooks* (2000) have the attitudes of "life is short" and "the important thing is not to get caught," as well as some of the other impulsive character traits, among them opportunism and lack of guilt. The charming character of the cat burglar played by Cary Grant in Alfred Hitchcock's *To Catch a Thief* (1955) is impulsive in his behavior. (The film is also worth seeing for the performance of the ravishingly beautiful Grace Kelly.) Claude Chabrol's entertaining film *Rien ne va plus* (1997) features Michel Serrault and Isabelle Huppert as partners in crime. They are modest, clever con artists who go around the countryside in their trailer, seizing every opportunity they can to bilk the unsuspecting out of their money.

THE PHALLIC-NARCISSISTIC CHARACTER
The main traits that constitute this character type, which is intermediate between a compulsive and a hysterical type, are:

1. Arrogance;
2. An impressive, sometimes overbearing demeanor;
3. Behavior that is "haughty, either cold and reserved, or else derisively aggressive";
4. Narcissistic — that is, self-involved and selfish — behavior, seen, for example, in sexual attitudes, which are without consideration for the sexual partner and solely concerned with taking pleasure, rather than giving it;
5. Exaggerated displays of "self-confidence, dignity and superiority";
6. There is much armoring in the chest area, hence the tendency to puff out the chest and to hold it forward unconsciously. They have a tendency to strut.

These types are provocative and aggressive, and whatever they say or do is expressed in an aggressive manner. Underneath it all is an infantile, demanding nature, unsatisfied and unfulfilled, covered over with a mask of contempt. They form attachments and have relationships on the basis of people they perceive they can dominate. They are often irrational but feel that they are behaving rationally in their relationships, although others perceive them as domineering and unpleasant. They seek power and are to be found among the military hierarchy and in positions of authority generally. These are the sorts of people who have to be right all the time, even when they are manifestly wrong, or else they feel they will fall apart. Passivity in others, even though they dominate the passive people in their environment, is very threatening, because it reminds them on an unconscious level of their own powerlessness and of the fear that they might regress to a state of passivity themselves.

AN "ARISTOCRATIC" CHARACTER
Reich describes a particular patient of his in *Character Analysis* who he says protects himself against violent emotions in the following way: His gait is controlled, slow, and steady; his speech equally slow and considered; and his whole manner is refined and elegant, with somewhat relaxed chest armoring. His gestures are elegant and he has exquisite manners. He is reserved and seems somewhat serious, and even a bit arrogant, as if he has a great sense of his own worth and social position. He is generally quiet and composed, and his responses are measured. In short, he appears to be the epitome of a refined lord, a true aristocrat, educated and knowledgeable, considerate and polite, serious in demeanor and bearing. And all of this gravitas is a mask for violent tendencies! This is a great lesson for actors in the playing of

opposites. It is also an important lesson in how to play the actions. And it is a lesson in the actual deportment of a member of the upper classes, who always treat others with courtesy and respect.

The fact is, however, that this person was by no means an aristocrat. He was from a petit bourgeois background, and he grew up hating his father, a Viennese Jewish tailor, and fantasizing that he was not really his son but the son of an English lord—his version of what Freud called the *family romance* (see page 196). He was aided in this fantasy by the fact that his mother was half English. The fantasy became reality for him, exemplifying once again Freud's idea that the unconscious id does not differentiate between the two, but arouses emotions, feelings, and actual bodily responses as if the fantasy were indeed real. This person was in the mold of the "as-if" personality elucidated by Helene Deutsch: The "as-if" personality is a species of pathological liar, who masquerades as something he or she is not, to the point of seeming completely convinced that the assumed identity is real, although the person really knows it is not. In this case, the "aristocrat" certainly knew he was not of high-born lineage.

Internally, he derided everyone and felt he was superior, and he also had a tendency to gloat over the misfortunes of others. None of this sadistic fantasizing was revealed to those with whom he came in contact, because it would have been too shaming and would have laid him open to being despised and derided in turn. And all of his behavior was really a mask for feelings of homosexuality that he found unacceptable. Underneath his hatred of his father was a deep desire for his love and a profound disappointment. His infantile Oedipal conflicts were resolved by a flight from the reality of his life situation.

He could easily observe the sort of aristocratic character he assumed in his native Vienna, where, however, the aristocrats' refinement and polite manners were real, although they may also have been a mask for aggressive impulses. You can utilize the traits listed above whether you have to play a real aristocrat or an imposter.

THE GENITAL AND NEUROTIC CHARACTERS CONTRASTED

For Reich, the most evolved character type is the genital type, who has overcome the Oedipal conflict, given up the unconscious incest wishes, and unambivalently replaced the earlier desired object with a new one. This character type is in touch with his or her sexuality and is *sex-affirmative*. In the genital character as Reich conceives it, earlier stages of psychosexual development have been sublimated in cultural arenas, and the actual evolved libido can be given full play as appropriate. The armoring is flexible and the pelvic area particularly free of tension.

To amplify the analysis of neurosis and its sexual etiology elucidated by Freud, Reich adds the following theoretical ideas: In contradistinction to the genital character, the neurotic character, no matter what the nature of the neurosis, is *sex-negative* and unable to experience sexual pleasure unambivalently and unambiguously. The interference of feelings of guilt and shame, due to unresolved Oedipal issues, is a hallmark of neurotic maladjustment. Freud said that every sex act took place between four people, even though only two were present in reality. As far as Freud was concerned, there was always a residue of unresolved incestuous desires that was a component of all sex acts.

This sex-negative feeling results in unsatisfactory, dissatisfying experiences and creates a stasis of libidinal energy, which is dammed up. Lack of discharge intensifies sadistic, aggressive tendencies, which have to be defended against because they induce too much guilt and are too threatening to the ego ideal. The defense consists very often of a particularly rigid morality. The neurotic has deep-seated feelings of insecurity and impotence, and compensates for them by social achievement, so neurosis is not always all negative. But the neurotic remains unsatisfied and unhappy, and finds it difficult to sublimate. The sex-negative defenses form the basis of characters who display a rigid, almost compulsive morality and who demand that it be adhered to.

THE MASOCHISTIC CHARACTER

Most masochistic characters do not behave in a sexually masochistic way (whips and chains, flagellation, bondage, etc.), but they do behave in self-defeating ways, with conscious desires that are thwarted by the unconscious. Their masochism is psychic and is accompanied by its repressed opposite: sadism. Masochistic traits may be found in other character types as well, such as the hysterical, and in non-neurotic people also in given circumstances. Groddeck writes in *The Book of the It* that we are all both sadists and masochists.

Masochistic characters want love but often choose to be emotionally involved with unavailable objects that do not requite their affection, which causes them great psychic distress and emotional pain; they constitute a punishment in themselves. The basis of the masochistic character is the fear of being abandoned. The message is given out: "I suffer so terribly that you can't abandon me. Please, no matter what I do, stay with me." Abandonment is punishment, and the masochist has an underlying need to be punished for unconscious Oedipal crimes. The compulsion to seek this punishment again and again in adult life represents a kind of disguised, veiled message: "Please don't hurt me." When punishment is actually administered—the lover abandons the masochist, for instance—it is actually experienced as a kind of relief and an unconscious proof that the masochist was right after all: "That person [the parent, originally, as the first object] did not really love me."

Masochists are sadistically provocative in their behavior with others, in order to bring about unconsciously desired punishment, which, in Freudian terms, may be seen ultimately as a defense against the castration complex. In other words, their masochism is actually a mask for sadism; hence the term *sadomasochistic.* Therapy consists in part of unmasking this sadism and making sure the masochist understands the real nature of his or her behavior.

The other distinguishing traits of the masochistic character are (the phrases in quotation marks are Reich's):

1. Inner feelings of chronic emotional *"suffering,"* of which the external manifestation is a "tendency to complain" and to look for what might be wrong in any given situation.

2. *"Self-depreciation"* and even damage to the self, manifested as putting oneself down and, in extreme cases, as being accident prone so that even cutting vegetables becomes the occasion for drama, as the masochist carelessly and clumsily cuts him or herself with the paring knife.

3. "A compulsion to *torture others*" (sadism), which does not necessarily mean physically torturing others but rather psychologically torturing them, as with the constant reproaches of a lover accusing his or her partner of infidelity, or being psychologically abusive in family situations. The torturer suffers internal torment perhaps as great as that which he or she inflicts on victims.

4. Masochists display "*awkward, atactic behavior* in their manners and in their intercourse with others." The movement of masochistic types is often clumsy and their facial expressions often pained. But the reply to the question "What's the matter?" will often be an indignant "Nothing! What's the matter with you?" The armoring is tight, particularly in the pelvic area, where the muscles are chronically tensed.

Playing Opposites and the Possible Meaning of a Smile: Another important and useful Reichian idea, based on Freud once again, is that the surface is a mask for opposite feelings. This is an idea that the actor can utilize in the technique of playing opposites. Someone consistently denied food might develop an attitude of greed and avarice that may be projected or displaced onto other objects, causing such an individual to develop into a miserly character, such as Harpagon in Molière's *The Miser.* Fear of being punished for being too gluttonous can lead to the displacement of the desire for food onto riches in general, which become a symbol or sign for food, and then to hoarding. A good actor's secret is to pretend that Harpagon is always hungry. But he doesn't dare eat, because he would be punished. The actor might pretend, too, that his chest of riches is food, so when it is stolen, he goes as frantic as if he is starving and miserable.

In Chapter IV: "On the Technique of Character Analysis, Section 2: e) The loosening of the character armor," Reich describes a patient who smiles perpetually and who has no idea why, where it comes from, or how it came to be his habitual mode of being in the world; he resists all attempts at interpretation. Yet the smile is strikingly in evidence all the time, even when the patient clearly is uncomfortable. Eventually, the smile is interpreted: It first represented an "*attempt at conciliation*" with his mother over an unpleasant incident, it had later taken on the aspect of being "a *compensation of an inner fear,*" and finally, "it also served as a means of *feeling superior.*" The smile itself was anchored, so to speak, in the musculature, and it was at first hard to interpret its meanings. It could have been ironic, friendly, sarcastic, or anything else. The expression in the patient's eyes must have been revealing as well. Every time Reich attempted to explain something to the patient — to interpret a dream or to offer an idea — the patient continued to smile, and often stopped talking. The reason the smile had turned from an attempt at conciliation into a mask for an internal fear is that the attempt at conciliation had not worked. The patient's mother had punished him, and the smile — not understood — had become, as it were, frozen in place, a sort of unspoken, pathetic message of love and desire. The smile thus came to stand unconsciously for the fear of loss of love. And to further repress all this knowledge from his consciousness and to compensate for the sense of loss and misery he had experienced, the patient, who continued to smile, had developed a sense of his own superiority. He felt he could overcome all adversities because he was really superior to those who had denied him what he wanted. He was overcompensating in this way for his deep-seated inner sense of lack of self-worth. Unconsciously what he really felt was that if his mother had punished him, he must have deserved it and deserved to lose her love. And so he continued to smile, masking the pain underneath, hiding it even from himself. The patient's unconscious tensing and relaxing of the muscles was automatic, and the fixed smile caused no particular stress, since it was warding off stress.

All of the above is by way of demonstrating the many possible meanings of a smile. A smile is not always simply the friendly or loving look it appears to be.

How do you delve into your character's psyche and come up with the playing of opposites: frowning when you are happy, smiling when you are angry? Matt Damon plays young Tom Ripley in *The Talented Mr. Ripley* (1999), and John Malkovich is an older Tom Ripley in *Ripley's Game* (2003). In both films Ripley hears himself being insulted. Matt Damon's fixed smile broadens in the scene where Freddy Miles (Phillip Seymour Hoffman), who enters the apartment where he expects to find his friend Dicky Greenleaf, unknowingly insults Ripley's taste. Matt Damon's smile is clearly a defense against unleashing his aggression and rage. John Malkovich appears not to react when, as Ripley, he shows up at a neighbor's house for a party just in time to overhear the neighbor insult his taste. Ripley's revenge is terrible. The smile in the first case and the seeming lack of affect in the second seem to have arisen spontaneously in the course of playing the scenes. Both reactions are chillingly effective.

BODY/CHARACTER ARMORING:
AN ACTOR'S EXERCISE IN AWARENESS

This exercise is meant to make you more aware of the physical sensations of your own body, including the streaming sensations of the blood, and to deal with the specific segments, so that you become more aware of them and of the emotions they bind. Applying Reichian principles to the body/character armoring of a theatrical or cinematic character, you might ask: How and where does the character hold tensions? How can they be freed, if they can be? Are they freed at any point in the play? Does the character break loose from her or his inhibitions? Do the inhibitions and armoring immediately return? If so, why do they return? If not, why not? Does the breaking of the armor represent a breakthrough to freedom or only a temporary manifestation of the emotional plague?

Lie comfortably on a bed or a mat or on the floor—anywhere, in fact. Close your eyes and relax as much as possible. Be aware of tensions in your body. Become aware of your entire body and its reactions by doing isolation exercises, from the feet up: Concentrate on each part or your body in turn, progressively. Now add to this awareness of each part of your body a consciousness of where the muscles are tightly held. Now concentrate on the specific segments:

1. **Ocular:** Open your eyes wide while breathing in and out until you feel the forehead muscles mobilized. Use your fingers, if necessary, to massage the muscles. What are you feeling? Do you feel frightened? Do you feel like crying? Roll the eyes around and from side to side, then focus on a distant point. What are you feeling?

2. **Oral, Including the Cervical:** Swallow hard. Move the lips up, down, and sideways in a circular motion. What do you feel? What emotions are aroused? Now try to activate the feeling of the gag reflex by sticking your tongue out all the way, holding it as long as possible, then pulling it in again. What do you feel when you feel like gagging? Notice all the physical sensations. Do you feel like screaming, in the manner of the *primal scream* as evoked in Arthur Janov's primal-scream therapy (an alternative, innovative therapy)? Now say something in a loud voice while being aware that you are holding back the desire to cry. How do you feel?

3. **Chest:** Breathe deeply in and out. What do you feel? Now take shallow breaths. How does this make you feel? Open and close your hands hard. Then open and close them softly. How do you feel each time? Make boxing movements with the arms. How does that make you feel? What emotions are aroused?

4. **Diaphragmatic and Abdominal:** Move your diaphragm up and down, as if you were doing breathing and support exercises in vocal class. Again, what feelings and sensations are aroused?

5. **Pelvic:** Tense and then relax the pelvic muscles and be aware of pelvic sensations. How do you feel? Are sensations of fear or of excitation aroused? If you were working on a character, how would this exercise make the character feel? How sexually repressed is the character?

Now just relax and remain stationary until you feel comfortable and able to get up with ease. The exercise does not require you to administer any kind of therapy or to do an in-depth self-analysis, merely to be aware of your body's sensations and reactions.

Chapter Seven

§

Existential Psychology: The Theories of William James, Ludwig Binswanger, Harry Stack Sullivan, Jean-Paul Sartre, and Other Pioneers

WILLIAM JAMES ON THE NATURE OF HABITS

*A*lthough considered the "father of American psychology," William James (1842–1910) — brother of the novelist Henry James, who was known for his realism and the psychological subtlety and depth of his character studies — thought of himself as a philosopher rather than a psychologist. In fact, the two disciplines were considered interrelated. A precursor of contemporary cognitive psychology, James taught at Harvard and published his major, long-awaited work *The Principles of Psychology* in 1890, after years of research and thinking about the subjects of the way the mind functions, of neurophysiology, of the nature of the senses, of consciousness — "primarily a selecting agency" and a "causal agency," according to James. He comes to no very definite conclusions regarding the existence of an unconscious as Freud understood it. And his vague ideas on psychological types have to do with whether someone is tough-minded or soft-minded. His elaboration of those attitudes was criticized by Jung as superficial.

It was William James who came up with the phrase *stream of consciousness,* the constant succession of images, ideas, feelings, thoughts, memories, and reactions that everyone experiences all the time as they go through daily lives. People are not usually aware of all that passes within, because of the fleeting nature of most sensations. As James says, "our state of mind is never precisely the same," and "the stream of thought flows on; but most of its segments fall into the bottomless abyss of oblivion."

Eugene O'Neill turned this concept into a playwriting technique in *Strange Interlude.* He created monologues that reflect the character's inner lives and interrupt their conversations as they talk to the audience while the play remains frozen in place until they have finished. In other words, we hear subtext, which itself has a subtext, reflecting layer upon layer of the unconscious. The system of repressions present in every character that Freud referred to and that it is one of the actor's tasks to analyze is readily apparent in this play.

James's functional psychology is mostly devoted to what Freud called in *The Question of Lay Analysis* "the physiology of the senses": the exploration of consciousness in terms of reaction time to stimuli, the difference between perception and sensation, and the like. This approach was exactly what Freud thought unproductive in nineteenth-century experimental psychology when it came to really understanding human behavior. Even though he was influenced to some extent by such great German experimental psychologists as Wilhelm Wundt (1832–1920), who studied the way conscious experience was structured based on biophysiology (*structuralism*), as far as Freud was concerned, this was severely limited. It didn't help solve the problem that was central to psychoanalysis, which is what motivates people to do what they do.

Within his field, James was brilliant and highly respected. Despite James's mechanistic views, there is far more to his book than a simple functionalist approach to human behavior. And James was very impressed by Freud both as a thinker and as a man. The two met during Freud's trip to America in 1909 to deliver a series of lectures on psychoanalysis at Clark University.

Questions and Considerations

Habit and Emotion: James describes habits in mechanistic terms but distinguishes those that we all have in common — such as walking upright — from those formed on an individual basis, such as swimming, reading Latin, or playing a musical instrument. It is primarily those of the latter sort that interest the actor: What is habitual to any character you are playing? What does the character's daily routine consist of? What happens if that routine is interrupted or altered? Does the character's objective change if this happens?

Sociologically, it is habit that rules society and prevents the mixing of social classes, even forestalling revolutions. People are brought up to behave in certain ways — that is, they have developed certain habits of behavior, and most people behave as they have learned to do. These habits prevent them from going beyond certain bounds and dictate their behavior in relationships. A question for actors to ask: What automatic, habitudinal behavioral patterns and responses has the character you are working on developed? Even the way someone speaks — a person's gestures, diction, and vocal patterns — are all habits. Habits, says James, are set by the time a person is thirty. Before that, they may be in flux. And this setting of habit is as it should be, because "there is no more miserable human being than one in whom nothing is habitual but indecision."

In Noel Coward's *Brief Encounter* (1945), both the "ordinary" housewife, played by Celia Johnson, and the "ordinary" doctor, played by Trevor Howard — whom she encounters at a train station and with whom she has a brief, intensely passionate love affair — have broken their habitual patterns of behavior. We see Celia Johnson at home and discover what the routine of her daily life is like: humdrum, a bit boring, but very comforting and comfortable nonetheless. She has longed for more—and she finds it, even if only for a short time—but then habit takes over, and she remains more or less contentedly in its thrall, with her memory of that brief encounter to sustain her.

As James points out, habit "simplifies the movements required to achieve a given result," so that, for instance, a beginner at the piano has a very different set of movements from someone who is an experienced concert pianist. Habit includes not only a set of learned muscular actions and responses but also a learned set of psychological responses. Equally important is the fact that habits usually entail a lack of necessity to concentrate on them consciously. A large part of what we do when we act in a habitual way is what James calls unconscious, but what Freud would perhaps think of as being prepared for preconsciously. Habit has more to do with learned sensations than with conscious thoughts or perceptions, James tells us. It is axiomatic that whenever you have to play someone who practices a particular profession, you will want to learn the habits of that profession as much and as well as you can, so that they appear to be second nature to you.

In a *New York Times* article of July 10, 2005, headlined "The 60-Day Course in Perfect Fake Piano Playing," Meline Toumani describes how Romain Duris learned how to fake playing Bach's exceptionally difficult Toccata in E Minor for the movie *The Beat That My Heart Skipped* (2005). He studied for two months with his sister Caroline, a classical pianist, who taught him the hand movements necessary to make it look as if he had the necessary professional habits and an individual style. In the film his playing looks absolutely real, but it is actually his sister who recorded the sound track. In addition to training three hours a day and practicing, he studied the habits, gestures, and demeanor of famous pianists available on video—at one point in the film, we actually see a video of Vladimir Horowitz's hands—in order to help himself feel like a musician and get inside the musician's mentality. One of the hardest skills to learn is the coordination of the left and right hands required for counterpoint. Margie Balter, a pianist and film coach, uses a physical method as part of the training for actors, actually putting her hands on top of theirs and playing a piece with them. She manipulates their wrists and elbows and puts their bodies into the correct centered, upright posture, much like the character of the young Chinese pianist Miao Lin, played by Linh-Dan Pham, training Tom (Romain Duris). She also makes sure they always keep their hands on the keys, as professional pianists do. In other words, she inculcates the correct physical and sense-memory habits. Of course, clever editing and camera work also play their part in making the piano playing appear real, as they did in *The Pianist* and *Ray* (2004) in which Adrien Brody and Jamie Foxx, respectively, look virtuosic, as have quite a few other actors.

AN AMERICAN SCHOOL OF PSYCHIATRY:
HARRY STACK SULLIVAN'S INTERPERSONAL RELATIONS

Spending his formative years in upstate New York, Harry Stack Sullivan (1892–1949) felt isolated, introspective, and lonely. He decided to seek life in the larger world. Sullivan studied medicine in Chicago and then worked with schizophrenics at St. Elizabeth's Hospital in Washington, DC, where he found himself disagreeing with the current ideas on how to treat them, which he felt were based on outmoded nineteenth-century concepts. He had been much influenced by his reading of Freudian psychoanalysis, and he discovered that Freud was far from the minds of the psychiatrists of the day, so he branched off on his own. Emphasizing existentialist questions and areas of personal relationships that he felt even Freud had neglected, he became a highly influential thinker, teacher, and psychiatrist.

The "influence of approval, disapproval, praise, blame, appeal to shame, and the inculcation of guilt are worth mentioning," he wrote in *The Interpersonal Theory of Psychiatry* (1953; posthumous). He was perhaps making a slightly ironic understatement, because he knew that those influential phenomena were more than merely worth mentioning, and that beginning in childhood, they all played a major role in shaping character and personality. For Sullivan, our reactions to the influence exercised by authority figures, in the first instance parents or caregivers, are the primary formative and causative experiences of the adults we will become. It is others who first show us and teach us our limitations, and the limits and extent of the possibilities of satisfying our desires.

And the influence of other people continues to be important throughout our lives in all areas. For Sullivan, character and personality are "the relatively enduring pattern of recurrent interpersonal situations which characterize a human life," he wrote in *Conceptions of Modern Psychiatry* (1940). In fact, we can never separate ourselves from other people, and our personality—our self—appears only in our interactions with them and is integral to those interactions. In other words, what happens outside the individual is as important as what happens inside. Nothing can be taken out of context, and we cannot look at past wishes and desires as if they were isolated from an interpersonal arena. We are enmeshed in relationships, and our fantasies, dreams, and wishes all revolve around other people and what we need and want from them. This is not to say that we are not individuals with our own character and internal structuring, but we cannot divorce ourselves from our environment.

These ideas were of enormous influence in later developments in psychology, such as the humanistic psychology of the American Carl Rogers (1902–87), who emphasized the need for approval from early childhood on and the need for existential living in an independent way. His idea was that we all strive towards self-actualization, in order to become fully functioning people in accordance with our ideal selves.

For Sullivan, there is another major influence on who we become, and it is biological: our gender. Sullivan does not mean our sexuality or sexual identification (although that eventually enters the picture of who we are) but rather the roles we are taught to play from infancy because of our biological gender. The parent of the same sex as the child feels familiar and comfortable with that child, more so than with a child of the opposite sex, and will treat the child of either sex in a way that will educate the child as to who he or she is and what sort of behavior is expected. Sullivan says this has nothing to do with the Oedipus complex, in which he did not really believe. He thought the "Jesuitical" idea of the first seven years of life as a determining factor in forming character mistaken, and maintained that the prepubescent and postpubescent childhood years, during which the child experiments with sexuality, were very important in determining adult behavior.

Rewards and punishments are meted out by parents for behavior that is considered appropriate to the social role played by members of a particular gender, and the "cultural prescription" for that gender is thus inculcated. This is undoubtedly one of the most important reasons that society's ideas about gender roles change so slowly: those gender-related constructs are inculcated and absorbed at a very early age.

The testing ground for gender is play, and whether a child plays with things and in a manner considered appropriate to gender earns approval or disapproval, applause or opprobrium. The expression of approval or disapproval can be masked by well-meaning parents who wish to allow their child leeway and do not wish to show the child what is or is not gender-appropriate, assuming that eventually the child will learn what is socially acceptable. Parents may fear that pressure from them might have a deleterious effect, but even if pressure is not applied, the child may get a sense that a parent is comfortable or uncomfortable, and absorb or introject the parent's approval or disapproval unconsciously.

In daily contact with other people, we are influenced by their moods and/or actions, which can be contagious. On a simple level, if someone yawns, we may want to yawn too. If someone applauds, we applaud as well—or we may boo, if we react in the opposite way; in either case, we will have been influenced and prodded into responding in some way. If someone is nervous or scared, we may become nervous or scared. If someone behaves seductively, our own sexual feelings may be aroused; or if we do not find the other person attractive, we may feel repelled.

This influence by other people comes partly from the desire we all have to relieve tensions that we all feel in the presence of someone else. These tensions come from needs that are unfulfilled, and we may feel that this other person, with whom we are in some sort of relationship, can fulfill our needs or desires. The conflict and tension have to be resolved in some way, either by the need actually being fulfilled or by our giving up on it and seeking satisfaction elsewhere.

To Sullivan, one of the most important things that others communicate to us is anxiety, which creates tension that has to be resolved somehow. The anxiety of a parent communicates itself unconsciously to a child, who may become anxious in turn, without knowing why. The child may then behave in a generally anxious way, feeling nervous and even fearful. Or the child's anxiety and unruly behavior, in which he or she may unconsciously act out the anxiety by being destructive, may arouse the anxiety of the parental figures or caregivers. They may become upset with the child and perhaps with themselves for reacting the way they do. This reaction may reinforce and anchor the anxiety, laying the groundwork for future upsets and for an unhappy relationship with the child during adolescence—and later, when the child has grown up. On the other hand, the child may learn how to behave in a way that relieves the parents' anxiety and consequently the child's own.

Questions and Considerations:
The Practical Application of Sullivan's Ideas to Character Interpretation

Different Faces: We often have different "faces" for different people. In other words, we relate in one way to one person and in a different way to another. We present ourselves to each person differently. This idea, which is also Proustian — he said we each have several selves and that we see one side at a time of other people, the way we see a photograph — is of course crucial for an actor putting the relationships of a character in their proper perspective. In analyzing a script, you will want to notice the different faces presented to different characters. Natasha in *Three Sisters,* for instance, presents herself in one way to the baby over whom she coos and oohs and ahs; at first in a fawning, self-effacing way, then in a more menacing, vulgar way to the sisters after she has married their brother and almost taken over the house; in an indifferent way to her husband; and in a nasty, dictatorial way to the old nurse.

Endings: For Sullivan, no ending is final. No objective attained is the end of the story, even in fiction. Once an objective has been reached and realized, another will take its place, unless death has intervened. Hamlet has no new objective after he kills Claudius, because he himself dies. Had he lived, he would have become king of Denmark, unless he had been dethroned by Fortinbras, backed up by his army. In any case, new troubles would have taken the place of the old ones. There is always a new objective, and there are always new actions to play.

The Psychiatric Interview: In analyzing a patient, Sullivan would want all the details possible. Aside from using free association as a therapeutic technique and having the patient prepare a chronology of his or her life, he would interact with the patient by asking the sort of questions listed here when the patient was talking about a particular relationship situation. I have arranged them as a questionnaire:

1. Who is the person you are in a relationship with, as you perceive that person to be?
2. If this is a person with whom you choose to be in a relationship, as opposed to family members with whom you are in a relationship from birth on, how did you choose this person?
3. What were your criteria?
4. What actually happened in the course of the relationship?
5. What events took place?
6. Where were you?
7. What did you say to each other?
8. How did you interpret the meaning of what was said?
9. What was the general emotional "climate" of the relationship?
10. How did you experience it?
11. Was there a change in this emotional climate?
12. If so, when?
13. How did it manifest itself externally — and internally, inside yourself?

14. What did the change mean to you?
15. Was it the beginning of the end or the end of the beginning?

Some other questions having to do with what Sullivan termed the *self-system* (patterns of behavior by which the self arranges its own security and avoids anxiety) might also be used for analyzing a theatrical character: What do you esteem and what do you disparage about yourself? What makes you feel vulnerable? How secure are you? Do you have reserves of security that will get you through a crisis? What do you do to restore your sense of equilibrium when something upsetting has happened?

Aside from the self-system, there is what Sullivan called the "rest of the personality," and he would study it developmentally. Again, he wanted every detail: When did a man first begin to shave? When did a woman first menstruate? How did the patient feel about those things? He would ask the patient for information about parents, siblings, other relatives, and people who were frequently in the family home as the child was growing up. He wanted as much detail as possible on all these relationships. Sullivan would ask the patient to describe both parents, and talk about what sort of people they were and what sort of images the patient had of them. He called the images people have of themselves and other people *personifications*. He wanted to know if the parents were respected in the community and what the family's economic circumstances were. He also wanted to know the patient's work and relationship histories. In short, he wanted to know the kind of information an actor wants to know in thoroughly analyzing a script.

Here are three examples of how someone might use the questionnaire for character analysis and interpretation, to help clarify issues and the overall arc of the part as well as objectives and obstacles. You can use the questions about events (4, 5, 6, and 7) to see how the scenes fit into the arc.

VANYA AND ASTROV (FROM VANYA'S POINT OF VIEW)

1. *Who is the person you are in a relationship with, as you perceive that person to be?* Astrov is one of my closest friends and, in fact, the only man I can talk to.
2. *If this is a person with whom you choose to be in a relationship, as opposed to family members with whom you are in a relationship from birth on, how did you choose this person?* He was there, he was our doctor, and he seemed intelligent and frustrated, like myself, so that we had something in common. We could talk about the stagnation of this provincial Russian life.
3. *What were your criteria?* I had to have someone in my life who was perceptive and intelligent, and not boring or stupid in his approach to life; someone who knew the value of being a considerate human being with moral values; and someone who cared about people and about bettering life. He went a bit overboard with his obsession with forestry, but although I make fun of that, it is at least the sign of a good-hearted person.
4. *What actually happened in the course of the relationship?* Fill in from script.
5. *What events took place?* Fill in from script.
6. *Where were you?* Fill in from script.
7. *What did you say to each other?* Fill in from script.

8. *How did you interpret the meaning of what was said?* Act 1: I thought he might be annoyed with me over my mocking of his interest in environmental issues, but I was just getting my own back because he was sarcastic with me over my feelings for Yelena.

9. *What was the general emotional "climate" of the relationship?* One of give and take and camaraderie, when we did see each other. One of empathy. We empathized with each other.

10. *How did you experience it?* I experienced it as warm, supportive, and genial.

11. *Was there a change in this emotional climate?* Yes.

12. *If so, when?* Act 3: When I saw him kissing Yelena. But it had probably been coming on for a long time before that, and I hadn't noticed.

13. *How did it manifest itself externally—and internally, inside yourself?* Externally I dropped the flowers I had gathered to give to her. Internally I was so upset that later on, when the Professor—her husband, of whom I was inordinately jealous—proposed his plan to sell the estate, I took out my rage on him by trying to shoot him. Of course, I was deeply angry with him anyway. But the person I really would love to have shot was my so-called best friend.

14. *What did the change mean to you?* It meant I could no longer really be friends with him. He knew I loved her. Of course, if they loved each other, he had no reason to control his passion on my account, but it still hurt deeply.

15. *Was it the beginning of the end or the end of the beginning?* It was the end! We had known each other for ten years. When I saw him kissing her, it was the beginning of the end.

ROMEO AND JULIET (FROM JULIET'S POINT OF VIEW)

1. *Who is the person you are in a relationship with, as you perceive that person to be?* Romeo is the handsomest, sweetest young man I have ever met. My husband. The only man in my life.

2. *If this is a person with whom you choose to be in a relationship, as opposed to family members with whom you are in a relationship from birth on, how did you choose this person?* It just sort of happened. It was love at first sight.

3. *What were your criteria?* A deep attraction, and then, once we got to know each other, a deep love for all he is, for his kindness, his gentleness—that's what I like in someone. And his charm, consideration, and sense of humor.

4. *What actually happened in the course of the relationship?* Fill in from script.

5. *What events took place?* Fill in from script.

6. *Where were you?* Fill in from script.

7. *What did you say to each other?* Fill in from script.

8. *How did you interpret the meaning of what was said?* I felt that he loved me.

9. *What was the general emotional "climate" of the relationship?* One of mutual trust, but fear also, because we couldn't let our families know about it, and if they found out, we would be in terrible trouble.

10. *How did you experience it?* I experienced it as blissful and anxiety provoking at the same time.

11. *Was there a change in this emotional climate?* Yes. Romeo was banished and had to leave Verona, and the anxiety grew even greater when my father wanted me to marry Paris, although unknown to him I had already married Romeo. We suddenly didn't know where we stood, and that's why I resorted to the stratagem of faking my suicide, in order to preserve my relationship with Romeo.

12. *If so, when?* He had to leave after the most beautiful night of our lives.

13. *How did it manifest itself externally—and internally, inside yourself?* Externally, I could not but acquiesce. Internally, I was distraught, anxious, and just plain unhappy, but I was determined nevertheless that our love would prevail.

14. *What did the change mean to you?* It meant I had to think of a way to deal with overwhelming, difficult conditions without his support or help.

15. *Was it the beginning of the end or the end of the beginning?* It was both—we hadn't been together that long. And when I awoke and found he had killed himself because he thought I was dead, I couldn't bear it...

THE MARQUIS OF QUEENSBERRY AND LORD ALFRED DOUGLAS IN "GROSS INDECENCY: THE THREE TRIALS OF OSCAR WILDE" (FROM THE MARQUIS' POINT OF VIEW)

1. *Who is the person you are in a relationship with, as you perceive that person to be?* Alfred, Lord Douglas, is a disappointing ne'er-do-well. A namby-pamby phony and a disgusting, effeminate snob who lives off my money. A revolting willowy insect!

2. *If this is a person with whom you choose to be in a relationship, as opposed to family members with whom you are in a relationship from birth on, how did you choose this person?* He's my son, unfortunately! My weak-willed wife *would* give birth to a sissy weakling!!!

3. *What were your criteria?* For him—I want him to be a man, damn it all!

4. *What actually happened in the course of the relationship?* He was born, and it made me sick to look at him—an effeminate little boy always clinging to his mother. He was a disgusting, sniveling brat and a sissy. And when he grew up, he wouldn't do anything I asked, wouldn't prepare himself for a career or study anything useful. We had nothing in common. What happened? A lot...

5. *What events took place?* We had scenes and screaming fights. I beat him when he was a child, but it didn't help. He went up to Oxford and became a disgrace!

6. *Where were you?* Home. Or at sporting events, or with the ladies. His mother wouldn't have anything to do with me. I believe in free love, and I wanted to move my mistress into the house. She wouldn't have it, of course, and Alfred thought it was disgusting!

7. *What did you say to each other?* I called him a miserable cur, and he said I was a "funny little man." Among other things. Oh, we said lots of things.

8. *How did you interpret the meaning of what was said?* He hates me and despises me.

9. *What was the general emotional "climate" of the relationship?* Tense. Riddled with anxiety. Terrible.

10. *How did you experience it?* Like being hit with a ton of bricks.

11. *Was there a change in this emotional climate?* Yes. It got worse.

12. *If so, when?* When I got wind of the fact that he was consorting with that posing sodomite Wilde. I don't say Alfred is it, but he looks it, and Wilde poses as it, and that's just as bad.

13. *How did it manifest itself externally—and internally, inside yourself?* Externally, I saw them together in the most loathsome, disgusting relationship, and internally, I was morally outraged and disgusted. It made me sick. I would be within my rights to shoot them!

14. *What did the change mean to you?* I knew I had to save my boy, and I was determined to do so at all costs. I would destroy Wilde, it that's what it took. I threatened to cut Alfred off without a penny if he didn't stop seeing Wilde, but that didn't work. He continued to defy me!

15. *Was it the beginning of the end or the end of the beginning?* It was the beginning of the end, because I knew Alfred would never speak to me again, but I had to do something to save him! My other son had been killed in a hunting accident. Some people spread the scandalous rumor that it was suicide, and that he had been having an affair with the Prime Minister. Well, I wasn't about to let anything like that happen to Alfred....

L U D W I G B I N S W A N G E R A N D E X I S T E N T I A L P S Y C H O L O G Y ;
V I K T O R F R A N K L A N D L O G O T H E R A P Y ;
S A R T R E A N D T H E L O O K I N T H E E Y E O F T H E O T H E R

Sullivan had raised existential questions and was in many ways a precursor of modern existential psychotherapy. He paid more attention to Freud than most of the existential psychologists—although they, too, could not entirely discard him, despite their here-and-now, basically ahistoric approach to psychotherapy, which does not deal with the patient's past in the same way Freudian psychoanalysis does and rejects Freud's psychic determinism. Existential psychotherapy is much more interested in solving problems in the context of their immediacy. The consequences of the past and the meaning and function of behavior in the present day, rather than the genesis of problems, are the main focus of existential psychotherapy and of existential psychology as described by the Americans Rollo May (1909–94), who called himself a psychoanalytical psychotherapist, and Irvin D. Yalom (born 1931) in his book *Existential Psychotherapy* (1980). May, whose ideas are very similar to Ludwig Binswanger's, was the best known of the American existential psychologists. He had studied with Sullivan, to whose ideas he did not entirely subscribe. Existential psychology, based first in Kierkegaard's philosophy and Heidegger's phenomenology and then in Sartre's existentialism, has a close relationship to the American school of humanistic psychology, as exemplified by Abraham Maslow (see pages 129–130) and Carl Rogers (see page 154).

Unlike most other schools of psychological thought, existential psychology, with its variations, had several founders in a number of European countries. Chief among them was the Swiss psychiatrist Dr. Ludwig Binswanger (1881–1966), a student of Eugen Bleuler and a student and colleague of Jung at Burghölzli. Jung introduced Binswanger to Sigmund Freud, and they became and remained close friends for more than thirty years. Indeed, Freud, who thought of Binswanger as a deeply supportive friend, considered Binswanger's disagreements with him intellectually honest and honorable, and Binswanger thought Freud the greatest human being he had ever met. In 1938 he offered Freud refuge in Switzerland from the Nazis. For forty-five years, Binswanger was the director of the Bellevue Sanatorium founded by his grandfather in Kreuzlingen. Incidentally, it was at that sanatorium, set in wooded splendor near Lake Constance, that Anna O. was interned while she recovered from her illness during the period when Robert Binswanger, Ludwig's father, was the clinic's director.

Becoming interested in the 1920s in such diverse philosophers as Kierkegaard, Martin Buber, Henri Bergson, Husserl, Nietzsche, and Heidegger, Binswanger based his *existential analysis,* as he called it, on both phenomenology and psychoanalysis. The idea of *Dasein,* meaning "there-being" or existence—in the sense of actually being present, which for him always included the idea of being with others—is central to his thinking. His psychology deals with phenomena as they presently exist. Indeed, his school of thought could be called phenomenological psychology. Rather than rejecting Freudian depth psychology, as some later existential psychologists were to do, Binswanger felt he was deepening it and expanding its parameters, but Freud disagreed and felt Binswanger was going farther and farther away from psychoanalysis.

Binswanger's concept of the unconscious, for instance, is that it exists as a realm of possibilities for self-realization, rather than simply as the repository of drives, affective organizations, cognitive processes, repressed ideas, and so forth. As in Sartre or Rollo May's thinking, people can see themselves as having the freedom to choose or not to choose. Well-being consists in part in being open to possibilities and open to the world. The *realization* of experience is subjective, filtered through the self. And since people do not exist outside their surroundings, they encounter others and have experiences in common, accounting for the phenomenon of *intersubjectivity,* which is inseparable from the knowledge of the other's existence. *Self-realization* comes about with reciprocity, in interaction with other people and especially in loving relationships—"being-with"—which provides us with the possibility of expanded awareness. Active involvement with others is thus a prerequisite of self-realization. Reciprocity depends on balancing relatedness with the simultaneous separateness of the individual, and on respecting and affirming the other person's differences from us in a positive way.

As in Sartre's idea, people deal with their experiences authentically or inauthentically. We have been "thrown" into the universe, so to speak—this is the phenomenon of *thrownness;* and if we give up the freedom with which we are born to somebody else or to conformity, we are then in a state of *fallenness.* This fallenness is inauthenticity exemplified; living the thrownness is authentic and involves making choices. Fear, guilt, and anxiety are existential experiences that Binswanger views in phenomenological rather than psychoanalytical terms, meaning that he deals with the actual experience of these things as they occur and with life as it is lived.

For Binswanger, we act on and can control the environment and are not simply conditioned by it. But anxiety, guilt, and regret arise in the face of uncertainty—for instance, when we don't know what course of conduct to pursue but know we must do something—and, more basically, in the face of nothingness—that is, confronted with the possibility of our own death.

One of the founders of later existential psychotherapy was Viktor Frankl (1905–1997), who named his school of existential analysis *logotherapy* so that it would not be confused with other schools of existential psychology. After World War II, Frankl, a concentration camp survivor, devised this form of innovative existential psychotherapy, building on, rather than repudiating, Sigmund Freud's psychoanalysis. He saw things slightly differently from Binswanger, and emphasized people's desire to find meaning in their lives and to accept responsibility for their actions, as well as helping people to cope with the traumatic events of their lives. His experiences in the concentration camps—in which he lost almost his entire family, and where everything came down to the naked attempt to survive and secure the most basic necessities of existence—led him to ask how he himself could find life worth living at all under such circumstances. Was life worth living under any circumstances? Did life have any meaning? Why did he not simply commit suicide? Later, as a psychiatrist practicing in Vienna (where he founded his famous Neurological Policlinic), he would ask despairing patients why they did not kill themselves. This was his way of entering into their mental and emotional lives; it was the beginning of an understanding of what was important to them. The answer they gave was that there was always something, someone, or some thread, however tenuous, that attached them to life, made living seem important to them, and made them want to go on even under the most adverse circumstances. There was always hope that things would get better. In the case of some Holocaust survivors, that thread was that they wanted to bear witness, to make known to the world the crimes their bestial captors had committed and bring the monsters to justice and, in doing so, to try to insure that such things could never happen again. Viktor Frankl's *Man's Search for Meaning: An Introduction to Logotherapy* (1984) is especially useful if you have to play a role in any of the many plays and films dealing with the Holocaust and World War II. So is Lawrence L. Langer's *Holocaust Testimonies: The Ruins of Memory* (1991).

In his seminal work on existentialism, *Being and Nothingness* (1953), the philosopher Jean-Paul Sartre (1905–80) deals extensively with psychology. As he famously said, existence precedes essence: we won't know who we are until we have lived. We know who we are and why we are here by what we do, by the actions we take. Being implies not-being, or nothingness—no-thing-ness. It is this inner sense of our possible annihilation that provokes anxiety. When we can confront the anxiety, we can have an authentic response to it, but when we flee from it, we are immediately in the realm of the inauthentic as we avoid its consequences for our existence, for our being. Inauthenticity implies that we have abandoned our search for authentic meaning in life. We have then condemned ourselves to search for meaning to bolster our inauthenticity.

One of the things Sartre says we seek in our search for meaning is a particular look in someone else's eyes, a look which we desire to have directed to and/or at us, a look with which we are familiar from childhood. Rob Bauer, a practitioner of the Rubenfeld Synergy Method of therapy (see page 212), said in an interview with the author:

> The look in the mother's eye is how we form our identity and sense of self or of separation from the other. We need to learn, and the way we learn is through contact with the other. We learn who we are through the mother or caretaker and through how the caretaker looks at us. Gazing into the face of the caretaker, I relate to the caretaker's connection with me. Do I see in their face love, frustration, exhaustion? Am I getting "You are the best little boy or girl in the world" or "I don't want you" or "You are too demanding" or "I don't have time for you?" Out of that contact we form our own identity.

Later, when we are adults, we seek that look we know, and that look spells rejection or acceptance of our love by the person looking at us. In either case, it will be the look we want. We seek the look everywhere, and when we find it, we cling to it, even if it is a look of rejection that betokens unhappiness for us. When we have found it, we introject the new psychic object who has given us the familiar look, but that introjection stems from irrational, magical thinking, as if there were an equation of the new object with the old, an unproven and perhaps unprovable assertion, a mystical construct that confuses and conflates new and old. The equation of one object with another is irrational, and it is also emotional. Therefore it has force and power—the force and power we have unconsciously given it. We scarcely feel able on a conscious level to accept or reject what we have automatically, magically introjected. The object as object is "unintelligible in itself," but it becomes a synthesis of itself with prior objects.

Some questions and considerations for the actor: What look is your character seeking from another character? Is it a look of love, of hatred, of indifference? How does your character conceive of love? Using the ancient Greek words, Rollo May distinguished *agape*, selfless love for others, from *eros*, love that desires the Other. Which kind of love does your character primarily experience?

But what do we seek from the object? We seek not only recognizability and familiarity but also an ideal. And most importantly, we seek to be an object for the other person—the Other, as Sartre characterizes other people, with a capital *O*. We want to be an object, but an object that controls the Other for whom we are an object. And we seek our own freedom. But the ideal is unrealizable. It partakes, once again, of magic and magical thinking. It is an attempt at realizing our own hidden projects (sometimes hidden even from ourselves), which the Other is not in a position to know. We therefore have to maneuver the Other into certain positions into which the Other may or may not wish to be maneuvered. There may be reactions against this attempt, or there may be acquiescence in our projects and enterprises, and we may acquiesce in theirs. Our personal projects put us in direct conflict with each other, because they concern the freedom of each individual. Paradoxically, a person wants to be loved freely, as the result of a free choice made by the Other, but demands at the same time that the lover give up his or her freedom. In giving love freely, one agrees to be in thrall to the Other and expects the Other to be in thrall as well. This situation is almost bound to lead to conflict sooner or later.

In addition to dealing with our relations with the Other as object, we also have to deal with, as existentialist psychologists such as Rollo May and Irvin D. Yalom inform us, certain more general aspects and concerns of existence:

1. Death and what the haunting prospect of our own death means to us from childhood on. People can either be resigned to and accept death or react against it, sometimes with defiance, always with ultimate anxiety. Sometimes we behave as if death did not exist, which, in a sense, it doesn't, at least when it comes to our own death. But sooner or later everything ends, which is tantamount to death. The day ends and we go to sleep, which is a simulation of death; on waking we scarcely realize how long we have been in an unconscious state. Yet sleep is the time when we renew the energy needed to lead our lives. We finish writing a book. And if we are lucky enough to have it published, it begins a new life. A love affair comes to a close. The paroxysm of the body in orgasmic release, with its instant of unconsciousness as the supreme excitation, finds relief in the supreme pleasure; it represents a kind of death, to which the Elizabethans likened it. And there is a phrase for it in French: *la petite mort*—the little death. We all die. And we all sublimate, which is also a kind of death, although it is a kind of rebirth and an entry into new life as well.

2. Freedom—what it is and what it means, whether or not we have free will or feel as if we have, and how we assume responsibility for our acts. Without the individual's acceptance of responsibility, continued existence is impossible. People are aware of themselves and others, and they can make intentional choices within the context of interpersonal experience. Rollo May emphasized that we wish for something and then implement our choice through the self-direction of our will. Will without wish is simply the assertion of power. Wish without will leads to neurosis and to the driven infantile personality.

3. Existential isolation, as we realize that we are actually, ultimately alone, imprisoned in our bodies, even if we have relations with others. We can be split off from others and also from our own selves, and this latter kind of splitting off must be dealt with either in therapy or by ourselves. In the encounter with others, we see the possibility of bridging the gap that isolates us or at least of feeling, however temporarily, that we have overcome the isolation that is a fundamental condition of existence.

4. Meaninglessness. People as objects, things, the world, and life in general only have the meanings we ascribe to them and have no essential or intrinsic meaning in and of themselves. Nor do we ourselves have any intrinsic meaning, but we give ourselves and our actions and activities the meaning we wish them to have.

All of these existential phenomena may give rise to internal, existential conflicts, as we seek to cope with the terrors they inspire and the sense of rootlessness and disorientation they impose in the face of a chaotic, fundamentally incomprehensible world. We must decide how to deal with these aspects of life and how to give meaning to our existence by being engaged—that is, committed to something or someone, some cause or some way of life, or to making some contribution to life.

The search for authenticity and the solution to problems of existence entails having to confront and overcome obstacles. It would be better for the maturing child in the throes of adolescent hormonal adjustments if the prospect of freedom and independence as an adult were viewed as exciting and attractive. People have fought and died in the name of freedom, but the actual possession of freedom can be frightening. What do you do with it? What does a character in a play do with it? As an actor, you will find it useful to explore how the character deals with his or her freedom or lack of it, and what the character wants to do with it. Is the character amoral or immoral, so that freedom means one can do anything? Is freedom limited by circumstance and responsibilities one has assumed? The mother played by Julianne Moore in the film *The Hours* (2002) flees, because she must be free and cannot stand the situation in which she is forced to live, which is false for her from beginning to end. Nora in Ibsen's *Doll's House* would seem to be her precursor, involved in a similar dilemma. In *Far from Heaven* (2002), Julianne Moore plays a woman who is the prisoner of her marriage. She is in love with a black man, and she dares not pursue her love to its inevitable, authentic conclusion. Her husband turns out to be gay and—deciding to live authentically, as he had not all the years of his marriage when he conformed automatically to everything he felt was expected of him—leaves her after the traumatic struggle of coming out. She learns who she is through these experiences.

As Rollo May points out, we are centered in ourselves and have the need and the possibility of being with others. The attempt at self-affirmation is the attempt to maintain the centeredness of the self. Some people rely on religion to give themselves and their lives meaning, while others engage themselves in politics. As long as these decisions are based on the authentic acceptance of the prevailing chaos, the person who has made them is living authentically. An acceptance of who one is can also either be authentic or inauthentic. One can live in a self-accepting (*ego-syntonic*) or self-rejecting (*ego-dystonic*) manner. Conflict and unhappiness arise from the rejection of authenticity.

For Sartre the dualism and opposition of *exterior* to *interior*—in other words, of subject and object—is nonexistent. The exterior is a superficial skin or cover of material existence separated from us by our own skin, which is contiguous with the rest of materiality and subject to absorption of elements from that reality. Think, for instance, of all the times you have developed a cold or felt a blast of hot or cold air. Sartre means that for every person, the perception of what is interior and what is exterior is equal: everything is actually interior or interiorized. At the simplest level, our insights and perceptions stem from our being inside ourselves, unable to escape. Everything in our lives depends on our own interpretation of appearance and of experiential phenomena. And everything depends most of all on our choices. We must choose. We have no choice in the matter. We are "condemned to choose," as Sartre says. Even if we think we are not choosing, we are. If we allow things to happen to us, that is a choice. We must choose to be engaged in our own lives, or we are lost.

Questions and Considerations

Ludwig Binswanger's Questions: Binswanger looked at the basic "directions" a person took, based on the "opportunities" in his or her life. What are the opportunities in a character's life? Part of the answer lies in the character's sociocultural and psychological background. Mental illness, for example, can be understood in part by looking at it from the standpoint of the original opportunities of the sufferer and the subsequent direction he or she took in order to deal with his or her issues. In Binswanger's therapy, he explored the meaning of phenomena without interpreting them to the patient or guessing at or attributing meaning to them. He wanted to know their meaning to the individual. He dealt with patients in preliminary phases by asking them to tell him about the following:

1. How they saw and experienced their *Umwelt,* their "around-world," the physical environment that surrounded them where they lived and worked in all its details, including the objects in it and their attitudes towards them. Were they attached to objects and, if so, which ones and why?

2. How they saw and experienced their *Mitwelt,* their "with-world," meaning their social world, their community and culture, and the people they were in some relationship with. How did they see their wives or husbands, their family, their friends, their coworkers, their society?

3. How they saw and experienced themselves internally, which was their *Eigenwelt* or "own-world." How did they feel about themselves? Were they comfortable with who they were?

4. What they thought and felt about time and space. Did they live mentally in the past, the present, or the future? Did they see life as a long adventure or as brief and finite? Did they see the universe and their world as comfortable or threatening? Did they feel they could be adventurous in space—traveling, for instance, and exploring the world—or did they feel they had to circumscribe their world and limit it to the confining space of their own narrow purview?

These are all questions and considerations that concern the actor interpreting a character. In fact, an existential schematic approach based on Binswanger's questions might be one of the most useful from an actor's point of view, as well as from a director's, establishing the environment of a play. And they are extremely useful for writers as well in creating both characters and environments.

Erich Fromm's Character Types: The German-born American psychologist Erich Fromm (1900–80), who fled the Nazis in 1934, tried to combine Marxism and Freudianism. His thinking is very close to that of the existential psychologists, but he has his own original ideas and analyses. Fromm believed that personality was in part the product of socioeconomic deterministic conditioning. People can attain freedom and transcend that kind of conditioning, but biology remains a determinant that cannot be overcome. As with the existential psychologists, for him, freedom is the principle human condition, and people either embrace it or escape from it, mostly the latter. Fromm categorized the following escape routes from freedom and the personality types they gave rise to: *authoritarianism,* which entails uniting oneself in some way with authority, either by assuming power or by submitting to it, perhaps in the extreme forms of sadism or masochism; *destructiveness,* which involves being involved in destroying the freedom of others or of oneself (self-destructiveness); and *automaton conformity.* Family relationships help determine which of these three basic behaviors will emerge. Families can either be *symbiotic,* meaning codependent and "swallowing up" family members, thus teaching dominance and submission, or *withdrawing*—that is, punishing—teaching conformity and not supplying nurturing and affection, engendering narcissism and sadomasochism. Families and societies also determine what orientation people have to the world, to the self and to other people. This orientation, which is largely unconscious, is their personality type. In addition, human beings need to have a sense of individual identity and to feel a sense of relatedness to others. They need to have a sense of belonging, which includes the idea of *rootedness,* or having roots, and a general sense of moral and sociocultural orientation. And they need to have a sense of creativity. Some types, such as exploitative and hoarding, may overlap. Fromm characterized the first four types as existing in the mode of *having* and the productive type as in the mode of *being:*

1. *Receptive,* meaning awaiting both personal and material satisfaction from external sources; submissive, or what Freud describes as oral passive. This type arises in symbiotic families as passivity. The escape from freedom is authoritarian and masochistic.

2. *Exploitative,* arising from the feeling that one has to nourish oneself, that nobody will do it for you and you have to take what you want. This is prevalent throughout history in economic imperialism and conquest, for instance, and is similar to Freud's idea of oral aggression. This type arises in symbiotic families in the form of active reactions, as opposed to passive acceptance. The escape from freedom is authoritarian and sadistic.

3. *Hoarding,* a type that includes many members of the bourgeoisie and upper classes, involves a severe work ethic and is much the same as Freud's idea of anal-retentive traits. Possessions, including the idea that other people can be possessed, are paramount. This type arises in withdrawing families. The escape from freedom is into destructiveness.

4. *Marketing*—that is, "selling" oneself as attractive and desirable, as in Freud's hysterical type; opportunistic, involved in fads and fashions, and business-oriented. This is the contemporary character par excellence. It arises in withdrawing families. The escape from freedom is automaton conformist.

5. *Productive,* the healthiest personality type, arising in loving families with rationality at their core; creative in various fields and contributing to the welfare of humanity, accepting freedom and the responsibility it involves.

FACING THE OPPOSITE:
AN EXISTENTIALIST EXERCISE FROM GESTALT THERAPY

Originally from Germany, where he trained as a psychoanalyst and which he was forced to flee to escape the Nazis, Fritz Perls (1893–1970), the California-based practitioner of Gestalt therapy, a form of existentialist therapy, had his patients do various exercises that can be of great use for writers, actors, and directors in creating and interpreting characters. The German word *Gestalt* means "form." Perls dealt with the form things took in people's minds and outside them, including the roles they played unconsciously. In Gestalt therapy, Perls worked with the split-off, repressed parts of the ego and the id, purely Freudian concepts, and he devised unique exercises for his patients: they played roles (often the role was that of patients themselves in relation to others), in order to "be real" and stop intellectualizing about their emotions and experiences, so that they could be in touch in a sensitive way with their feelings. The clichéd popular image of a Gestalt exercise is beating a pillow with one's fist to get out the anger one feels towards somebody. Cliché or not, this is a real exercise and can actually be quite effective.

One of the most famous of the exercises was the *empty-chair exercise,* during which a person sat opposite an empty chair, which was imaginatively filled with someone the person wanted to talk to. The person would then talk to that other person as if he or she was really there. Much emerged from the unconscious, revealing the nature of the conflict with that person and many of its details.

Perls wanted people to "own" who they were and their life experiences, and to become whole as a result of acknowledging what had gone on in their lives; how they had reacted to it and developed and behaved as a result. Gestalt therapy dealt with the subjective in other people and in the self, and tried to objectify and externalize the inner world, making people aware of the nature of their thoughts, emotions, and feelings.

And now, here is the exercise, which involves the "empty chair" and the famous Perls exercise of role-playing, which we all do, for ourselves and for each other:

Put paper and pen on a table. Next to the table, place two chairs opposite each other. Having read and studied a part you are playing, a role you are writing, or a play you are directing in which you want to make all the roles fit into the story as you wish to tell it, sit facing the empty chair, and talk to it as if someone you wish to communicate with is there.

If you are acting a role, this is another character with whom you are in a relationship, whether a primary or secondary relationship; you can do this exercise for each of the characters you relate to in the script. What do you want that person to say to you? What do you want to say to them? How do you feel about them? What do you want from them? What do they want from you? Are you prepared to give them what they want? If so, why? If not, why not? Do you think you will get what you want from that person? If so, why? If not, why not? You can think of many questions to ask that other person. What do you think their responses would be?

If you are writing or directing, you will switch roles and do the exercise at least twice. In fact, you should do the exercise for all the characters you are writing or directing and for all the relationships. Whether you are writing, directing, or acting, be sure to write down anything that occurs to you as you evoke the person. Talk to that person, telling him or her everything you really want to say, whether you as the character would actually be able to say it or not and whether or not the script allows you to say it.

Brief Psychodynamic Psychotherapy (BPP) and the Core Conflictual Relationship Theme (CCRT) Method

The term brief psychodynamic psychotherapy (BPP) refers to a number of schools of contemporary, innovative therapies that have their origins in earlier psychoanalytic practice. The pioneer psychoanalyst Franz Alexander (1891–1964) wrote in *Psychoanalytic Therapy* (1946) that the therapeutic process took much too long and that with certain disorders, a briefer therapy was just as effective in bringing about change as was a protracted course of analysis. Alexander felt that patients could be cured without either the analyst or the analysand understanding in depth all the causes of their disorders. If the patient changed for the better, that was all that was necessary. He was by no means alone in feeling this way, but more traditional psychoanalytic circles considered his views scandalous.

BPP is not to be confused with crisis intervention or emergency psychotherapy, both of which deal with immediate specific incidents and necessities. What BPPs have in common is the brief number of therapeutic sessions, from twelve to fifty, and the goals of eliminating symptoms and effecting some character change that is meaningful and significant but also limited. Dealing with childhood conflicts that are at the origin of adult conflicts is at the heart of this therapy, which is psychoanalytically oriented, although it avoids any deep analysis of the issues involved in the Oedipus complex or the sexual etiology of neuroses, just as it avoids object-relations issues such as separation and individuation, partly because of such practical considerations as the time the therapy will last. In addition, it avoids the development of a transference neurosis by immediately dealing with resistances and transference phenomena as they arise. The patient sits face to face with the psychotherapist in one weekly session, and the duration of the therapy is always less than a year.

Questions and Considerations

The CCRT Explained: One method of brief psychodynamic psychotherapy is the use of the core conflictual relationship theme (CCRT), devised in the late 1970s and refined over the course of twenty years by Lester Luborsky, Ph.D., Professor of Psychology in Psychiatry at the University of Pennsylvania. The CCRT Method deals with immediate existential issues in a patient's life, even if its orientation is not strictly existential. The heart of the CCRT is the tripartite analysis of any relationship from the point of view of the patient, guided by the therapist. It deals with what it conceives as the unconscious core component of personality, based on the idea that patients are usually concerned with a specific conflict that preoccupies them. They may wish to avoid conflict or to be confrontational. Other patients are concerned with issues of dependency or commitment, or with their ability to function well in a close, intimate relationship. The procedure is reminiscent of Harry Stack Sullivan's summation for his patients of what he calls the "reconnaissance" sessions: He would tell the patient what the sessions had taught him was his or her major or central life difficulty.

The use of the CCRT method for actors, directors, and writers wanting to do a quick analysis of relationships in order to put them in perspective will be immediately apparent. The method can also be of great use in honing and clarifying character motivations and actions.

The therapist (or actor, writer, or director) looks for the following information:

1. **Wish (W):** What does the patient or the character wish for in the relationship—the character's objective(s)?

2. **The Response of the Other (RO):** What is the expected response of the other person? In theatrical terms, if negative, this response could constitute an obstacle. If positive, the response could help the character achieve the objective.

3. **The Reaction of the Self (RS):** What is the patient's or the character's reaction to the response?

All three categories can be expressed as verbs, showing that they are actions: "I wish to do _____." The response of the other is "to do _____." "My reaction is to _____." The categories can also be expressed as adjectives descriptive of feeling: "I wish to feel _____," or as nouns: "I wish to have _____." For actors, the verbal expression is perhaps the most serviceable, but adjectives can also help clarify what is going on in a scene or in a relationship as a whole.

While it may seem too formulaic at first glance, the CCRT is susceptible of endless variations. Any individual actor can use it to interpret a role in a way that will be different from any other actor interpreting the same role—because first, everyone will have an individual approach to the interpretation of a role, and second, each individual will be using his or her own substitutions to personalize the role.

In the course of the therapeutic session, the therapist listens for what is called the *relationship episode* (RE), which begins to reveal the nature of the patient's conflict. The episode is an actual event revealing feelings and behavior, much like a scene in a play, as opposed to a general account of the emotional climate of the relationship and the patient's general desires revolving around it. The therapist, having listened and perhaps asked some questions during the session, later extracts the W, RO and RS from the episode, so that he or she can begin to zero in on the patient's core conflicts.

Similarly, a writer creating a script or an actor analyzing a scene can look for the actual event or episode and find the spine of the scene. The writer or actor can then extract the same things a psychotherapist does from a session with a patient and zero in on the character's core conflict.

In the scene (the RE) where Hamlet confronts Ophelia, she wishes to return his letters. The response she expects from him is anger and rejection, and she feels guilty at betraying him because she still loves him. He does indeed become angry, because he realizes he is being spied on from behind the arras. Her reaction is fear at his display of temper, and she is more deeply upset than she expected to be, although she is upset even before the scene begins.

His wish upon seeing her is to have a tender, intimate conversation. The response he expects from her is that she wishes the same thing, which is illogical given his recent strange, rejecting treatment of her. When she offers to return his missives, and he realizes her father and Claudius are observing everything from their hiding place, his reaction is one of anger; and he feigns erratic behavior, if not madness, in order to deceive them and to mask his deep disappointment in his love for her. One of the things the scene shows is how much Hamlet and Ophelia love each other and how dysfunctional they are when it comes to expressing their love or to acting on it.

An Exercise: Using the Core Conflictual Relationship Theme (CCRT)

*F*or any character you are working on, whether as a writer or an actor, here is an exercise that will help you map out not only the specific scenes but also the entire arc of the story, as you deal with each relationship episode in it. Write down your responses:

1. In a particular scene (relationship episode—RE) pick five verbs, nouns, or adjectives—or a combination of verbs, nouns, and adjectives—to express the character's wish (W—you can think in terms of objectives) for any one relationship. The scene could have two or more characters in it. Do this for all the relationships in the play.

2. Pick five verbs, adjectives, or nouns, or a combination, describing the expected response (RO) from the other person. Do this for all the relationships. What is the actual response?

3. Pick five verbs, nouns, or adjectives, or a combination, describing the character's reaction to the expected response (RS) in question 2. Pick five adjectives describing the character's reaction to the actual response. Then pick five verbs. Do this for all the relationships.

4. What action does the character take next? What action is warranted by the actual response? Is the character's action appropriate or inappropriate, and why? Is the character's reaction productive of desired results or counterproductive—in other words, is the objective obtained or not? What is the next expected response? What is the reaction of the character to it? What is the actual response? What is the reaction of the character to it?

Here is the exercise as it might be done for the last scene of act 1 of *Uncle Vanya,* which is a relationship episode between Vanya and Yelena. She has been staying on the estate all summer with her husband the Professor, and Vanya has fallen deeply in love with her:

For Vanya: My wish is to express my love for Yelena. My wish is to confront her with her indolence. My wish is to have her love me. My wish is to run away with her (I know that is not realistic). My wish is to stay alone with her in the garden while everyone else is inside. The responses I expect from her are, in order: indifference, annoyance, anger, rejection, and departure from the scene. The reaction to all this will be that I will feel wounded, hurt, unhappy, miserable, and depressed. Her actual response when I express my love is to tell me that I am torturing her and that she feels agonized, then to leave. My reaction to her actual response is exactly the same as it is to the expected response, because things happened more or less as I expected them to. I don't know if my actions were appropriate or inappropriate. I only know that I love her and that she rejects me. And I don't know what I am going to do next. In act 2, I appear in the bedroom to relieve her of her duty in attending to her husband and to let her get some sleep. Actually, what I really wish for is to be close to her and to have an exclusive relationship with her. I want her to take me seriously, and I want to feel important in her eyes. I want her to admire me. We shall see…

For Yelena: My wishes are that he leave me alone or at least that he stop pestering me with his attentions; that he treat me in a respectful way; that he simply be a friend and that he stop being so unhappy, because it makes me feel guilty, but it also makes me want to avoid him. He should know by now that I don't find him attractive as a man. The response I expect from him is that he will declare his love, which will drive me up a wall; that he will be clingy, annoying, tenacious and obnoxious. My reaction will be to express my anger, to tell him off, to make sure he realizes that there is no hope that I will ever return his affection, and maybe even to insult him if he goes too far, and then to flee. What actually happened was close to my expectations, and I simply asked him not to "look at me like that," and he said he could not look at me otherwise because he loved me. My reaction was to tell him that it was agonizing, that he was tormenting me. I meant that I knew he was torturing me because I did not return his love, and I hope he understood that. I could not bear to reject him outright, however, and to tell him to stop loving me, so I simply fled back into the house, to my husband. What can you say to people like that? What I am going to do next is to avoid him as much as I can, while being diplomatically friendly when I am forced to be in his company—at dinner, for instance. I think that action is warranted, appropriate, and productive. At least it will procure me some peace of mind, I hope. Why can't he just leave me alone?

To round out the characters and give them even more depth, add to these stream-of-consciousness inner monologues an analysis of the ambivalent side of the characters' feelings: On some level, Vanya hates Yelena, because she has rejected him and because he can't have her. His masochistic need for punishment is one reason he continues to annoy her, to dream about a relationship with her, and to press himself upon her. And his love/hatred (ambivalence) is aroused once he discovers her in Astrov's arms. She, on the other hand, much as she finds Vanya's attentions maddening, is flattered by them on some level. After all, his falling in love with her shows that she is still an attractive, desirable woman. Because she is afraid of being punished, she also finds it difficult to confront people in general, even when doing so would lead to desirable results.

Chapter Eight

§

Psychological Terms and Topics

*T*his chapter is a grab bag of topics not generally covered elsewhere in the book, such as cognitive psychology. Some of the topics are meant simply to give you information about other schools of psychology you might wish to explore. But most of the terms and topics are meant to have practical applications in the work of interpreting character, as in personality/personality theory. There are also suggestions for further reading, and recommended films and plays to help you explore such subjects as the "as-if" personality. And there are a number of topics dealt with at greater length, such as addiction and group psychology.

abreaction: in Freudian psychoanalysis, the verbal expression of an emotion underlying a trauma. When the ability to express what has been unconscious because of the trauma is achieved, its conscious verbal expression constitutes a breakthrough and may have a healing effect. Bringing about an abreaction was an early goal of psychoanalytic therapy, but it is less important in contemporary psychoanalysis than other aspects of treatment.

When Hamlet kills Claudius, saying as he does so, "Here, thou incestuous, murderous, damned Dane, Drink off this potion;— is thy union here? Follow my mother," he is finally expressing in an abreaction what he has felt throughout the play. The trauma of his mother's marrying his uncle is finally expressed verbally directly to Claudius. We know that Hamlet found the marriage traumatic and was able to express his anger to his mother in the "closet" scene, whereas previously he had only been able to talk about his feelings to himself or his closest friend, Horatio; but only now do we see the full force and fury of his rage unleashed. In *A Doll's House,* Nora finally frees herself from the constraints of her unworkable marriage and is able to leave, telling Helmer that she can no longer stand the life she has been leading and wants to be free. Juror Number Three in *Twelve Angry Men* breaks down when he realizes that he is condemning the boy on trial because of the pain he has felt over his relationship with his own son, and not because he is certain of the boy's guilt beyond a reasonable doubt.

accommodation: a form of adjustment or adaptation, which, in psychological terms, means an anticipatory repositioning of the internal defense mechanisms, when particular stimuli are expected or received. For instance, when a person falls in love at first sight, there may be an accommodation based on the person's life and other relationships in order to make room and time for a new relationship, which is anticipated as pleasurable. The adjustment may be quick or slow, and is often unconscious at first, then conscious, and cemented by ruminative thinking, the results of which then recede into the unconscious. In sociological terms, accommodation means adjusting to a group situation, so that a person can fit into the group and help maintain its harmonious relationships and smooth functioning. Accommodation and compromise often go hand in hand, and altruistic sacrifice, the defense mechanism described by Anna Freud (see page 76), may be one of the compromises necessary to accommodate certain situations. Whole nations may find it necessary to accommodate or to be conciliatory in order to maintain peace and harmony in international relations.

In *Romeo and Juliet,* all the characters have to accommodate to new relationships and situations. Depending on their original attitudes towards each other, they do so in different ways. The feud between the Capulets and the Montagues requires accommodation of both Romeo and Juliet. Their various friends and relatives either accommodate to the situation or choose not to, so that, for instance, Tybalt — Juliet's cousin — and Romeo's friend Mercutio fight duels and are killed. They are unwilling or unable to accommodate. Romeo cannot accommodate to Juliet's death, so he kills himself, and Juliet, awakening after the effects of the drug that caused a simulation of death have worn off, similarly cannot adjust to Romeo's death and commits suicide.

Another form of accommodation is an adjustment to adverse circumstances, when some form of adaptation to them is seen as necessary for survival. The accommodation may or may not achieve the desired results. For instance, in World War II, many people in the German heartland and in occupied countries felt that if they simply went peaceably about their daily lives, accommodated the Nazis, and appeased them by obeying them and their restrictive laws, they would live through the war. In many cases, their behavior was a form of denial: "Oh, this can't last," or "They don't really mean what they say about the Jews," and so forth. Tragically, this accommodation did not assure the survival of those who accommodated. Among other things, there were reprisal massacres of innocent civilians; nobody was safe. In another form of accommodation that involved more than simple obedience to a tyrannical master, some people survived by actually embracing the conquerors and serving them in subordinate capacities (secretaries, servants, etc.). Some, such as Bernard Grasset, the publisher, who had had many fruitful connections with Jewish authors before the occupation and was condemned as a collaborator after the war, actually went running to the Nazis in order to accommodate to their demands in the most subservient, fawning, and self-serving manner possible. He wanted to be on the winning side, and indeed, due to his obsessive-compulsive compliance, Grasset was the czar of French publishing under the Nazis. His relationship with them was sadomasochistic, to say the least. France's most important publisher, Gaston Gallimard, on the other hand, accommodated to the Nazis in public but used his Paris offices as headquarters for the Resistance. After the war, he was accused of being a collaborator but was, of course, exonerated. The role of one of the pioneers of psychoanalysis in France, René Laforgue (1894–1962), a correspondent of Freud and a friend of Princess Marie Bonaparte, was more ambivalent: he spent the war sequestered on his estate, where he hid a number of Jews. But he also attempted to establish a French branch of the infamous Göring Institute, which was the central Nazi psychological organization in Berlin. Not a single French psychoanalyst would join Laforgue in this enterprise.

For an interesting play about accommodation and adjustment, read Michael Frayn's *Copenhagen,* about the 1941 meeting between the Danish Nobel Prize–winning physicist Niels Bohr and his former student, then head of the German atomic bomb project, Werner Heisenberg (whose famous contribution to physics was the *uncertainty principle,* which states that an observer influences what is being observed, so that you can never know anything with absolute exactitude; you cannot determine the exact position of a particle, for instance). Bohr was of partly Jewish extraction, and Heisenberg was not. Before the Nazi takeover, they were fast friends, but things were more difficult afterwards, of course, especially once the Nazis occupied Denmark. They remained friends, nevertheless, until after that meeting. No one knows quite what transpired, despite various accounts by the two participants themselves. Why did Heisenberg go to Copenhagen? What did he want from Bohr? In any case, it is worth noting that afterwards, Heisenberg told the Nazi authorities that it would be exceptionally difficult to make the bomb, and they underfunded the project, which made it impossible. This was, perhaps, Heisenberg's form of resistance to the hated regime. Or it might have been that he simply couldn't quite figure out how to do it, although that is less likely for a physicist of his stature and attainments. All these issues are raised in the play, as is that of Heisenberg's discomfort with and tacit accommodation to the anti-Jewish policies of the government he supposedly served. The underlying moral question in the play is how a scientist can serve the nefarious ends of an evil regime, when it is clearly in aid of unethical policies. In Heisenberg's case, the answer was to pretend that he was serving them but to undermine the bomb project by making sure it would be underfunded, and by working as slowly as possible, making as many errors as he could reasonably hope to convince the authorities were unavoidable.

On a less serious, more entertaining note, see the Jurassic Park series of films, in which the people have to adjust instantly and accommodate to the dinosaurs, who have adapted to their habitat and multiplied, despite efforts on the part of the scientists who bred them to prevent their reproducing.

acting out: This term is often used in talking of children's behavior when their unconscious inner conflicts have caused them to behave provocatively. For instance, a young child, angry that his or her parents have gone out for the evening but unable to verbalize that anger, may throw food or toys, not necessarily at the parents but around the room, or may scream or make a fuss about something that seemingly bears no connection to the parents' evening out. The parents would have to be mind readers to know what is really going on, but intuitively, many parents do realize what is happening. Someone may act out only at one or more moments, but not at others and not in general, or acting out might indeed be someone's general mode of behavior, as in addiction.

adaptation: Similar to accommodation and adjustment, *adaptation* means dealing or coping—usually in a positive, advantageous way—with new circumstances in the physical or psychological environment. These might require severe changes in lifestyle or psychological or behavioral adjustments. A poor or unsuccessful adaptation is called a maladaptation. For example, if someone who is extremely wealthy suddenly goes bankrupt, the new circumstances require the person to adapt in order to survive. Obviously, some people are able to adapt well, whereas others may adapt poorly or not at all. For a seriocomic look at what could happen in such a situation, see Mel Brooks's *Life Stinks* (1991), in which a heartless, unscrupulous tycoon, played by Mel Brooks, bets that he can survive without a penny for a full month on the mean streets of Los Angeles. As a result of his experiences, he develops some sympathy for the plight of the homeless.

In Alexandre Dumas' *The Count of Monte Cristo,* a novel much filmed and dramatized, Edmond Dantès, a young sailor, suddenly finds himself in prison for reasons beyond his comprehension, since he has done nothing wrong that he is aware of. He discovers that his imprisonment is the result of conspiracy by envious, covetous, duplicitous people, some of whom he thought were his friends. Eventually he escapes and finds the treasure on the isle of Monte Cristo that another prisoner, an abbé who had befriended and taught him in prison, has left to him as his sole heir. He assumes the title of count and wreaks vengeance on his persecutors. Throughout the novel, the vicissitudes of his life require him to adapt both physically and psychologically to many changes. He has first to adapt to life in prison, when perforce his life and expectations change completely, then to the knowledge that the people he thought were his friends are his enemies. Each new revelation is a shock to him. He has to adapt to the idea that he will never have the happiness he dreamed of. Once he recovers the treasure buried on the isle of Monte Cristo, he has to adapt to the fact that he has suddenly become a very rich man. And he has to adapt his behavior so that he will seem to be an aristocrat. In prison the abbé had educated him, so that he is now a cultivated man and can pass himself off as someone who grew up with wealth. He makes no mystery of the fact that he has purchased his title, because that can astonish nobody, since it was not so unusual in his day. And he has to adapt to new relationships and to the change in his relationship with Mercedes, the love of his life, who, believing him dead, has married one of his enemies, not knowing that her husband had betrayed her first love.

In real life, people thrown into concentration camps and ghettos during World War II had either to adapt or perish. Adapting meant not only that at least some people survived longer in situations in which all were condemned to death but also that in some cases, they survived the war and were able to resume life afterwards. Some, like Anne Frank and her family, adapted by going into hiding, only to be betrayed and caught.

If you ever have to play characters such as Władysław Szpilman, the pianist poignantly portrayed by Adrien Brody in Roman Polansky's deeply moving *The Pianist* (2003) — an object lesson in adaptation and in surviving the worst adversity, based on a true story — one of the questions you have to ask yourself is how anyone could survive in such circumstances. What is it that enables people to be resilient enough to adapt and change with the times so that they can remain alive? And what is it in others that prevents their doing the same? It must take a certain temperament and ego and the ability to relate to others to be able to live through the worst horrors, and nobody can know how he or she will react unless forced into those kinds of situations.

Another object lesson in resilience, adaptation, and survival is Steven Spielberg's 1987 inspiring, moving adaptation (to use the word in a sense other than psychological) of J. G. Ballard's novel *Empire of the Sun*. Christian Bale plays a young, pampered British schoolboy in Shanghai who proves to be adaptable, heroic, and unconquerable, and so manages to survive World War II.

addict/addiction/addictive personality: The general psychological term *addictive personality* applies to someone who is dependent on something — whether a substance, an activity, another person, or a thing — and who attaches him or herself, often obsessively and compulsively, to whatever appears to best alleviate suffering and psychic pain. We cannot refer to people who occasionally use drugs such as marijuana for recreational purposes, occasionally take a drink, or even go on a drinking bout, as addicts, because these people are not generally dependent on these substances. Addicts involved in substance abuse are self-destructive (masochistic), usually have low self-esteem, and are acting out conflicts. They are sometimes involved in codependent relationships, in which two or more people are involved in supporting each other's addiction.

One can be addicted not only to substances but also to any kind of sublimated activity, such as collecting things, gambling, religion, work, food, sports, or exercising, sometimes to the point of exhaustion. Sometimes such sublimated activities do betoken more serious emotional problems: Ed Harris in the film *Pollock* (2000) plays the quintessential obsessive, the modern artist Jackson Pollock, destructive and self-destructive, addicted to practicing his art at any price. And one can be addicted to another person, as in the case, for instance, of someone deeply in love. When that love is unrequited, it indicates a masochistic addiction. Some addictive personality types are also stalkers, but these latter are not just addicts; they are obsessive-compulsive sociopaths.

There are whole subcultures that have grown up around drugs and quite a few films and plays on the subject. Among them is *The Trip* (1968), with Peter Fonda as a man taking an LSD trip. Jack Gelber's *The Connection* (1961), shot in black and white in a semidocumentary style, about junkies waiting to secure their heroin "connections," shows the drug culture of the 1960s in a naturalistic manner. Jack Nicholson, Peter Fonda, and Dennis Hopper play motorcycle riders—disaffected alienated youths on a cross-country trip, always getting high on "grass"—in *Easy Rider* (1969), a film considered shocking when it was released. And for further reference, should you have to play anyone involved in the drug culture, see the early, very silly, but amusing antimarijuana film *Reefer Madness* (1938); *Panic in Needle Park* (1971), which deals with heroin addiction; and the 1995 Scottish film about heroin addicts, *Trainspotting*. Frank Sinatra's memorable performance as a junkie in *The Man with the Golden Arm* (1955) is outstanding, in a film about drug addiction that is now a bit dated but was considered very advanced for its time. In *Clean and Sober* (1988), Michael Keaton portrays a drug addict in a rehabilitation program. Keaton thinks he is merely hiding out, because he refuses to admit that he is an addict and has a problem—often the case with addicts.

It seems clear that the legal solution of imprisoning addicts and drug dealers is not only less than efficacious but is actually harmful, provides no solutions, and serves certain political and economic interests more than it does society as a whole. In some countries, addicts can obtain their drug by prescription and must also get treatment for their addiction, which makes more sense than sending them to jail. The criminalization of these substances, driving them underground, simply exacerbates the problem, as was the case with the prohibition of alcohol in the United States in the 1920s, which resulted in the careers of some of the most famous gangsters in history and provided Hollywood with a great deal of cinematic material, and the great gangster characters played by James Cagney and Edward G. Robinson. And in our own day, the drug lords of Colombia and other Central and South American countries and American drug culture have been portrayed in such movies as the exciting action adventure *Clear and Present Danger* (1994) and the graphic, brutal *Traffic* (2000).

Gambling is another common addiction, and you may remember scenes of horse racing in such films as *Seabiscuit* (2003); pool playing in *The Hustler* (1961) or its sequel *The Color of Money* (1986); casino gambling in *Rain Man* (1988), with people sitting bleary-eyed at card or roulette tables, or staring glassily at slot machines of which they automatically pump the arms, putting in coin after coin in an effort to make money or, more likely, to recoup their heavy losses. They are usually not even under the illusion that they will become rich, but they indulge in their self-destructive activity anyway, living in hope that resembles despair. They can hardly be induced to leave their slot machines even to eat: they feel they may strike it lucky at any moment.

If you are called on to play the part of an addict who is a substance abuser, the first thing you have to do, of course, is research the nature of the particular addiction. Is it a physical dependence? Is it an emotional dependency on a non–physically addictive substance? Physical dependence always includes emotional, psychological dependence. What are the manifestations of the addiction—that is, its physical symptoms and behaviors? How does the character justify the addiction to him or herself and others?

How does a person act in various stages of drunkenness or when high on heroin or marijuana? How does the person feel about the addiction—ashamed, for instance, or all right about it; arrogant, defensive, guilty? In *Long Day's Journey into Night*, Mary Tyrone's shame is coupled with the typical self-justification of the addict. Lillian Roth's alcoholism is superbly acted by Susan Hayward in the film *I'll Cry Tomorrow* (1955). There are many other films dealing with alcoholism, among them *Days of Wine and Roses* (1962), about a "lost weekend"—which is also the title of the Academy Award–winning best picture of 1945, *The Lost Weekend*, in which Ray Milland plays an alcoholic insightfully and chillingly; *The Country Girl* (1954); and *Come Back, Little Sheba* (1952).

How do you play drunk? Uta Hagen, who describes how to do this in eminently practical terms in *Respect for Acting*, used to do a superb exercise in class, in which she demonstrated the behavior resulting from the desire for physical control when someone is drunk. People who are drunk do everything in a slower, more controlled fashion than usual. They will set down a glass of whisky very, very carefully—and just miss the table. Hagen created the role of Martha in the original production of Edward Albee's *Who's Afraid of Virginia Woolf?* so memorably and convincingly that it was hard to believe she was not actually drunk through the entire play. It was truly an astonishing performance. And it was even more astounding to think that she was doing it live on stage every night! She talks about her preparation for the role in *Respect for Acting*, and it is well worth reading. You can see the 1966 movie, with Elizabeth Taylor and Richard Burton (almost too strong for the part of the professor who goes along with his wife in everything in their codependent relationship); they both won Oscars.

adjustment: The word *adjustment* means adaptation to one's physical and psychological environment, and includes how someone positions him or herself in relation to immediate or more long-term circumstances. A person may be generally *well adjusted* socially, meaning he or she gets along well in the environment, or *maladjusted,* meaning he or she appears incapable of coping with either changing or stable circumstances. In negative terms, a person who is adjusted may be viewed as too conformist. In *The Shawshank Redemption* (1994), based on a Stephen King story, all the characters have to adjust to their life in prison. This film is a study in morality and ethics as well, and Tim Robbins, Morgan Freeman, and Bob Gunton all make different adjustments and accommodations.

In acting terms, this word is also used to mean changing the way in which an actor approaches a moment or beat in a scene, or even a whole approach to the interpretation of a role. In auditions, an actor may be expected to show how well he or she "takes direction" by instantly accepting and accurately interpreting a director's instruction to "make the following adjustment."

adjustment disorder: a maladaptation to stressful circumstances involving a severe disturbance in the individual's sense of security and well-being, resulting in a failure to assimilate and overcome the anxiety and stress caused by what has happened, and occurring immediately after the circumstance that caused it. Such traumatic horrors as suicide bombings or the taking of schoolchildren in Ossetia by fanatical, psychopathic terrorists can bring on an adjustment disorder on the part of the victims. The disorder can be very long lasting or less severe and temporary, depending on circumstances. If it is long lasting, it may even be characterized as a traumatic neurosis or as a post-traumatic stress disorder (PTSD), much more than simply an adjustment disorder.

affect: The nouns *affect, emotion,* and *feeling* are often used interchangeably, but *affect* means a general constellation of feelings and emotions obtaining in any specific situation, including the unconscious, unperceived part of the emotions as they have "affected" the whole biophysical and psychological system of the individual. These may involve secretions or hormonal discharges into the system, and include reactions that result in behavioral manifestations. Affect is perceived subjectively as pleasurable or unpleasurable, positive or negative. In metapsychological terms, affect refers to the qualitative discharge of psychic energy involved in fulfilling the demands of the drives. Such conditions as manic-depressive or bipolar disorder and severe depression are called *affective disorders.* In acting terms, affects are involved in such actor's considerations as how strongly or passionately a character desires a certain object or objective and how strongly a character plays an action.

Ajase complex: The Japanese pioneer psychoanalyst Heisaku Kosawa (1897–1968), who had been analyzed by Freud himself, interpreted the Buddhist myth of Ajase as illustrating a specifically Japanese Oedipal relationship pattern — which actually might apply equally to many non-Japanese families. The myth concentrates on the ambivalent relationship with the mother, as opposed to the Freudian emphasis on the troubled relationship with the father. In the myth, Prince Ajase draws his sword in rage on his mother when he learns that she had tried to kill him soon after he was born because of a prophecy that he would grow up to kill his father. Ajase is then stricken with guilt. He seeks advice from the Buddha, who comforts him, and Ajase and his mother forgive each other. In some versions of the myth, he has imprisoned his father in order to gain the throne, and they also forgive each other. Forgiveness, reconciliation, anger, ambivalence, guilt, and resentment are important symbolic themes in the myth, which also illustrates the concepts of *amae* (dependence, unwillingness to be separated from the mother, and the desire to be loved passively that all infants experience) and *ningō* (the necessity to put aside personal feelings when they conflict with social obligations). According to Kosawa, the Ajase complex revolves around the tendency of children to be orally dependant on and submissive to the mother. The child growing up and going through the process of individuation resents this dependence and has to resolve the resultant guilt and ambivalence in order to reestablish a healthy mother-child relationship. The mother also has feelings of pre- and post-natal anxiety, resentment, and guilt that she must deal with.

alexithmia (n.); alexithmic (adj.): An affective disorder involving a person's refusal, usually on an unconscious level, to acknowledge somatic and psychological signals that require attending to, such as symptoms of illness. The alexithmic person denies that anything is wrong and will not take medications or see a doctor, even when it is apparent to others that he or she ought to do so. In general, alexithmic people have an incapacity or inability to distinguish clearly among different affective states. In simpler terms, they don't know if they are happy or unhappy, sick or well; they are not ambivalent, just genuinely out of touch with their bodies and themselves generally. They may have symptoms of illness that they do not know what to make of or what to do about. Often, such people are what we would call bores. They dwell on the trivial and the banal, much like those people whom Karen Horney described as neurotically involved in the lifestyle she calls *shallow living*. And we describe such people as robotic or automatons, both in their relationships with others, with whom there is a kind of automatic quality, and in relation to themselves as they mechanically go about the unvarying routines of their daily lives. Any variation in routine, which might be cause for alarm in some neurotics, leaves people with alexithmia simply blank and unresponsive. They may take time to adjust, but they do, because one routine is much like another to them. One cinematic character who seems alexithmic is Henry, the childlike gardener played with a blank smile by Peter Sellers in *Being There* (1979). He appears completely lacking in affect and almost autistic. He is unresponsive, blank, and bewildered, as we can see by the expression in his eyes. In an ironic twist, his monosyllabic replies and general failure to respond are taken for wisdom, if not brilliance.

altered ego state: a condition caused by any number of circumstances, of which the result is a change in the ego's perception of itself and consequent disorientation. The ego can adjust and maintain a sense of being intact. The term also applies to the hallucinatory condition induced by such consciousness-altering drugs as LSD, which change not only perception but also moods. Lady Macbeth in the "sleepwalking" scene is in an altered ego state. Macbeth also seems to be in a hysterical altered ego state in his soliloquy "Is this a dagger that I see before me," almost as if he has been projected into another world. And at the end of the play, after he learns of Lady Macbeth's death, his state of mind alters again under the shock, as he muses pessimistically, "Life's but a walking shadow...."

Othello about to murder Desdemona is also in such a state and hardly seems to know what he is doing until afterwards, when it is too late. In George Cukor's 1947 film *A Double Life,* Ronald Colman plays an actor whose roles affect his personality. Othello takes over his life, and he, like the character, does not realize what he is doing but seems to go around in an altered ego state.

amphimixis: The cause of a number of sexual problems, *amphimixis* is the (usually) unconscious equation of excretory—particularly anal—functions with sexual functions and a concomitant unconscious disgust with sex. For more on this subject, read Ferenczi's brilliant analysis in his 1938 classic *Thalassa: A Theory of Genitality.*

"as-if" personality: a particular kind of pathological impostor and liar, whose chameleon-like personality changes with his or her object choice. The concept of this specific sort of impostor was one of Helene Deutsch's most famous contributions to psychoanalysis. "As-if" personalities behave as if they were somebody they are not, but unlike actors playing parts and following the Stanislavsky dictum to behave "as if" things were happening to them for the first time, "as-if" types do not take on personalities and identities at will. Rather, they unconsciously allow another personality to take over, although they remain paradoxically aware of who they really are. They change particularly when they relate to somebody else as an object of attraction and become the person the other wants them to be: if they fall in love with a criminal, for instance, they adopt the lifestyle, attitudes, and personality of a criminal. This character type is severely disturbed, and the hallmark of these people is the ability to seem as if they are sincere, whereas they are really a kind of pathological liar who does not believe a word they utter. They are completely untrustworthy and hard to detect. And they are unlike simple impostors, who are often confidence tricksters and criminals well aware of their real identities, or more complicated instances of impostors — disturbed people who have to aggrandize their fragile self-image by means of their particular imposture.

In *Emotional Growth,* (1971), Phyllis Greenacre explains Deutsch's concept: The psychological basis of the "as-if" imposture derives from an interference with the spontaneous childhood development of reality testing, because of the paramount need to please others, even to the point of lying in order to obtain affection. These people unconsciously identify with the person from whom they need affection, usually their parents — not in the way children usually identify with their parents, trying to emulate them so as to gain approval, but rather in order to ward off their fear of their parents, whom they emulate and lie to out of resentment and, in extreme cases, terror. In other words, their approach to reality is through the other person, rather than being direct. Their adult imposture is a kind of acting out of the twisted, encoded message, "This is what I went through in my childhood. Understand and pity me, or love me, although I can't believe you love me, any more than 'they' did, because you, like 'they,' are loving someone I am not, so it is not really me you or they can love, because you can never know the real me." The "as-if" person who can never admit who he or she really is or give up his or her adopted persona is actually a species of psychopath.

"As-if" personalities are masters of manipulating other people to their own ends. Their will to power is exceptionally strong and overwhelming. Bette Davis in *A Stolen Life* (1946) takes the place of her twin sister. The character is very close to the "as-if" personality, forced as she is to live a lie once she has made her choice. *All About Eve* (1950) provides another example, in the ambitious liar and schemer played by Anne Baxter as Eve Harrington, who assumes a name and a persona, posing as a naïve, adoring fan in order to inveigle herself into Bette Davis's life and take her place as a star in the theater. She molds herself into exactly the person Bette Davis wants her to be. The implication of a homosexual attachment is understated but present nonetheless. In fact, she is all things to all people, as circumstance requires, and she uses sexuality as a weapon to get what she wants. The film begins with her acceptance of the prestigious Sarah Siddons award and flashes back to show us how she got there. She used and betrayed all the people who had befriended her out of sympathy, for whom she had played the waif, the stray in need of love and protection.

Matt Damon as the pathological Tom Ripley in *The Talented Mr. Ripley* (1999) plays an impecunious young man who, through a chain of events that he sets in motion because he can't help lying in order to bolster his image in others' eyes, ends up not only committing a series of murders but also masquerading elaborately as Dicky Greenleaf, the first of his victims. He hadn't planned to kill Greenleaf, with whom he was in love, but he loses his temper and commits a crime of passion. Essentially, he wanted to be Greenleaf, whose persona he assumes after the murder, although he actually has passed himself off as Greenleaf earlier. Obliged to weave a continual web of deception in order to survive, he enmeshes himself increasingly in the necessities of adjusting in order to maintain his "as-if" personality, as one lie and one murder lead to another. In a classic "as-if" maneuver, he behaves to the women in his life as he thinks they would wish, so that he is sweet Tom Ripley to Marge (Gwyneth Paltrow), Dicky's fiancée, and the sophisticated Dicky to Meredith (Cate Blanchett). In a sequel, *Ripley's Game* (2002) — in which John Malkovich plays an older Ripley, who has never been caught for the murders he committed — Ripley is no longer masquerading as Greenleaf, but he continues his psychopathic, manipulative behavior.

Matt Damon's characterization of Tom Ripley is particularly interesting: he seems so innocent and presents himself so charmingly and ingratiatingly. The exterior persona is altogether sweet, and as audience members, we actually sympathize with him until he commits murder. And even then, the reaction tends to be one of "Oh, this poor guy is so sick — if only he would get professional help!" Ripley feels trapped and cannot see his way out of the dilemma he has created. He justifies everything to himself from the beginning when he tells his first lie to Dicky Greenleaf's parents about being a Princeton graduate and a classmate of his. A talented pianist, he meets them at a private recital party where he has been asked to accompany the singer, but he is actually an impoverished washroom attendant at a concert hall and cannot bear the humiliation of telling the truth. He simply falls naturally into telling that first lie, which seems harmless enough because we don't yet know him or what he is capable of; probably, neither does he. We can all sympathize with Tom Ripley at first, but we have a growing sense of horror as Ripley goes from crime to crime, unable to stop himself.

An even more disturbing, indeed terrible, "as-if" personality is the bizarre, outwardly ordinary character Jean-Marie Faure, played by Daniel Auteuil in the film *L'adversaire* (2002), based on an almost unbelievable, appalling true story. Faure (the real person was named Romand) passed himself off as a doctor but spent his days sitting in roadside car parks or cafeterias doing nothing, deceiving everyone he knew. Inevitably, suspicion was aroused. When he was about to be unmasked, unable to bear the ignominy and shame and what he knew would be the look of incredulity, anger, and disappointment in the eyes of those he knew, he murdered his wife and children and his parents, and then tried to kill himself by setting fire to his house. He had constructed an entire edifice of lies, a tangled web of deception, and once he began lying, he simply couldn't stop. He absolutely had to pass himself off as the respectable, hard-working medical doctor everyone thought he would become and took him to be. For years nobody suspected a thing. Having been told all his life that he was brilliant and would be a great success, he deeply needed to be perceived as brilliant by others, when he was in reality a complete failure in his own eyes. He dared not reveal the truth for fear of being despised and falling apart, and yet inside he had already collapsed and just didn't know how to get out of the trap he had set for himself. He was empty and hollow at the core of his being. Along with his enormous, deeply wounded narcissism, he had an extraordinary lack of affect and an incapacity to enter into real relationships with anybody—even the wife he pretended to love and perhaps did on some level, and to whom he revealed nothing of the truth, or the best friend with whom he had been to medical school and to whom he had lied about passing the medical exams he had failed. Even more extraordinary, he was completely unable ever to feel depressed about any of this, according to a psychiatrist interviewed on the subject on the DVD. Had he only been able to experience real depression and seek help, his story might have turned out very differently.

Phyllis Greenacre's very interesting essay "The Impostor" in *Emotional Growth* discusses "as-if" personalities as part of the general picture and distinguishes the diffuse nature of their imposture from that of more focused impostors.

association: in psychological terms, any functional bond between two or more separate aspects of a situation, such as an association of a particular food with a particular event. Proust's Narrator in *In Search of Lost Time* swallows a spoonful of tea with crumbs of madeleine in it and involuntarily awakens memories of childhood, for example. Associations may be conscious or unconscious. An association may be a substitution or, to use Uta Hagen's later term, a transference of emotion from one's own life into that of the character's, thus lending the character reality. Actors might ask what associations the character makes when food is mentioned—or sex or love.

autosuggestion: 1) an image, idea, or affirmation about oneself, which may be destructive or constructive and is believed to be true, so that it becomes true over the course of time, like a self-fulfilling prophecy; the result that one brings about unconsciously in order to prove to the self that one has been right about the prophecy, then leads one to believe the prophecy has been true after all; 2) a simplistic system of affirming to oneself something one wishes were true, such as the famous "Every day in every way I am getting better and better."

behaviorism: a school of psychology that rejects all cognitive or psychoanalytical approaches to understanding human behavior in favor of a biophysiological, deterministic, mechanistic view of human beings, who are seen essentially as responding to conditioning. Sexuality is considered only in its hormonal—that is, its biological and physical—manifestations, and is seen as a set of conditioned responses to stimuli. The best known practitioner and innovator in the field of behaviorism was its founder, the American B. F. Skinner (1904–90).

bipolar disorder: This affective disorder, characterized by alternation between extreme emotional states, used to be called manic-depression. In fact, despite the manic phases some people typically experience, it is basically a depressive disorder, and those subject to it experience anxiety as a major condition of their affective lives. It is a condition that can now be treated with lithium salts (lithium chloride, lithium carbonate), because the major components of this syndrome are known to be physiological, but its underlying construct also responds to psychoanalytic therapy. Atypically, someone afflicted with mania (elation, exhilaration), with severe depression, or alternating between the two (those are the three basic kinds of bipolar disorder), may veer towards the psychotic or have psychotic episodes.

The literature on the subject is vast. In terms of theater or film, the typical romantic-era hero, the passionate Byronic young lover alone on a mountaintop, his long hair blowing in the wind, in love and veering between the extremes of exaltation and elation, fear and joy, pleasure and pain, may be said to typify the syndrome—although that was scarcely the intention of romantic writers. In the 2002 French film made from Benjamin Constant's romantic novel *Adolphe,* the eponymous hero, played by Stanislas Merhar, and his lover, played by Isabelle Adjani, go from one extreme to another of passion and dejection, anger and appeasement, abject despair and exalted ecstasy.

borderline personality disorder: Characteristic of this disorder on the borderline between neurosis and psychosis is a pattern of instability in relationships; a range of shifting affects; and a nebulous, shifting, and unstable self-image. These people tend to alternate between idealizing and devaluing the person they are in a usually intense relationship with, even if it is only a fantasized and not a real relationship. Impulsive behavior is another hallmark of this disorder. Other people are perceived as rejecting. At the basis of this illness is a fear of abandonment, and there is constant manipulation of people and circumstances in an attempt to avoid being abandoned. These people feel hollow and empty at the core and are not in touch with their feelings. They veer at times towards a dissociative, psychotic delusional state, and they can be violent and uncontrolled.

It is possible to classify Solyony in *Three Sisters* as having not only obsessive-compulsive aspects of his character but as actually having a borderline personality disorder. His erratic, sometimes violent, always intense behavior and the fantastic nature of his relationship with Irina, who has no interest in him, would seem to indicate as much. His awkward attempts to be ingratiating fail, and his behavior shifts to sneering, cold hostility. The fear of abandonment and the feeling of being unloved and unlovable would constitute a very good actor's secret.

character: The word *character* originally meant "a letter of the alphabet" and, when used as a verb, "to write." Polonius exhorts Laertes: "…these few precepts in thy memory / Look thou character," or "See that you write these precepts down in your memory."

In psychological terms, the word means the ensemble, taken as a whole, of traits, inner constructs, and typical personal adjustments to internal and external circumstances that result in an individual being the person he or she is and having the specific personality he or she has.

Character gives rise to more or less stable, or at least enduring, habitual patterns of behavior, and includes the way people usually think, feel, react, and act to themselves and to the world. Early reactions to other persons and events—absorbed and, when threatening to the id, repressed—and the resultant components of the superego and ego that have arisen from reactions in the id form character and give rise to traits that we associate with a particular person. These components and traits are the result of compromise formations at various psychosexual developmental stages, and account not only for character in general but also for that specific aspect of character that we usually perceive and describe as someone's *temperament.* Perhaps an inborn disposition, temperament is a person's habitual way of being: someone may be calm and easygoing, for instance, or highly anxious and reactive.

Character traits and patterns of behavior are usually *ego-syntonic*—that is, people are comfortable with themselves and their reactions and behavior. But when people are *ego-dystonic,* or uncomfortable with themselves, the resulting problems can be more or less severe; it is in such cases, for instance, that we speak of someone's having a bad self-image. But most people are ego-syntonic in some areas and ego-dystonic in others.

In theatrical terms, a character is the literary and dramatically realized creation of a fictitious person, written by an author with as much specificity as possible and brought to life by an actor, who infuses the character with his or her own personality and incarnates the person with the help of a director.

codependence: mutual emotional reliance of one person on another. When people who are codependent are separated for a time, they experience more or less acute anxiety. Codependence may be healthy and productive, as it often is in work-related situations that function for mutual benefit, or it may involve a mutually unhealthy addiction of two people to each other. In abusive situations, the unhealthy aspects of codependence may include physical and/or psychological abuse; physical abuse always includes psychological abuse. It can be extremely difficult to end an unhealthy codependent relationship, because both parties are emotionally invested in it. When Nora in Ibsen's *A Doll's House* ends her codependent relationship with her husband, it is a shock to both of them. In the film *The Hours* (2002), codependency informs the entire psychological basis of the characters' relationships.

In any relationship you are writing or acting, how much is one person dependent on another? In other words, how much does one person need the other? In *Three Sisters,* Vershinin leaves with his regiment because he has to and because he is more dependent on his life in the army than on his love for Masha. In fact, Vershinin and his unpleasant, demanding wife (an offstage character much discussed), whom he no longer loves, have a codependent relationship, in part because of their children, and he will not leave her, showing that there is a something in him of the self-destructive but also of the honorable.

cognitive psychology: Very important and influential in contemporary thinking in many fields, *cognitive psychology,* with its various branches, is the study of mental processes, which include thinking, reasoning, deduction and inference, logic, analyzing error, rationalization, mental representations, language and psycholinguistics, ideas, beliefs, motives, attention, intentions, intentionality, and the nature of memory. There are three important types of memory: *episodic*, which is the memory of actual events; *semantic*, which is the memory of the sorts of "scripts" Silvan S. Tomkins talks about (how we talk to ourselves, what we say, and why we say it) and that has to do with interpersonal relations and what we tell ourselves about them; and *procedural*, prelinguistic, nonverbal memories of infantile experiences. Memories in this latter category are something few people remember with any specificity, but we know they have left their mark because that is apparent in current behavior, relationships, and the way we see the world around us (trustingly, suspiciously, etc.). Memory can be distorted, falsified, or invented; in the latter case, events from episodic memory appear to be real but are not. These distortions or inventions may be pathological.

Like all schools of psychology, which each have their own ideas on the subject, cognitive psychology, too, studies motivational theory. See reactance theory on page 211 for a specific cognitive motivational theory, derived from Leon Festinger's influential *cognitive dissonance theory* (detailed in his 1957 book *A Theory of Cognitive Dissonance* and researched and elaborated on by many others). The simple basis of the theory is that pairs of cognitions (perceptions, thoughts, ideas, or other elements of knowledge) are either relevant to each other or irrelevant. If they are relevant to each other, they may be consonant or dissonant. If relevant cognitions are consonant with one another, the person feels comfortable. If they are dissonant, people are uncomfortable, and they avoid confronting or even knowing about the dissonant element that arouses their anxiety. Information that would tend to increase the dissonance and the anxiety is avoided. But the person is under (self-imposed) pressure to reduce the dissonance. Festinger uses the example of a smoker, who learns that smoking is bad but cannot or does not wish to stop smoking. The dissonant cognitions must be resolved somehow. This can be done by bringing cognitions into line with each other and making them consonant: the smoker could decide to wish to stop smoking, for instance. Or the relevance of one of the dissonant cognitions could be minimized: the smoker might decide that health risks are less important than the pleasure of smoking. Resistance to change can be strong and depends in part on the amount of pain and anxiety that someone has to go through in order to effect a change in cognitive perceptions. There must be a strong incentive or gain in order to change one's behavior. As an actor, writer, or director, you can readily see how such questions could be relevant.

Behavior can be explained at least in part as a direct result of all the mental processes listed above. Decision making, for instance, based in whatever motivations may underlie it, leads from the internal mental process of thinking and deciding to its externalization as behavior. People have certain expectations (*expectancy theory*) about the possible results of their cognitive processes. Some of the questions cognitive psychologists ask are: How do we know what we know? How do we process information? How do we retain the knowledge we acquire? How do we recognize someone or something? How do we retrieve memories? How do we form concepts of space and time? What is the nature of consciousness?

Cognitive psychologists distinguish between *deep* and *shallow processing* of information. Shallow processing leaves fragile memory traces, which is why it is easy to forget vocabulary in another language or what you had for dinner the night before. Deep processing, on the other hand, leaves more lasting memory traces, because the acquired knowledge has real meaning to the person who has learned it and who has given the learning process sustained attention.

In the version of social cognitive theory proposed by Canadian Albert Bandura (born 1925), people are seen as the agents of their own actions, not as simply reactive or influenced by the environment. There are internal, learned models of events that are among the determining factors in how a person makes decisions regarding similar events. Motivation in the decision-making process is based on incentives of various kinds. For Bandura, psychoanalysis and behaviorism, which are at opposite theoretical poles, are both limited in scope, and both are incomplete explanations of human behavior.

The highly influential Swiss child psychologist Jean Piaget (1896–1980), who studied how we acquire and retain knowledge, was particularly interested in the cognitive development of children. He distinguished four stages in their growth from infancy to adulthood:

1. The sensorimotor period, lasting until about the age of two, when the child learns to perceive and to coordinate reflexes and muscles, but does not yet really think;

2. The period of preoperational thought, lasting from about two until about age six or seven, when the child learns language and representational skills, and is narcissistically self-involved;

3. The period of concrete operations, lasting from six until approximately eleven or twelve, when the child begins to realize the point of view of other people, learns to solve concrete problems, and is beginning to reason abstractly as well;

4. The period of formal operations, which lasts from about eleven through adulthood, when the child learns to reason abstractly and theoretically, and to make decisions independently. People's learning and acquisition of knowledge does not stop, but their way of looking at things may be pretty well set during the early part of this stage.

Although less concerned with character and personality than with mental operations and processes that may or may not lead to behavior, cognitive psychology is nevertheless useful for actors, writers, and directors. If you are creating the character of a detective in a mystery story, of which there are so many in television series and in movies, it is very important to understand the processes of deductive and inductive reasoning, logic, and inference in order to make the character real and convincing. In any case, for all characters the following questions are useful: How does my character think? Is my character good at reasoning things out? Does my character have a sense of logic? What areas of knowledge or expertise does my character possess? Is my character clever or dull when it comes to understanding what is going on around him or her? How quickly does my character grasp the meaning of events? Is my character capable of thinking quickly in an emergency? Is my character flexible or rigid when it comes to thinking things through? Can my character convince others by using logic? Can my character be convinced or persuaded to change his or her point of view?

Attention, including getting and keeping attention, is another area cognitive psychology studies: What does the character pay attention to? How concentrated is the attention? Does the character appear to be paying attention to something while really paying attention to something else? Is the character easily distracted? How does your character get others' attention? Does your character need attention? How does your character hold the attention of others?

One of the concepts explored by cognitive psychologists is *rehearsal,* both *maintenance rehearsal* and *elaborative rehearsal,* which are internal mental processes that help us remember something. In maintenance rehearsal, a person simply repeats by rote information that has been acquired. Or someone may repeat a series of actions—such as a proposal of marriage, as Lomov in Chekhov's *Marriage Proposal* does so that he will not forget what he has planned. In elaborative rehearsal, something that needs to be remembered is given a structure, such as a series of numbers that are memorized, as someone's phone number.

In cognitive psychotherapy, the therapist wants to know the patient's cognitions, including among other things what thoughts are at the core of any conflict or problem, what automatic thoughts arise in various situations with regard to the problem, and what the patient's assumptions are regarding those situations. An actor or writer might ask similar questions. What does the character assume about his or her situations and about the other characters in the play? What are the character's automatic thought responses, and where do they come from? What is the core thought that gives rise to them?

compensation/overcompensation: making up for some loss or absence, or perceived deficiency or shortcoming. For Freud, compensation was an important basic defense mechanism, in which people prevent the knowledge of their deficiencies in a particular area from filtering through to consciousness. They do not want to acknowledge their shortcomings, and they build up a self-image that allows them to be in a state of denial. Helmer in *A Doll's House* thinks consciously that he is a good, principled, loving husband. He treats his wife like a child, and his lack of respect, not to say his unconscious contempt, for her intellect and personality is hidden from him by the compensatory thought—which is not simply compensation, but rather narcissism and denial—that she loves him and that he provides her with everything she needs, which he certainly and obviously does not do on an emotional level, even if they are materially comfortable enough.

For Adler, compensation was a way of overcoming the inferiority complex. He talks of the *masculine protest* that he feels exists in every woman, because women are born into a society that makes men important and gives them power. Women compensate for this in various ways, either by asserting their own aggressiveness and taking power themselves, or else by backing away from power and retreating into the home.

It is often said—perhaps inaccurately—that blind people compensate for their lack of sight by developing a more acute sense of hearing, and deaf people for their lack of auditory sensation by a more developed visual sense. In emotional terms, a person may compensate or overcompensate for a loss, such as that of a loved one, whether that person has been lost through death or separation. For instance, overcompensation might involve someone's sliding into alcoholism or drug addiction, rather than simply compensating for the loss by taking up activities that might prevent sitting around and being miserable. People who overcompensate overshoot the mark; they do more than is necessary to make up for any deficiency or perceived inferiority. An office worker who thinks he or she is inferior in the job may volunteer for endless hours of exhausting overtime and run to fetch coffee for the boss even when not asked to do so. An overcompensatory person is usually overanxious and tense, nervous and insecure.

defensiveness: an acute oversensitivity to criticism or to insults or slights, real or perceived, giving rise to an overreaction; touchiness. Responses vary from hostile, hurt silence to more violent reactions of anger and rage, including the desire for revenge, whether immediate or long planned. Tom Ripley in Liliana Cavani's film of Patricia Highsmith's *Ripley's Game* is an example of an extremely defensive psychopath, who bides his time before carrying out an elaborate revenge for a minor insult—a revenge that he then tries to undo because he has received sufficient recompense from his victim. John Malkovich, for whom Ripley's defensiveness was only one deadly trait in a brilliantly observed portrayal of his psychopathic personality, played the role with uncanny reality.

deference behavior: sociologist Erving Goffman's phrase. This behavior comes from an attitude of subservience or even servility towards people considered superior to the self, whether because of the hierarchal position they occupy in relation to the deferent person or for some other perceived reason. It is a kind of unconscious role-playing. The question is often asked in theatrical productions: How do we know the king is the king? And the answer is that we know because of the way other people treat him. There is a conscious consent to play the role assigned, which includes treating someone with deference if he or she is in a position of authority. If everybody were to treat the king disrespectfully, you would have a different play, perhaps one about a revolution, which happens when the authority figures are deemed unworthy of respect and perceived as not fulfilling their duties, and/or as being corrupt and undeserving.

dehumanization (n.); dehumanize (v.): the process of viewing someone as less than a person, less than a human being, someone without feelings and desires, a thing. For the Canadian psychologist Albert Bandura, this was an important cognitive process that explained a great deal about the way prejudice functions. Dehumanization is a necessary phenomenon when a person wishes to bend another to his or her will or to commit murder: the victim must first be dehumanized and is then seen as someone deserving no consideration. The ability to dehumanize, a hallmark of the psychopath, is a component of the psychological makeup of historical and contemporary psychopathic murderers and terrorists, who kill indiscriminately. To view the victims as pestilential objects and therefore no more deserving of consideration—let alone life—than vermin such as lice, cockroaches, or rats (a metaphor constantly employed by the dehumanizer) would seem to be a necessary concomitant of the ability to carry out the individual and mass murders of people of all ages and both genders. Ordinary human impulses of compassion, empathy, and sympathy are deadened and, indeed, completely absent in such inhuman human beings, who have simply become monsters and are killing machines. On the most superficial but deeply believed level, the killers justify their actions internally for various delusional ideological reasons that are divorced from any semblance of commonly accepted rules of ethics or morality, and are completely self-serving. The killings essentially accomplish nothing except to cause outrage, horror, misery, and deep grief and mourning for the victims. Survivors of these kinds of events and the families of the victims suffer terribly for the rest of their lives.

delusion: As distinguished from an *illusion,* which is a mistaken perception that something is true when it is untrue (although it may possibly be true, and one can understand why people believe in certain illusions, whether philosophical or optical, as in magic tricks), a *delusion* is a belief in something that is patently untrue, at least to everybody who does not share the delusion. It may be part of a person's neurosis or a manifestation of psychosis.

The *DSM-IV-TR* lists seven kinds of delusions in its category of *delusional personality disorder,* not classified as schizophrenic, which is a psychosis deliberately excluded from this class of disorders: *erotomanic,* in which someone believes that "another person, usually of higher status, is in love" with him or her; *grandiose*—that is, having delusions of grandeur (see below); *jealous,* in which a person believes that his or her "sexual partner is unfaithful"; *persecutory,* which can be the delusion that a particular individual is "out to get me"; *somatic,* in which someone believes hypochondriacally that he or she has a medical condition, such as cancer, or something else that is wrong with the body; *mixed,* meaning that someone may have two or more of the above delusions; and *unspecified,* which covers everything else you might think of.

Delusions can take all forms, from mild paranoia to a more severe dissociative disturbance, such as a belief that everyone is out to do harm. Some people have delusions of grandeur, thinking themselves wealthier or more brilliant than they are, or having convinced themselves that they are actually of aristocratic origin and will be recognized some day as the duke or count of something or other, even though they are now as poor as church mice. Others think they are Napoleon or Jesus Christ. In Joseph Kesselring's *Arsenic and Old Lace,* one of the Brewster brothers thinks he is President Teddy Roosevelt. The irrational nature of such beliefs is readily apparent, but the deluded have convinced themselves of the truth of their conceptions, and nothing will shake the firmness of their beliefs.

Even escapist delusions are a form of self-punishment—Napoleon is being persecuted, and who could be more harshly punished than Jesus Christ? Other well-known persecutory xenophobic, racist, or anti-Semitic delusions involve the idea that evil people belonging to certain groups aim at the destruction of the person harboring the delusion. In this way the deluded person unconsciously punishes him or herself, out of deep feelings of unworthiness and inferiority, and then compensates for that punishment by projecting him or herself as a victim of other people, when it is actually other people who are his victims. Delusions also entail denial—principally of the truth about the external world, perceived inaccurately; and in the kind of denial called self-deception, the deluded person projects his or her own wishes and fears onto an innocent.

depersonalization: a change in self-perception, so that one's usual attitude and orientation to oneself and the world, and the sense of one's place in the world, is lost. The condition is usually temporary, as when one wakes from a dream in unfamiliar surroundings: "Who am I? Where am I?" In a severe form, it may be an aspect of amnesia and require treatment, as in Hitchcock's film *Spellbound* (1945). This phenomenon may include *derealization,* meaning a view of the external world as strange, forbidding, and unfamiliar, if not actually unreal. Depersonalization is a kind of splitting off of the consciousness of the self, so that someone is simultaneously a detached observer of him or herself and the person being observed. Not surprisingly, one of the symptoms is dizziness. Parts of the body may seem to have changed and not belong to the person who is in this state. The observing part of the person is stronger than the observed and takes over, so that one performs actions as in a waking dream. Depersonalization also occurs in situations of danger and constitutes a denial of the menace: "I am not really in this situation; it is somebody else. Can that really be me out there?" People who are ordinarily well adjusted and stable may be shocked into depersonalization in unusual situations. For instance, someone on a battlefield who has been shot and is traumatically shocked may experience depersonalization. Certain other kinds of situations may also give rise to depersonalization: a person doing something out of the ordinary, such as participating in certain sexual acts that had been forbidden by the interplay of ego, superego, and id and been disavowed, may experience depersonalization: "It is not I but somebody else who is doing these things." Or someone may commit a murder, especially a crime of passion, and feel depersonalized, even as they are cleaning up the scene of the crime in an attempt to escape its consequences: "I can't remember having done that. It was somebody else. What is going on here? What am I doing?" A drug-induced high may also cause such a temporary disorientation as well as derealization. An example of depersonalization from theatrical literature is the famous "sleepwalking" scene from Shakespeare's *Macbeth,* in which Lady Macbeth appears to be sleeping but is really in a kind of depersonalized waking dream of herself, one that will not go away, unlike most phenomena of depersonalization.

detachment: a lack of emotional involvement in any given situation or with regard to another person. In Karen Horney's interpretation, detachment is a defense mechanism that prevents someone from forming an intimate, bonded relationship. With detachment, a sense of aloofness is maintained, and that sense acts to preserve a person's freedom. Detachment may also entail a lack of empathy, as well as downright insensitivity to others. The character of Doctor Chebutykin in *Three Sisters* is deliberately as uninvolved as he can be, but his detachment results from his deep disappointment in love, and he lives in the past, as is apparent from the few allusions he makes to his unfulfilled love for the mother of the three sisters. His defense against his deep hurt has caused him to maintain a cynical attitude toward life in general and never to seek out another relationship. When he is drunk, his true feelings emerge: "In vino veritas," as he says. Detachment, depending on circumstances, can be a perfectly rational solution to a problem; or it may be a neurotic response to a situation, as in the case of Chebutykin, whose solutions to problems are based entirely on previous disappointments—the rationality of the neurotic. He takes no risks, and his disengagement from everything leads to disastrous consequences: he probably had the power to stop the duel between Solyony and Tusenbach, but he chose to do nothing except sit it out.

effeminate: In contrast to the word *feminine,* which usually has desirable connotations applied to women, the word *effeminate* is usually applied to males, and means having the behavioral characteristics and comportment associated with females in any given society or sociocultural setting. It carries the pejorative, denigrating connotation of weak, willowy, and cowardly, showing the idea's male-chauvinist, patriarchal origins. So-called effeminate men are often thought to be homosexuals, but this is not always so, and so-called effeminacy, including cross-dressing, is not a good indicator of sexual preference. It remains a mystery to me why the characteristic limp wrist and wilting, drooping manner, as well as a mincing walk, raised eyebrow, tilted head, and lisp should be thought of as typically female—except, as stated above, for prejudicial male chauvinist reasons. I don't know women who act that way, and I can hardly associate such characteristics with them. Effeminate mannerisms can be a conscious way of joking among some homosexuals. So-called effeminacy has been an offensive cliché indicating homosexuality in Hollywood, where certain character actors such as Franklin Pangborn or Clifton Webb were known for their "effeminate" characteristics, which were a kind of code. It was never overtly stated that they were gay, but it was up the audience to understand that they were. The audience usually did and often found them amusing, and at the same time felt superior to these men, whom they perceived as being less than "real" men, because they were feminized. In some quarters, the cliché still persists.

emotion: This word is surprisingly nebulous and diffuse in its meanings, and consequently difficult to define. It means literally a "movement outward," from Latin *emovere.* Emotions are feelings aroused by external and/or internal stimuli. They are responses to those stimuli arising from the depths of the unconscious. The word is usually not applied to purely physical responses, such as feelings of hunger, but to psychological responses. For instance, a person may respond to hunger with pleasurable anticipation of a meal about to be served or with disgust at some dish that he or she dislikes.

failure neurosis: René Laforgue's term—based on an idea of Freud's—for a disturbance in functionality characterized by the inability to accept success, due to underlying feelings that one is undeserving and unworthy, and the consequent self-destructive behavior that ensures someone's downfall after they have achieved something they desired. Many a tragic hero in Shakespearean and other plays suffers from this neurosis.

family neurosis: René Laforgue's term for a disturbance in families where individual neuroses complement each other and have a pathological influence on all the family members, particularly when neurotic parents impact their children, who then become neurotic in turn. Ibsen's *Hedda Gabler* and *A Doll's House,* particularly the relationships between the daughters and their fathers, and Chekhov's *Three Sisters* provide examples.

family romance: the common enough escapist childhood fantasy that one is the offspring of another family, rather than of the disappointing family one was supposedly born into. Such fantasies may indicate the child's desire to escape unpleasant circumstances. They attribute low status to the parents, but they may also indicate the unconscious wish to restore the parents to their original ideal status as demigods. In addition, these idealized corrective fantasies may include the unconscious desire to overcome the incest taboo. These fantasies have their origin in the Oedipus complex.

feeling: *Feeling* can be distinguished from *emotion* as being a sensory impression, which may give rise to emotion, which is the reaction to the impression. But the word *feeling* is also generally used to refer to a state of being—such as happiness, euphoria, depression, sadness, or misery—in which case the word means an affective state including emotions. A third meaning is that of a general idea, intuition, impression or notion about something, as in the sentence, "I have a feeling something is about to happen."

fixation: specific obsessions to which the ego has attached itself. Any number of characters in theatrical literature have fixations, from Iago to Uncle Vanya. Iago is fixated on his revenge against Othello, even though Othello has not done anything at all to Iago that calls for revenge. Vanya has become fixated on Yelena as a love object.

gender identity/gender nonconformity: the identification by a person of him or herself as belonging to a particular gender (masculine or feminine), which involves assuming the roles and behavior socioculturally associated with the person's biological sex. But there are people who are physiologically masculine or feminine but who identify so strongly psychologically with the opposite gender that they behave in the sociocultural manner associated with that gender, in some cases dressing like persons of the gender they psychologically identify with and, in fewer cases, going so far as to have a physical operation to change their gender physiologically. There are terrible prejudices against people who do not conform to societal "norms," and the consequences can be horrible indeed. There have been several films on the topic. *Soldier's Girl* (2003) is based on the true, heartbreaking story of a young soldier who falls in love with a woman who is a transgendered cabaret performer, biologically a man who will later have a sex change operation. The uncomprehending, bigoted reactions of his army buddies cause him immense suffering and lead to his death. The tragic, wrenching true story of a young girl who felt she was really a boy and lived as one, trying to make a life with her soul mate, and what she suffered until murder put an end to her misery at the hands of trailer-trash bigots among whom she lived in rural Nebraska, is heartbreakingly brought to life in *Boys Don't Cry* (1999), with an unforgettable, deeply moving performance by Hilary Swank. The transvestite homosexual character Dil, played by Jaye Davidson, in *The Crying Game* (1992), set in Northern Ireland, is also notable, and the film is worth seeing for its compassionate look at the problems some people face. Another film dealing with gender identity is *Yentl* (1983), based on an Isaac Bashevis Singer story. Barbara Streisand plays a young woman from an ultra-Orthodox Jewish background who wants to become a yeshiva student and study the Talmud, which is the province of males only. She successfully disguises herself as a young man and pursues her studies.

group psychology: As far as Freud was concerned, individual and social or group psychology did not have severely marked boundaries, because, for one thing, an individual from the very beginning of life was involved with other people and developed mental models of others who could be inspirational and helpful or inimical, an object of love or hate. We are always in the realm of group psychology. It is clear that individuals are born into groups and acculturated into their surroundings. Nevertheless: "The contrast between social and narcissistic...mental acts falls wholly within the domain of individual psychology."

It also appeared true to Freud that a member of a group (which could be the individual's family) is subject to influences from other people in the group that alter his or her mental activity. In the course of this process, feeling or affect dominates and intellect recedes, as the person gives in to suggestion. Freud asked why this should be so. His answer was that leaders of groups have prestige in the eyes of their followers, who therefore act on suggestions from the leaders. But why do we not react in the opposite way? Why do we give in to this phenomenon (of course, we don't always), which Freud characterizes as contagious? He concludes that giving in to suggestion is actually a primitive phenomenon, a survival from humanity's past—and groups are often perceived as behaving primitively in crowds or mobs. Giving in to suggestion comes about due to the functioning of the libido and its primitive narcissism, which is then transferred onto the leader of the group.

In *Group Psychology and the Analysis of the Ego* (1921), from which most of the quotations in this section come, Freud distinguishes several kinds of groups: temporary and long lasting, homogeneous and unhomogeneous, natural and artificial (the church and the army being two cases in point), "primitive and highly organized."

Artificial groups depend on some external force to keep them together. In the case of the church, it is faith in Christ and his love for all, and the principles of the religion—love for one's neighbor, equality before God, etc.—that are inculcated from a very early age. In the case of the army, it is the state and political necessity that watch over the formation of the group. In both cases, people have very little choice as to their actions within the group. Those who watch over the group do not often tolerate deviations from its principles, and the individual's needs are subsumed in the group's needs to preserve its coherence and efficient functioning.

There are groups with leaders and groups without leaders. When there is a leader, each individual in the group has "introduced" the leader into his or her superego, and on this basis, they have each "identified themselves with one another in their ego," as Freud says in *New Introductory Lectures on Psycho-Analysis*. The group's functioning well depends on the group members sharing the illusion (and for Freud, it is perforce an illusion) that the leader loves each one of them equally and has their best interests at heart. Such is the case with the church and the army, where the faithful have to respect and trust their priests and the soldiers have to revere and trust their commanders. These leaders are father substitutes, so that there is an unconscious necessity to obey, partly out of fear of punishment. An atavistic "herd instinct," if it exists, is possibly based in contemporary society on children's fears of being left alone, and the group appears in general to be a revival of the primitive horde, but "individual psychology must be just as old as group psychology." It is also important to bear in mind that in contemporary society, "each individual is a component of many groups," and that people are capable of rising above their groups and being more or less independent, original, and creative. And as a most important final generalization, adherence to a group requires the play of the libido, which is sublimated and based on early identifications with objects (the boy identifying with and wanting to be like his father, the girl identifying with and wanting to be like her mother) and later Oedipal adjustments, with their ambivalences.

The British Kleinian psychoanalyst Wilfred R. Bion (1897–1981), expanding on Freud's ideas, made great contributions to the study of groups, not only about their collective psychology but also about the dynamics and functioning of individuals and of leadership and authority within groups. Bion held that individuals could only be understood in the context of the groups within which they lived. For a group to exist, members have to come together through an awareness of their common relationship. He theorized that there were two ideas prevalent in any group: the *work-group modality* and the *basic-assumptions style*. In the work group modality, the task of the group is defined, and everyone agrees as to the purpose and necessity of accomplishing the task. And the group's members are called on to cooperate with one another in order to effect that end. The group's valid purpose and the necessity to cooperate in fulfilling it are two of the basic assumptions operative in every group. The assumptions also include such mundane matters as obeying established rules, including those governing polite manners; or how to behave with other members, how to dress for the task in hand, and what the hierarchical nature of the group is, whether it is a large or small group, a club, a political or religious entity, a business enterprise, or the like. The group has to provide for the collective and individual security and safety of its members, and for defense against external threats of whatever kind, whether natural or man-made. The group is thus greater than the sum of its parts, and it has a life of its own.

Why, then, does the "work" group not always conduct itself according to the work-group modality, the necessity of group survival, and the basic assumptions? Why are the dynamics within a group seldom perfect, so that members of the group often interfere with the accomplishment of the task or perform inefficiently? Bion's theory of groups holds that there are several dynamics at work in any group, which has its overt aspect—the accomplishment of the task, survival, and so forth—and its hidden, covert aspects. These latter are based on the fantasies of the individual members of the group and their individual needs and desires, and serve to focus the group inward upon itself, rather than outward, and to interfere with the basic assumptions set up at the outset.

The dynamics of any group include:

1. *Dependency,* which has three aspects: the first being that everyone depends on everyone else to do the jobs assigned to them; the second being that everyone depends on a leader, who is thus open to hostility and criticism that may be based in part on unresolved Oedipal complexes and the difficulty some individuals have in dealing with authority; and the third being a dynamic in which the individual's unconscious needs are asserted and acted out with other members of the group, so that although a sense of bonding is created with one or more members, a member may be perceived by others as demanding or obnoxious in some way. The bonding may not be shared by all members of the group or may be rejected by some. Cliques may form, or a disliked member may be partially excluded, either of which interferes with a group's functioning as a whole entity.

2. *Fight/Flight,* in which, for various reasons, the survival of the group is seen as depending on either fighting an outside force or fleeing from it. Members of a group may disagree internally and fight or quarrel with each other, and then take flight from each other, which also interferes with group functioning.

3. *Pairing,* which is similar to dependency but may happen for reasons other than the need to depend on another member, and has to do with the need for affection, resulting in a relationship between two members, whether a man and a woman, two women, or two men.

Any or all of these dynamics may obtain at any given time and may interfere with efficient group functioning in furtherance of accomplishing the task the group has set itself.

Another of the dynamics of groups consists of what is called the basic assumption of *oneness,* or the belief (which may be psychotic and delusional, as in the case of the Nazis) that the group is striving after a higher purpose, is superior to other groups, and is united forever in its wholeness. Each individual may more or less subscribe to this belief, or keep quiet within the group if he or she doesn't. This belief entails an unshakable, irrational faith in the group's goals and task and, often, an idealization of an all-powerful group leader. Examples from the history of nations abound.

Sociologist Erving Goffman's books dealing with group psychology and the engagement of the individual in groups are listed in the bibliography. In *The Presentation of Self in Everyday Life* (1959), he describes how people alter their personalities when in the presence of other people and how they perform, in a theatrical sense. The following observations of Goffman's are quite useful for writers and actors: When somebody first enters the presence of another person, they do one of two things. Either they immediately seek information about the other person, especially if it is someone they are encountering for the first time, or they remember information they already have and bring it "into play." This is particularly important to keep in mind when writing exposition. Too often we hear people telling each other information they have in common, and that always strikes audiences as particularly unreal. Also, people usually seek information for quite practical reasons, and they develop expectations based on the information they acquire. And they interpret clues about who the other person is based on their impressions of that person's appearance, behavior, manners, and general comportment. The information can only be very general at first, but of course further acquaintance supplies much that was perforce unknown, if indeed the person is telling the truth.

A person always wants something from another person—this is axiomatic for actors—even if it is only for a stranger on the subway in New York to keep his or her distance, for example, or to be quiet during the showing of a movie. This is a negative kind of wanting, to be sure, but it contains within itself the potential for action, such as changing one's seat.

Directors might bear all of the above information in mind when dealing with the group known as a cast in rehearsal situations, as well as when analyzing the plot of a play. *The Closet* (2001) is a hilarious, wryly satiric film that takes place against the background of a factory where condoms are manufactured and clearly shows group dynamics as well as individual psychologies. For a different kind of group, the upper-class English school where spies for the USSR revolted against their background and what they saw as the evils of class society, see the fictionalized play and film account *Another Country* (1984). This film is in part about what it means to be an outcast within one's group. The British television miniseries *Cambridge Spies* (2003) is a dramatization of real incidents.

For actors, the following questions should prove useful: In what way or ways is my character involved in whatever groups the character belongs to? What are the relationships within the group, and how do they affect my character? What are the dynamics of the group's functioning? How do I feel about the group? Do I feel part of it or alienated from it? What is my function or task within the group? Do I do it well or badly? Do I feel I have the respect of the other members of the group? Do I respect the other members of the group? *Uncle Vanya* is about a family group, and the relationships in the play depend on each character's attitude towards being a member of the group. In the family council scene in act 3, the characters all come together to hear the proposals of their "group leader," the Professor, and each character has reactions to those proposals that have to do with group functioning and what will happen if the group breaks up. It is at the end of this act that Vanya attempts to shoot the Professor.

illusion: The terms *delusion* and *illusion* are very close in meaning but distinct nevertheless. *Delusions* are cognitive beliefs consisting of irrational constructs that are patently, demonstrably false, whereas *illusions* are perceptions (or misperceptions) that actually could be true but are not, and (like delusions) involve deception and/or self-deception. Both delusions and illusions are the result of the desire to overcome overwhelming fears. The result of this desire is wishful thinking, taken for reality.

impostor: A "very special type of liar," says Phyllis Greenacre; she discusses many famous, intriguing historical impostors in her 1958 essay "The Impostor." *Impostors* are people who pretend to be something they are not and take on another identity, personality, and name. Some impostors are simply confidence tricksters with a flair for acting and assume their chosen identity for purposes of criminal deception or fraud. But there are many examples of another kind of impostor: people with severely disturbed ego disorders who have to aggrandize themselves and appear great in the eyes of others because they appear insignificant and unworthy in their own eyes. Their enterprise is not always criminal, although it may be. The impostor exaggerates his or her status and accomplishments and makes implausible claims in the hope of gaining prestige or some other advantage, whether of a material or ego-gratifying nature. Impostors mask their contempt for what they consider the stupidity of those they manipulate and take advantage of. While impostors are clever, they are often very crude, although they can be great showmen and masters of illusion and con games.

On the other hand, many impostures succeed because the people imposed upon want to believe in the imposture. For instance, an eligible, wealthy young lady may wish to believe that the handsome but impecunious young man who seeks her hand in marriage really loves her. She will do anything for him, even when others try to help her by revealing his true motives. This is the plot of the play and film *The Heiress*, based on Henry James's novel *Washington Square*. The story is complicated by the fact that her father thinks the admittedly impoverished suitor is an impostor, while her hysterical, romantic aunt is charmed and taken in by him. The questions of whether Morris Townsend is sincere or shamming and of what his true motivations are remain open.

The basis of the impostor's personality is a strong libidinal investment in the family romance and an almost overwhelming internal pressure to maintain it, beginning as childhood fantasy of belonging to a much better, more prestigious family than the one he or she is born into. The impostor can have an acute perception of reality, but there is an internal pressure to live out the fantasy nonetheless and thus to relieve the deep feelings of fragility, insecurity, and unworthiness. During their periods of imposing on other people and being perceived by those they impose on as superior and accomplished, they have a great sense of calmness and relief from tension.

Leonardo DiCaprio plays the reformed impostor Frank Abagnale in the delightful, heartwarming *Catch Me If You Can* (2002), based on his true story. He was an appealing but confused kid setting out on a path in life that led him, out of desperation and economic deprivation, from scams and identity impersonations as an airline pilot, a lawyer, and a doctor (as opposed to the crime of identity theft, which steals other people's identities in order to rob them) to a highly successful and lucrative career in law enforcement, once he had finally been caught and decided to change his life. He had a chameleon-like facility for adopting other identities and adapting instantly to situations, and clearly was sane and not psychopathic at all, so that he was a good candidate for productive rehabilitation.

There were a number of cases of criminal imposture solved by that remarkable real-life Sherlock Holmes, Eugène-François Vidocq, a master of disguise. A friend of Balzac, Dumas, and Victor Hugo, he served as the model for several of their literary characters, among them both Jean Valjean, the escaped convict who makes good and is an impostor by necessity, and the implacable Inspector Javert who always gets his man in Hugo's *Les Misérables*. Alexandre Dumas' Count of Monte Cristo (who shares Vidocq's ability to disguise himself) is in reality the wrongfully imprisoned sailor Edmond Dantès, who escapes from the fortress prison the Château d'If and passes himself off as an aristocrat, but also as an Italian priest and an English banker. His conscious imposture is for the purposes of revenge, and at one point, having accomplished most of what he set out to do, he questions his own motives.

Vidocq, a convict who escaped from prison five times, went from being a criminal to becoming a law enforcer, and unmasked several impostors who were able to take advantage of the chaos prevailing after the defeat of Napoleon and during the Restoration, and had passed themselves off as aristocrats at the court of Louis XVIII. Among them was the Count of Sainte-Hélène, another escaped convict, a brazen thief and master forger who boldly forged his own patents of nobility and became an intimate friend of Louis XVIII and a military leader. At the same time, he was the chief of a band of robbers who systematically burgled Paris *hôtels particuliers* (townhouses) in a series of spectacular robberies. He was sent to prison for life, and continually claimed to be innocent and denied that he was of plebeian birth, despite the overwhelming evidence against him. To the end of his life, he insisted on being addressed as a count. At least the so-called count always avoided violence and was never guilty of hurting other people physically or of murder, and at times did indeed more or less admit that he was the escaped convict, forger, and thief Pierre Coignard. He left those who came into contact with him in an ambivalent state, not knowing if he really thought of himself as a count or was shamming.

For a famous case of imposture, see the film *Anastasia* (1956), with the ethereal Ingrid Bergman as Anna Anderson, who passed herself off as the czar's daughter and claimed to have escaped when the rest of the czar's family was executed during the Russian Revolution. In the film she is clearly manipulated by criminals who simply want to enrich themselves, but in real life she stuck to her story, and many people believed her. DNA evidence conclusively disproved her claims.

innovative therapies: There are two kinds of contemporary innovative therapies: 1) valid, scientifically based depth therapies, such as the Rubenfeld Synergy Method and physical therapies including Rolfing, Feldenkrais, and many others; and 2) simplistic quick fixes and quackery, so-called therapies for which there is no scientific basis or criteria for workability. Some of these latter have caught hold among certain unhappy, insecure people who hope to find a rapid cure for what ails them; to feel loved, accepted and, quite possibly, superior because they are knowing members of an in-group. Most of these schools are not only lacking in integrity; they are unhelpful because they do not deal in any kind of depth psychology, which means they never get to the heart of any problem and so are unable to be truly therapeutic in the long term. These so-called therapies are no substitute for the real thing. Should you have to play either the provider of such a therapy, out to make a quick buck from the gullible, or the recipient, convinced illusorily that he or she has been raised to some higher level of consciousness, or if you are writing or directing material on this subject, I advise you to look at the DVD of the first season of Penn and Teller's television show *Bullshit!* They debunk certain schools of self-help and alternative medicine. The personalities involved can be very useful character studies.

Many self-help books that advocate self-administered psychotherapy are in the category of simplistic, superficial innovative therapies. They are broad without being deep, and most of them do not deal with root causes. Some "New Age" concepts that talk about spirituality and "transformation," as opposed to psychotherapeutic healing, are eclectic and derivative. The use of *affirmations,* which are positive statements meant to be autosuggestive repetitive mantras, is a widespread practice in a number of schools of thought.

insecurity: a feeling of uncertainty and vulnerability. People who are insecure lack assurance and the feeling of being protected. They feel anxious and unconsciously think that anything may happen to them at any time, and that they are not effective human beings whose actions will lead to the results they want. If they constantly feel attacked or threatened when there is no discernible external cause, we say that they are paranoid. Everyone feels insecure from time to time, but if the insecurity is a general unconscious character trait, it is the basis of neurotic behavior.

lay analysis/lay analyst: Freud supported the recruitment and training of psychoanalysts who were not M.D.s and who were therefore called *lay analysts,* but he found much opposition to the idea of lay analysis among colleagues who were M.D.s—in the AMA, for instance—and who felt that only medical doctors were qualified to administer psychoanalysis; hence, in part, the distinction between psychologists, who are Ph.D.s or Ed.D.s, and psychiatrists, who must be M.D.s. In *The Question of Lay Analysis* (1926; *Postscript,* 1927) Freud eloquently defended his ideas. He thought psychoanalysis too important to be left to doctors, who often had a very different outlook from that required of a psychoanalyst.

maladaptive: unable to make necessary adjustments; ill adjusted. The term *maladaptive behavior syndrome,* which does not necessarily indicate a mental illness, refers to comportments that do not fit a given situation or are more generally nonproductive of desired and desirable results. People who cannot change their behavior when a situation requires change and adjustment are maladaptive and dysfunctional.

maladjustment: a specific maladaptation to the environment. The term *maladjusted* refers to people who have not adapted well to the sociocultural environment in which they live. Internally, they are unable to do so. Maladjustments vary from the severely dysfunctional to situations in which the maladjusted person may be mildly uncomfortable. Maladjustment may be accompanied by feelings of awkwardness and/or inadequacy, as well as an actual inability to function productively.

mania: Resulting frequently in highly erratic, not to say neurotic, behavior, a mania is an obsession with something particular, such as amassing a collection, and it may be psychotic. Most collectors of records and CDs, stamps, the memorabilia of particular authors, composers, or historical figures, and so forth are simple hobbyists. When the hobby becomes an all-consuming passion or fixation, we say that such a person has a mania for collecting this or that. A hypochondriac, fixated on the self, may develop a mania for a particular kind of remedy. The card-playing character in Chekhov's *Ivanov* concentrates on little else and is always talking about cards.

metapsychology: the overall theory that is the basis of psychology and psychoanalysis. Metapsychology consists of the most basic concepts, such as the existence of the unconscious, ideas about the structure of the mind, and the idea of the dynamic nature of character and mental processes.

mood: a state of being characterized by a particular emotional coloration. Edith Jacobsen tells us in *Depression: Comparative Studies of Normal, Neurotic and Psychotic Conditions* (1971), which contains an excellent, useful discussion of the topic, that moods are the result of conscious or unconscious reactions to psychological or psychophysiological events. There may be inborn predispositions to certain moods, as we can observe from babies who may have a generally placid or else a more truculent temperament. A mood is temporary, however long lasting it may be. In any particular mood, there is a concentration on a narrow aspect of events and their possible influence on the future.

Moods are a focus of the discharge of emotions "induced by significant emotional experiences," writes Edith Jacobson. A mood is "attached to all feelings, thoughts and actions." It is pervasive and "may indeed be called a barometer of the ego state." A mood "may be significant either in terms of the current reality or because it is associated with significant conscious or unconscious memories."

Moods arise regardless of general personality or character structure, and may either be typical or atypical manifestations of feeling that results in behavior that is either typical or atypical. The most salient component of any mood is its subjective emotional content, the externalized aspects of which—such as facial expression, demeanor, and physical carriage—are usually apparent to external observers as well. A mood is an unconscious attempt to integrate experience and deal with it, but there are people whom one calls moody who fail to do so. They may have uncontrollable mood swings because they find it difficult to cope with their emotions, if they even understand them. Such people can be very upsetting to the people around them. People may or may not be aware of their own moods or of what sets them off. Someone may trigger a mood in someone else by consciously or inadvertently "pushing their buttons," which evokes an unconscious reaction that gives rise to a mood.

Directors might want to consider the general mood or emotional climate of a scene so that they can integrate each character into it and create the mood or atmosphere they wish by directing the actors to carry out their actions in certain ways.

For actors: What mood is your character in at any given moment? Is the character aware or unaware of those moods? Do such physical conditions as heat or cold affect the character's mood and consequently color the character's response to other characters? Are the character's moods and/or changes of mood the result of internal circumstances and reactions to external events, as they are, for instance, when Hamlet sees Ophelia alone in the castle corridor and realizes that Polonius and Claudius are hiding behind the arras and spying on them, or when Vanya sees Yelena and Astrov kissing?

neo-Freudian: deriving from but significantly altering Freudian psychoanalytic theory, thus forming a new school of psychoanalytic thought. Hans Loewald and Jacques Lacan, who actually thought of themselves as Freudians, are two examples. Karen Horney, Melanie Klein, Erich Fromm, and Harry Stack Sullivan depart from Freudian thought, while still paying tribute to it and using much of it; in a way, they are also neo-Freudians.

Immigrating to the United States in the 1940s, Hans Loewald (1906–93), who made important studies of the nature of language development and worked with Sullivan, altered Freudian thinking on such subjects as the results of the Oedipus complex and sublimation. He emphasized the positive influence of childhood experiences on adult relationships, rather than their negative impact. Jonathan Lear's discussion of Loewald's ideas in *Open Minded* (1998) is most illuminating.

Neo-Freudians are not to be confused with Freudians, such as Marie Bonaparte, Anna Freud, or Theodor Reik (1886–1969), who amplified, extended and added to Freudian theory, clarifying it without discarding it.

True departures from Freudian theory include the schools of psychology and psychotherapy founded by Reich, Adler, and Jung, and the secessionist theories of Otto Rank (1884–1939) and Wilhelm Stekel (1868–1940). All of them were former adherents of Freud and ultimately derive their ideas from Freudian psychoanalytic theory. Skinner's behaviorism, on the other hand, is a total departure from Freudianism.

parapsychology: Parapsychology has nothing to do with psychology, despite the last part of the word, and everything to do with quackery and charlatanism. So-called parapsychological, paranormal, occult phenomena, such as the existence of ghosts; communicating with the "spirits" of the dead; telepathy; witchcraft; fortune telling of divers kinds, such as the predictions of astrology (a nice party game); interpreting tarot cards, palmistry, or the reading of tea leaves; and other such absurd manifestations of so-called spirituality have long been debunked by scientific enquirers, who have conclusively proved the nonexistence of any truth or reality to these fictions. They are nevertheless often believed in by the gullible, the naïve, the superstitious, and people who are terribly troubled and upset by various things, such as the loss of a loved one and the inability to cope with that loss in ways that will take them beyond their grief. The practitioners of such nonsense often believe in what they are doing, having convinced themselves of the truth of their assertions, however irrational they may be. In Penn and Teller's TV series *Bullshit!* there is one program in which the researcher and world-famous investigator James Randi, president of the Randi Educational Foundation, which offers a million-dollar prize to anyone who can prove the existence of a ghost (so far nobody has even come close), details the ridiculousness of believing in the prophecies of the fifteenth-century fake and charlatan Nostradamus, which were so general that future generations of idiots interpreted them as foretelling events in their own times and marveled at his perspicacity and acumen. He used specific names of places and of people about whom he was making predictions only 107 times, and he was wrong about every single one of them! It is worth noting that Hitler and many other top Nazis took this blatantly absurd stuff seriously, and remembering that they were delusional psychopaths.

Parapsychological phenomena have provided amusing and even disturbing premises and pretexts for plays, such as Noel Coward's *Blithe Spirit*, beautifully filmed in 1945 with Rex Harrison, Margaret Leighton, and Margaret Rutherford, as well as the moving psychological dramatic film *Séance on a Wet Afternoon* (1964), with meek, subservient Richard Attenborough married to a severely disturbed "medium" Kim Stanley, whom he loves very much and is powerless to help. Henry James's novella *The Turn of the Screw,* often dramatized, filmed, and even made into an opera, and *The Others* (2001), a very well-done film reminiscent of Henry James and starring Nicole Kidman, are also highly entertaining and instructive, with the psychological element predominating. The Ghost of Hamlet's father, the three witches, and Banquo's ghost in *Macbeth* are some more examples of the dramatically effective use of parapsychological phenomena, during which the audience must suspend its disbelief.

The only way to play such characters and situations believably is to act them as if they were absolutely real and you believe in them completely, of course. Directors can make clear in the staging that they are dreamlike phenomena, not to be taken literally. Only Macbeth, who believes in the witches' prophecies, sees the ghost of Banquo. And only he, Lady Macbeth, and Banquo know about the weird sisters. Hamlet is more problematic, since several people see the ghost. Shakespeare lived in a superstitious age that burned so-called witches at the stake; he may have believed in these things himself. Sometimes people just believe what they want to believe, I guess.

personality/personality theory: Someone's *personality*—or their *character;* the words are often used interchangeably—is the result of the sum total of individual psychological characteristics as they have developed from childhood on, in combination with inborn temperament, and the way in which those results manifest themselves in a person's presentation of the self to the world. One aspect of personality, temperament, is the habitual manner in which a person usually behaves, whatever mood he or she may be in. It may be characterized adjectivally: he or she is, or is perceived as, charming, truculent, taciturn, lugubrious, gloomy, cheerful, and so forth. He or she has, or is perceived as having, a charming or truculent personality and/or temperament.

Since the days of Hippocrates' personality theory in ancient Greece, people have been characterized as being of certain personality (or character) types. His categorization was considered correct and useful well through the eighteenth century and even into the nineteenth. The four temperaments he distinguished are the *choleric* (quick and easily prone to anger), the *sanguine* (calm and not easily ruffled), the *melancholic* (stationary, depressive), and the *phlegmatic* (lethargic, slow, and not easily aroused). The adjectives are used to this day, although we have now discarded the idea of using them as characterizing types in any real analytical sense. The idea of a *Type A personality* (hypertense, driven, competitive, prone to heart attacks) and of a *Type B personality* (the opposite of Type A: calm, easygoing, relaxed) might fit into Hippocrates' types of choleric and sanguine, respectively. And there are many more adjectives to describe personality and personality types.

The Nobel Prize–winning Russian physiologist Ivan Pavlov (1849–1936) distinguished four personality types: *extreme excitatory, extreme inhibitory, balanced excitatory,* and *balanced inhibitory.* They correspond, in order, to the choleric, melancholic, sanguine, and phlegmatic temperaments of Hippocrates.

Agreeing with Pavlov in his idea that personality was a biologically based balance between the excitatory and the inhibitory, Hans Eysenck (1916–97) based his own personality theory firmly in biology. He saw personality as a result of neurological functioning. He also thought that Jung's categories of introvert and extravert were accurate, and had to do with the neurological tolerance of stimuli: introverts were *stimulus shy,* while extraverts were *stimulus hungry.* Personality was partly a function of visceral response to arousal in particular centers in the brain. Eysenck also analyzed personality from the point of view of Hippocrates' four temperaments, in which he saw neurological functioning as the prime explanation for them.

Another way of looking at personality is to describe character traits, rather than typing or categorizing. This approach is often used in literature, where people are portrayed rather than analyzed. In the theater, where actors and directors deal with particular traits or manifestations of character, Stanislavsky often used the descriptive approach in his directing. And the American psychologist Gordon W. Allport (1897–1967) was famous for his "Trait and Self Theory," as well as for his studies of the nature of prejudice. For Allport, who called his school of thought *personalistic psychology,* personality was a system composed of traits. The whole personality, dominated by a powerful *cardinal disposition,* or tendency (it might be that of generosity or miserliness, of Don Juanism or constancy), together with *central* (important and salient traits) and *secondary dispositions* (peripheral traits), is more than the sum of its traits, and each trait affects and is affected by the whole. Allport defined a *trait* as a neuropsychic structure that amounts to a predisposition to behave in certain ways. As people develop a sense of self and seek autonomy, personal motives and behavior may change, and may no longer be subject to original infantile narcissistic wishes. For Allport, personality is dynamic, evolving, and self-regulating.

In cognitive psychology, personality is seen partly as the result of all the mental processes as they have developed over time. The contemporary concept in cognitive psychology of a *schema,* which is the way a person reacts to and evaluates stimuli that lead to behavior, is similar to Allport's concept of traits.

An early member of Freud's circle and, like Jung and Freud, a student and interpreter of myth in psychological terms, Otto Rank was at first a proponent of Freudianism and then a dissident from it, although he never founded a separate school. Freud had said that birth was the prototype of the experience of anxiety and separation. Rank took up this idea and made of it the central *birth trauma,* which he said was a universal conditioning force. (Freud thought this notion useless.) Rank distinguished three basic personality types: the *adapted,* the *neurotic,* and the *productive.* They all have to do with *will,* which is the ego wishing to free itself from the domination of others. The adapted type is basically passive and average, and wills itself to obey what it has been taught, identifying the will of others as its own, obeying society's morality, and restraining sexual desire. Neurotic types fight incessantly against domination and feel guilty about doing so, expending energy in the fight against their own and others' wills so that they have no time for freedom. The productive type, such as the creative artist or the scientist, affirms his or her will and creates his or her own being in accordance with the *life instinct,* which is opposed to the *death instinct* and the fear of our own demise.

Freud's approach to personality theory is, as we have seen, the psychodynamic one (how people function; the relations among the id, the ego and the superego; etc.), which includes the questions of why people function as they do psychodynamically; the psychosexual development of the personality; interpersonal relations and their influence on personality development; and so forth. See the various chapters in this book for the different personality theories of Adler, Jung, Horney, Klein, Reich, Sullivan, Binswanger, Fromm, and others. The psychoanalytic approach is distinguished from behaviorism, which sees everything in terms of responses to stimuli and eschews character analysis in psychological or cognitive terms.

personality disorder: a general term for psychological disturbances in adaptation and functionality in which someone's entire character is impaired; character disorder. It includes neuroses and sociopathy as well as psychoses and other conditions.

phrenology: Originally a serious attempt to read personal characteristics from the bumps on the head, this elaborate pseudoscience was devised in all honesty by Francis Joseph Gall in the nineteenth century and was widely believed in and practiced. However, it is acutely unscientific and fraudulent.

possessiveness: the overwhelming desire to control completely the object of one's attention. Possessiveness is the product of massive insecurity, which includes at its base primary masochism, jealousy, lack of trust, and the feeling of not being loved. For an extreme example, read about the Narrator's virtual imprisonment of Albertine in his apartment in the volume of Proust's *In Search of Lost Time* called *La Prisonnière* (The Captive), which contains a wealth of psychological detail and descriptions of the characters' jealousy, hypersensitivity, and defensiveness, as well as the implication of primary sadism under the mask of primary masochism. Helmer in *A Doll's House* is very possessive with Nora. Kulygin in *Three Sisters* tries not to be possessive with Masha, but he can hardly help himself.

primal scene: the universal fantasy or the actual recollection of having seen one's parents or other primary caregivers engaged in sexual intercourse. The fantasy (not only an invented fantasy, but also the real, witnessed event, which can be relived in recollection and has elements of fantasy as it is recalled) usually includes an element of sadomasochism, because the child, not understanding what is really going on, perceives the father as mistreating the mother or one partner as mistreating the other. The repressed result of the fantasy or the actual scene really witnessed by the child may result in unconscious identifications and judgments about either or both parents and/or about sex, and may even be traumatic in certain circumstances. In the course of psychoanalytic treatment, the primal scene at some point may become a matter for analysis with regard to its effects on the analysand. There is a good account of this in the film *Princesse Marie,* in which Marie Bonaparte comes to grips with the primal scene in her life.

primary relationship: a relationship between two people of long duration and emotionally involving, and often intimate and close. There is a sense of commitment and the feeling that one person cannot simply be replaced by another. Friendship and marriage are two obvious examples.

psychodrama: developed by J. L. Moreno (1889–1974), a kind of psychotherapy in which a patient acts out his or her situation in a therapeutic setting, under the guidance of a psychotherapist, who may ask leading questions and/or play a role of someone in the patient's life either sitting silently or else engaging in a dialogue with the patient. The patient is encouraged to express conflicts unreservedly and to say what he or she really thinks without fear of repercussions. In group therapy, patients may play roles for each other under the therapist's guidance. This is reminiscent of the empty-chair exercise devised by Fritz Perls in his Gestalt therapy.

There is also a form of theater called psychodrama, in which actors play parts improvisationally. The audience asks them to act out situations and play certain roles, and presumably learns something from the drama unfolded before them. In some ways, psychodrama is similar to role-enactment therapy, except that the patient in the latter plays roles under hypnosis.

psychosomatic disorder: a physical disease or condition brought on for psychological reasons, as when a person catches a cold because he or she has been working overly hard, due to stress and anxiety arising out of the desire to please an overexacting, tyrannical boss. The somatic part of the condition must be dealt with on the somatic level, of course. Georg Groddeck in *The Book of the It* maintained that all diseases are ultimately psychosomatic. Dealing with psychosomatic illnesses at his clinic in Baden-Baden was one of his special areas of expertise, but this assertion is probably one of his most problematic and questionable. The hypochondriac, imaginary invalid of Molière's play is a case of someone with psychosomatic diseases. He's not really sick, but he has convinced himself he is to such an extent that he actually develops symptoms. The quack doctors he calls in to help him—Molière seems generally convinced that all doctors are quacks—apply the most ludicrous remedies.

Pygmalion effect: Named after Shaw's play, the term refers to behavior that results from the attempt to influence someone to change, when the person trying to exert control is perceived as authoritative, powerful, and worthy of deference, and the person being influenced is overawed and not sure how to react. The Pygmalion effect may be seen in anyone who behaves in accordance with another's expectations in order to gain the approval of that person, even if the behavior in question actually goes against the grain. But the influence can work in both directions, so the term also refers to anyone who falls in love with his or her own creation; this latter condition can be pathological.

In the ancient Greek myth, Aphrodite, in revenge for the sculptor Pygmalion's misogyny, makes him fall in love with his own statue of a beautiful woman named Galatea. Moved by the depth of his passionate love, the gods take pity and reward him by bringing her to life.

rational-emotive therapy (later renamed rational-emotive behavior therapy): Albert Ellis's (born 1913) practical school of direct, interventionist, confrontational psychotherapy. Ellis's therapy is devoted to direct problem solving, without necessarily going into depth analysis. He asked what the patient's actual thoughts and beliefs were, and how he or she continued to entertain irrational thinking, but he did not explore the origins of the thinking. His is an innovative therapy, with its own approach and vocabulary (*self-downing,* meaning to disparage oneself; *love slobbism,* the term for an approach to life in which somebody thinks they must have love in order to feel happy and validated, etc.). Rational-emotive therapy bears some relation to self-help movements, although it is clearly more efficacious and less superficial. Ellis distinguished between unhealthy, unrealistic demands a person made on the self, and preferences, or choices based on rational thinking as opposed to emotion or feeling. There were appropriate, healthy emotions and inappropriate, unhealthy emotions—such as guilt, to which concern was a healthy alternative. Rational-emotive therapy deals, among other things, with making patients confront their problems forcefully by taking action. The patient is sometimes given homework to do between sessions, such as "antiprocrastination" exercises (if procrastination is a problem), including making lists of the advantages and disadvantages of procrastination; visualization exercises; and keeping a journal of daily activities.

rationalization: The original meaning of the word is the process of reasoning by which the obscure is clarified and the nonreasonable made clear and rational. But its more usual meaning turns the original definition upside down: the false justification, arrived at through self-deception, for a person's immoral actions; convincing oneself of the rightness of reprehensible, unethical behavior. Rationalization is a defense mechanism, a form of intellectualization that serves to make a person feel justified, good, or at least all right about doing something that is morally wrong. Many characters in films and plays rationalize their actions. They include Lady Macbeth, justifying the murder of Duncan; Natasha in *Three Sisters,* mistreating the old Nurse and taking over the house; Stanley's seduction/rape of Blanche in Tennessee Williams's *A Streetcar Named Desire;* Antonio's spurning of Shylock because he is a Jew; and Shylock's demand for a pound of flesh from Antonio because he is an anti-Semite.

reactance theory: An area of cognitive psychology's motivational theory, based on and derived from dissonance theory (see page 189), the idea was first proposed by J. W. Brehm in 1966: people react against someone or something they perceive as unfairly controlling their choices of objects or actions by choosing or doing the exact opposite of what they think of as an unjust imposition. In other words, people who feel their freedom is being unfairly restricted will rebel against being controlled and want to regain their freedom.

Reactions vary from extreme rebellion to mild, sullen, furtive disobedience. Telling children they may not do something, for instance, may provoke an angry and rebellious—but honest—reaction. As a way of asserting independence and refusing to be controlled by someone else, the child may do exactly what he or she has been told not to do. An adolescent whose parents have restricted him or her from dating, particularly if this restriction involves not seeing a particular person, may sneak out of the house if possible and have a clandestine meeting. A driver may speed simply as a rebellious reaction against the legal restrictions of a speed limit. Such an adult or even an adolescent driver clearly has problems in dealing with authority.

If some people are allowed to do something and others are not, the perception of unfairness will provoke an angry or even furious reaction. The reasons for such angry reactions and subsequent provocative behavior, which may result in punishment (perhaps unconsciously desired), are many and varied.

The desirability of an action or an object is seen in relation to the opportunity to choose it. The more it is perceived as actually being available, but with the access to it limited because of external pressures, the more attractive it becomes. In the case of Romeo and Juliet, the two are restricted from seeing each other by the ongoing feud and bad blood between their families, and this, as much as their deep physical attraction to one another, may be a factor in arousing their love, partly as a rebellion.

The choice and attainment of an object that has been forbidden may have to be secret, and all kinds of devious and even criminal behavior may be the result. The gangster activities in connection with the Constitutional prohibition of alcohol and the contemporary problems with drug smuggling are extreme cases in point. Trying to persuade someone to pursue a certain course of action for his or her own good, such as trying to get someone to give up smoking, may arouse rebellious reactions if the person misinterprets good intentions. The moral of all this is: asking someone politely to refrain from doing something gets far better results than ordering someone not to do something, or as the proverb says, you catch more flies with honey than with vinegar.

retrospective falsification: the distortion and modification of past events and experiences, so as to make them conform to the memory one wishes to have, such as the memory of being loved or of having been innocent of some crime or provocation. Retrospective falsification arises out of the *unconscious* need to reinforce positive images of past events that may have been deeply disturbing, or else is a defensive *conscious* lying about the past so as to present the self in the best light possible. This pathological lying, which can take other forms than lying about the past, is a symptom of a deep disturbance. However, ordinary people who are by no means pathological liars or disturbed and in need of therapy often are in denial and remember things as they wish them to be. They idealize past events — their childhood, for instance — repressing the memory of abuse, whether emotional or physical. For more on this subject, see Alice Miller's books, listed in the bibliography. Such repression — and even the justification of the abuse by the person who has been abused and remembers the abusive situations, either accurately enough or in a distorted way — is common enough. People see either through rose-colored glasses or through a glass darkly and dimly, but seldom through clear and undistorted lenses.

Rorschach test: a psychological, diagnostic, projective test designed by Swiss psychiatrist Hermann Rorschach (1884–1922), consisting of showing ten standard inkblot drawings to a patient and observing the patient's reactions to them. Among laypeople, this famous test amounts to a cliché symbolizing psychology. Dianne Wiest examines Brendan Fraser with similar tests in *The Scout* in one of the funniest, scariest scenes in the film.

Rubenfeld Synergy Method: Drawing on the work of Freud, Reich, the Alexander Technique and the Feldenkrais Method of physical psychotherapy, and created by Ilana Rubenfeld in the 1960s, the Rubenfeld Synergy Method is a form of therapy that combines bodywork and psychotherapy, including depth psychology, touch therapy, and body-mind exercises to help release tensions and psychic conflict stored somatically. In accordance with the title of Ms. Rubenfeld's book, *The Listening Hand: Self-Healing Through the Rubenfeld Synergy Method of Talk and Touch* (2000), there are, among other therapeutic techniques, "talk and touch duets that allow you to 'hear' the nonverbal messages of your body." Rob Bauer, LCSW (Licensed Certified Social Worker), a body-centered psychotherapist who practices the Rubenfeld Synergy Method and was trained by Ms. Rubenfeld herself, adds that the method provides the "release of chronic physical holding patterns." The method, which is scientifically based and highly effective, provides group therapy and therapy for couples as well as individuals.

schizophrenia: Once perceived as a purely emotional or mental illness, *schizophrenia*, which is an umbrella term for a number of similar conditions, including those with multiple personalities, is now known to depend partly on chemical malfunctioning and is treated with medications. It is classified as a psychosis. Schizophrenics typically hear voices, have visual hallucinations, or both. The diseases vary from mild to very severe. Some schizophrenics have the delusion that a higher power talks through them and makes them communicate their theories to the world. Others say the voices they hear make them do things, often evil things, such as committing murder. In *A Beautiful Mind* (2001), Russell Crowe plays the Nobel Prize–winning Princeton University mathematician John Nash, who was diagnosed as schizophrenic. The film is based loosely on his life. He had a much milder disease than that depicted in the film. Nash did not have visual hallucinations, but he did hear voices that caused him to be dysfunctional at times. For more details on schizophrenia see the *DSM-IV-TR*.

screen memory: Also known as a *cover memory;* a fleeting return of childhood or other memories that serve to mask or cover more disturbing ones, which the ego has repressed. The so-called memory may actually be an unconscious invention and not a real memory at all, although it seems like one, or it may combine incidents that really happened or turn two people into one. Adult witnesses from the period that is being recalled may be in a position to corroborate or deny the truth of these memories.

In his essay "Screen Memories" (1899), Freud talks about the difficulty or even the impossibility of remembering events from early childhood. When we try to do so, he says, either we remember nothing at all or else we remember something so trivial and uninteresting that it is hardly worth remarking. However, what we remember can sometimes serve to prevent us from remembering "occasions of fear, shame, physical pain, etc." For instance, he describes one person (mentioned in a paper by some other psychologists) who remembered a table set for a meal, with a basin of ice on it, when he was about three or four years old. What he did not remember, which his parents did, was how upset he was over the death of his grandmother at that time. But he had no recollection of that at all. The screen memory is a diversionary tactic of the ego, deflecting the return of repressed memories.

In her book *Emotional Growth,* Phyllis Greenacre wrote an exhaustive, thoroughly researched essay called "'It's My Own Invention': A Special Screen Memory of Mr. Lewis Carroll, Its Form and Its History." Carroll, Alice Liddell (the real-life inspiration for the Alice of the famous books), and Carroll's fellow Oxford don, Canon Duckworth—who accompanied them, along with Alice's two sisters, on the famous rowing expedition during which Carroll was prevailed upon to tell the stories that led to his writing the Alice books—all remembered the day of that journey on the Isis as being a bright, golden, sunny day and quite hot, so that they had to shelter from the sun under trees growing on the bank. ("Insistent overbrightness," according to Greenacre, is a typical characteristic of screen memories.) But the meteorological records of Oxford on that day, July 4, 1862, indicate that the weather was in fact "cool and rather wet" with over an inch of rain falling! Thus, what appears to us now to be a collective screen memory is quite a bizarre discrepancy. Furthermore, it is worth noting that the theme of the golden day appears throughout Carroll's writings, particularly in the introductory and closing poems that frame not only the Alice stories, which are told as dreams Alice has when she falls asleep, but also in other writings of his.

In the course of inventing the Alice stories, Carroll created several poems that deal with the relation between a younger and an older man, from whom the younger man seeks advice—a theme that also appears many other times in his writing. The younger man is often rebuffed in some way by the older man, an exception being the famous Jabberwocky poem, in which the young man is received with joy by the older man after having slain the monster (forbidden sexual desire?). In all the poems, this scenario represents Carroll and his father, concludes Greenacre.

The young Carroll, the third of eleven children, must have wondered what was going on as he witnessed his mother becoming pregnant over and over again, depriving him of the love he needed because she had no time and was always too distracted and feeling too poorly to pay attention to him. And then, to his despair, she died when he was only nineteen, just a few days after he had started as a student at Oxford. He felt responsible somehow. And he must have blamed and resented his beloved father for all that had happened, and especially for upsetting him by keeping everything such a mystery, even after repeated questioning on the subject of sex and what it all meant.

As he told the stories and invented the poems for the little girls, Carroll must have felt these memories awakening, even if only dimly. Alice Liddell's and Canon Duckworth's anxiety must also have been aroused, for different reasons. And the brightness of the day they misremembered (suggested, perhaps, to Alice and Canon Duckworth by Carroll having first elaborated on the "golden afternoon" in his prefatory poems) served to screen the real memory of what had been awakened and perhaps of the tensions among all the people in that little boat, despite the pleasure they took in the story.

All of Lewis Carroll's inner turmoil and repressed thoughts must have been very near the surface: the constant distress and guilt and fears revolving around his mother and around sex; his appeals to his father for comfort and advice, and his rage at being put off or rebuffed in some way by the older man; his inadmissible, never-to-be-talked-about attraction to little girls and simultaneous dislike of little boys....The stories about Alice, who escaped for a brief time from the cares of this world into a dreamland of wonder, had nothing to do with all that! Playing croquet in their garden, the ineffectual but kindly King and the fierce Queen of Hearts, who had no time and was always rushing about, were a world away from the old family home....And here was the real little Alice, beautiful Alice, sitting and listening with rapt attention as he wove his story for her... just for her....It was not a dark and rainy day....No, it was a day of bright golden sunlight, and everything was wonderful....

The film *DreamChild* (1985), with Coral Browne as the elderly Mrs. Alice Liddell Hargreaves on a trip to New York to be honored on the occasion of Carroll's centenary, and Ian Holm as Lewis Carroll, is very revealing and beautifully observed, and the sexual undercurrents in the flashbacks with Carroll and Alice are extraordinary. The film also contains startling, almost surrealistic dream sequences.

Actor's questions: Does your character talk about memories? Are those memories accurate? Do other characters confirm or deny them? Are there other interpretations of what happened in the past that are different from various characters' points of view?

secondary relationship: a temporary, limited relationship between two people, such as that between a temp and a permanent worker in an office. There is little if any emotional involvement. Behavior may be limited to superficial if polite interchanges and may be friendly or hostile, depending on circumstances.

self-analysis: The study by someone of his or her own psyche and personality with the aim of understanding the self and solving personal problems, *self-analysis* is undertaken without the help of a professional psychotherapist. The most famous self-analysis in history was undoubtedly Freud's. He described it minutely in letters to Wilhelm Fliess. Self-analysis required the utmost rigor, discipline, and above all, absolute honesty about who he was and how his character had been built up. But Freud thought complete self-analysis ultimately impossible.

self-fulfilling prophecy: a prediction that comes true because the person making the prediction behaves in such a way as to ensure that it will. The behavior is often unconscious. An example: somebody, believing that he or she is not worthy of love and that nobody could possibly love him or her, behaves in such a way as to court rejection.

self-image: an imagined and sometimes imaginary positive or negative mental picture of the person one supposes oneself to be, frequently of the person one wishes to be in order to live up to the ego-ideal. The image of the self includes physical appearance as well as moral characteristics. It is an adjustable inner construct. Most people want to be thought of as attractive and want to think of themselves that way. Most people want to think of themselves as well meaning and their acts as justified. Even psychopaths usually justify their behavior, no matter how much harm they do to others. It is axiomatic that villains, at least in the theater, do not think of themselves as villains. Who one really is can be quite different from the person one thinks one is.

sentimentality: As opposed to true sentiment or empathy with people or situations, sentimentality is the maudlin, saccharine indulgence in often false feelings of sympathy or nostalgia, masking feelings of hostility and anger. The words Pollyanna—a byword for sentimentality—and hypocrisy leap to mind. "If you can't say something nice about someone, don't say anything" is a form of sentimentality, in which one is encouraged not to tell the truth or rock the boat, even when talking of an evil, warmongering politician. People who say they have had an absolutely wonderful time at a prestigious, high-powered event where they didn't really fit in and have been virtually ignored if not mistreated are sentimental. Snobs are sentimental. Characters given to sentimentality can have a comic, rather silly side. The cynical aesthetic poet Reginald Bunthorne is sentimental underneath his sneering exterior, and so are the twenty drooping lovesick maidens who adore him in Gilbert and Sullivan's charming comic opera *Patience.* The arch arch-romantic, recently widowed Popova and the sentimental antisentimentalist Smirnov who falls in love with her in Chekhov's outrageous farce *The Bear* are, well, sentimental. And Telyeghin in *Uncle Vanya* is a prime sentimentalist. Sentimentalists are frequently in a state of denial, out of fear. The hysterical sentimentalist Telyeghin simply wants everything to remain the same, which is not possible, and he cannot bear to hear unpleasant truths.

separation anxiety: extreme discomfort and distress over the necessity of temporarily or permanently leaving someone. In adulthood this feeling is based on the child's need for the parents and the anxiety occasioned by separation from them. Young children sometimes experience a version of this anxiety when parents go out for an evening and leave the child in the care of a babysitter. Masha in *Three Sisters* experiences severe, almost traumatic separation anxiety when her lover Vershinin is leaving with his regiment. She thinks she will fall apart, but of course she does not.

The first-person narrator of Mark Haddon's fascinating novel, *The Curious Incident of the Dog in the Night-time* (2003), is an autistic child, and the novel deals with separation anxiety, among other things. In the autistic condition, separation anxiety is severely repressed and unacknowledged, and this takes the reader aback. Its absence where we would expect it is startling, like the curious incident of the dog in the night in Sir Arthur Conan Doyle's story "Silver Blaze": What gives Sherlock Holmes his clue is that…but, no, you must read the story, and Mark Haddon's novel, for yourself.

sexism: the attitude that one is superior because of one's gender; the word usually refers to discrimination against women, which is the behavior resulting from the attitude. This prejudice includes a delusional belief in the existence of specific psychological traits and behavior common to a particular gender. That belief is derived irrationally from the fact that there are obviously real biophysiological differences. Based on feelings of inferiority, sexism, like other forms of bigotry, is a kind of stupidity, with the most unfortunate social and cultural consequences. Generally speaking, it is men rather than women who are sexists (male chauvinists) and who have lorded it over women partly by using physical force and coercion, since men are often though not always physically stronger than women. Feminism, on the other hand, is not sexism, but rather a sociopolitical movement aimed at redressing injustice and securing equality, which is not to say that there are no women who are sexists.

sex therapy: This term covers a number of different types of therapy, both physical and psychological, that deal with helping people overcome their sexual difficulties and dysfunctionality. When attitudes exist that interfere with sexual functioning and feelings of guilt and shame prevail, sex therapy may be of direct help, even though depth psychology, which can take a long time, is not used in such treatments. There are individual therapies for those who want to solve the problem of impotence or premature ejaculation, and couple and family therapy.

situational stress reaction: a temporary condition in response to a new situation, whether a new job or school or something potentially violent, such as a soldier's going into battle. The conflict and tension created in the new situation give rise to dynamic behavior in which the person involved acts against the inner stress by doing something to overcome it, such as really doing the job or making an effort to make friends at school.

Stockholm syndrome: A variation of the defense mechanism known as "identification with the aggressor," the *Stockholm syndrome* is one in which hostages begin to identify with and develop sympathy for the point of view and actual persons of their kidnappers, jailers, and torturers. The reactions vary individually, of course. The hostage takers who have imprisoned their victims may torture them and afflict them with sensory deprivation, refusing to give them food and drink and blindfolding them or keeping them in dark rooms, but the victim, overcome by feelings of guilt and shame based on early psychic conflicts, may nevertheless begin to feel that on some level, the actions of the hostage takers are justified.

superstition/superstitious behavior: an irrational belief, one not founded in reason or requiring any kind of proof of its veracity, in omens and portents of future ill or good luck, and in the efficacy of some form of "magical" behavior to ward off the ill luck that many superstitions portend and to calm the fear of the unknown and the mysterious. The behavior is a kind of defense mechanism, as in *undoing,* which is the attempt to undo some event or action from the past by such means as saying prayers, uttering incantations, or holding various ceremonies. Such phenomena as séances, during which one contacts the spirits of dead loved ones, and futuristic predictions based on dream interpretation (since Freud, we know better), astrology, Ouija boards, Tarot cards, or the I Ching (Book of Changes; the fascinating Chinese book of Taoist and Confucianist philosophy much loved by Jung) are also included in this category.

In *Julius Caesar* (and in many other Shakespearean plays), superstition plays a major role, and nearly all the characters pay attention to prophecies. Caesar himself claims to discount such things as augury or the prophecy of the Soothsayer to "beware the Ides of March," but he is assassinated. Gee, maybe he should have paid more attention....And don't forget Calpurnia's prophetic dream!

There are many theatrical superstitions, aside from the phobia about not quoting from the Scottish play, among them the idea that whistling backstage brings bad luck. In the nineteenth century, when British sailors were often hired as stagehands and the signal for lowering flats from the flies was a whistle, this might have made some sense, since whistling could result in being hit on the head by a sandbag. But the superstition is actually much older, and whistling was considered a way of summoning the Devil. Such phenomena as not walking under a ladder or having a black cat cross one's path were considered, and no doubt still are by some, omens of ill luck. The number thirteen is considered unlucky, and Friday the thirteenth is supposed to be an especially bad day. The wary choose to stay indoors, and even then....Spilling salt requires one to toss salt over the shoulder to ward off bad luck. And so forth and so on. All most amusing, but hardly to be taken seriously. Those who are superstitious are clearly projecting their unconscious fears, which have resulted from some psychic conflict, in a phobic way onto some phenomenon or object.

syndrome: a group or cluster of symptoms that, taken together, indicate the existence of a particular medical or psychological condition. The syndrome may contain variables but nevertheless fits into a particular category. In medical terms, a syndrome may indicate the existence of a particular disease. An example of a psychological syndrome is the Stockholm syndrome (see above).

type fallacy: The fallacy consists in treating people and character as being absolute manifestations of a particular category describing a character type, without taking account of specific variations in functioning and temperament, or of the possibility that particular reactions depend on particular circumstances and not on particular character traits.

voyeurism: There can be few people who do not enjoy the visual stimulation of watching sex acts and/or seeing in the nude the person they are in love with, have a relationship with, or simply find physically attractive. But when the preferred mode of sexual arousal is clandestine observation, whether of people one knows or of complete strangers, to the exclusion of other forms of gratification, we speak of voyeurism and of the person who indulges in this activity as a *voyeur,* from the French, meaning "one who sees." Voyeurs, often colloquially called peeping Toms, prefer that the person they are observing remain unaware that he or she is being watched. They are often not aroused by public exhibitionistic displays, such as striptease shows.

war neurosis: a stress-related anxiety disorder that is a variation of traumatic neurosis. The term, which is a generic one for all kinds of syndromes resulting from the traumatic shock experienced on the battlefield or during war generally, even when one is not on the front lines, was first introduced after World War I. Its symptoms include severe general anxiety, which may come and go and vary in its intensity; suspiciousness and lack of trust, sometimes amounting to paranoia; general withdrawal from society, even when surrounded by people; and recurrent nightmares and occasional waking flashbacks of the war experiences, either generalized or relating to the particular traumatic incidents. Today it is usual to speak of war neurosis as a post-traumatic stress disorder (PTSD).

If you have never served in a war and seen its horrors firsthand—and I sincerely hope you have not—and you have to do a play or a film about war, or if you are directing or writing a war drama, look at the extras containing interviews with soldiers and documentary footage of the war in Iraq, as well as at the film itself, on the DVD of Michael Moore's 2004 prizewinning documentary *Fahrenheit 9/11.* The footage of the war is graphic and sickening, and if it doesn't horrify you and turn you into a pacifist, unalterably opposed to war, nothing will. Although a fictionalized account of actual historical events surrounding D-Day in World War II, Steven Spielberg's deeply moving film *Saving Private Ryan* (1998) presents accurately observed, terrifying details of the invasion and gruesome occurrences on both a massive and an individual scale. There are so many other films dealing with various wars that it seems unnecessary to mention many more of them here, but I cannot refrain from drawing your attention to three others: the 1942 Academy Award–winner for best picture, *Random Harvest,* with Ronald Colman as a shell-shocked, amnesiac World War I soldier interned in an asylum; the Australian epic depiction of the doomed British invasion of Gallipoli in World War I, *Gallipoli* (1981); and Oliver Stone's masterly *Born on the Fourth of July* (1989), based on the true story of Ron Kovic, the Vietnam veteran who was first a gung-ho patriot marine and then became an antiwar activist. In one of his greatest performances, Tom Cruise plays Kovic with heartfelt passion and conviction.

People who have served in war have many and varied reactions to what they went through, and by no means all of them suffer from traumatic reactions. Most adjust to returning to peacetime conditions and are proud to have served their country. The question is: Does killing someone change the murderer forever, whether in war or peace? It seems there are wars that had to be fought, such as World War II, because it was forced upon the world by maniacal, unscrupulous dictators, and the world had no choice but to fight back. In such a case, there are many instances of real heroism, such as what took place in Denmark, where the Danish resistance to the Nazis was on a national scale, or the rescue of resistance fighters under the nose of the Gestapo in 1943 in Lyon, France, as in the real-life events depicted in the stirring film *Lucie Aubrac* (1997). Even in a war that many people thought should never have been fought, Vietnam, there were amazing instances, amid the horrors and the crimes, of incredible heroism, like Senator John Kerry's saving of lives during the stress of battle. Finally, one of the best films ever made about the effects and ramifications of war is Marcel Ophuls' riveting 1970 documentary *The Sorrow and the Pity*, portraying the Nazi occupation of the French city of Clermont-Ferrand during World War II. People in all situations, conditions, and walks of life are interviewed. For actors, writers, and directors, the lessons are invaluable.

PART TWO

§

INTERPRETING CHARACTERS:
THE PRACTICAL APPLICATIONS
OF PSYCHOLOGY

Introduction

§

Psychology and Psychoanalysis in Plays and Films

The theater and the cinema have dealt directly with psychology and psychological subjects ever since Freud penetrated public consciousness. Psychiatrists and psychoanalysts are frequent characters in films, from the psychiatrist at the asylum in *Random Harvest* (1942) treating Ronald Colman's war neurosis amnesia; to the analysts played by Ingrid Bergman and Michael Chekhov in Hitchcock's *Spellbound* (1945); to Billy Crystal's character in the satirical *Analyze This* (1999) and *Analyze That* (2002), with Robert De Niro as his mobster patient; reminding one of *The Sopranos,* the HBO series in which a gangster (James Gandolfini) consults a psychiatrist (Lorraine Braco).

Sigmund Freud himself has been portrayed on film by actors a number of times. John Huston's *Freud* (1962), with Montgomery Clift excellent and thoughtful in the title role, is a highly fictionalized account of the beginnings of psychoanalysis. Alan Arkin plays Freud in the amusing Sherlock Holmes film *The Seven-Per-Cent Solution* (1976). Freud spoke fluent, clear English with a rather heavy Austrian accent, as you can hear in recordings of him in an A & E Home Video Biography DVD.

I have already discussed the 1977 German television film *Young Dr. Freud* and the 2003 French television film *Princesse Marie* in chapter 1 on page 68, and Nicholas Wright's *Mrs. Klein,* which depicts situations in the life of Melanie Klein, on page 93. These films and the play did not oversimplify psychoanalysis, as it would have been all too easy to do. There have been a number of films and plays that did just that, among them Terry Johnson's *Hysteria* (1993), which puts Salvador Dalí on stage with Sigmund Freud—the two met in London in 1938; and Willy Holtzman's *Sabina* (2005) about a patient of both Jung's and Freud's, Sabina Spielrein, a very disturbed young lady who was cured and became a psychoanalyst, returned to her native Russia, and was killed by the Nazis during World War II. Christopher Hampton's *The Talking Cure* covers much the same ground as *Sabina* but is less simplistic. Richard Brockman's play *5 O'Clock* (2003) concerns the arrest and interrogation of Anna Freud by the Gestapo; she tries to convince her father to leave Vienna. The title derives from the fact that Anna's training analysis sessions with her father always began at five o'clock in the afternoon.

Among the most interesting films directly influenced by and dealing with Freudian psychoanalysis is Alfred Hitchcock's *Spellbound,* with Gregory Peck as an amnesiac patient. The view of psychoanalysis is somewhat oversimplified, but the story is very effective, the acting is superb, and the film is beautifully made. It includes a spectacular and famous dream sequence based on designs by Salvador Dalí. Hitchcock's *Strangers on a Train* (1951), based on a novel by Patricia Highsmith, is another psychological thriller, in which a psychotic, Robert Walker, thinks he has made a bargain with a fellow traveler, played by Farley Granger, to exchange murders. Barry Sonnenfeld's hilarious comic remake *Throw Momma from the Train* (1987) stars Danny DeVito as a misfit; Anne Ramsey in a tour de force as his cranky, abusive mother; and Billy Crystal as DeVito's writing teacher, with whom DeVito thinks he has made an agreement to swap homicides.

In *Vanilla Sky* (2001), a complicated, compelling dream fantasy, Tom Cruise's character is being treated by a psychiatrist, played by Kurt Russell. Stanley Kubrick's *Eyes Wide Shut* (1999) with Tom Cruise as a doctor who gets involved in a strange orgiastic society, as an outsider, is based on a story by Freud's contemporary and acquaintance, Arthur Schnitzler, who used Freud's ideas constantly in his writing. A psychiatric institution and psychiatrists figure largely in another Tom Cruise film, *Rain Man* (1985), in which Dustin Hoffman plays Tom Cruise's long-lost idiot-savant brother.

The classic psychological thriller *Gaslight* (1944) stars Charles Boyer as a sadistic, psychopathic character, who, for mercenary motives, terrorizes his lovely, sweet-tempered, compliant wife, played with depth and passion by Ingrid Bergman, into believing she is going insane. *All About Eve* (1950), made at the point when psychology was beginning to be understood by the general public as something more than simply the treatment of the mentally ill, shows the direct influence of Freudian ideas, particularly in its portrait of the title character, Eve Harrington, an "as-if" personality (see page 183). *Fatal Attraction* (1987) with Glenn Close as a woman obsessed with a married man played by Michael Douglas, with whom Close has had a brief affair; and *Dream Lover* (1994) with James Spader as the victim of a woman with an "as-if" personality who manages to have him committed to an asylum, deal with psychosis. And who could forget Humphrey Bogart's performance as the paranoid Captain Queeg, with his narcissistic personality disorder, in *The Caine Mutiny* (1954), set during World War II? The ship's communications officer, Lt. Tom Keefer (Fred MacMurray), compares Queeg— "a Freudian delight," as he says— to Captain Bligh in *Mutiny on the Bounty,* the Academy Award winner for best picture of 1935. Based on historical events, the film was made only three years before the Second World War, and Charles Laughton's classic performance as the paranoid, obsessive shipboard tyrant echoes the personalities of the psychopathic dictators then in power in Europe. Audiences must immediately have made the connection. Bligh was apparently quite a typical eighteenth-century officer, when tyranny was the order of the day, and living and working conditions in the navy were horrible. He was also an unusually courageous seaman, making a historic voyage to safety in the ship's longboat after the mutineers had cast him and other members of the crew adrift.

The chilling psychopath who begins as an innocent pathological liar on a superficial, self-protective level and becomes a murderer is so sympathetically portrayed that one could almost pity the unhappy Tom Ripley played by Matt Damon in *The Talented Mr. Ripley* (1999), based on Patricia Highsmith's novel, were it not for the horror of what he has done. There are no doubt people like that, and one would never suspect them, because they present a terribly sweet exterior to the world. John Malkovich plays him when he is older, as a brilliant psychopath already ensconced in his psychological otherworldliness, in *Ripley's Game* (2003). The 1960 French version of *The Talented Mr. Ripley, Purple Noon,* with Alain Delon as Ripley, is also quite good and tells the story very differently from the American version. There have also been films about real-life people with severe narcissistic personality disorders, among them the sociopathic serial killers Aileen Warnous (*Monster*), Ted Bundy, and Jeffrey Dahmer.

Mel Brooks's *High Anxiety* (1977), a parody of Hitchcock's psychological thrillers, is awfully silly and absolutely hilarious. Brooks is a psychiatrist who takes over the direction of an asylum that seems to be run by its inmates, so insane is the former director, a psychiatrist played by Harvey Korman, who is having a sadomasochistic affair with the outrageous Nurse Ratchett, played by Cloris Leachman. The extremely funny *What About Bob?* (1991) stars Richard Dreyfuss as a tense, narcissistic psychiatrist and Bill Murray as his loony patient. Diane Wiest plays a psychiatrist in the dramatic comedy film *The Scout* (1994), with Albert Brooks as a baseball scout and Brendan Fraser as the world's greatest baseball player, the emotionally needy and repressed Steve Nebraska; this is a brilliant, moving, funny film, and the performances are superb. In the sensitive, wryly amusing, bittersweet *Little Man Tate* (1991), Wiest plays the director of a school for genius children, and she is a very different character than in the later film; here she is rigid and inflexible, dealing with a boy genius, beautifully played by Adam Hann-Byrd, and his working-class mother, played by Jodie Foster, who also directed.

Such psychological thriller films as *The Shrike* (1955), with June Alyson and Jose Ferrer, or *Whirlpool* (1949), with Ferrer again, this time as an evil hypnotist, portray the possibilities of using psychology for evil purposes. The horrifying *Snake Pit* (1948) showed in a most painful manner the indignities, humiliations, and maltreatment to which insane-asylum patients were often subjected. And the question of who is mad—the patients in the local asylum in a French town or the people who make war—is raised in the satirical and moving antiwar French/British film *King of Hearts* (1966), set during World War I.

For a look at how brutally mental patients were treated in the late eighteenth and early nineteenth centuries, see *Sade* (2003) with Daniel Auteuil as the Marquis de Sade, imprisoned in the asylum of Charenton, or, less good, *Quills* (2000) with

Geoffrey Rush as Sade. And the film of Peter Weiss's play *Marat/Sade* (1966), with Patrick Magee as the keenly intelligent and bizarre Marquis, is set in the same place, during which the question of what it means to be insane is proposed, as the infamous Marquis de Sade puts on a play with the inmates that includes the assassination of the radical French revolutionary Jean-Paul Marat. Maurice Lever's *Sade: A Biography* (1994) is a mine of information about the treatment of the mentally disturbed in the French Revolutionary era, as well as a fascinating look at the strange and complicated Sade.

The Story of Adele H. (1975) is based on the real-life story of Victor Hugo's daughter, played by Emmanuelle Béart. Possibly psychotic, Adele Hugo was obsessively, delusionally in love with a young English soldier, whom she followed to Halifax, Nova Scotia. In the subtle psychological drama *Nelly et Monsieur Arnaud* (1995), Béart plays a young woman in the throes of separating from her husband. A courtly, dignified older gentleman (Michel Serrault) is introduced to her by a mutual friend and hires her as a temporary secretary to help him with his memoirs. He has fallen in love with her at first sight and never tells her so. "There are some desires that should never be expressed," he says to her in his usual offhand but reserved way. Underneath his serene, unruffled, somewhat inhibited exterior lurk anger and quite a temper. This man has had a past.

The greatest master of psychological drama in the theater was Anton Chekhov, whose plays are discussed in chapter 11 and elsewhere in this book. In Harold Pinter's plays and films, among them Joseph Losey's *The Servant* (1963), about a sadomasochistic relationship between a master (James Fox) and the servant (Dirk Bogarde) who controls him, the text is clearly the tip of the psychological iceberg and the subtext is everything. Paul Schrader's film *The Comfort of Strangers* (1991), with a screenplay by Pinter, stars Rupert Everett and Natasha Richardson as a young couple victimized by two psychopaths, played by Christopher Walken and Helen Mirren. The film is set in the most forbidding Venice you ever saw, brooding, dark, and gloomy. It harks back to an earlier period when the Doges ruled the Republic of Venice with an iron hand, and intrigue, mystery, anonymous denunciations, and murder were the order of the day.

I have already had occasion to discuss briefly some of the work of two great American masters of the psychological drama, Tennessee Williams and Eugene O'Neill. Williams's *A Streetcar Named Desire, Cat on a Hot Tin Roof,* and *Summer and Smoke* are only three of his many memorable journeys into what Freud called "the psychopathology of everyday life." As we have seen, O'Neill drew on William James's stream-of-consciousness idea for *Strange Interlude,* both a stage play and a film (1932), and on his own family background for the searing, brutally honest *Long Day's Journey into Night* and its sequel *Moon for the Misbegotten. Mourning Becomes Electra* is a scary psychological drama, very Oedipal in nature, based on the Greek myths of the aftermath of the Trojan War.

In the twentieth century, such plays as Arthur Kopit's *Oh, Dad, Poor Dad, Mama's Hung You in the Closet, and I'm Feeling So Sad* (it could hardly have a more Oedipally complex title) and Christopher Durang's zany, satirical comedy *Beyond Therapy* dealt in absurdist ways with psychological ideas. Twenty-first-century plays with psychological themes include Martin Moran's *The Tricky Part,* discussed in chapter 12, and *I Am My Own Wife,* the one-person show about a transvestite who survived first the Nazis and then the East German Communist regime. Based on a true story, it was superbly directed by Moisés Kaufman and brilliantly performed by Jefferson Mays in a virtuoso tour de force. He played thirty-six characters completely and convincingly, seeming simply to become the characters instantaneously.

All of the modern and contemporary films and plays mentioned above are an indication of how pervasive thinking in psychological terms has become. And there are so many more that could be cited as examples. The use of such terms as *ego, persona, introvert, unconscious,* or *Freudian slip* is another sign of how much psychology has been accepted into mainstream consciousness. Gone are the days when Freud was vilified for daring to speak his mind on the unspeakable subject of sex.

The 2004 film *Kinsey,* directed by Bill Condon and starring Liam Neeson as Alfred Charles Kinsey (1894–1956) and Laura Linney as his wife, portrays the groundbreaking research scientist who revolutionized ways of looking at people's sexual lives in America with his books on male and female sexuality in the late 1940s and 50s. He exploded commonly believed societal clichés and revealed what people actually did and how they lived their lives.

Freud had exploded clichés about sexuality long before Kinsey came on the scene. Like the dog that does not bark in the night in Arthur Conan Doyle's Sherlock Holmes story "Silver Blaze," any mention of Freud, Wilhelm Reich, the magisterial 1886 study *Psychopathia Sexualis* by Richard von Krafft-Ebing (1840–1902) — on which Freud relied for information when he was writing *Three Contributions to the Theory of Sex* — or the pioneering work of the Berlin sexologist and early gay rights advocate Magnus Hirschfeld (1868–1935) is noticeable by its absence in the film. But then, their revolutionary ideas, conclusions, and attitudes about sex had not sufficiently penetrated mainstream American consciousness some fifty years ago. It took Kinsey, who was as excoriated and vilified as Freud, Reich, and Hirschfeld had been, to open people's eyes.

I went to a SAG screening of the film, after which there was a question-and-answer period with Lynn Redgrave, whose portrayal of the last interview subject in the film is a poignant, heartwarming conclusion, pointing up the benefits of Kinsey's studies. The interviewee had been divorced by her husband. Her children were adults, and she had decided to get a job, where she met and fell in love with another woman but did not dare to express her feelings. After reading Kinsey's study of female sexuality, she realized how many women out there had the same kind of feelings and worked up the courage to tell the woman she loved her. The feelings were mutual, and they had been together for three years when Kinsey interviewed her. She says to him: "You saved my life."

Asked about her preparation for the one-scene role, Ms. Redgrave talked about having worked out the character's entire biography, deduced from the text, including the fact that she had been a Westchester soccer mom and that her three children were all boys, which explained why she had no women in her life to confide in, no grown-up daughter who might have been able to help her or at least to understand. Her analysis forms the entire subtextual context of the scene. And in order to play the scene, which begins *in medias res,* Liam Neeson, taking a hint from Kinsey's own practice of always putting his interview subjects as much as their ease as possible, suggested they improvise everything that happens in the interview before the scene begins. When she felt comfortable, Ms. Redgrave slipped naturally into starting the scene with the lines in the script, as the camera rolled.

❧
Shakespeare's Timeless Psychological Themes

A Psychopathic Personality: Shakespeare's Richard the Third

*W*hy have generations found Shakespeare's Richard the Third attractive as a personality? What enables audiences to identify on some level with such a monstrous villain? In "The 'Exceptions,'" (part of a longer essay, "Some Character-Types Met with in Psycho-analytic Work," 1916) Freud discusses Shakespeare's genius in creating this character. He informs us that patients must often make some sort of temporary sacrifice of their pleasure, as part of their therapy, in order to work on their problems with their doctor's guidance. Some patients categorically refuse to do this on the grounds that they have suffered enough and are entitled to pleasure, because they are exceptional people. Freud sees this attitude in Richard, Duke of Gloucester.

At the very opening of the play, Shakespeare does not reveal all the contents of his character's psyche. The audience perceives that Richard's grandiosity and overweening pride mask deep insecurity. And the opening soliloquy "merely gives a hint" of what is to come. The full extent of his ruthless megalomania and regressive narcissistic feelings of entitlement will only gradually be revealed as the play progresses. And this is part of Shakespeare's genius, as Freud says: he knows exactly how to arouse the audience's empathy by revealing at first only something with which we can all identify—namely, Richard's deformity, which is such a curse to him. It has forced him to renounce love. This renunciation already makes him an exception among men. He sees his deformity as a "congenital disadvantage," imposed on him through no fault of his own, and he has suffered terribly because of it. He rebels against this injustice and claims special privileges. Richard feels that life and nature owe him something, and we feel, watching him, that we are like him in some way, because we all have reasons "to reproach Nature for congenital and infantile disadvantages." And that is how Shakespeare immediately involves us in the world of the play. This identification with Richard allows us to hold onto our fascination with him as the play progresses. Here Freud ends his analysis, and it is a pity he did not go farther.

Richard's deceitful, cynical, manipulative, exploitative behavior will become increasingly erratic and repellant, forcing us to renounce as repugnant our early feelings of identification with this intimidating "psychopathic" personality. (The term *sociopathic* is sometimes used interchangeably with the term *psychopathic,* which is older; you will find neither in the current *DSM-IV-TR,* which does list *narcissistic personality disorder* and *antisocial personality disorder.*) The bases of this narcissistic personality disorder are the compulsive desire to manipulate and control other people — because the psychopath lives for power, due to an underlying feeling of powerlessness — and the incapacity to form meaningful, personal, emotional attachments. Psychopaths can counterfeit or imitate warmth and love for manipulative purposes, as Richard does with Anne, but they are internally cold and unfeeling. In fact, they avoid feeling. They don't want to feel, since feeling causes anxiety and threatens their stability. Feelings of anxiety, provoked by the slightest contradiction or challenge to their authority, can result in generalized rage that the psychopath attaches to a specific convenient object. This rage acts out the terrible physical abuse such people experienced as children. It is thus a coded message about their childhood.

Richard is able to see into others' emotions and desires and to perceive reality clearly, but only uses his knowledge for purposes of manipulation and control. His underlying hollow feeling of powerlessness thus receives vast overcompensation. The mechanism by which he inveigles the unsuspecting into identifying with him and doing his bidding is to invoke their sympathy and appeal to their self-interest. From there it is an easy task to persuade them that his self-interest is also theirs. Buckingham does his bidding for those reasons, only to be disabused too late of his illusions about Richard, whom he cynically thought he was using, whereas in reality Richard was using him.

Among the further characteristics of psychopathy are overweening self-love and profound insecurity. The awareness of all this is defended against and therefore hidden from the psychopaths themselves. Aside from a lack of self-knowledge, the psychopath displays a complete lack of conscience and has a distorted sense of reality, although some criminal psychopaths may perceive reality perfectly clearly. Nancy McWilliams tells us in *Psychoanalytic Diagnosis* that psychopathic personalities range from "psychotic, disorganized, impulsive, sadistic people…to urbane, polished charmers."

Everything in Richard's life must be sacrificed to his ambition. Everyone in his life is there to be manipulated to his ends and is seen as weak-willed, miserable, puny, and motivated by greed and the desire for power and therefore untrustworthy. His contempt for people is as boundless as his ego. And he shares another characteristic of psychopathy: the defensive projection and displacement of responsibility for anything that goes wrong onto other people.

Psychopaths can be very charming and seductive, despite their malignant narcissism. They put on a good act: they don't really feel charming inside. They just think that the people they have charmed in order to use, control, and manipulate them are stupid. The cynicism of the act Richard puts on for Lady Anne in the scene where he seduces her is revealed later in his callous line, "I'll have her, but I will not keep her long." The murderer of her husband and her father, Richard has convincingly counterfeited a passionate love he is incapable of feeling and pretended that he killed them because it was the only way he could get her, whom he adores more than life itself. If she doesn't believe him and still hates him, he tells her to stab him with his sword (of course he doesn't mean that either).

The grief-stricken Anne is really a good, moral woman and a good-hearted, kindly person who looks with affection on her fellow human beings, and is at the same time gullible and naïve. Richard catches her at a particularly vulnerable moment, both emotionally and as a defenseless woman in a dangerous, unprotected position now that her husband and father are dead, and takes full advantage of the situation. Even if she perceives his slimy hypocrisy, she has little choice but to succumb.

Here are some of the further hallmarks of the psychopath. These traits indicative of a toxic narcissistic personality disorder apply not only to Richard the Third but also, in varying degrees, to several other Shakespearean characters, among them Macbeth, Lady Macbeth, and Iago:

1. The view that other people don't count and don't matter unless the psychopath can use them in some way, and then they count for the psychopath only insofar as he or she can use them. After the psychopath has used them and is finished using them they cease to be of any interest and can be discarded with impunity, as Richard does Buckingham. Psychopaths do not see people as terribly real, with their own fears and desires. People are to them only pawns in the vast game of chess they play. In fact, they think life is a game.

2. They have little or no sense of acceptable social limitations. They will say and do anything they wish if it serves their purpose. They think the ordinary rules of fairness and morality don't apply to them.

3. They cannot bear to appear weak in others' eyes, since they feel unconsciously weak in their own eyes. Any feeling of weakness is turned into rage.

4. Psychopathic manipulations, which are meant in part to preserve the psychopath's wavering sense of personality and ward off danger, may enable him or her to appear charming one moment and terrifying the next. Patterns of behavior are unpredictable. One never knows what will set psychopaths off, so that everyone within their purview has to be constantly on his or her toes.

5. They are arrogant, grandiose, and self-aggrandizing pathological liars who habitually overestimate their abilities.

6. Because they are not as powerful as they would like to seem to themselves and as they have convinced themselves they are (which creates confusion that they repress), they overcompensate by overdoing their dominant, domineering behavior, and by a show of arrogance that seems even to themselves to be an act they are putting on for the benefit of others.

7. And psychopaths don't learn from experience, so that there is in them an element of self-destruction, along with elements of internal disorganization.

8. They rarely have a sense of shame, remorse, or regret for their unconscionable actions, unless they are caught, and then they are full of self-pity and only regret being caught.

The psychopathic aspect of Richard's character was emphasized in Ian McKellen's performances on stage and screen (1995), set in the fascist era, and Laurence Olivier's 1955 film interpretation, set in the historical era of the play.

Some examples of psychopathic characters in film are the frightening psychotic played chillingly by Kathy Bates in *Misery* (1990); the bizarre con man played by Michael Keaton in *Pacific Heights* (1990); the deeply disturbed young Jewish man who becomes a neo-Nazi played by Ryan Gosling in *The Believer* (2002), based loosely on a true story; the murderers played by Ryan Gosling and Michael Pitt in *Murder by Numbers* (2002); and the kidnapper played by Adrien Brody in *Oxygen* (1999). What a superb contrast he gives us between that psychopathic criminal and the character he played in *The Pianist* (2002), a man who has to deal with Nazi psychopaths and whose life is finally saved by a German army officer who is neither a Nazi nor a psychopath. There are a number of psychopathic criminal "enforcers" for crooked real-estate interests who drive people out of their homes in the riveting *The Beat That My Heart Skipped* (2005), in which Romain Duris tries to break out of the criminal underworld in order to pursue a career as a concert pianist, which had been his mother's profession. Jack Nicholson is positively seething with inner fury as the single-minded fanatical Col. Nathan R. Jessep in the film of Aaron Sorkin's hit Broadway play *A Few Good Men* (1992), starring Tom Cruise as the navy lawyer who proves Jessep's undoing. For a study of the genesis of a psychopath, see *Apt Pupil* (1998), in which Brad Renfro plays a high school student fascinated by the Nazis and tracks a psychopathic war criminal, played by Ian McKellen, who is hiding in the United States.

Another film that deals with psychopathy, but in a satirical vein, is the highly amusing *No Way to Treat a Lady* (1967), with Rod Steiger as a serial killer and George Segal as the detective who eventually nails him when he makes the fatal mistake of trying to kill Segal's girlfriend (Lee Remick). The film gives us some insight into the bizarre mentality of a psychopath who hates his mother so deeply he cannot even begin to acknowledge the hatred and instead comes to her defense when necessary. Rod Steiger's performance is an object lesson in how to play such characters with absolute sincerity, reality, and conviction. Psychopaths are really convinced that they and they alone have a monopoly on the truth, that their every action is justified, and that the world as they see it is the real world.

For a truly frightening real-life example, see the story of the Mafia hit man Richard Kuklinsky, known as the Iceman, in *The Iceman: Confessions of a Mafia Hitman* (2002), and *The Iceman Interviews* (2003), which contains three documentaries on the DVD. You will not believe what you are seeing and hearing. The films will freeze the very blood in your veins. And there are a massive number of films and documentaries about the most horrendous example in modern history of a psychopathic personality, Hitler.

Well worth reading should you need to explore the psychopathic character further, Florence R. Miale and Michael Selzer's *The Nuremberg Mind: The Psychology of the Nazi Leaders* (1975), with an introduction by Gustave M. Gilbert, Ph.D., provides a historical record of unparalleled value. Using the Rorschach diagnostic technique, the psychologist Dr. Gilbert examined the Nazi leaders on trial at Nuremberg in 1946–47. This book is a detailed analysis of the record of the examinations of sixteen of the war criminals; the other six were not available. Dr. Gilbert conducted extensive interviews with the criminals and took copious notes. And he concluded that they were all psychopathic in varying degrees and ways. Psychopaths are functional and often phenomenally energetic human beings, and when they choose to go into politics, they display an uncanny ability to rouse insecure, unhappy people to follow them, as Richard the Third does.

In conclusion, here is some of what the nineteenth-century critic William Hazlitt has to say in *Characters from Shakespeare's Plays* (1817) about the performance of Edmund Kean as Richard:

> There is at times an aspiring elevation, an enthusiastic rapture in his expectations of attaining the crown, and at others a gloating expression of sullen delight, as if he already clenched the bauble, and held it in his grasp. The courtship scene with Lady Anne is an admirable exhibition of smooth and smiling villainy. The progress of wily adulation, of encroaching humility, is finely marked by his action, voice and eye. He seems, like the first Tempter, to approach his prey, secure of the event, and as if success had smoothed his way before him....Mr. Kean's attitude in leaning against the side of the stage before he comes forward to address Lady Anne is one of the most graceful and striking ever witnessed on the stage. It would do for Titian to paint. The frequent and rapid transition of his voice from the expression of the fiercest passion to the most familiar tones of conversation was that which gave a peculiar grace of novelty to his acting on his first appearance....His manner of bidding his friends "Good night," after pausing with the point of his sword drawn slowly backward and forward on the ground, as if considering the plan of the battle next day, is a particularly happy and natural thought. He gives to the two last acts of the play the greatest animation and effect.... The concluding scene in which he is killed by Richmond is the most brilliant of the whole. He fights at last like one drunk with wounds; and the attitude in which he stands with his hands stretched out, after his sword is wrested from him, has a preternatural and terrific grandeur, as if his will could not be disarmed, and the very phantoms of his despair had power to kill.

"The Merchant of Venice": The Psychology of Prejudice

The word *prejudice,* meaning a preconception that is not based on either knowledge or rational thinking, most often refers to hostile prejudgments and phobic reactions regarding people because of the group they were born into. Associated with fear of the unknown, prejudices are phobic neuroses in which unconscious psychic conflicts, self-loathing, and threatening feelings, principally those revolving around sex, are disowned, split off from consciousness, and projected onto a convenient external object—namely, individuals and their groups to which negative attributes are ascribed a priori. These split-off conflicts and feelings then feel like threats from an external source. In their extreme forms, prejudices are paranoid psychotic delusions.

The phobic hater's own group is uncritically evaluated and sacrosanct, while the despised, prejudged group is disparaged and vilified. The haters compensate for their own masochistic, self-punishing feelings of inferiority (inextricably bound up with Oedipal guilt, according to Freud) by maintaining that they are superior and the hated, feared group is inferior. Reality testing is avoided: it would reveal the stupidity of the prejudice and upset the hater's psychological apple cart, because somewhere in their unconscious, the prejudiced know they are being moronic.

The bigot's displacement of unconscious feelings of hatred, homicidal anger, and rage that have their origin in early childhood conflicts is an attempt to deny that those feelings exist and to avoid being punished for them—"for who shall 'scape whipping?" Being sadomasochistic cowards and bullies, haters either avoid confrontation with the people they loathe or typically pick on someone they perceive, rightly or wrongly, as powerless and weak. It is not enough for them to hate someone: they must have their Oedipal revenge, and the target of their hatred must be made to feel their loathing and punished, provided there are no repercussions.

If Antonio had not thought Shylock weak and in an indefensible position, he would never have voided his rheum upon Shylock's beard or spit upon his Jewish gabardine. Voiding the rheum and spitting are unconscious symbolic imitations of the discharge of seminal fluid. To make the orgasm into an act of contempt is to denigrate sex itself as contemptible. Its "dirty" product, like excrement or urine, must be "voided." The symbolic seminal fluid is discharged onto the Jew, who is thus unconsciously seen as a sexual object and therefore as dirty and worthy only of contempt and detestation. This is exactly how anti-Semites, Antonio among them, unconsciously view themselves, their own sexual feelings, and sexuality in general.

In addition, the circumcised Jewish male is seen as not quite being a man, because circumcision is equated unconsciously with castration, and the unconscious castration anxiety of the anti-Semite is aroused. It is no accident that in grotesque images of Jews, the nose, a phallic symbol, is the outstanding facial feature. The noses in caricatures of Jews do indeed resemble hanging penises.

Nobody could be more surprised than Antonio when Shylock chooses not to relent in his demand for the pound of flesh. He thought he had picked a passive victim on whom to void his rheum, and lo and behold, the victim has turned on him! But how could this happen? Had Shylock not said that sufferance was the badge of all his tribe? In Antonio's unconscious, this remark had given rise to the inadmissible analsadistic fantasy of sodomizing Shylock or, worse, of Shylock's sodomizing him. The Jews have been "taking it" for centuries. These unacceptable paranoid fantasies are displaced and appear disguised in Antonio's sadistic verbal abuse of the moneylender:

he is right to condemn Shylock as a usurer! He will continue his persecution! He will spit on Shylock again, he says, and spurn (kick) him, too, presumably in his behind! And what does Antonio fantasize unconsciously about doing to Bassanio, with whom he is in love, for whom he would do anything? What does he unconsciously want Bassanio to do to him? He overestimates the rather shallow if charming Bassanio's worth in the typical manner of someone who makes a narcissistic object choice and then idealizes the object. Masochism is sadism's intimate partner, and in his relationship with Bassanio, Antonio is nothing if not masochistic, afraid that Bassanio will abandon him, just as he is sadistic with Shylock, whom he goads into punishing him so that he can create a sadomasochistic scenario. He wants to have the pleasure of suffering and feeling self-righteous. He is, of course, unconscious of his true motivations. No, the Jew is simply a devil and delights in making him, poor Antonio, miserable out of the crassest, meanest motives, because he is a Christian and that's how Jews are: nasty and vindictive! This must be how Antonio saw his father, but he could never consciously acknowledge that. He must have gone through hell with his parents in the Oedipal phase to have become so paranoid.

Paranoia, based as Freud tells us on unconscious, unacceptable homosexual tendencies, is another trait always found in the prejudiced mentality, whether that paranoia is a component of a neurotic personality disorder or of a psychotic illness. But otherwise, prejudices cut across characterological lines, although they may manifest themselves differently in different character types. Either an obsessive-compulsive or a histrionic personality may harbor the psychotic, analsadistic delusions of racism or anti-Semitism. But the histrionic person might generalize in abstract ways when talking about people who belong to a so-called different race or about Jews, while an obsessive-compulsive individual might perform certain rituals connected with Jews, such as crossing him or herself (if he or she is a religious Christian) whenever an individual perceived as a Jew is sighted. A director who wants to emphasize Gratiano's obsessive-compulsive side might direct him to cross himself every time he sees Shylock or Tubal.

Recently, an acquaintance of mine informed me that his father was Jewish and his mother was a Christian. "Even though the Nazis would have considered me Jewish," he added, "under Jewish law, I am not a Jew." (Orthodox Jewish law is matrilineal — that is, it traces descent and confers the status of being a Jew through the mother.) I smiled and said, "Well, a lot of Jewish people don't agree with that law, and if you want to be considered Jewish . . ." "No, I just want to be thought of as a human being." "Isn't that the Jewish problem par excellence?" I said. I might have added that it is the problem of all those members of so-called minority groups who are perceived as "different" and less than human by someone else and who experience prejudice and discrimination. It is Shylock's problem.

Anti-Semitism in its most virulent form is not merely prejudice against or phobic neurotic dislike of Jews: it is an obsessional psychosis in which fear and envy are mixed. The psychosis of anti-Semitism consists of a persecutory delusional system of ideas about Jews that is divorced from reality and passionately believed in. The so-called Jewish conspiracy to dominate the world holds the central position in this judeophobic madness. All evidence proving the contrary is rejected or reinterpreted in order to allow it to fit into the psychotic system. Jews are dehumanized and demonized. The psychosis is manifested in what Elizabeth Young-Bruehl characterizes in her magisterial *The Anatomy of Prejudices* (1996) as "analsadistic chimeria." The sadomasochistic ravings of the anti-Semitic Baron de Charlus in Marcel Proust's *In Search of Lost Time* are a perfect illustration of what she means.

Homophobia and general fears of sexuality are integral parts of racism and anti-Semitism. Most anti-Semites prefer to avoid confrontation with Jews, whom they fear, and to confine themselves to talking in the most negative terms about them. In both the neurotic and psychotic varieties of anti-Semitism, they project onto the Jews their sense of their own weakness and vulnerability, their own sense of not belonging anywhere, and their own aggressive and exploitative tendencies.

Considering the Christian characters in *The Merchant of Venice*, I would say that Shakespeare clearly understood the nature of the delusional projection of the unacceptable, disowned, and split-off qualities of the anti-Semites onto Jews. This extraordinary insight was especially unusual for an Elizabethan Englishman who could not have been acquainted with Jews in general, since they were not permitted to live in England, although many converted Jews and others lived there anyway. Among them was Queen Elizabeth's personal physician and frequent confidant and agent, Dr. Rodrigo Lopez, a Portuguese-Jewish convert. In 1594 he was wrongfully accused by his enemies of trying to poison her, found guilty, and publicly tortured and executed. In fact, he had promised his correspondent King Philip of Spain that he would poison her for fifty thousand gold ducats if the king paid him in advance, but the king refused to do so. Dr. Lopez told the English—who knew all about his contacts with the Spanish, to whom he had often fed false information at their request—that he had never intended to murder the queen and only wanted the Spanish gold. Elizabeth believed him, but his enemies at court prevailed. This notorious case was still fresh in the public mind a few years later when Shakespeare produced his play, in which there are allusions to it. The first Shylock, probably Richard Burbage, may have made up to look like Dr. Lopez.

His insight into the projective mechanisms of the anti-Semitic mind notwithstanding, Shakespeare painted the satanic portrait not just of a Jew but of *the* monomaniacal Jew expected by Elizabethan audiences, which was fundamentally that of an antipathetic alien hellbent on avenging the insults to his "tribe." Shylock's forced conversion to Christianity and the treatment he receives at the hands of the Christians was considered entirely justifiable. Unthinking prejudice against Jews, seen as treacherous and untrustworthy like Judas, was simply part of the culture. The ingrained hatred of Jews was justified on religious grounds, like the hatred for other religions, particularly Roman Catholicism. But Shakespeare, being the great humanist and perceptive thinker that he was, could not help but add a realistic human touch to the stereotypical character of the Jew prevalent in his day. He seems to be saying, "Yes, the Jews are horrible, but what do you expect, given how they are treated? And are the Christians *really* any better than the Jews? Do they really live by Christian principles? Are they better than Jews just because they are Christians?" The Christian characters in Shakespeare's play think they are. But every group into which humanity has divided itself has a positive identification that does not fit the stereotypes prejudiced outsiders have about it. And Shylock is certainly not a Jewish character in any real, positive sense that a Jew would recognize as making him Jewish, such as taking pleasure in the traditions, the joy, the humor, the laughter, the sense of love and kindness, and the strong family ties; as well as in Judaism itself, with its holidays and rituals and the moral approach to living an ethical life based on a firm commitment to the Torah.

"…[A] pound of his fair flesh / to be cut off and taken in what part of his body pleases me…" Thus does Shylock laughingly demand his jocular, very un-Jewish bargain of Antonio—such a bargain, clearly leading to murder, is forbidden in the Torah. Theodor Reik sees Antonio as being an analogue of Christ, whom the Jews have been historically accused of killing. And the audience makes the unconscious identification of Antonio with Jesus and Shylock with the Christ-killer.

Any psychoanalyst will tell you, as Reik points out in his chapter "Jessica, My Child!" in *The Secret Self: Psychoanalytic Experiences in Life and Literature* (1953), that the fear is not that the flesh will be cut from Antonio's chest but that he will be castrated. For Freud, castration anxiety is at the root of anti-Semitism: all non-Jews learn that Jewish males are circumcised, and as previously noted, circumcision is unconsciously equated with castration. Castration anxiety is projected onto Jewish males, who are not quite seen as men but rather as emasculated and feminized, and therefore as inferior. Of course, Jews have the same castration complexes that non-Jews do. Certainly Shylock does.

Some Jews have internalized the attitudes anti-Semites have about them, thus unconsciously humiliating and punishing themselves. At the same time, they magically try to ward off the hatred directed at them by adopting anti-Semitic attitudes and projecting them onto other Jews and away from the self. Feelings of self-hatred and inferiority arising from Oedipal-phase hatred of the parents redirected at the unconsciously guilt-ridden self are so devastating that they are disowned, split off, and projected onto other Jews. They are convenient objects with whom the projector unconsciously identifies and whom he or she consciously rejects, thus implicitly rejecting him or herself. This is paradigmatic of what self-hating people belonging to other hated groups do to themselves, but not all self-hatred is turned into hatred for members of one's own group. In Shylock's case, it is directed towards members of the other group, to which he does not belong, the Christians, and this is another reason the play is considered anti-Semitic: it presents Shylock's hatred of Christians as paradigmatic.

Jessica's self-hatred, on the other hand, is redirected at other Jews and at herself as a Jew. Her hatred for her father is reinforced because he is overprotective, sending her the message that she cannot take care of herself or be independent, that she is somehow still an unruly child who needs to be carefully guarded. Out of guilt over her hatred, because it was born out of her repressed love for him—she hates herself for hating him—she has distanced herself from him, so that they barely communicate. She is embarrassed by her Jewish father, but really by herself, because she too is Jewish, after all—but no, no, she's not like *that*: "Alack, what heinous sin is it in me / To be asham'd to be my father's child! / But though I am a daughter to his blood / I am not to his manners." In order to ward off her feelings of self-hatred and so as not to be hated by others, she has developed an ingratiating, almost overly sweet persona with everybody including her anti-Semitic servant. That way, they have to love her, as her ego narcissistically demands. And if they hate Jews, she will go along with it and not protest, just so they don't put her in the same category. Harold Bloom says in *Shakespeare: The Invention of the Human* (1998) that she is "insufferable." He also finds her "charming." And Bloom feels that "she gets what she deserves in her playboy, Lorenzo."

It is clear that even those who find Shylock's desire for vengeance understandable, and who quote his famous speech "Hath not a Jew eyes…" about the common humanity of Jews and Gentiles as one sympathetic to Jews, see him as ultimately contemptuous of the rest of humanity: inveterate, inflexible, unforgiving, and permanently involved in his hatred of those who hate, despise, and mistreat Jews. Shylock is bent on their destruction, and all Jews are to be seen as imbued with this same desire to destroy others in some measure, when those others are perceived as anti-Jewish. The anti-Semite knows, after all, that every Jew feels personally attacked by anti-Semitism, because every Jew *is* personally attacked.

Both Morris Carnovsky, whom I saw in television excerpts from his interpretation at the American Shakespeare Festival, and Dustin Hoffman, whom I saw on stage in a Broadway production, tried to humanize Shylock and play him as sympathetically as possible. Each in his own individual way played the part brilliantly. Carnovsky was impressive, dignified, and even majestic; deeply hurt, proud, and not to be trifled with. Hoffman was slightly overwrought, almost verging on hysterical at times, and very passionate, clearly deeply upset and goaded almost into madness by the anti-Semitism directed against him. In his scenes with Jessica, he showed his anxiety and his love, even while being extremely strict with her.

Humanizing Shylock was very difficult for them to do, given not only his reprehensible demand in the trial scene for the pound of flesh but his entire troubled relationship with Jessica. The literary phenomenon of the ugly, evil, controlling, manipulative, wicked Jewish male and the sweet, lovely, caring, compassionate, exceptionally beautiful, desirable Jewish female—or the hard-hearted Jewish father and his innocent, sweet, lovely Jewish daughter—is ubiquitous in European literature from Shakespeare through Balzac and beyond, and is obviously Oedipally based: the bad father whom the child wants to be rid of and the good mother whom the child desires.

Whatever the interpretation, I have always been left with the old idea that Shylock is crazy and villainous. This was something that emerged in Laurence Olivier's effective if undignified and jovial, almost comic interpretation (until his tragic near-collapse at the end) in a production set in nineteenth-century Venice and directed by Jonathan Miller (who is Jewish) for the theater and for television. Miller tried to make the play about anti-Semitism rather than anti-Semitic. The Christian characters were horribly prejudiced; hypocritical, as Shylock points out to them; and generally pretty awful, but that hardly helped dispel the impression of Shylock's deliberate wickedness. For one thing, Shylock dances in glee when he learns of Antonio's misfortunes, which mean he will be able to take his pound of flesh. This gloating clearly shows Shylock's self-loathing, since to project such extraordinarily deep hatred onto someone else can only mean that one has a self-hating side—the moment is horrifying. Self-hatred is an aspect of Antonio's personality as well, and that is also clear in this production. Still, ending the play with the Kaddish (the Jewish prayer for the dead) sung in the background to underline the injustice done to Shylock didn't help dispel the nastiness of the play. It is obvious that Shylock is by no means content, despite his line, "I am content." He could never really become a Christian, nor, Shakespeare implies, could any Jew, which is anther reason the play is perceived as anti-Semitic.

However, there is an exceptional, fresh, and eye-opening interpretation of *The Merchant of Venice*, adapted for the screen in 2004, which changed the distasteful impression this play always makes on me. The film was directed by Michael Radford, with a superb cast, headed by Al Pacino as Shylock. He had been asked to play the role many times but had always refused because of the play's anti-Semitism. But when he saw the film script, he changed his mind.

For the first time in my experience, I found Shylock to be one of Shakespeare's towering and most powerful tragic characters, thanks to Pacino's passionate, haunting performance, which is riveting from beginning to end. Shylock has been pushed over the edge by his daughter's betrayal, and in the trial scene, we see that he has gone quite quietly mad. When we first see him, Antonio voids his rheum on Shylock's beard on the Rialto against the background of other shocking and violent anti-Semitic incidents taking place there. As the film goes on, we continue to side with Shylock, especially in his deep despair over losing his daughter (an aspect of the character that is also movingly described by Theodor Reik in "Jessica, My Daughter!") Only in the trial scene does our sympathy turn to antipathy and chilled horror as he prepares to commit murder, until he loses everything, and then our sympathy and outrage on his behalf are reasserted. The self-righteous, hypocritical obtuseness of forcing Shylock to convert to Christianity has never been more apparent than it is in this film. And we perceive as horribly unjust the confiscation of all his possessions when he has actually been prevented from doing any harm; the law has said it is his intention in wanting to take a Christian's life that counts against him and justifies the sentence.

In any case, throughout the film we see Shylock as an individual and not as a stereotypical portrait of a self-loathing, hateful Jew applicable in some measure to all Jews. This is an incredible achievement by both Radford and Pacino, especially when you consider the play's history. In the trial scene, for instance, Radford makes clear the fact that Shylock is an individual and not a representative of all that is Jewish by doing something one can only do in film and not in the theater: as Shylock is whetting his knife, Radford cuts to a shot of Shylock's friend Tubal (Allan Corduner) looking deeply distressed and dismayed, as if he had not expected Shylock to actually take the pound of flesh, an action Tubal and the other Jews in the trial audience clearly deplore and find terribly disturbing. And Tubal is profoundly saddened at his friend's deterioration.

Cutting the play for the screen adaptation was a necessity, of course. Happily gone is most of Shylock's servant Gobbo's anti-Semitic so-called humor. The choices for cuts in Shylock's part softened him, while preserving him and all the other characters as portraits of flawed human beings.

The Christians as portrayed in the film are a mixed group, many of them less than sympathetic. Gratiano is a boor and eminently dislikable. Bassanio's other friends are decadent, when they are not corrupt. Antonio as interpreted by Jeremy Irons is a typical neurasthenic, always tired and anxious: "In sooth, I know not why I am so sad: / It wearies me; you say it wearies you; / But how I caught it, found it, or came by it, / What stuff 'tis made of, whereof it is born, I am to learn…" He is also positively unpleasant, bitter, and constantly depressed because of his unfulfilled love for Bassanio (that is why he is "so sad"), and he is anti-Semitic to the core. For Antonio, Jews are inherently evil, so treating them sadistically is perfectly all right. Bassanio as played by Joseph Fiennes is very intelligent, as well as kind and even sweet, although he uses Antonio, which makes him too less than sympathetic. Even his love for Portia hardly redeems him in our eyes.

Portia (Lynn Collins) is vivacious, delightful, and brilliant; levelheaded and mentally healthy. She fulfills her obligations out of a sense of duty. But in the suspenseful trial scene, the character actually arouses our disgust with her goading, sadistic treatment of Shylock, however hateful we may find him in his murderous sadomasochism and however much he deserves to lose. She has, perhaps, displaced her resentment at having to stick by the terms of her father's will, which forced her to take a husband who chose the correct casket (even though it all worked out for the best), onto the unfortunate Shylock, a father figure in her unconscious mind. That may explain why she is so forthright and vicious with him. Her ingrained anti-Semitism, not stated but part of the cultural ethos that forms her background, is a further explanation.

The relationship of Shylock and Jessica in this film is deeply troubled, especially given Jessica's self-loathing. Shylock talks to her on a restrained, soft-spoken note, behind which we sense his deep love for her. He is never harsh and never scolding, but he is clearly in charge and worried for his daughter's virtue. But of course, she cannot stand to be treated like a child, and she wants her independence. And she obtains it by the worst of means, stealing her father's money and eloping with the judeophobic Lorenzo, who is nothing if not venal. And later on we see how alienated and uncomfortable she feels in the Christian society of Portia's Belmont. The sense of personal betrayal and the agony at her desertion—the deep, permanent sadness that settles over Shylock after he loses her—have never been more heartbreaking than in Al Pacino's dignified performance.

SOME CHARACTERS IN "OTHELLO": PARANOIA AND WOUNDED LOVE

Venice is enthralling, exhilarating, and incredibly beautiful, its ethereal, gossamer architecture shimmering in reflection in the Grand Canal, but once again Shakespeare transports us to a Venice that is brooding and dark. *Othello* begins at night, when people are asleep and dreaming—an appropriate opening for a play about the dark undercurrents of the human psyche. All the characters in this tragedy of wounded love are ambivalent in their feelings about one another and about themselves. That is what gives the play not only its impetus but also its atmosphere of constant uncertainty.

Does the cynical Iago, who hates so deeply, love? He certainly does not love his wife, Emilia, whom he merely tolerates. He has paranoid suspicions about her, if we can believe what he says, which seems so absurd to us that we find it difficult to believe he believes it. He doesn't seem to love himself, but rather to be full of self-loathing and of rage over his offended narcissism. He feels that he is an exceptional person, worthy of respect, and that people should appreciate and love him, but they don't. In any case, everyone around him is worthless and a fool. (Would that change if they loved him?) Perhaps he admires Othello, but he can find ready proof that Othello too is a fool: he believes all the falsehoods Iago knowingly tells him, and he can therefore be easily controlled.

Perhaps Iago really does have a jealous delusion and believes that Othello slept with his wife, which is patent nonsense. He thinks the same about Cassio. Iago has displaced and projected his desire to sleep with Cassio and with Othello onto Emilia! He is paranoid and, as previously stressed, two of the hallmarks of paranoia according to Freud are repressed, unacceptable homosexual desires and the conscious hatred of someone the paranoiac unconsciously loves. The paranoiac who has a male as an unconscious sexual object displaces sexual feelings and projects them onto that male in the form of a suspicion that he wants to sleep with the paranoiac's wife.

Iago is a bigot, and paranoia is one of the components of bigotry, although one may question how much bigotry is a basic motive for his nefarious actions. It clearly plays a part in his insane love/hatred of Othello, who is of African origin, as we all know. In fact, Brabantio, Desdemona's father, is a typical racist and was opposed to his daughter's marriage. Bigotry is indeed an important theme in the play. And Iago's bigotry, which seems so unconvincing even to himself and is so incredibly stupid, may, on the other hand, play the largest part in his psychopathic, warped mind — that is a decision for the actor to make. Although called a Moor, Othello is a Christian, not a Moslem, so religious prejudice can play no part. Nor can religion be an obstacle to his marrying Desdemona. She has fallen madly in love with him. Brabantio the bigot finds this incomprehensible, but his daughter sees Othello as beautiful, and she loves his character and his mind. If only Othello had trusted himself more, he would not have trusted her less than he should have.

In "Note on Desdemona" in *The Secret Self,* Theodor Reik deals insightfully with the relationship of Othello and Desdemona. He discusses the manifestations of Desdemona's identification with the masculine and the vestigial survival of her penis envy as two motivations for her falling in love with Othello, who is the ideal man — chivalrous, brave, courteous, and considerate; charming and masculine. As Othello says to the Venetian Senate when describing the course of his courtship with her, Desdemona said to him in admiration, almost enviously, having listened to his stories of his experiences, "…she wished that heaven had made her such a man," a line that clearly expresses what Reik meant and that is his clue as to that aspect of her personality.

The description of the psychopathic character traits of Richard the Third also contains much that would apply to the manipulative, game-playing Iago, in all his ambivalence. He has, for instance, exorbitant narcissism. It is unjustified by external circumstances, since he has accomplished nothing or at least very little in his life. And he has the incredible sense of entitlement that is a common trait of psychopaths and of the "exceptions" Freud mentioned in his consideration of King Richard.

Iago is completely obsessed with his hatred for Othello. He is in fact obsessed with Othello altogether. Why? Unconsciously at least, if not consciously, he is mad about Othello, one might say. He is madly in love with Othello, and it is a very threatening thing to him, this love. It is actually Desdemona, of whom he is insanely jealous, who is his intended victim. He hates her because Othello loves her, and Iago wants Othello to love him. Iago will destroy them both, and in doing so, destroy his own homosexuality. That may be one motive…or, since Iago is constantly suspicious and terrified of punishment, and (as Freud says is true of paranoiacs) hates consciously the person he unconsciously loves, it may be that he is really obsessed with Desdemona and that his obsession with Othello is an unconscious mask for that overwhelming desire for her. Or perhaps he is obsessed with both Othello and Desdemona together. In other words, Shakespeare has presented us with a riddle in portraying the nihilistic Iago's supposedly motiveless malignancy. But no malignancy is motiveless, and there are many possibilities as to what his motivations might be.

I remember being quite struck and a bit shocked at the age of thirteen, when my father took me to see *Othello* as a birthday present, with the lines where Iago talks of "lying" with Cassio, of throwing his leg over his, of the dream Cassio has. This dream is Iago's invention. It is therefore actually Iago's dream, his fantasy: he unconsciously lusts after Cassio, or perhaps not so unconsciously. At the time I thought, "Oh, that's just the way the Elizabethans talked. They were just being extravagant. It didn't mean anything." Now, of course, I know better. At any rate, the evidence in the lines is quite clear, and Othello is not even shocked by the incident, which means he is not surprised to hear of an at least latent bisexuality (of course, the word did not exist in the Elizabethan era, but the behavior certainly did) in both these men. He is deeply troubled only by what Iago appears to reveal about Cassio's relationship with Desdemona. This attitude about the incident involving two men sleeping together actually speaks volumes for Othello as a tolerant man who understands a good deal about the manifestations of human sexuality, although he is constitutionally incapable of dealing rationally with his own obsessions, and especially with his own obsessive jealousy regarding his wife.

Iago's hatred is not mitigated or mollified by what he has done. His revenge appears to bring him no satisfaction, and he does not seem to feel guilt or shame, let alone remorse. We cannot even trust that his motives were simply those of revenge for being passed over for the ensignship or of racism. Maybe he is just deeply angry because Othello doesn't really love him, and everything else is cynical rationalization.

Whatever the interpretation, Iago's behavior when in the presence of Othello is fawning and servile; cunning, cleverly manipulative, and controlling. But he shrinks from actual murder. Certainly most people shrink back when it comes to committing homicide. So deep is his hidden terror that Iago himself dare not murder, except in a panic, when he kills Emilia. Instead, he incites people to murder for him.

Othello, the brilliant, accomplished general and military expert, a man of passionate temperament — easily given to emotion in private life, although greatly coolheaded in a military situation — is capable of great extremes of goodness and badness. He is a splendid, generous, wonderful man with one fatal flaw: he trusts Iago. He is not gullible or naïve, simply manipulated. Iago plays upon Othello's underlying fears, and he does not perceive that Iago is deranged and evil. Nobody in the play does! And this is a clue as to how Iago should be played, whether he is interpreted as a rough-and-ready career soldier with a lower-class background and crude manners, or a silky smooth would-be aristocrat, unconsciously involved in his "family romance" and the fantasy that he was really born into a higher social class. In any case, he must appear forthright and honest, if not charming. As Hamlet says of Claudius, "A man may smile and smile, and be a villain." Nobody should be able to tell what Iago is really like. Even Emilia, who probably knows him best, only suspects his true nature, until near the end of the play. And she pays with her life.

Othello, who has some (but not all) of the phallic-narcissistic traits described by Reich — a certain display of arrogant self-confidence, masking insecurity; armoring in the chest area; aggressive demands and domination of the love object, as in the handkerchief scene with Desdemona; irrationality at times — is easy prey for Iago because he feels insecure. Part of his insecurity is unconscious, and part of it is conscious: as a foreigner and a black man, he knows that he doesn't quite fit into Venetian society. He knows that he is accepted provisionally and that he is the object of bigotry in spite of his military prowess and service to the state. It is this vulnerability that enables Iago to take advantage of him, which he does with all the characters whenever he wants something from them.

There have been splendid productions of this play, notably a Broadway production with James Earl Jones and Christopher Plummer, and another originally mounted at the American Shakespeare Festival in Stratford, Connecticut, with Moses Gunn and Lee Richardson. There is a recording available on CD of one of the best productions of all, the 1943 staging with Paul Robeson, deeply impressive in the title role, and Jose Ferrer as a particularly evil-minded villain. The young Uta Hagen, married to Ferrer at the time, plays Desdemona. Olivier's rather offensive interpretation of Othello as a stereotypical African complete with an unaccountable Caribbean accent is best avoided, as is Orson Welles's rather hammy version, both with good performances in other than the title role. The scenes from *Othello* in *Stage Beauty,* although anachronistically done in a contemporary method style, are riveting. And Lawrence Fishburne is also quite excellent as Othello in his 1995 film version of the play.

In *Stanislavsky Produces Othello* (1948) — an object lesson for directors and actors — compiled from his extensive production notes, Stanislavsky dwells at great length and in exhaustive detail on all the technical aspects of his production, on what the audience will see: the costumes, lighting, and scenery; such effects as the Venetian gondola that rows Iago and Rodrigo to the quayside at the opening of the play; and even on the sound level the audience should hear, as in this stage direction for act 1, scene 1: "The scene begins with two subdued voices in heated argument…

and the splashing of oars (which must not interfere with the words)." Stanislavsky writes a great deal about what we would now call the back-story of the play and describes, for instance, how Rodrigo's rejection by Desdemona caused him to lose his head. And Stanislavsky dwells at length on Iago's past and the actual circumstances and actions of his life, and on the nature of his past relationship with Othello. But he does not go into detail about his character in any psychoanalytical sense. His descriptions of character are in adjectives, rather than in analyses. He talks also in terms of the characters' "lines" (through-lines), and he tells the story of such events as Othello passing over Iago for promotion from the purely descriptive point of view of conscious motivations. Nevertheless, he does talk sometimes in more psychological terms, as when he tells us that Iago has hypnotized himself into believing that Othello had slept with Emilia, Iago's wife. And he exhorts the actors, or will exhort them — these are his director's prerehearsal notes to himself — to play scenes with the utmost passion and ardor, giving certain scenes, such as the opening, quick, lively, and nervous tempi. As a director, he is deeply concerned with the physical actions the actors will play and with what the audience will see them doing.

A Classic Freudian Interpretation: Ernest Jones's "Hamlet and Oedipus"

*E*xpanding on Freud's ideas about Hamlet, Ernest Jones in his book *Hamlet and Oedipus* sets forth the idea that Hamlet's Oedipus complex is the basic explanation for his hesitation in avenging his father's murder. Hamlet, like everyone, has difficulty in seeing his parents as sexual beings, in part because of the ancient repression of his proscribed Oedipal desires, which would arouse his disgust if reawakened. Unconsciously, they are indeed reawakened when he observes his mother with his uncle — with whom he had never identified as he had with his father, whose relationship with his mother he had learned to accept. In fact, in a reaction formation in which he turned his rivalry for his father into admiration, he had supposedly learned to love that relationship, and even to profess to admire the exclusive, deeply tender love the king displayed for Gertrude. This was what he consciously told himself. In reality, it was not so.

Gertrude has a sexual passion for Claudius, who fully returns it. Hamlet's deep, bitter jealousy of Claudius, who has replaced Hamlet's father in his mother's affections and bed, should be one of the factors that lead him to carry out the revenge, but it does not do so. According to Jones, this is because unconsciously he has been deeply jealous and resentful of the almost exclusive relationship of Gertrude and his father, King Hamlet, who excluded the young prince from his mother's affections. Consciously, Gertrude expresses her love and tender solicitude for her son. Unconsciously, she distances herself from him, partly to avoid the guilt of her remarriage and also out of the need to assert her maternal authority. When Hamlet repressed his Oedipal strivings, he sought to gain his father's love, but his father's coldness — the king was jealous of Hamlet's striving to win his mother's affection and so kept him at arm's length — wounded him, although he continued to respect and admire his father.

Perhaps he wanted his father to love him as tenderly as the king loved Gertrude, so that Hamlet is jealous of his mother too. (This complicated emotional situation with regard to the father figure is known as a *father complex,* with all its ambivalences and ambiguities.)

At the same time as he was jealous of his son, the old king really loved him, so that his ambivalent feelings must have confused him as well as his son at some points in their relationship. But despite the undeniable love between father and son, which the father had great difficulty in expressing, unconsciously Hamlet continued to resent and even to hate his father. Out of the unconscious fear that he would simply fall apart and/or be terribly punished (the fear of castration), he had to defend himself against any admission of such shocking, undesirable feelings of hatred, and so the principle traits and inhibitions of his personality—his shyness, his timidity, and his ruminative thinking—were generated. His father's death struck Hamlet with such great force because unconsciously it was a fulfillment of his inadmissible homicidal Oedipal desires, which could never be consciously admitted, and because in actual terms it was the terrible loss of the man whom he loved. He felt such guilt and shame, as well as such profound love, that he went into the most profound mourning, making a great show of the outward signs of grief, but indeed, he also had "that within which passes show"—and which he could not even begin to verbalize. As the old saying has it, be careful what you wish for: you may get it.

Jones's deductions made so much sense to Laurence Olivier that he used his interpretation when playing Hamlet in the 1951 film, which he also directed. In *The Secret Self,* Theodor Reik says he feels it is too obvious that Olivier has read Jones and Freud, and that Gertrude, admirably played by Eileen Herlie, is cast too young, so that Hamlet looks older than his mother. Reik also felt that there was too much physical contact between them. I didn't feel that way, but actually, in one respect he is probably right: the incest taboo alone, as well as the force of the emotions repressed in the Oedipal phase, would probably prevent such close personal contact. The sociocultural factor of behavior in the late medieval era in which the play is set in Olivier's film might also actually preclude certain kinds of touching. It might have been better to see how physically restrained Hamlet is with his mother, which would make the force of the repressed feelings even more apparent.

Anyway, Olivier did not pay strict attention to everything Jones had written. In his addendum to the book, "A Note on the Acting of Hamlet," Jones says that Gertrude's age should be forty-five. Wonderful as she is in the role, Eileen Herlie is nowhere near that. Jones describes Olivier's stage performance as one of "robust vehemence," but this is less apparent in the film version, although he is still occasionally quite energetic, and he does fulfill Jones's idea of Hamlet's "intense suffering," which Olivier emphasizes.

Another result of Hamlet's Oedipus complex is his abortive love for Ophelia, which must fail. He unconsciously identifies her with his forbidden mother, so that his inhibitions come into force, while consciously comparing her unfavorably to Gertrude. She is weak and untrustworthy in his eyes and all too ready to betray him, which he feels she does. He finds every excuse to alienate a woman who obviously adored him but does not understand him or know what is going on in his mind, which he does not reveal. Amazed at and put off by his frightening behavior, she does give him an excuse for his offensive actions towards her when she obeys her father Polonius and Claudius, and lends herself to their will as they spy on Hamlet, whose erratic behavior they consider a sign of madness. She is a frightened girl and does not dare disobey them.

Nor can one leave out of the picture the possibility of Hamlet's unconscious repressed homosexuality as a factor in his failed relationship with Ophelia. His relationship with Horatio is one of friendship, but if one may judge by his words in act 3, scene 2, his feelings are implicitly those of love. Hamlet's longing for his father's tender affection has been transferred to Horatio — the only person who never betrays the unhappy prince — from whom he expects complete support. "Give me that man / That is not passion's slave, and I will wear him / In my heart's core, ay, in my heart of heart, / As I do thee," says Hamlet to his dearest companion.

There is another question, scarcely posed by the unquestioning cultural premise in which the play moves but which must move the moral philosopher who is Hamlet: What is so wonderful about killing the man who killed your father? Is the cycle of violence never to end? The all-too-human desire for bloody revenge, thwarted in the play by the Oedipal strivings that have not been worked through, is a base desire in any case. Justice is more important, and Claudius should have his crimes brought home to him. He deserves punishment, but somehow we must find a way to end the cycle of violence.

The murder of his brother is evidence of Claudius's own Oedipus complex and the sibling rivalry it engendered. In winning crown and queen, he has triumphed over his brother and through him, symbolically, over their father. He has won a woman away from the man who was her husband. Of course, he has not actually won anything: he has stolen everything he now possesses. And because of his guilt, he cannot enjoy his victory. He is pursued by feelings of inadequacy, like Chekhov's character Ivanov, who thinks of himself as a superfluous man. But Ivanov is not a Claudius; he is a Hamlet.

In fact, Anton Chekhov created his own Russian version of Shakespeare's play, his variation on a theme, with the title character in *Ivanov*. To make the point even clearer, Ivanov says, "I've become another Hamlet." Here too is a man who cannot make a decision to better his life. He broods on his fate, ruminates and rationalizes. So depressed and troubled is he that he commits suicide, in an implicit answer to the famous question: "To be or not to be." His neurotic approach to life is passive and he feels weak, just as Hamlet does in Shakespeare's play.

David Shapiro describes this way of behaving in his book *Neurotic Styles* (1999) when he talks about a character style that is a variant of the impulsive style: the "Passive, 'Weak' Character." People who are impulsive do things without necessarily being aware of their motivations, as in "impulse buying," which can fill an emotional lack temporarily. When Hamlet kills Claudius after Gertrude's death, it is on impulse, rather than in a premeditated, calculated way. Everyone sometimes does things on impulse, but when someone's entire style of living is based on doing things without thinking about them, we can say that such a person is impulsive. They do not do anything in a sustained way that would require deliberation and planning. They may ruminate, as Hamlet does, but they do not act on their ruminations.

It is odd to think that passive people can be as impulsive as action-oriented people, but such is the case, because these types ruminate impulsively but without real reflection. This seems paradoxical, until you consider that their ruminations consist of avoidance, as in Hamlet's case. Such people feel impelled to turn things over and over in their minds without taking action. This is because they feel weak and give in to circumstances, rather than attempting to control them. On the other hand, they may give in to temptation, as Hamlet does when he impulsively treats Ophelia badly. Hamlet had not intended to be unkind to her, but on impulse, he is.

The play within the play is another impulsive last-minute idea, which he enthusiastically puts into action, only to revert to his passive mode of behavior after it has revealed the truth to him in no uncertain terms. When he kills Polonius, he does so once again on a last-minute impulse, because he mistakenly thinks Polonius is Claudius. Under temptation, he indulges in hasty, precipitate action because of his vague intention to kill Claudius. He then reverts to his usual passivity again, even though he disposes of the body in an active way. This is a recurring pattern that now becomes clear.

It is partly this impulsive avoidant behavior that enabled Freud to characterize Hamlet as a hysteric in the same letter of October 15, 1897, to his Berlin friend Dr. Wilhelm Fliess in which he discusses *Oedipus the King*. Hamlet certainly has histrionic personality traits, and his love for the theater and the art of acting is only the most obvious example of this side of his personality. Among other typical histrionic traits is Hamlet's intense level of anxiety, which threatens to overwhelm him as he goes from crisis to crisis. And he has an extremely high level of guilt and shame that propels him into a state of inertia at times. His guilt over his sexual feelings for Ophelia is very strong: he loves her but unconsciously identifies her with his mother, so that he cannot bring his love for her to fruition. Hamlet also has to be the center of attention, as in the court reception scene previously mentioned where he is in his mourning cloak. And in his philosophical, speculative soliloquies, he deals in generalities, after the typical manner of the hysteric, alternating between bitter and even suicidal musings and unbalanced moods along with self-castigation. In describing one of his patients, Shapiro says something that applies very well to Hamlet: he "exaggerates the extent to which his life actually has been determined by force of accidental, external circumstances; the circumstances bear too many marks of consistent selection."

In a display of ambivalence, Hamlet loves Ophelia and hates her for her supposed betrayal of him. She loves him and hates him for the way he behaves with her. Claudius too is a model of ambivalence. The murder he committed to win the crown and Gertrude leaves him ultimately dissatisfied and full of guilt. He is thus incapable of enjoying his ill-gotten gains, which actually shows that he has a conscience, weak as the moral sense in him is. He feels he deserves punishment, fears it, and has no real means of justifying his foul deed. Gertrude loves Hamlet and hates him, because through him she sees her own faults. She lusts after Claudius, but does she really love him? Is there some love in Hamlet for Claudius that is a key to his deep rage and disappointment, even before he knows about the murder?

OTHER APPROACHES TO HAMLET

You can read what Hazlitt has to say about Kean and Kemble in the part and about Edwin Booth's Hamlet in detail in the Variorum edition, where some of his prompt script, giving every intonation and gesture, is reproduced, and he must have been truly the "melancholy Dane," to judge by his Othello recording. He delivers Othello's speech to the Venetian Senate, justifying his marriage to Desdemona in a most lugubrious tone with a quality of realism I did not expect to hear in a nineteenth-century actor. Although he recorded "To be or not to be," I have not heard it; apparently the sound quality is so bad that nobody has seen fit to release it to the listening public.

Among the innumerable modern interpretations of the role (I have actually seen thirteen Hamlets), John Gielgud gives a glorious delivery of the verse in several recordings. Richard Burton in a 1964 Broadway production directed by Gielgud—filmed live and available on an Image Entertainment DVD—seemed to be a passionate prince who was generally overemotional, but somehow Burton was not terribly moving or even convincing. Eileen Herlie plays Gertrude once again, and Gielgud himself is the Ghost.

In 1969 Brian Bedford played him at the American Shakespeare Festival in Stratford, Connecticut, as truly mad in a generic sense. He and the production were enjoyable to watch, but Morris Carnovsky was the real star: Polonius in his interpretation was a narcissistic egotist. Carnovsky was so funny from his first entrance on, and one laughed so heartily, that one anticipated his future entrances with delight. When he first came on, he looked all around him, almost as if he were the king, to see who had noticed him and who had not, and whether or not they respected his power at court.

There are more than one hundred film and television versions of *Hamlet* listed on the Internet Movie Database (IMDb) web site, among them Franco Zefirelli's (1990), with Mel Gibson, effective and low-key; and Kenneth Branagh's brash, narcissistic interpretation (1996). Nobody really expected Ethan Hawke's performance in Michael Almereyda's high-tech, modern film (2000) to be very moving, but it was. He was simple and clear in his delivery and very real psychologically, able to involve us in his predicament in a most sympathetic way. But the most extraordinary and compelling version I have seen is the 1964 Soviet Russian film adaptation, *Gamlet* (there is no *h* in Russian), directed with great insight by Grigori Kozintsev, with Innokenti Smoktunovsky absolutely remarkable in the title role and a superbly evocative score by Dimitri Shostakovich. It is available on a Russian Cinema Council (RUSCICO) DVD, and if you love the play as much as I do, you must see this artistically photographed, sensitively and realistically acted rendition. The first appearance of the Ghost made the hair stand up on the nape of my neck!

Stacy Keach, serious, understated, and empathetic in the 1964 Central Park production by the New York Shakespeare Festival, was clear and convincing in his motivations, seemingly as Oedipal as Olivier's, and James Earl Jones's beautifully observed, magisterially played Claudius was outstanding, in company with Colleen Dewhurst's Gertrude, but the rest of the supporting cast was uneven.

The funniest Hamlet I have ever seen was Jack Benny in Ernst Lubitsch's 1942 film *To Be or Not to Be.* In his imperturbable, deadpan manner, Benny walks on stage to recite the famous soliloquy…and forgets the first line. Talk about resistance! That's the only excerpt from the play that we see, several times, and it is hilarious. Also funny is the scene where he orders a corned beef sandwich over the phone dressed in his Hamlet costume. Mel Brooks in the 1983 remake is over the top, as one might expect, and very funny in quite a different way, in his Jungian persona as a clown.

A serious Jungian approach to *Hamlet* might begin with the salience of the characters' shadows. Certainly the extraverted Claudius is prey to his archetypal shadow's desires, and taking Gertrude to wife represents for him the mystical triumph that is realized in his intense sexual relationship with her. Gertrude's shadow too is apparent in her behavior: she has abandoned the role of archetypal mother, which she continues to play out in a formal but uninvolved way, in favor of her role as the love-goddess archetype for Claudius. In doing so, she has blinded herself to the truth about Claudius, whom one can view as the archetype and one of the manifestations of the Dark Lord, and abandoned as well the allegiance she felt for her dead first husband, the archetypal father. Gertrude's image of the ideal man, the animus, has led her to Claudius; and his image of the ideal woman, the anima, has seized him and driven him to his shadow side to obtain her by the worst means, that of murdering his rival.

As for the Prince himself, his shadow leads him to a profoundly pessimistic expression of a philosophy about the nature of man, "this quintessence of dust." An introvert, Hamlet is alternately thrown back and forth among the four functions of feeling, which is often primary for him; sensation, as in the scene where he observes the passage of Fortinbras's army; intuition, as when he guesses the true role that Rosencrantz and Guildenstern have been asked to play; and, perhaps least and most seldom of all, thinking, despite his philosophical discourses on the nature of man. Although critics often emphasize the thinking side of the character, I would say that Hamlet does not really think. He only appears to do so. But what is the nature of his so-called thinking? He ruminates, muses, philosophizes, reproaches himself, complains, and bemoans his fate. His thinking hardly deserves the name. It is really all intuition, feeling, and sensation, rather than intellectual reasoning. It is agonizing emotion externalized in words.

Hamlet has a complicated imago of his father and an equally complicated imago of his mother. These imagoes are compounded of ambivalent images and desires, and further entangled with an early incest complex. This is what motivates his actions and his lack of action.

Claudius's public persona is that of rational, reasonable head of state and loving husband and uncle. His private personality is almost the opposite: he is prey to irrationality and guilt over the fratricide he committed and lust for Gertrude, and he fears and hates his nephew.

Gertrude's public persona is that of loving wife and mother and regal queen, but in private she falls apart and is miserable over her son's behavior. To get to the root of it, she summons the archetypal philosopher and sage teacher, Polonius—who, like the other characters, is the opposite of what he appears to be. His wisdom is superficial, and he is an extraverted thinking type—in fact, he is a bit of a windbag—but his thinking is shallow and he relies on appearances, by which he sets great store.

Hamlet's persona is more difficult to pin down, because he alternates among the four functions so frequently. In fact, he has many personae. The actor who takes this approach has to decide which persona to adopt in which scene. This will give variety, subtlety, and nuance in the playing. When we first see him, he is in mourning, and he presents himself in public as the grieving son. He is deeply involved in the imago of his father. To Polonius he presents himself as antic and almost mad. To Claudius he is sarcastic and cold, and to the players who come to perform at the castle, he is simple and friendly, as he gives them advice and shows his admiration for them. To Ophelia he is the cold and distant former lover. Since the incest complex is so strong in him, his love for Ophelia must fail, because his personal unconscious has identified Gertrude as the archetypal anima of his dreams. Hamlet is one of those individuals whose incest complex Jung might have characterized as being a "personal complication," rather than only spiritual and symbolic.

If you choose to study the characters from the point of view of Karen Horney's categorization of neurotic lifestyles and ways of being, refer to pages 85–88, where you will find some possibilities for this approach as specifically applied to *Hamlet*.

The use of part-objects and Kleinian object-relations theory for this play is another possibility. To remind you of her point of view, Klein thought in terms of positions unconsciously adopted by people. These were unconscious stances they took as attitudes towards themselves and the world. She distinguished two positions, based in childhood fears and imaginings: the paranoiac and the depressive. There is a "flight to the good" from those two positions to a more rational view of life. But both of those positions in their adult forms are characteristic of Hamlet, who finds himself incapable of a real flight to the good because of the circumstances in which he finds himself. He is ultimately afraid of his own death, as he tells us in the most famous speech in the play (the paranoiac position). This dread might be one of his unconscious motivations for not wishing to carry out his revenge against Claudius, for which Hamlet fears he would be punished by expiating the deed with his own death. But for much of the play, he is in a depressive position, perceiving external objects as separate and feeling guilty about wanting to destroy them. He surmounts this depressive position by taking all kinds of actions that are not to the point, and by disparaging and demeaning many of the objects of his attention, whom he represents as reprehensible in some way. This is true of his representations of Claudius, Polonius, Gertrude, and Ophelia.

Hamlet splits off and represses his uncomfortable, threatening emotions. He then envisions the objects of his attention not as whole but as part-objects, and concentrates on what has symbolic meaning for him: the medallion portraits of his father and his uncle that he shows Gertrude in the "closet" scene, the letters he has written Ophelia, the physical appearance of the ghost with its wan visage. In splitting off the negative feelings he has about his father and mother, he is able to idealize his father and love his mother, but the negative feelings reassert themselves because of her marriage to Claudius. Underlying all of this is the Oedipus complex that gives his behavior its shape.

The splitting off of unwanted emotions swirling around objects and their repression from and subsequent return to consciousness is one of the cores of the play — something directors might want to bear in mind in controlling how the repression and return happen, and how they are revealed to the audience as the story unfolds.

Guilt about her relationship with her dead husband's brother (was there a love affair going on behind the old King's back?) and her betrayal of her first husband is split off from Gertrude's ego, and she concentrates on Claudius as an object of sexual desire. Her guilt returns during the "closet" scene. Claudius too has split off his guilt feelings over murdering his brother, and they return in the scene where he is praying — "my offense is rank." As for Hamlet, he has more split-off feelings about the objects of his love and attention than any of the other characters, and this is what makes him so complicated and difficult. His unconscious shame and guilt are apparent in all he does, as is the depth of his disappointed love.

Whatever the psychological approach to the play, it is interesting that each and every one of them leads back inevitably to the Oedipus complex as a prime motivating factor in Hamlet's psychic life and external behavior. It seems that all roads lead to Rome — one of Freud's favorite cities!

Chapter Ten

❧

Sheridan, Strindberg, and Ibsen: The Development of Feminism

MRS. MALAPROP AND SIR ANTHONY ABSOLUTE IN SHERIDAN'S
"THE RIVALS": TWO NARCISSISTIC EGOTISTS

*R*ichard Brinsley Sheridan's *The Rivals,* written in 1775, the year the American Revolution began, takes place in Bath, where the gentry go to take the waters. Not accidentally, it is a play about the beginnings of a social revolution. Sir Anthony Absolute and Mrs. Malaprop, who is Lydia Languish's aunt, both want Lydia to marry Sir Anthony's son, Captain Jack Absolute. But Lydia is in love with "Ensign Beverly," who is really Jack Absolute in disguise. He has disguised himself as a poor person in order to win Lydia's love, because he believes that if she loves him as a poor person, she will really love him, even when she discovers who he is and that he has money — a great deal of money, in fact. In addition, Lydia Languish is extremely sentimental and unrealistic and has her heart set on marrying a poor man, so that Captain Jack Absolute must pretend to be poor in any case. But all of this is unknown to Mrs. Malaprop and Sir Anthony, who have learned of Lydia's romantic attachment to "Beverley" and strongly disapprove of the impoverished ensign, without ever having met him, of course. To complicate matters further, if Lydia marries without her aunt's consent, she will lose her fortune to Mrs. Malaprop. Of course everything works out perfectly in the end.

The name "Malaprop" comes from the French phrase *mal à propos,* one meaning of which is "inappropriate." Her most famous malapropism is "as headstrong as an allegory on the banks of the Nile." Here is another example:

MRS. MALAPROP: Ah, and the properest way, o' my conscience! — nothing is so conciliating to young people as severity...prepare Lydia to receive your son's invocations; — and I hope you will represent her to the captain as an object not altogether illegible.

Mrs. Malaprop is pompous, stuck up, and unconscious of her misuse of language. Julia, Lydia's cousin, speaks in act I, scene 2 of "her select words so ingeniously *misapplied*, without being *mispronounced*." The humor comes partly from the air of authority she gives to even her most trivial utterances while making the most egregious mistakes. And everything she says is absolutely serious. She means it! When preparing Mrs. Malaprop, you have first of all to figure out what she actually means, then to give the words she uses the meaning she actually intends. The reason for such Freudian slips is the existence of an unconscious conflict, which reveals itself in them.

What is it in Mrs. Malaprop that leads her to be so imprecise and anal expulsive, throwing her words about loosely and unconsciously undermining her own authority? Deep insecurity and a feeling of not being loved are at the core of this character. And the underlying feeling that she does not deserve to be loved leads to the unconscious, masochistic desire to be punished, which would take the form of being mocked, if anyone dared to point out to her how absurdly stupid her warping of the English language makes her appear. But nobody would dare indulge in bold-faced mockery to her face, because she preserves her air of authority as a defense.

She and Sir Anthony Absolute are both authoritarians who try to control and manipulate others. This is not psychopathic manipulation of the kind Richard the Third uses to gain his own ends but is rather manipulation arising from the fear of losing the person being manipulated. The manipulator often conceals from the self the nature of the manipulation by the invention of the fiction that he or she is simply out for the good of the person being manipulated. And the manipulator believes it, too. Most of the time, the manipulator is not even aware of how controlling he or she is being.

Sir Anthony Absolute's name, like many names in seventeenth- and eighteenth-century plays, represents the basis of the character: everything he says is absolute, as if it were a divine, oracular utterance. He is so completely convinced that he is right and that the world should be as rigid, unbending, and ordered as he is that he can't see anything but what is straight ahead of him. The tone in which he speaks is compulsively dictatorial, and there is little give and take between him and his interlocutor, to whom he often barely listens. He is a narcissistic, anal retentive, egocentric personality, but while in real life this might make him eminently dislikable, here it makes him slightly pitiable, because should he not bend, he would be destroyed. So we smile at him, and we know he will get his comeuppance. And underneath it all, he loves his son and wants what is best for him, so that his severity is tempered by his affection and is, indeed, a result of it.

One of the major themes of the play is that of older people choosing who shall marry younger people. The idea of arranged marriages is called into question in this play, although it would be a common custom through at least the first two decades of the twentieth century in Western culture and still is in some cultures. Women are always in a subordinate position in such a sociocultural situation, treated like chattel to be bought and sold.

The questions of authority and guilt over disobeying it come into play, but the younger people in *The Rivals* are so strong in their desire to assert their independence and fulfill their desires that their guilt is overcome. In the end all is forgiven, and love is triumphant. Society is beginning to change, and the play seems prophetic of a later day when the position of women would be one of greater equality, and they would no longer be expected to behave in a passive and humbly obedient way.

AUGUST STRINDBERG'S "MISS JULIE"

Considered scandalous, outrageous, and controversial because of its frank portrayal of sexual passion and its iconoclastic view of the rigid social class system of the day, the naturalistic one-act drama, *Fröken Julie* (Miss Julie, 1888) by August Strindberg was staged for the first time in Sweden only in 1906, eighteen years after it was written. Its themes show a blatant disrespect not only for the conventions of class and gender but also for the sexual hypocrisy prevalent in society. The play was banned in most of Europe but had been privately produced in Copenhagen. In Great Britain, the ban was only lifted in 1939.

The two protagonists in this study of sadomasochism (one of Strindberg's favorite things) are the aristocratic Miss Julie and Jean, her father's servant, who is a bit of a snob and an iconoclast. Julie, a histrionic personality, behaves extremely seductively with the ambitious Jean, and they have a brief affair. But they have nothing in common, and once the sex is over, they have no idea how to behave with each other.

Sexual intercourse in the play is a physical act of pure lust that does not necessarily have anything to do with love. Commonplace enough today, that idea was considered shocking in 1888, at least when expressed in public: one didn't talk about such things, although men went to brothels to satisfy their lust and women had affairs.

A passionate sexual encounter—only described in the play and not acted out on stage—between an aristocrat and a servant was also considered deeply shocking and not to be mentioned. Strindberg, like Freud, was an iconoclast, shattering accepted notions about what actually occurred behind the scenes in society. After all, such encounters were not unusual, and also served the upper class as a means of assuaging their unconscious sexual guilt, since they could split off that part of their lives and divorce it from the usual high social spheres in which they circulated. They could pretend that such encounters meant nothing. Relations with the great unwashed masses, as they were thought of, were also titillatingly lowlife and dirty, which is how many people thought of sex anyway, no doubt because of unconscious amphimixis, which is the association of sexual and excretory functions because of their somatic proximity. The attitude that sex is dirty is Miss Julie's as well underneath her hysterical, seductive, flirtatious manner. Even the rebellious Jean feels this way unconsciously. Despite his rage and loathing for the sociocultural attitude that decrees his inferiority, he remains conventional in his attitudes about sex. He, like Miss Julie, is full of repressed guilt and shame.

The snobbish Miss Julie does not fit in with her social class and rebels against the inferior status to which women are relegated, just as Jean rebels against class conventions. Women of her class are expected to behave in an aloof, respectable, nonsexual way, and there are endless restrictions placed on them as to whom they may even talk with. Miss Julie's libertarian attitudes and behavior alienates her fellow aristocrats, and even the class-conscious servants, who "know their place," disapprove. She is flighty and inconsistent in her behavior, disregarding convention one minute and demanding the respect and deference due to an aristocrat the next. She thus loses everyone's respect and brings about her own downfall. Ultimately, she is driven to suicide.

It is by no means certain that the deeply misogynistic Strindberg approved of his character Miss Julie's sexuality or considered her attitude a healthy manifestation of a new social consciousness and egalitarian principles. But despite Strindberg's phobic neurosis about women, we can now see the play as making a case for the liberation of women from subservience and for a healthier, freer attitude towards sexuality, as well as towards social-class differences.

FEMINISM AND IBSEN'S "A DOLL'S HOUSE" AND "HEDDA GABLER"

*I*n H. L. Mencken's introduction to the Modern Library edition of *Eleven Plays of Henrik Ibsen,* Mencken quotes Ibsen as saying that "a dramatist's business is not to answer questions but merely to ask them." According to Mencken, Ibsen was an artist first and a social commentator second. Nevertheless, at the time when Ibsen was writing and producing his plays, he was considered a shocking iconoclast, and audiences were heard to gasp and left the theater shuddering at what they had seen. How dare Nora simply abandon her husband—the respectable bank lawyer, soon to be bank manager Torvald Helmer—and their children at the end of *A Doll's House* (1879)? Such things simply weren't done! A wife's duties were to be a homemaker, raise the children, and serve as a helpmeet to her husband—whom she was expected to honor and obey, even if she could not love him—and that was that. And writers certainly did not have the effrontery and unmitigated gall to talk about sexually transmitted diseases, as Ibsen did in *Ghosts* (1881). Ibsen was viewed much as Freud would be later in the century.

Henrik Ibsen exploded all the convenient received ideas of his era on the subordinate position and subservient condition of women, and the hypocrisies of the sexual and social order. And he did this by creating real characters, among whom were those obliged to live their real lives in secret for fear of the social repercussions, should their true desires and actions become known by others. Their fears leave them open to the predations of the unscrupulous. Blackmail is a major plot theme of both *A Doll's House* and *Hedda Gabler* (1890), and other Ibsen plays as well.

Yet lending credence to Mencken's point of view, Ibsen said he did not want to deal in *Hedda Gabler* "with so-called problems." He wanted simply "to depict human beings…human destinies" against their societal background and to show what society had done to them, how it had shaped and molded their characters. Both *Hedda Gabler* and *A Doll's House* deal with women trapped in unhappy marriages, and both plays have problematic Oedipal relationships between fathers and daughters as their background. We learn about those relationships in penetrating dialogue with just enough detail to provide us with a psychological sketch of what went on in the two women's premarital homes.

Judge Brack in *Hedda Gabler,* who resembles Hedda's father in certain ways, is an authority figure of no mean accomplishment, but he is also neurotic, a secret lecher, and a corrupt seducer; hypocritical and cynical. Despite Mencken's idea that Ibsen is not really a social commentator, it is hard not to see Brack as representative of his upper-bourgeois class, or at least of certain smug, hypocritical members of that class. And the cynical, destructive, and self-destructive Hedda Gabler herself, with what Freud might call her masculine identification and Adler her "masculine protest," is misunderstood by all around her and is supposed to play a role that she despises. She is not the typical personality of her era, but she is in a typical social position. Her internal rebellious reactions to her situation make her different from everyone she knows.

Unlike Nora in *A Doll's House,* who has the courage to escape, Hedda's only escape from Brack's attempted blackmail is suicide. Hedda does not lack courage, but she is in despair and sees her entire life as miserable and pointless. The occasion for the blackmail is that she had given one of her father's pistols, which she used to love fooling around with, to the poet Lövborg. He had killed himself, almost driven to do so by Hedda. Brack, guessing her complicity, demands that she become his mistress, or he will reveal her secrets and bring her into disrepute.

The further reasons for Hedda Gabler's suicide include the indifference of the people who surround her, with whom it is impossible for her to have a decent intellectual conversation, so dull and bourgeois are they, let alone to discuss what is bothering her. She would only be met by complete incomprehension. She is especially disappointed and ultimately completely bored by her head-in-the-clouds husband: the scholarly, withdrawn Tesman, who knows nothing about her and has no real interest in her, certainly not a sexual interest, even though he professes to love her. He is obsessive-compulsive in his devotion to his scholarly work, and he treats Hedda as Torvald Helmer does Nora: as a mere appendage, something to be shown off like a new watch or shining jewel—something that assures his masculine self-image and validates his masculinity in his own eyes and the eyes of others.

And Hedda is in love, in any case, not with her would-be seducer, Judge Brack, but with the romantic poet Eilert Lövborg, who adores her. Despite that, or perhaps because of it, she pushes him over the edge with her teasing and seductive manner and the orgiastic activities she invites him to participate in. He represents iconoclasm and the freedom to be. He has not chosen the rigid path of conformity, and it is his choices in life that so intrigue and attract Hedda and that so repelled her parents. Yet although she is attracted to him, in her psychopathic self-centeredness and sadomasochism, she betrays him. Deep down, she feels unworthy of being loved. Her anger is disowned, split off, and displaced into destructiveness. Guilt is a feeling that seems foreign to her as she goes about proving that nobody, not even Brack or Lövborg, really loves her. Brack is just out to take advantage of her and try to manipulate and control her. And how could Lövborg really admire her when she behaves as she does? She has a strong streak of paranoia in her personality. She suspects that nobody sees her as a human being—a sentient, feeling person—not even Lövborg, who seems to do so. George and Hedda Tesman live in the lap of luxury, yet all the material comforts in the world cannot supply what Hedda is lacking in the way of emotional, psychological comfort.

Hedda is the daughter of General Gabler, who is a rigid, authoritarian, phallic-narcissistic personality of the type described by Wilhelm Reich. No doubt this arrogant, overbearing man was as cold as he could be to his only child and possibly even abusive, since he had wanted a son to carry on the military tradition. Hedda grew up feeling unloved. The ungratified Oedipal desire for her father's love and her dislike of her mother have left her feeling alone in the world and abandoned. Confused and upset as a child, she has developed a reaction formation, whereby she denies the unhappier aspects of her childhood, in much the same way Alice Miller describes in her books. When Hedda goes riding with her father, it appears that all is well in their relationship and that she is the suitable, admiring daughter of an accomplished general, whom he can show off at balls and society events. All this activity amounts to a severe denial of her deep disappointment, a profound sadness that, as she grows older and surrounds herself with people she ultimately dislikes and who do not understand her in the least, will lead to her suicide. All of this has only partly to do with the position of women in society. It also has to do with the nature of the strict parenting in her particular social class, where children of both genders were brought up inflexibly, sometimes with military precision.

Surrounded by admirers and indifferent to them all, Hedda marries a person she thinks is the opposite of her father, an intellectual who studies cultural history, and she marries him with the high hope that he will appreciate her, but he too leaves her feeling abandoned. The man who really is the opposite of her father, the poet Lövborg, was considered an unsuitable match by her staid, inflexible, bourgeois parents. Even during their nearly six-month long honeymoon, Tesman has been at his scholarly pursuits, collecting copies of documents from archives and neglecting his young bride. Their sexual relationship is virtually nonexistent, since this largely asexual pedant has sublimated his libidinal energy into his work, in the classic Freudian manner.

Tesman has been raised by two maiden aunts, one of whom is an invalid and to both of whom the mere mention of sex is shocking. Aunt Berta can speak of Hedda's admirers but avoids the sexual innuendo and connotation of the word, and even though she is already sixty-five, she cannot speak directly of the Tesmans becoming parents. Tesman has avoided even thinking of sexual satisfaction, because he is deeply afraid of sexual contact, almost as if he has remained stuck in prepubescent anxiety. His narcissistic self-involvement blinds him to the outside world and especially to Hedda, who might like to enter his world but to whom the way is barred by his obtuse lack of concern. Oh, he is a nice enough man, but…there's nobody there, in a way. His sexual repression is very severe, to the point of neurosis, as the rather odd but comic conversation he has with his aunt near the beginning of the play shows. He is in his thirties, yet he obtusely fails to understand her allusions to the possibility of his becoming a father. This obtuseness does not prevent him from being functional in his scholarly work, where his ego and superego allow him full play. Tesman is also rather anal-retentive when it comes to money, and worries over expenses, much like Torvald Helmer.

Nora's father, a banker, was irresponsible, according to Torvald, who thinks of himself as responsible and ethical although he is merely moralistic, opportunistic, and smug. Aside from his streak of casual irresponsibility, Nora's father was actually very much like her husband, as Nora reveals to Dr. Rank, the family friend who is in love with her and finally shocks her by telling her so.

She tells Dr. Rank that she loves Torvald best but prefers spending time with other people, just as she did when she was a child. Of course, she loved Daddy best, as she says, but she enjoyed spending time with the servants below stairs much more, because they did not preach at her. Socially conventional, her father was a male chauvinist who treated women as if they were children, or dolls, and who felt he could lay down the law. What he said was sacrosanct, and he used to "preach" constantly at his daughter, who grew up as a result accepting the social conventions into which she was born. But she always felt resentful and vaguely uncomfortable. Nevertheless, she was able to cope with her life up to the point where she committed the gravest of errors and forged her father's signature on a paper guaranteeing a loan she had taken out from Krogstad, an impoverished widower with two children to raise. The loan was necessary in Nora and Torvald's straitened circumstances in order to pay the bills that would ensure his recovery from a dangerous illness.

Nora is obliged to keep all of her past actions secret from Torvald, which makes her an easy prey to Krogstad. When he does find out, Torvald hits the ceiling and calls her "You stupid woman!" over and over again. He screams at her that she has ruined him and put him at Krogstad's mercy, because Nora's crime can never be revealed: it would be too dishonorable and shaming. It is this narcissistic egotism that finally opens her eyes. She realizes that he is concerned about his social reputation and does not really care about her or what she has had to go through. She may be his little doll, but he doesn't really love her; he merely feels he owns her. He doesn't know what love is. Instead of offering gallantly either to take the blame or to discuss a reasonable way out of the situation, Helmer behaves like both a coward and a male chauvinist. As soon as the letter from Krogstad is opened, revealing that he will no longer pursue his goal of being not only reinstated but also promoted at Torvald's bank, Torvald does a complete about-face.

The reason for Krogstad's renunciation is that he has discovered happiness and is about to marry Kristine, the woman he loved years ago. She will also be a mother to his children. Kristine is a widow after an unhappy marriage and an old friend of Nora's, to whom Torvald has given employment at his bank. She was to have replaced Krogstad, but in an act of unselfishness that is also selfish, she tries to save Nora, who has confided in her, by proposing marriage to Krogstad and saves herself as well by doing so. Krogstad is a basically good, moral man, driven to evil by desperation.

After Torvald's histrionic temper tantrum and dramatic reversal of his attitude, Nora sees in the clearest possible way that he does not look upon her as his equal, something she always knew but accepted as natural, even though it made her unhappy. But now she is no longer able to accept his not seeing her as a person in her own right, with a mind that deserves respect and consideration, but as a doll, a plaything, someone to control. Torvald is indeed very controlling with Nora and is always preaching at her, just as she says her father did. But she too, in her own way, is very controlling with him. Only she hides it and manipulates him from behind the scenes, as it were, while his attempts to control her are out in the open.

Helmer has scolded her for frittering away money and indulging in her passion for macaroons, as if she were still an irresponsible little girl and not a particularly bright one, who needed disciplining. She was only fit to dance the tarantella for him, and even then, he felt he had to control her lest she become too emotional. Any strong emotion arouses anxiety in Torvald, who prefers to remain placid and restrained and presents a staid, stolid, respectable persona to the world, for the world's edification. Beneath his slightly forbidding, self-controlled exterior and his seeming superiority complex lurks a seething cauldron of feelings of inferiority, lack of self-worth, and massive insecurity. But not until that fateful confrontation had Nora seen him finally in his true light and realized viscerally how he looked upon her and the effect this had upon her. Her father had looked upon her in much the same way. Unlike Hedda Gabler's father, however, Nora's father had spoiled her and treated her like his little pet.

In addition to treating Nora like a slightly dimwitted incompetent, Torvald, unlike the asexual Tesman, who couldn't care less, is sexually demanding. Nora has to resort to lies sometimes in order to put him off, because she doesn't really find him attractive. Unconsciously, she has been out of love with him for a long time, because of the way he treats her. And her persona, in the Jungian sense, is different in any case with him than it is with other people, at least when he is not there. When he is, she feels obliged to play the role in which he has cast her. She is much more her real self with other people, and is not afraid to appear as the intelligent if troubled woman she is, worried because of the transgression she had committed, since she knows her husband and what he is capable of. Still, she hopes for something from him that will show what an admirable, understanding man he is. He, of course, does not know her or what she is capable of, never having thought it worth his while to find out. In fact, it never would have occurred to him that the object representation he has of her is anything but an accurate perception of who she is: a slightly irresponsible, flighty, spendthrift woman, which he thinks are typical feminine characteristics anyway. She is a bit of a spendthrift, true, but she is nevertheless quite levelheaded. And she feels forced to lie to him all the time because she doesn't dare be herself, so much is she terrified of his disapproval, exactly as with Daddy.

In his essay "Nora," written in 1910, Georg Groddeck says that the actress who plays Nora, for whom lying is a habit, must lie with a "disconcerting sureness," and the actress must not make Nora appear embarrassed. Lying has become a necessity to her, after all. To lie is an essential trait of her character, says Groddeck, and even Dr. Rank does not suspect it.

When Torvald discovers what she has done, he says that her father's irresponsibility has been passed on to her, although Torvald himself is so much like him in his intransigent, rigid, moralistic sensibility. In his fury, he is physically abusive as well. He forgives her, he says, once they are out of danger, but he does not ask her forgiveness.

That too would never occur to him. He doesn't think he has done anything wrong. He is master in his own house and entitled to behave as he does.

She finally realizes that he does not even begin to understand her; that they have never talked seriously. And they have certainly never been on an equal footing, because he would not allow it. In short, they have never really been married. She finally has the courage to say that Torvald and her father have done her great wrong. Neither of them loved her, but they both used her. She now has to educate herself, and she has to do it by herself. Helmer accuses her of being a hysteric, but it is he who has behaved hysterically.

Nora has been fed religion and morals and no longer believes they are necessarily right, as she was taught. And she has the courage finally to say to Helmer that she does not agree with his opinions. She tells him that she no longer loves him. Helmer has the nerve to find Nora's attitude unreasonable:

> TORVALD: No man would sacrifice his honor, even for love.
> NORA: Millions of women have!
> TORVALD: You talk like an ignorant child!

Torvald, as Groddeck says, has nothing of the hero in him. Earlier in the essay, he characterizes Helmer as "that absolute zero": he is hollow to the core. But he warns actors quite rightly, as a stage director might, that it would be a stupid mistake to play him as a caricature or a villain. Helmer is simply "a perfectly ordinary man such as one meets every day." He is a man of grand words and a petty soul, and he has finally become "a doll in Nora's hands," as she appeared to be in his. The image of all these dolls in a dollhouse is a really useful one for a director to keep in mind. How are all the characters dolls and why do they belong in the doll's house?

Groddeck makes another point directors might find useful: to take the title as simply underlining what Nora says about being treated by her husband and father like a doll is to make the piece purely into a "thesis play," and both the title and the play are far more than that. To begin with, the title evokes childhood pleasures, and when we enter the world of the play, we enter what appears to be a happy childhood environment. It is Christmas, and the presents will soon be under the tree Nora will so charmingly decorate—as indeed she has decorated the entire house, chosen the furniture and the pictures. In fact, she is generally in charge. All seems pleasant and warmly comforting in the sumptuous dollhouse interior to which we have been transported at the curtain's rise. And Nora herself is immediately adorable, rosy-cheeked from being outdoors in the cold, merrily and furtively popping macaroons into her mouth like the slightly petulant little squirrel Helmer says she is. The audience is immediately won over.

For Groddeck, Ibsen's genius as a playwright consists in part of not revealing at all what will happen later in the play, and in creating characters that are ambivalent and therefore real. We immediately accept that we have before us a contented, happy woman, the very type of homemaker and mother who spreads joy and cheer all around her.

But at long last, Nora realizes she has been living with a stranger. Helmer says he can change, but of course, such a promise is empty, since he doesn't even really know what would be required to effect change, let alone what changes to make. He is married to his work and to his reputation, but not to her. This too Nora realizes. Knowing he is incapable of change and that they will never really be married gives her the courage to leave him. At the same time, while she can justly accuse him of not loving her, she too has never really loved him. Instead, she has lived in a dream world, in a chimera of love. What will become of her after she leaves the doll's house? Ibsen leaves the question open.

A director or actors interested in applying ideas drawn from object-relations theory to *A Doll's House* might consider the following: for Torvald, Nora is a subjective object, in Winnicott's sense of the term — the object onto which subjective desires and needs are projected. He is incapable of viewing her as an objective object: "the object as an external phenomenon, not as a projective entity." Nor has Torvald progressed beyond what Klein calls the paranoiac position, in which he fears his own annihilation and defends himself against this knowledge with an attitude of omnipotence. The evolution to the depressive position, which represents the ability to accept ambivalence and see good and bad in the same person, is beyond him. Everything in his basically schizoid-paranoid thinking is either black or white; there are no grays for him. That is why he can explode at Nora when he thinks he is lost because of her actions, and immediately turn round and treat her once more as his little doll once he is saved by Krogstad's renunciation of his threat to expose Nora.

Nora, on the other hand, has indeed progressed to the depressive position and is able to view objects objectively. She has evolved while her husband has remained static. It is her realization of her position and her feeling that Torvald is incapable of evolving that has enabled her to reach the depressive position. She has internally destroyed the object, as Winnicott says we all do, and yet it continues to exist. She perceives his otherness for her and hers for him, and realizes that she has a long way to go in becoming an individual. And in devaluing the object (Torvald), she is able to remove its power over her and take the important step towards being a free individual.

Indeed, Nora at the beginning of the play lives only for her husband and their children. Everyone else is a stranger; everyone is a subjective object. She knows other things are important to Helmer besides the family, but she is convinced that at bottom, she is as much his universe as he is hers. For Groddeck, the psychological truths in the play reside in the fact that it is more than a simple study of characters: with this attitude of Nora's, the play gets to the heart of the basic relationship between men and women. For women it is often the family that is their world, but for men this is not so, at least in turn-of-the century Europe when Groddeck was writing. This theme, which leads directly to the idea of women's liberation, is what accounts for the play's perennial appeal, according to Groddeck. And as for Nora, who has evolved to the point where she can perceive objective objects, she is no doll. She is possessed of a strength and power of domination that will enable her to change the world! No, Torvald could never have understood Nora.

Claire Bloom's evanescent stage performances as both Nora and Hedda remain etched in my memory after more than twenty years. Everything she did was specific and individual. She had thoroughly understood the unconscious part of her characters' minds. And in the course of her performances, she went from conscious thought to conscious thought, from moment to moment. The most amazing thing was that you could read every thought in her eyes at every moment with lucidity, clarity, and precision, as if you were reading a book.

As Hedda she was sweet and ingratiating with the other characters. But when they were not paying attention to her, she looked daggers at everyone or suddenly dropped a smiling mask of civility to appear utterly lost and miserable. The only thing that enabled her to get away with her game playing was that most of the time nobody looked at her. It was a startling way to bring out one of the themes of the play—that of isolation as a fundamental condition of existence—and the atmosphere was disconcerting and troubling.

She repeated her famous performance as Nora in the 1973 film *A Doll's House* with Anthony Hopkins as Torvald, Sir Ralph Richardson as Dr. Rank, Dame Edith Evans as the children's Nurse, Anna Massey as Kristine, and Denholm Elliot as a moving, sympathetically played Krogstad. The screen adaptation by Christopher Hampton is particularly effective. The film is available on DVD and video.

Chapter Eleven

§

Anton Chekhov

CHEKHOV'S PHILOSOPHY; "THE CHERRY ORCHARD,"
"THE SEAGULL," AND OTHER PLAYS

*A*t the end of his story "Lady with a Dog," Chekhov wrote, "You can't figure out anything in this world." Objecting to this, his friend and former classmate Scheglov-Leontyev told him that the writer's job is to figure out his hero's psychology; otherwise it will remain unclear. Annoyed, Chekhov disdained to disabuse his obtuse friend and wrote back ironically, "A psychologist should not pretend to understand what he does not understand. Moreover, a psychologist should not convey the impression that he understands what no one understands."

Chekhov understood psychology as only a handful of other writers ever have. His view of all his characters is deep and complex, and he is able to imbue them with a very real, carefully observed and constructed unconscious life. He points out to the discerning audience the unconscious nature of people's unhappiness. Chekhov's characters are often so involved in their personal situations and problems, and in their egotism, that they don't see that the solution to their problems lies right in front of them. Even if they did, they might not be capable of changing their ways of dealing with their situations.

People are, indeed, generally unaware, as the Scottish existential psychologist R. D. Laing was to point out in *The Divided Self* (1965). Most people are unconscious of the causes of their own depression and misery. We go through our lives as in a waking dream, he said. That we live our lives in a state of waking dreaming is also one of Chekhov's main themes. And everything takes place against the background of nature's indifference and of time's onward, uncaring march, as Chekhov states in "Lady with a Dog"; in the plays, this theme is subtextual.

Chekhov was a believer neither in religion nor in human progress, yet he was by no means indifferent to people and how they lived. He hated pettiness, lying, cruelty, violence, and superstition, "in whatever forms they might take," he wrote. Another of Chekhov's major themes is the manner in which people orient themselves to the world and the manner in which they behave: this is their ethical, moral viewpoint.

People live out their lives with a certain idea that they can plan for the future. They are filled with illusions. When these plans don't work out, when these illusions prove to be what they are, their disillusion with life can be just as false as their original illusions were. Somewhere in between is the view of life that leads to equanimity, if not to happiness. But Chekhovian characters, like most people in real life, are incapable of living in an unexciting limbo. They need drama and they create it.

In *The Cherry Orchard,* moral and ethical viewpoints are called into question, and time clearly marches on, indifferent to the fate of the protagonists. Selfish and demanding, Madame Ranevskaya, the once immensely wealthy owner of the estate with the famous orchard, and Lopahin, the once impoverished serf, now a self-made millionaire who purchases the orchard on the very estate on which he had suffered so much under serfdom, are often seen as contrasts, as opposites, but they are really very much alike. The new order of capitalism compared to the semifeudal order that went before it is supposed to represent progress, but does it? Is capitalism better than feudalism? For Lopahin it is, but he will find no happiness in life. The progress he stands for destroys the old (the cherry orchard and the estate itself) without replacing it with anything better. For Madame Ranevskaya, capitalism is the unfortunate ruin of a social system from which she has benefited enormously without having taken any responsibility, living only for herself and paying no attention to its consequences for those less fortunate. Is Madame Ranevskaya's pretended refinement and nostalgic regret not a mask for a boorish or at least narcissistic insensibility, as her authoritarianism, self-pity, and miserliness show? And is Lopahin's rough boorishness and readiness to exploit others not a mask for basic kindness and a rebel's desire to see justice and progress prevail against the semifeudal class system, with all its misery, even if capitalism will certainly not turn out to be a more just system? Narcissistic characters do not think of themselves as egotistical or selfish: everything is justified in their minds, and this is how they get through life without feeling guilt or shame. So in this play, good is not pitted simplistically against bad.

The Cherry Orchard is based quite consciously in Chekhov's experience of the social order and the complexes of the former serfs, of whom his grandfather was one, and in his childhood experience of being beaten "for his own good" by his religious fanatic father. In *The Negative Affects—Anger and* Fear (1991), volume 3 of his magisterial *Affect Imagery Consciousness,* Silvan S. Tomkins has written insightfully on the inner "script" that Chekhov "wrote" and on how he experienced his childhood in ways that consciously and unconsciously influenced his personality and the inner workings of his mind.

Anton Pavlovich Chekhov (1860–1904) was born into a family that had been serfs until his grandfather, Yegor Mikhailovich, saving his money in spite of deprivations and suffering, purchased freedom for himself and his wife and children. Yegor Mikhailovich entered the next highest social class in Russia, the lower middle class. Chekhov's mother's family had come from the same roots and done the same thing. The ambitious Yegor Mikhailovich forced his sons into a higher class still. So Chekhov's father became a merchant, and the family moved eventually to Moscow, where they did not do well. As a young man with a sense of responsibility, Anton Pavlovich felt he had to help support them. To do so, he became a doctor. He started writing in order to earn extra money.

Chekhov knew from the firsthand experience of his own and his family's struggles all about the intolerance, bigotry, inhumanity, and brutality of the economic system. He was able to translate his insights and portray human beings with an uncanny reality in his short stories and plays. So real were his characters that people used to say not "I am going to see *Three Sisters*" but "I am going to the Prozorovs.'"

His first great play in its first great production by Stanislavsky and Nemirovich-Danchenko at the Moscow Art Theater was *The Seagull* in 1898. The domineering, egotistical, miserly actress Madame Arkadina tramples on the ambitions of her son Constantine, who wants to be a playwright. He is in love with the insecure Nina, who wants to be an actress. There is something Oedipal about this attachment to a young woman who wants to pursue the same profession as his mother but whom he feels he can protect and take care of, which he cannot do with his rejecting mother. Nina ruins herself by having an affair with the writer Trigorin, Arkadina's lover, who turns out to be a cad, a typical Don Juan with a charming persona. Chekhov portrays such a type as weak willed enough always to give in to his instincts. From a Freudian point of view, he is the erotic-narcissistic libidinal type, very sexual and preferring to love, or at least to fulfill his erotic desires, rather than be loved, because he wants to remain in control. When Nina falls in love with him, he sees her as demanding and throws her over, because he cannot bear to be at the mercy of anybody's demands. His infidelity to the controlling Arkadina is a rebellion against her attempts to control him, even though he had previously found her physically irresistible. But she is growing older and losing her looks and her charm, which is mitigated in any case by her tendency to meanness, and he prefers younger women as sexual objects. He doesn't care whose heart he breaks. He simply wants what he wants. His indifference to people's fates, which is the moral position he unconsciously takes about life in general, is a precursor of the Doctor's cynicism in *Three Sisters*. And yet even he cannot but be affected, if not moved, by Constantine's suicide.

In the one-act play *Swan Song*, an aging actor falls asleep in his dressing room after a benefit given in his honor on the eve of his retirement from the theater. He has been left alone. Everyone has already forgotten him. Chekhov deals here with the psychology of the discarded old actor, which is actually the universal psychology of everyone who grows old and has to give up everything that was meaningful in his or her life, is abandoned, and is living thenceforth on the verge of death, feeling useless and unwanted. And the old man has been unhappy in love. Because her family objected to his profession, much looked down upon in Chekhov's day, he was not able to marry the girl he adored. As he wanders groggily and disconsolately onto the stage, he inadvertently awakens the prompter, who sleeps in the theater because he is too poor to afford lodgings. Together the two old-timers reminisce, the actor reliving the days of his triumph, now gone forever; the sycophantic prompter, with his vast inferiority complex, his understanding of human vanity—typified in the narcissistic old actor—and his kindness, listening to a man he admired suffering the humiliation of being discarded and thrown onto the scrap heap. This play evokes the fears we all have of what might happen to us in old age, even as it shows us the distress caused by human failings and the limitations of the ego. And all the internal actions result in a drama that is poignant because of the actor's and the prompter's situation, and funny because of the actor's still monumental ego: he performs some of his famous monologues, such as the "storm" scene from *King Lear,* and expects adulation from his audience of one.

In *The Marriage Proposal,* the painful shyness of Lomov, the suitor, his passive-aggressive beating around the bush and his endless other neurotic symptoms (his dry throat and unquenchable thirst, his blinking eye, his aches and pains), which are a mask for his sexual desires and his aggression, are so side-splittingly funny that when I first saw this play, I nearly fell on the floor, literally. (I was a high school student, and I had been standing at the back of the theater on the Princeton University campus where I had been ushering for the Princeton Players, a group that performed there every summer.) Lomov's sexual desires are sublimated and assert themselves as soon as his land is discussed, when he immediately projects them onto the disputed part of his estate. He is confronted with the obstinacy of Natalia Stepanovna, the prospective bride, who sublimates her sexual desire for him by being equally aggressively possessive about the estate. But there is nothing shy or passive about her aggressivity. When she realizes she has made a mess of things, she has hysterical fits that are hilarious to the audience. Her father (a role I later played), who thinks he is so clever and can't wait to get his daughter married, is simply obtuse, even more so than the two obtuse young protagonists. The young couple, both of them hysterics, are at immediate cross-purposes as soon as a subject arises about which they can argue and forget the real reason they are talking, so that Lomov never gets around to proposing. This is a way of avoiding the true topic of discussion, which is sex. The audience sees this clearly, and that is why the play is so painfully funny, quite aside from the unconscious activation of the audience's sadistic and masochistic feelings.

In *The Bear,* Smirnov's boorishness and male chauvinism are contrasted with the widowed Madame Popova's romantic posing and fake mourning for a man who obviously treated her like dirt when she was alive but whom she feels it her duty to mourn. She only appears to be in a state of denial, however; underneath it all, her sexual instincts, easily aroused, are as alive as ever. Chekhov has been seen as misogynistic for his portrait of Popova, with her pretensions and her masochism. But Chekhov is far from being misogynistic, and his genial satirical portrait of the "battle of the sexes" is tempered by his guying of male chauvinism, and Smirnov, with his posing as a macho sadist, is just as pretentious, exaggerated, and silly as Popova. When he generalizes about women, he is ridiculous. Chekhov has him deliberately deal in clichés, and it is those Chekhov is making fun of and having fun with. The audience immediately sees what is really going on between these two histrionic, hysterical personalities. Again, the topic of the play is how two people who are sexually attracted to each other avoid the subject of sex and are in denial at first, but pushed forward finally by overwhelming desire for each other.

Chekhov's characters exist for us in all the complexity and depth of actual living human beings even in his most outrageous farces. And farce is a genre that is often completely unreal because of the hysteria of the characters overreacting in real situations. In Chekhovian farce even the overreactions seem real—as they do, for instance, in another classic of the genre, *The Anniversary* (also known as *The Jubilee*). A bank president is trying to prepare for his jubilee while dealing with his narcissistic wife, who insists inopportunely on telling him everything that has happened to her. She is a hysteric who lives in flights of romantic fantasy that are clearly sexual, and are not about her husband but about a stranger she flirted with outrageously on a train. At the same time, he has to deal with an outraged, obsessed, tenacious customer and with the misogynistic bank clerk who is trying to get rid of her and write a report. The committee sent to congratulate him enters in the midst of chaos, much to everyone's consternation. All these people are at the ends of their tethers in this awfully funny and silly farce, but once again, it all seems so real.

"On the Harmfulness of Tobacco"

*A*n inveterate smoker, Ivan Ivanovich Nyoukhin (the onomatopoetic name means "sniveler" in Russian) has been told by his wife to give a lecture on the harmfulness of tobacco at the local social club in the provincial town in which they live. Nyoukhin can't help instead launching into complaints about his life, as one thing leads him on to another almost in a Freudian free-association exercise. He suffers, but he is almost unbearably funny at the same time, and he is a complex creation: sometimes ridiculous, sometimes pathetic, sometimes poignant, and full of nuances and subtleties, even though the line of his story and the situation in this one-act play are simple. Nyoukhin says the most ridiculous things, but he is unaware that they are silly, and he is certainly not trying to be funny. One of his objectives is to maintain his dignity, and despite his sadness, he is not self-pitying.

Nyoukhin, who is just a little drunk (later on, he surreptitiously takes a sip out of a flask) and has no idea what to say, because he had probably not begun to prepare his lecture, hems and haws his way through the first part of his talk and, except near the beginning, speaks about everything but tobacco. A teacher in his wife's boarding school, he is a miserable, henpecked husband and an unhappy father, whose daughters laugh at him. When he says that they went into raptures over his article on the harmfulness of certain insects, or at least over the part about bedbugs, what really happened was probably that they went into gales of laughter. One gets the impression that his wife suggested the topic of the lecture after she too had seen his article. She probably screamed at him something like, "You idiot! What a stupid article! Why don't you give a lecture on the harmfulness of *tobacco?!* On that you're an expert!!! And stop stinking up the house! Put out that cigarette!" Gradually, Nyoukhin reveals just how miserable and upset he is and how much a failure he feels. His only desire, he tells us, is to run away and forget everything. The monologue ends on an ironic note when his wife shows up at the back of the lecture hall and, terrified, he reverts to the subject he hasn't actually talked about and ends the lecture.

What must his parents have been like? What was his childhood like? How did he end up marrying someone who treats him abusively and has him under her thumb? Why doesn't he have the courage to escape? What sort of introjected mother object must he have that he doesn't dare fight back? Was he ever in love with his wife? Did he really hope to make contributions to science? What must his dreams be like?

He is furious at his wife and depressed about his life, and he turns his rage and frustration against himself, just as Freud describes depressed people doing in "Mourning and Melancholia." Karen Horney's idea of neurotic styles of living suggests an approach to this character: resignation is Nyoukhin's style. And Groddeckian ambivalence in his character is quite a salient feature of his attitudes. These underlying aspects of his personality go some way towards arriving at an answer and providing an explanation for the questions about why he stays in a situation that is so painful to him and from which he feels he cannot escape. He feels paralyzed even when he thinks about it, so he avoids in-depth thinking on the subject, but he complains about it nevertheless.

Wilhelm Reich's explanation of masochism suggests the basis of Nyoukhin's character: fear of abandonment is an answer to the question of why he stays put. He feels alone, even when surrounded by people, but he dare not really be alone. He couldn't deal with it. He couldn't cope with life. The familiar is better than nothing, as it so often is with neurotics invested in retaining their neuroses rather than ameliorating their situations.

And what can we ask about his immediate circumstances as he prepares to give his lecture? What is it like in the lecture hall? Is it too hot? Is it stuffy? What has he just been doing before he walks on stage? He has been taking a wee drop, probably, and having a smoke. In a two-character version of this play, which I performed on tour in 1973 with the National Theatre of the Deaf,* Nyoukhin walked on stage with the stub of a cigar in his mouth, which he immediately removed in embarrassment, having forgotten it was there, and concealed it by shoving it into a pocket.

What is the first thing Nyoukhin wants (aside from running away to the ends of the earth the moment he sees the audience?) Perhaps he wants a glass of water. But there is none available, or in some productions, there may be. If there is, Nyoukhin wastes as much time as he can by drinking as long as possible, so as to avoid having to start the lecture. If there is not, he is simply stymied. Alcohol is dehydrating, and only alcohol allows him to confide in the group of strangers before him as the lecture goes on. Of course, he would never confide in anyone he knew personally. But then, whom does he know? He has no friends. He feels completely alone and alienated. He has no one to talk to. No one understands or appreciates him, let alone loves him. He started life with dreams, but they have all been shattered, and his life has

---

* I played the Chairman of the Lecture Committee and briefly introduced Nyoukhin, then sat at the side of the stage in the dark and spoke the monologue—my translation—while Patrick Graybill played Nyoukhin in American Sign Language. I served as his voice and played vocally the emotions he played physically, mirroring his performance.

become a disappointment. As he comes out onto the lecture platform, his discomfort is compounded by his thirst.

It is almost as if Nyoukhin at the beginning is talking to himself at the same time as he is addressing the audience, so his first action, once he is past the introduction of himself to the audience, might be, "I am talking to myself." And after that, his train of thought runs like this: "I am trying to make sense of the things in my life that make no sense, and because I feel incompetent and unworthy, I am trying to convince the audience that I am, indeed, a competent lecturer and worthy to appear before them. Of course, they see right through me."

If you are preparing this piece, you might try an imaginative exercise of the sort the writer's nephew, Michael Chekhov, would have suggested. Tell yourself: "I am standing here in front of the audience completely naked, and I want to hide, so I am looking around for a hiding place," or: "I desperately want to run away, but there is a ball and chain attached to my ankle and tied to a post right there on stage in front of me."

See also the discussion of Nyoukhin's nervous tic on page 51.

"Three Sisters"

*I*n his book about Chekhov, *If Only We Could Know,* Vladimir Kataev points out something that directors in particular should find very useful in structuring their interpretation of this play: it is full of interruptions and contradictions. All the characters interrupt each other, and whenever a character expresses an ideal or an idealistic point of view, the character with whom he or she is talking contradicts in some way the ideal that has been expressed. This is true even if in the next minute the contradictor expresses his or her own ideal, which is contradicted in turn. The characters are all critical of one another and think they know how life should be lived, and in this connection, it is worth remembering Groddeck's dictum that we do not live, we are lived by, the It. When it comes to the love these characters experience or have experienced, this is certainly true, and things seem to be beyond their control.

Another note for directors: In *The Chekhov Theatre: A Century of the Plays in Performance* (1997), Laurence Senelick points out a discovery of Stanislavsky's associate at the Moscow Art Theater, Nemirovich-Danchenko, when he was directing a 1940 production of *Three Sisters.* He decided that one of Chekhov's secrets as a dramatist was that every scene was written in a tempo, like a piece of music, "one in 4/4 time, another in 6/8 and so on." Finding the rhythms of the internal (psychological) and external actions in the scene added enormously not only to the pacing but also to the variety and texture of the play.

Among other things, *Three Sisters* is all about love and the frustrations and vicissitudes of relationships. Masha falls in love with the handsome, depressed army officer Vershinin. Her husband, the pedantic Kulygin, is still in love with her. Andre, the three sisters' brother, falls in love with Natasha, whom the sisters consider vulgar and an inappropriate choice—and indeed, she turns out to be Chekhov's version of Lady Macbeth. Natasha has an affair with Protopopov, who has to be one of the most famous offstage characters in theatrical literature. Chebutykin, the old army doctor, was in love with the three sisters' mother and has never gotten over his obsession with her. The unprepossessing, philosophical, kindly, mild-mannered army officer Baron Tusenbach is in love with Irina, the youngest sister, who does not requite his love but is willing to settle for a life with him that she knows will be calm. The sullen, obstinate, narcissistic, sadomasochistic, obsessive-compulsive Solyony, who takes himself for a hero out of the pages of the Russian romantic writer Lermontov, is obsessed with Irina and consequently loathes Tusenbach, to whom he is unconsciously attracted in typical paranoid fashion (see pages 54–56). All of these people appear to be lived by their It. But none of them know that.

How does Kulygin—Masha's bland, pleasant, pedantic, not-very-bright schoolteacher husband—really feel about his wife's platonic affair with Vershinin? And is the affair platonic? He goes around saying, often to nobody in particular, "I am content." But is he? I played the part—another actor will, of course, play it differently, and may well come to different conclusions than mine—and I think he is not only upset at what he considers his wife's betrayal but also deeply angry, although his rage, threatening to his ego ideal, is repressed. Kulygin cannot, perhaps, feel anything that deeply, because he has a certain lack of affect, defending himself against any threatening strong feeling. All such feelings are threatening and unacceptable to him, because they have Oedipal connotations of rage towards men and desire for women. At any rate, he cannot bear to admit that the woman who once obviously loved and admired him no longer does either and may even despise him. Naturally, Kulygin cannot see himself as boring, tedious, pedantic, placid, limited, narrow, rigid, and provincial, his life running along in the same groove year after year. He has no wish to change (change is threatening; it might arouse strong emotions) and constantly says, as if to convince himself, "Masha loves me. My wife loves me." Kulygin thinks himself clever, a paragon of enlightenment and an educated, cultivated intellectual. He seems to feel superior to the people who surround him, but underneath it all, he feels terribly inferior, in the way Adler describes. His way of asserting his superiority is to quote phrases in Latin, without translating them, that he knows others cannot understand—the uneducated, ignorant boors, from his point of view. Since he is a high school principal, he even feels superior to Olga, his schoolteacher sister-in-law, although she clearly is miles ahead of him in intellect, as is Masha, his cultivated, sensitive—perhaps oversensitive—wife. She loves literature and is reading Pushkin's dramatic poem *Russlan and Lyudmila* as the play opens. Kulygin really loves her, and his love is a far stronger, more absorbing feeling than his hate. So he is able to forgive her and offer her a peaceful home once again after Vershinin's departure with his regiment. This certainly shows that he is goodhearted and perhaps has a bit more depth than he usually given credit for, particularly with the damning phrase that often describes him: "He is a nice man."

Kulygin is resigned to his fate. He exemplifies Karen Horney's ideas on resignation. He might also be seen as an example of what Horney calls shallow living. He would rather deal with triviality than comprehend his situation, and all his Latin quotations are superficial—there is nothing apt that might illuminate or even apply to his situation. He carries out his actions hesitantly and presents a mild-mannered persona to the world. His movements are automatically slightly stiff, awkward, and atactic.

From a Jungian perspective, Kulygin is primarily an introverted thinking type. He is not particularly intuitive, and he defends himself against both feeling and sensation. He can occasionally be extraverted, as in the opening party, during which he gives a toast. But for the most part, he is given to sitting silently and thinking, but not terribly deeply.

Vershinin, the unhappily married officer who falls in love with Masha, as she does with him, will not abandon his demanding, manipulative, controlling wife, who goes to the most terrible extremes to maintain her hold on him. He has a strong sense of duty but not of what might be best, and his ambivalence gives him an inertia that he finds it difficult to overcome. He must need that sort of masochistic, codependent relationship on some level. Perhaps his mother was that way with him, and the only way to retain her love was to give in to her demands, however excessive they were. He would have felt too guilty if he had not and too awful if he were to abandon his wife.

With all this psychological baggage, it is therefore impossible that his relationship with Masha will be complete and fulfilling. Unconsciously, he cannot allow it to be—this is a function of his masochistic side. But in addition, he knows that he must leave with his regiment, and that Masha cannot and will not follow him. She too has a masochistic streak, as we know because she has stayed so long with Kulygin, a man she does not love. Remaining married to him is partly because she cannot see what else she could do and partly a function of living a limited provincial life, as well as of the sociocultural prohibition against what was seen as the scandal of divorce at that time.

Both Masha and Vershinin have sensitivity and intelligence, and are really lovely, sweet people: considerate, kind, and not so narcissistic as to be insensitive to other people's needs, wants, and desires. It is paradoxical that their good qualities fail to make them happy. Their unhappiness comes from unconscious interference from their strict superegos, which prohibit them from asserting themselves when self-assertion might mean hurting someone else. And neither of them desires to hurt another person, if it is at all possible to avoid doing so.

Masha feels guilty about hurting Kulygin, who is, after all, a good man, even if he is terribly limited. And Vershinin would feel horribly guilty about abandoning his mentally disturbed, neurotic wife and leaving his children in her care. The similarity of Masha and Vershinin is one of the things that attract them to each other. His resemblance to her father is another. So it is not only their masochism that is operative here but also their sense of morality and ethics, which their intelligence perceives as paramount. There is something admirable in this ultimately futile, doomed attempt to avoid hurting others, and something tragic as well, because they end up hurting themselves.

The situation of Irina, who agrees against her better instincts to marry Tusenbach, is quite similar. She is a true Prozorov. She has the example of the loveless marriages of Masha and Kulygin, and Andre and Natasha, before her eyes. And she lives with a sense of duty and resignation. She does not want to hurt Tusenbach, so she will end up hurting herself. Perhaps Olga, who will remain a spinster, is better off than her siblings: better to be alone and unhappy than involved unhappily with someone else, whom one inevitably ends up hurting.

All three sisters and their brother have a masochistic streak in them, as well as sensitivity to others and intelligence. This is a family characteristic, a family neurosis. Among themselves, however, they communicate on a level of love and familiarity, even though there are times when they have to avoid saying anything, lest they hurt someone. The sisters avoid criticizing their brother for having married Natasha, whom they have rejected—perhaps out of unconscious sibling rivalry for their brother's love—and whom he loved partly because she appeared to be the opposite of his sisters, with their intellectuality, with which he felt in competition. He feels he cannot live up to them and that he is in some way inferior to them; has failed them and not lived up to his promises. Nor can he overcome his Oedipus complex and do better than his father did in life. His sisters do not wish to hurt his feelings, but of course, their anger and resentment come out anyway. As a result, Andre does not communicate with them, until finally it all comes rushing out of him, and his unhappiness, sorrow, resentment, and anger come pouring forth. And in one way, he actually agrees with them about Natasha: he too actually finds her unrefined and even coarse. One unconscious reason for his marrying her is that he could feel superior to her, as he could not with his sisters.

Adler's analysis of the importance of birth order is exemplified in this play as a conditioning factor. Despite the inevitable and obvious sibling rivalry, the sisters are very close, perhaps as a defense against what would otherwise be a bitter, aggressive competition for power in the triad. From a Freudian point of view, this would result from competitive Oedipal strivings for their parents' love, and those strivings are sublimated in different ways by each of the three sisters.

Olga, the eldest, who sublimates her desires into her work as a schoolteacher, is the most withdrawn from the triangular relationship.

Masha, the middle sister in the triad, who sublimates her feelings by reading and fantasizing, does not appear to suffer so much from her birth-order position as one might expect, but on the other hand, she gets herself involved in unhappy relationships. Her love affair with Vershinin is temporarily fulfilling in some ways, and so was her marriage to Kulygin at first. They both indicate her repetition complex and her early competition for her parents' affection. As a child, she had felt herself replaced by her younger sister—Irina, the most adored and doted on of the three, as is often the case with the baby of the family—so that Masha has floundered in life and does not always know what to do with herself or where or how to look for happiness.

Irina will sublimate her anxiety and timidity in work and resignation, and in this, she exemplifies Karen Horney's idea.

The family quartet, of course, includes Andre, but he appears to remain apart from the triad. He does not wish to confront their disappointment, which makes him anxious and gives him the feeling of being unloved and rejected. From the point of view of character formation, he had his own Oedipus complex to deal with. Andre, the only son, was undoubtedly doted on by their father, the general—who must, however, have been disappointed in his son for not following a military career and for being what he might have considered overly sensitive for a boy, in an era when male chauvinism and patriarchal thinking dominated society even more than they do today. He plays the violin, but only as an amateur, and he is withdrawn and shy.

What must their father, the dead General Prozorov whom they mourn, have been like? There must have been an unconscious streak of sadism in him (not surprising in a military man), some difficulty relating to people, and also awkwardness and shyness perhaps, for all his children to have had a streak of masochism in them. It developed perhaps when they sought his love and approval and were met with some coldness, due to his shyness. But he must have been very different from another offstage character we never see, the overtly sadistic martinet who wanted a son, General Gabler, whose daughter Hedda is psychopathic. General Prozorov was clearly an educated man and wanted not only his son but also his daughters to be cultivated and refined. His sensitivity and his endearing quality of shyness—ironic, considering his murderous profession—has been passed down to his children, communicated by osmosis, as it were, absorbed at their father's knee as a way of being and behaving in the world. Their long-gone mother, whom they barely talk about, must have been a more or less passive presence in their lives, although she must have taken care of them in basic ways. It is possible that she too lived resigned to her fate, married to a man she did not really love.

One of the themes of the play, lived out in the lives of its characters, is the indifference of the march of time and nature. Doctor Chebutykin, the pessimistic nihilist who has defended himself against ever being hurt again after the failure of his love for the mother of the three sisters and Andre, seems to express a unity with that indifference—and with the difficulty of understanding the world with all its complications. His lines are a kind of musical counterpoint to the other characters' passionate involvement in their dilemmas. And he even sings a popular 1890s music hall tune with its nonsense refrain: "Ta Ra Ra Boom-de-ay," with its words changed to suit the situation of the play. His ethical and moral orientation to the world and how one behaves in it—what one does with one's life and how one does it—are a matter of indifference to him because of his deep rage and disappointment in love. In a reaction formation to his rejection by the one woman he ever really loved, Chebutykin has turned his passion into indifference, as if denying that it mattered at all. Did she love him in return? He no longer remembers....Does it matter? Does anything matter?

"UNCLE VANYA"

*I*van Petrovich Voinitsky, familiarly called Vanya, is introspective, shy, and ruminative. Unhappy and frustrated, he is also humorous, warm, and sensitive. His depression leads him to be ironic and self-deprecating. Vanya is intelligent, even brilliant, but he feels that he has wasted his life and squandered his intellectual gifts, that he is a failure—and that it is not his fault. He could have been somebody, or so he thinks: a contender instead of a bum. Vanya is the first victim of his own illusions and his own inferiority complex. Underneath his self-depreciation are feelings of superiority, implied but not expressed verbally. He talks to himself in an act 2 ruminative soliloquy that is eloquent, masochistic, and...not to the point. He dreams of a better life and of love, but Hamlet-like, he takes no actions, except for inappropriate, unproductive, dysfunctional ones. In fact, he seems functional only when it comes to his work in managing the estate.

Vanya's immediate subobjectives in his soliloquy are to resolve issues and relieve his feelings. But he solves nothing. He simply ends up where he started, full of self-pity, which is the same sentimental, maudlin, self-serving defense mechanism that he despises in others. And at the end of the play, despairing, he will continue working as he has done all his life, but with an added feeling of bitterness and disillusion.

In spite of or even because of his failings, the audience takes him to their hearts. At some point in his or her life, everyone has felt the way Vanya feels. Everyone has felt frustrated and desperate and been thwarted in love. So every woman in the audience wants to mother him and every man to console him and to be a loving father to him. And sometimes everyone wants to give him a good slap and say, "Wake up!"

Vanya's relationships with everybody—except his niece Sonya, whom he loves dearly—end up by being distant, if not downright cold. He is judgmental and critical, as he unconsciously projects his feelings of self-criticism and self-hatred onto everyone around him. In some cases, he has a ready target. He had admired and revered his widowed brother-in-law Professor Serebryakov, a renowned professor of aesthetics who had published books about art. But now the Professor is remarried to Yelena, whom the frustrated Vanya has fallen in love with. And he feels that the scales have fallen from his eyes. He now sees the Professor as a no-talent egotistical windbag, a hollow empty shell, and a nonentity. Of course, he would never dare say this to the Professor. But he complains loudly to Astrov, in Waffles's presence, about the Professor's pretensions. And Vanya despises the Professor's shabby, egotistical imposition on the entire household, which has to cater to his dictatorial whims. "I believe you're jealous," says Astrov, teasingly. Vanya admits as much. He is jealous as well of the success the Professor has had with women—a regular Don Juan . . .

With the exception of Ilya Ilyich Telyeghin, known as Waffles—an easy target of Vanya's scorn—and his own mother, Vanya can talk about people behind their backs, but not to their faces, because he fears the punishing consequences should he tell them how he really feels. Ultimately, in fact, all his negative judgments about the other characters come from his frustration and his deep need to feel loved. But since he doesn't love himself, he feels that nobody could love him. In Yelena he has masochistically picked an inappropriate object on which to transfer his libidinal strivings, proving to himself unconsciously that he is unattractive and unlovable, and the choice has developed into a transference neurosis. Perhaps part of his pity and love for his niece stems from the fact that she does the same thing, and he projects his self-pity onto her. She is the one person in the play whom he doesn't end up hating.

On the other hand, Vanya genuinely finds Waffles endlessly irritating and expresses his annoyance more than once. Waffles was a pivotal character in Vanya's family's past. It was from his uncle that Vanya's family bought the estate that Vanya has managed since his sister's death (he had left her his entire share, because he loved her), on behalf of the Professor, sending him the proceeds regularly.

The impoverished, shabbily clad Waffles now lives there on the estate, as a barely tolerated quasi member of the family, on Vanya's, or rather the Professor's, charity — a word Waffles cannot bring himself to utter, since it awakens feelings of deep shame and inadequacy. He would fall apart if he were to acknowledge the truth — namely, that he is a shallow hanger-on who does nothing but try to be ingratiating and agreeable and who has nothing to offer. In a severe state of denial, the pockmarked, unattractive Waffles wants to avoid anything unpleasant or threatening, particularly to his self-image, so he tells the truth (as he sees it), which is good for his ego ideal of himself as an honest, caring human being. But he lies about how he feels concerning the truth! In his displays of sentimentality and self-pity, he lies to himself, as well as to everybody else, but others see through him where he is incapable of seeing through himself.

"My wife left me on account of my unprepossessing appearance, but I feel sorry for her," he says. No wonder people think Chekhov writes comedies! The line is very funny, but it evokes a wry and even sympathetic smile from audiences, rather than a loud laugh. It is obvious to everyone but Waffles that he hates his wife. Freud would have understood: this is the same mechanism he describes in "Mourning and Melancholia" of turning anger at the lost love object against the self, because it is too threatening and unacceptable to the self to acknowledge. His wife not only didn't love him but also awakened his feeling of being ugly and sexually unattractive. He is the most heavily defended, narcissistically wounded person in the play, and he salves his wounds and asserts his superiority by generously supporting his wife and her offspring by her lover, who has deserted her as she had Waffles.

The physicality of the character is important. When I played the part, it took me over forty-five minutes to do my makeup. The pockmarked skin had to be painstakingly stippled, and I used collodion to create wrinkles. I also wore padding. Doing nothing, Waffles puts on weight.

And how Waffles handles his unconscious rage and anger is of paramount importance. The Marquis of Queensberry, discussed on pages 290–293, is the almost diametrical opposite of Waffles in the way he handles his anger: he acts out and even glories in all his feelings of rage. Since I played both parts, I had to find within myself two ways of dealing with rage and anger: 1) defensive repression: the denial that one can even be angry, the binding of anger physically, and the consequent inability to express rage, except passive-aggressively (Waffles); and 2) overwhelming sadomasochistic and ultimately futile and counterproductive rage that the ego ideal permits to be expressed, because the self-image allows it — nay, demands it (Queensberry).

At one point in act 1, as Vanya inveighs against the Professor, Waffles says to Vanya, "I don't like it when you talk like that." Consciously, he feels that such talk is beneath contempt and dishonest as well, that one should only say nice things about other people, as in the old adage, "If you can't say anything nice, don't say anything at all." But unconsciously Waffles identifies with the Professor, a father figure whom he continues to admire. He projects his own feelings of inadequacy into what Vanya is saying and remains unaware of his preconscious reality, which is bubbling just below the surface. He feels the same way about himself that Vanya feels about the Professor. Waffles cannot bear to acknowledge that he is imposing on the household and that he is unloved and not admired. Unconsciously, he feels that anything nasty said about the Professor is really said about him. But Waffles is not paranoid; he does not consciously realize all this, nor does he think Vanya is actually talking about him. Unconsciously, he makes the connection between how Vanya feels about the Professor and about him.

The Professor himself has no idea he is making himself hated. He too is in a state of denial and feels put upon at times. He pities himself for being old and ill, which he is in most interpretations, although in others, such as the 1970 Soviet film of the play, he is not so very old at all, even if he feels ill and is not shamming. But he uses his illness, like Molière's imaginary invalid, to impose his will and feel that he is loved after all, because people take care of him.

Vanya's entire relationship with his mother is implied in the few lines he addresses to her and in the way he relates to Yelena. Freud's remark that if you are your mother's favorite you have every chance of being successful doesn't mean that this is always going to be the case, and with Vanya in particular, it proves not to have been. He takes her remarks about his having been a person of high ideals—whom, by implication, she admired—the wrong way. Vanya cannot bear to have his own shortcomings pointed out to him. He is one of those people who were made to feel as if he were unusual and special, until everything went wrong. And then, Vanya's mother admires and even reveres the Professor, whom Vanya detests and resents, as we have seen. In the scene where the Professor proposes to sell the estate, Vanya's mother betrays him by siding with the Professor, increasing Vanya's suffering. From a Freudian point of view, his agony is rendered even more painful to him by the early Oedipal strivings and love for her that remain deep in the recesses of the unconscious.

Yelena, a beautiful woman, the cynosure of all eyes, claims to be the faithful wife and rejects Vanya's advances. "This is agonizing," she says to him when he refuses to leave her alone. Vanya is not the only one in love with her. The Professor loves—or at least, did love—his wife, whom he takes more or less for granted. And Astrov, Vanya's closest friend (if Astrov can actually be said to be anybody's friend) falls in love with Yelena. She falls in love with him, but although she would ultimately have preferred to be married to a younger man, as she admits to her stepdaughter Sonya, she will not allow herself to give in to passion. Sonya confides in her that she loves Astrov, and Yelena, of course, keeps quiet about her own interest in the country doctor. She does not believe in any case that Astrov is in the least attracted to her. Yelena only really discovers the true state of affairs when she approaches Astrov to plead Sonya's case, and Astrov thinks she is there on her own behalf. In a rare moment of letting go, Yelena allows herself to return Astrov's ardent kiss—and Vanya sees them. It is this that sends him over the edge, so that he will shortly afterwards try to shoot the Professor.

The theme of the characters' boredom runs throughout the play. Everyone is bored in some way. Boredom is a state of being that often involves listlessness and a lack of desire or ability to do anything to overcome the situation, or it may involve taking actions in order to attempt to alleviate the unpleasant feelings of not being interested in anything. It is often temporary but may be chronic and/or pathological.

Boredom is not to be confused with depression, although they may be close to each other. But in a depressive state, a person is full of emotions and ideas about the self and feels deeply, whereas in a bored state, by contrast, a person seems almost incapable of feeling or being interested in anything. This may be a defense against allowing oneself to experience feelings.

Yelena maintains that there is nothing to do and that she is terribly bored living in the country, to which her stepdaughter Sonya replies that there is plenty to do, if only she cared to do it: teaching the peasant children to read and write, gardening, and so forth. But to Yelena all those activities are simply boring. Vanya tells her she is too indolent to live. Is it boredom or laziness? Is her laziness a symptom of her boredom? There is perhaps a certain defeatism in her character, which has resulted in what the French call *je-m'en-foutisme* and the Italians *me-ne-fregismo*—"I-don't-give-a-damnism." Perhaps she has simply given up on life because she is so disappointed in where her choices have led her, and she feels stuck in a rut from which she cannot escape. It is axiomatic that an actor cannot play boredom—that is, being in a bored state—so one must ask: What is Yelena doing? She is walking about, looking at the scenery; sitting down; restlessly wandering about; playing the piano; ministering to the wants of her ailing husband; or having conversations that don't interest her with people who don't interest her. Yelena avoids being in touch with her feelings both because they threaten her sense of well-being and so that she won't have to act on them. When they are pointed out to her, she is more uncomfortable still, but in the late-night scene with her stepdaughter Sonya, she manages to confide her feelings of unhappiness over her marriage, although she is only able to do so to a very limited extent. She can't even be bothered to remember everyone's name, so she calls Ilya Ilyich Telyeghin "Ivan Ivanovich," and he is mortally offended. The only person who rouses her from her lethargy is Astrov, for whom she feels a sexual and intellectual attraction that she doesn't want to admit and to which she yields briefly, to her later regret.

Sonya is in a most unfortunate position: not only is her love for Astrov unrequited and therefore painful, but she has a complex about being sexually unattractive because she considers herself to be plain or, to put it more bluntly, ugly. Those around her reinforce this complex about her looks. Nobody goes out of his or her way to tell her how beautiful she is, and everybody buys into her own self-image. Astrov considers her plain, but beauty is in the eye of the beholder, and she simply isn't his type, whereas the glamorous Yelena, who is aware of how attractive she is, is very much his type. And he doesn't even have to say as much for either woman to realize how he feels. Sonya has overheard remarks about her looks at the church she goes to from people who did not know she was listening. Probably at some point in her early childhood she was made to feel that she was not beautiful. Perhaps her mother felt a rivalry with her for her father, the Professor's, affection. Perhaps he doted on the little girl at first and then, to please his wife, agreed with her that they had an unfortunately plain daughter but that looks aren't everything. Unconsciously her mother must have reinforced Sonya's feeling of plainness. She seeks out this reinforcement, this early conditioning, by looking for it in the other's eyes, much as described by Sartre and by psychotherapist Rob Bauer—see page 163. Her psychic devastation has been repressed, and she has compensated for it by developing into a sweet—perhaps overly sweet—young lady, and a helpful, industrious hard worker. She needed her parents' love and approval, so she had to bow to their feelings about her looks and make them right. In doing so, she felt right about herself, and avoided punishment by repressing her anger and resentment over not being viewed as a sexually attractive being. Along with Waffles, Sonya is probably the most unhappy person in the play, more so even than Vanya. She is sexually miserable and deeply angry and resentful underneath her sweet persona. But she does indeed have good, moral, ethical instincts.

By rights, this wonderful person deserves to be loved. Astrov should return her affection. But...she is not attractive in his eyes and is usually played made up as plain and unattractive, or at least unprepossessing. Astrov likes her as a person but does not love her as a woman. The Oedipal origin of her feelings about herself was apparent in the Soviet film, in which the ethereally beautiful, very young Irina Kupchenko played Sonya, thus making it quite apparent that this attractive girl has a neurotic complex about her looks, a complex which must have its origins in early conditioning. It is no exaggeration to say that Sonya's complex about her looks and not being sexually attractive conditions everything in her life and all her behavior. People love her for her intelligence and her kindness, but that is not good enough, since she wants to be loved for her looks. She is therefore incapable of really feeling how much she actually is loved.

In the same film, her father, the egotistical Professor Serebryakov, played by Vladimir Zeldin, does not appear old, despite his graying hair—merely middle-aged, and he sports an elegant mustache. He is trim and handsome, vain and narcissistic, and one can see in him quite the ladies' man—we sense that he must have a "past"—so that Yelena's attraction to him becomes not only intellectual, as she describes it, but clearly and obviously sexual. Vanya, with his insecurities and diffident manner, cannot compete with him on that level. The Professor is usually played as a crabby old man, a bit of a crackpot, and probably just as unpleasant and as much of a charlatan as the jealous Vanya describes him, but why accept Vanya's views? He has every motive to downplay Serebryakov's good side. Vanya is so frustrated and unhappy that he is incapable of being fair or just, or of viewing either himself or the Professor objectively. And many actors and directors dealing with this play have accepted Vanya's interpretation of the Professor's character because of their own Oedipus complexes, unconsciously identifying him with the negative images of their fathers when they were hostile to them during the Oedipal phase.

We usually sympathize with Vanya, and dislike the vain and vainglorious professor of aesthetics who "knows nothing about art" and who has cheated the now disillusioned Vanya out of a life that he was willing to sacrifice for the great man's benefit, for much the same Oedipal reasons, but that interpretation is perhaps too simplistic. They are not necessarily polar opposites, the villain and the hero, any more than the idealistic ecologist Astrov and the sarcastic Vanya cynically mocking Astrov's ideas are complete opposites. It is true that Vanya whines and Astrov doesn't, and Chekhov told the Moscow Art Theatre actors who were creating his play, "Uncle

Vanya is crying, but Astrov is whistling!" But Chekhov is never so one-sided or simple in his approach to human beings as such an interpretation of Vanya as sympathetic hero all the way and Serebryakov as narcissistic villain would indicate, or of Astrov as high-minded, noble idealist and Vanya as masochistic cynic. Vanya too has his ideals, and Astrov has his coarse and even sadistic side. As Yelena tells Vanya when he says he hates the Professor, "There is no reason to hate Alexander. He is no worse than anyone else." Of course, she also has her biases, but directors and actors might take a clue as to Chekhov's meaning and how to interpret the role of the Professor—and indeed the entire play, by extension—from that line instead of from Vanya's diatribes.

Serebryakov may be the Chekhovian version of a villain, because of the insensitivity of his unthinking plans to sell the estate out from under Vanya and the others (plans that are not going to be put into effect), which betrays his lack of consideration, but Vanya is ultimately responsible for himself and his own life. And that is exactly what he doesn't understand.

Astrov is probably the figure in the play that most represents Chekhov himself. However, Astrov is a rather satirical portrait of an idealist, whereas Chekhov was a realist at the same time as he was an idealist. Georg Groddeck in *The Book of the It* has a very interesting analysis of the general character of doctors: "There you have the essential quality of the doctor, a propensity to cruelty which has been just so far repressed as to be useful, and which has for its warder the dread of causing pain." This might apply perfectly to Astrov. He is defensive and remorseful for having been there at a patient's death, even though he had not really caused the death, but he sadistically teases his friend Vanya. His cruelty comes out as well in his attitude to Sonya when Yelena reveals to Astrov that Sonya is in love with him, and he dismisses her, although he also displays "the dread of causing pain"—in this case, emotional pain. But he immediately jumps to the not entirely unjustified conclusion that Yelena is really attracted to him herself, and he acts on his supposition. As they are embracing, Vanya enters, and Astrov is not particularly sympathetic to his friend's distress.

Set in the Australian outback in the World War I era, *Country Life* (1994), directed by Michael Blakemore—he also plays the Professor—is a superb updating of Chekhov's play, with psychologically well observed, moving performances by John Hargreaves as Uncle Jack, Sam Neill as the local doctor and village playboy, and Greta Scacchi as the stunningly beautiful woman with whom everyone falls in love at first sight. In its interpretations of Sally/Sonya (Kerry Fox) and the Professor, the film seems to have been inspired by the 1970 Soviet version.

But the best English-language Chekhov I have seen is the 1960 Chichester Festival staging (available on DVD and video), with Laurence Olivier as a wry, slightly coarse, and somewhat cynical but sentimental Astrov; Michael Redgrave as a genuinely tortured, sensitive, appealing, intelligent Vanya; Rosemary Harris as a gorgeously beautiful, bright, refined, feeling Yelena; and Joan Plowright as the warm-hearted, psychologically scarred Sonya, making her complex about her looks painfully apparent, and filled with a sweetness that made everyone love her. All of the psychological complications of the relationships in the play emerged in depth.

In this production, we have in the Professor, as superbly played by Max Adrian, a rather typical interpretation of the part: the portrait not only of a narcissist who takes advantage of everyone but also of an aging man who doesn't want to let go of life and is full of self-pity as his body begins to betray him. As he loses physical power, the Professor tries desperately to hang on to what mental power he has, but in his paranoia and self-pity, he mistreats even those who love him. In act 2, he is nasty, mean, and sarcastic, theoretically directing his sarcasm at himself but really torturing those who have to listen to him, as he projects his own unhappiness onto them, blaming them for it. Serebryakov, in this interpretation, lacks dignity and self-respect—two qualities that he had earlier in his life—and therefore exacerbates Vanya's contempt for him, especially as he also rejects Vanya, talking to him about "our former friendship." The remark not only surprises Vanya (this is before the scene where Vanya tries to shoot him) but also enrages and infuriates him, particularly in light of his love for the Professor's wife. On the other hand, it is quite obvious that he and the Professor are no longer close, and his rage arises partly from the fact that it is the Professor, and not he, who acknowledges a fact that Vanya himself had implied in his remarks at the opening of the first act, when he talked behind the Professor's back. He can now blame the Professor for what he himself feels. But the Professor isn't supposed to know all that! He is not supposed to feel that way! How dare he?

It seems that in analyzing Chekhov's characters, we never finish exploring the subtleties of those whom we take for real people. With what craftsmanship and brilliance Chekhov conveys his knowledge of how human beings behave, and why! His insights are so extraordinary and vivid that one wonders how he could have been so perceptive as to arrive at them. Even Silvan S. Tomkins's explanation of the inner "script" that Chekhov unconsciously "wrote" about his own life and an analysis of the artistic temperament do not suffice to explain the mystery of his genius. The mystery will always remain, which Freud was convinced was universally true when it came to the enigma of artistic creation.

Chapter Twelve

The Artistic Temperament: Six Modern Plays

INTRODUCTION: THE PSYCHOLOGY OF THE ARTIST

*I*n Ronald Harwood's 1980 West End play, *The Dresser*, made into a film in 1983, the character Sir (Albert Finney), the temperamental actor-manager of a Shakespearean company touring England during World War II, is the stereotype of a vain, narcissistic, egotistical artist and actor. When he is informed that the left-wing political member of the company, whom Sir despises, has written a play he wants Sir to read, he disdainfully tells Norman, his dresser and general factotum (Tom Courtenay), "I won't read it." Norman: "I've read it." Sir: "Is there a part for me?"

Sir was once idealistic and began his life in the theater with the lofty idea that he was doing the work of the gods and would be admired and even adored, idolized, and adulated for his brilliance. The audience, however, can see that he is really a second-rater. And now he is past his prime and on his way to oblivion, but perform he must! The world may be falling apart around him, but the show must go on. The public will have forgotten him, just as it will forget the old actor in Chekhov's *Swan Song*. Sir's death in the theater after a performance of *King Lear* is as fitting as Molière's death on stage during a performance of *The Imaginary Invalid*. He is the artist eternally chained to his art, like Prometheus to his rock, eternally gnawed by self-doubt and yearning for approval: Do I have what it takes? Am I talented? Was I good tonight? Did the audience love me?

It is a given that art of whatever kind is produced by the artist (meaning the creative person involved in any field of artistic endeavor) for an audience—even if that audience is solely the artist. But why does the artist want to create art? Because he or she is searching for something and has a deep need to externalize that search and receive approval. Approval received means implicitly that the artist does not deserve punishment, which is always equated in the unconscious with castration, as Freud says, and can breathe freely—as Marcel Proust with his asthma could not, for example. It is significant that it was only after his parents' death that he could truly set to work on his novel, with its critique of social attitudes that implied a criticism of his upper-middle-class parents.

What the artist is ultimately looking for is inner harmony in the light of "the artist's own changing and developing life situations," as Phyllis Greenacre informs us in her essay "The Childhood of the Artist" in *Emotional Growth*. One of the sources of this harmony is precisely the validation of the self represented by external approval.

The classic analysis of the artist's psychology holds that artists were unusually given to daydreaming as children, a trait that carries over into adult life. Also, they are generally emotionally fluid and flexible, if not chameleon-like, and more than usually passionate. It appears that all artists have experienced more than average childhood awe in the face of sex. And they have such a deep disappointment over Oedipal rejection that they retain a greater than usual unconscious desire to return to the less aware pre-Oedipal phase, when the parents or caregivers were perceived as gods and the infant's needs were met as if the world were there only for that purpose. The future artist, like everyone else, moves away from the original Oedipal objects and towards an expression of desire into the world. But in the case of the artist, the movement away is accompanied by unusually vivid dreams, fantasies, and screen memories, which assume tremendous importance as mechanisms that prevent the ego from being flooded with painful, wounding recollections. These unconscious memories nevertheless find their outlet and expression in artistic creation in a form that may be unrecognizable to the artist and is therefore safe.

Another aspect of the artist's personality is greater sensitivity to stimuli than is found in most people. Artists generally have acute awareness of relations among things and people, and an extra sensitivity to nuances and changes. They possess a tremendous ability for expressive emotional discharge of built-up conflict, born partly of the pressing necessity to sublimate because of threatening strong drives, which nevertheless must find expression somehow. This greater sensitivity may also be due to ambivalent experiences in the anal phase. Pressure in the as yet mysterious phallic area is associated with early pleasurable masturbatory fantasies that are not understood. And the feces are viewed as both good and bad. They are associated with a representation of the good self—when the toilet training goes well and the stool is produced—and the bad self, when the training is difficult and the stool not easily excreted. Nevertheless, where the greater sensitivity and what Greenacre describes in her essay "The Family Romance of the Artist" as an "inborn heightened perceptiveness of the outer world (including intensified and precocious awareness of form and rhythm)" come from actually still remains a mystery.

The fantasized, escapist genealogy of the family romance of the artist assumes great importance in the unconscious. The artist often imagines that he or she is from a richly endowed noble family, powerful and respected in the world, rather than the one the artist was born into that does not respect or understand him or her. In fact, the artist very often has to struggle to feel respected and self-respected and, especially at the beginning of a career, often feels unworthy and even like a bit of an imposter, unsure of gifts and abilities. This accounts in part for the overwhelming need for approval, validation, and praise from external sources in order to bolster the somewhat slender inner resources of a fragile ego afraid of punishment for daring to express what should be inexpressible—namely, sexual desires, especially Oedipal wishes and fantasies. While Oedipal strivings are of necessity relinquished, they remain strongly cathected nonetheless and are a source of danger as far as the ego is concerned. See, for example, *Gods and Monsters* (1998), with Ian McKellen as the film director James Whale, famous for the 1931 Hollywood *Frankenstein* and *Showboat* (1936). Whale escapes as boy into a world of fantasy and imagination, building a story about his family he will later tell as if it were the truth, which we the spectators believe until we see the first flashback into the reality of his childhood.

The longing for love and the necessity of resolving internal conflicts by externalizing them in ways that allow them to be expressed and do not threaten punishment for shameful, guilty thoughts or actions is exemplified in poetry. The poet's personality is always reflected in her or his work. Poetry, with its highly libidinal content, comes evocatively flowing out of the unconscious and awakens the unconscious of the reader to its nuances and psychological subtleties. Sometimes the sounds are the sense and arouse feelings in much the same way as music does, by providing an immediate visceral experience.

Among the many psychoanalytic attempts to understand creative artists is a fascinating and important long paper by Karl Abraham called "Giovanni Segantini: A Psychoanalytic Essay" (1911), about a Swiss painter who lived from 1859 to 1899 and was manic-depressive—a specific kind of case, since by no means all artists fit into this category—and whom Abraham characterizes as powerful, original, and independent. His mother died when he was only five, and the despairing Segantini felt unconsciously guilty because he resented her death, which he saw as abandonment, and he wanted revenge. Unlike other children who have lost parents at an early age and who have assimilated the loss, however painful the process, Segantini, bereft and forlorn, simply could not let go of her image. He says as much in his autobiography, but without being aware of the implications, as later analyzed by Abraham. It is striking and strange, Abraham tells us, that Segantini never talks of tender maternal solicitude or affection, or of how much he missed his mother, but only of how very beautiful she was. Unable to acknowledge his rage, Segantini poured all of his narcissistic longing and love and his desire for vengeance into dark, mournful paintings—for instance, one he named *Bad Mothers*, which is an empty landscape with a lone tree in the foreground.

Freud's contributions to the understanding of the artistic personality and the nature and origins of creativity include his essay "Dostoevsky and Parricide" (1929), about the Oedipus complex that wreaks havoc throughout *The Brothers Karamazov*, and his book *Leonardo da Vinci: A Study in Psychosexuality* (1910)—mentioned by Abraham as precursive of his essay on Segantini. Freud did not claim to understand why da Vinci was a genius but felt at most that he could explore the artist's process of sublimation and its background, insofar as the artist's work reflected and revealed them. Abraham similarly disclaimed the idea that in applying psychology to someone "who is no longer with us"—and who is not and never was a patient—one could do more than deduce and speculate from available material. Just as Segantini left documents, as well as his works of art, so did da Vinci. In the case of this greatest of Renaissance intellects, there were clear indications in his notebooks about childhood fantasies indicating oral passivity and his deeply emotional early relationship with his mother. One of Freud's interesting speculations is that the Mona Lisa's enigmatic smile may represent the one da Vinci saw on his mother's face. Despite his mastery in so many fields, Leonardo trembled with terror every time he began a painting. He was a perfectionist, whose inability to finish his works was legendary and who deeply needed his audience's approval.

Alice Miller, a contemporary Swiss psychologist, explores certain areas of childhood and the psychology of abused children. As Miller tells us in *The Drama of the Gifted Child* (1981), if you are the gifted, talented child of narcissistic parents, you have an emotionally difficult situation to deal with. Such parents unconsciously require their children to fulfill the parental needs for self-validation, so that the child's marks in school, ability in sports or in the arts, and other accomplishments are seen unconsciously by the parents as direct reflections on themselves, as marks of their own self-worth. Hence, if the child does well, he or she is inordinately praised and made much of; if badly, he or she can be severely punished. Often the punishment consists of being grounded, going to bed without supper, or being deprived of watching a favorite television program. But there are many cases where the child is abused physically, sometimes quite severely, by sadistic, uncontrolled, emotionally sick parents who have a narcissistic personality disorder.

As children grow up, they inevitably begin to perceive their parents not as ideal beings but as fallible humans—in other words, as real. If the children are able to, they realize that their parents did the best they could and were conditioned by the parenting they received. But children are not always able to understand things in this way, because their resolution of childhood conflicts may have included an idealization of the parents that is sacrosanct. The title of one of Alice Miller's books, *Thou Shalt Not Be Aware* (1984), indicates the inculcated necessity of repressing knowledge about one's parents, whose faults the child is not supposed to notice.

Stephen M. Johnson puts matters regarding such parents and children succinctly in *Character Styles* (1994). In "Chapter 7, The Owned Child: The Symbiotic Character," he writes: "Natural attempts [by the child] at separation are blocked, causing parental anxiety, or are actively punished." On the other hand, should the child express the slightest sympathy or empathy with the parent(s), the child's reaction is "overvalued and reinforced" by the parent(s) who unconsciously wish to see the child as an extension of the self.

Many gifted children who have had careers in the arts come from this kind of background and are psychologically abused in varying degrees and ways, and in some cases, physically abused. This is apparent in such characters as Rimbaud in *Total Eclipse* (1968), A. E. Housman in *The Invention of Love* (1997; Broadway, 2001), Emily

Dickinson in *The Belle of Amherst* (1979), and Elizabeth Barrett Browning in *The Barretts of Wimpole Street* (1931). And all the poets and writers in this chapter can be seen as specific variations on the theme of the psychology of the artistic temperament with the kind of vivid imagination they all have in common.

The general tendency of artists is to escape from the overwhelming sensations aroused by the reality of the external world into a world of fantasy, in which the satisfaction of what is longed for is realized. Of course, such satisfaction has its limitations: how satisfied is any poet with only the poetry and not the reality it represents? The fact that the satisfaction must be continually renewed is an indication of the continuing force of the emotional needs of the poet and the compromise of sublimation.

MARTIN MORAN'S "THE TRICKY PART"

Sándor Ferenczi laid particular stress, as Freud tells us, "on the conservative nature of the instincts, which seek to re-establish every state of things that has been abandoned owing to an external interference." Children who have been physically or sexually abused try to reestablish, reintegrate, and reform their wounded egos, and to adjust to the revelations of sexuality that have come to them too early in their lives, before they are in any psychological position to handle or process it. This idea is exemplified in actor/writer Martin Moran's deeply moving, eloquent one-person play, *The Tricky Part* (2004), which is about his own life. Sensitively directed by Seth Barrish, Martin performed the piece in New York, where he won an Obie, and other venues throughout the country to great critical acclaim. He says about the real-life experience on which the play is based, "It was deeply agonizing and traumatic, but by the grace of God, I am moving through it."

As he comes somewhat shyly but ingratiatingly onto the stage, Martin leads us gradually and artfully into his story in a most gentle manner, and we are first charmed by him, then amazed and shocked at what he has to tell us about what he went through. The play lets us into the world of Catholicism and repression in which he was steeped as a child, and takes us through his painful experience of being abused more than once by Bob, a trusted and admired camp counselor (who would later serve part of a five-year sentence in prison for having abused another child), whom he sees again years later when the man is old and ill in a veteran's hospital.

This important play is emotionally wrenching, but he has written and performed it with such gentle, emotional sweetness and such vivid, humorous intellectual hindsight and insight that we in the audience were moved to compassion and profound empathetic understanding. Martin even describes the molester—whom I as an audience member found disgusting and hateful—with a degree of compassionate understanding that is a tribute to Martin's humanity.

In working on the play, he wrestled for several months with the problem of how to end it. He decided to finish it without a sense of closure for either himself or his audience, leaving us with the idea that his feelings are not resolved, however much he may have forgiven his abuser, and that they continue to be part of him and emerge from his unconscious to trouble and disturb him from time to time, because they exist just below the surface. They always will.

The closing that is not a closure for Martin—or for us—leaves us pensive and reflective. The revealing ending is perfect, because even though he has moved beyond his childhood, has a fulfilling life as an actor, has found a wonderful life partner, and is a forgiving, loving person, the psychic scarring remains to be dealt with. Adjustment to what happened is a lifelong, never-ending process, as it must be for all abused children. And the unresolved ending makes that point graphically and viscerally. For Martin, what is important is "that sense at the end when I remember the notion of grace—a gift from the beyond that moves us towards our own salvation. What feels pivotal to me is that I want grace to let Bob go. Get him out of my psyche! What I realize is that I am actually talking about someone else: the twelve-year old I was." But as Freud points out, the unconscious is "timeless"; therefore, in some way the child still exists, concurrently with the adult. Martin wants to "stop focusing on Bob. I am not sure how in the world to let him rest. Not yet, anyway."

He is very aware of how powerful and deep his feelings about his parents are as well. But, he says, "It's hard to talk about that mysterious, primal stuff. Somewhere in the heart of this entire play is the yearning for father. There is a humming engine underneath this play that has to do with the longing for father, both as protector and as one who embraces."

Freud said that the strongest need of the child is for the father's protection. And Martin proceeded to tell me about a dream: He is in a truck with Bob, driving to the campground, and Bob puts his hand on Martin's neck—this is the beginning of the "touching" that took place. Bob turns into his father, who protects Martin and "stops the whole thing from happening." But of course, his father never knew what was going on, and Martin felt powerless to tell him.

The Tricky Part is a constructed theatrical presentation of events that took place over a number of years. "The reverberations of this play are many," he says. The play goes back and forth in time, and its characters represent a sort of distillation of Martin himself and his abuser, by means of which what happened can be examined and understood more clearly. Martin says, "In a sense Bob is emblematic, and I am emblematic." So are other characters: Sister Christine, for instance, is a composite, conflated from the nuns who were his teachers. Fortunately for him, putting the play together and writing it, revisiting his childhood, and performing the piece were cathartic and healing to an extent, even if perforce not completely. He has had the immense courage and honesty to look at what many people would be too terrified to hold up to the light of day, because it is so painful and so threatening. But the play also gives us hope that people can overcome and go beyond such dreadful happenings. Through courage and compassion and learning to forgive themselves, and by ceasing to think unconsciously that what happened was their own fault—that the child they once were was to blame—they can begin to put to rest, uneasy as that rest may be, the ghosts of their childhood, and to get on with their lives.

Sándor Ferenczi published a paper about child abuse called "The Confusion of Tongues between Adults and Children: The Language of Tenderness and Passion"

(1933). Children need tenderness, affection, and nurturing from adults, and they need to feel loved. What they do not need is sex. And children are easily, sometimes traumatically, confused by adult language, which is that of passion, whether conscious or unconscious, when they, the children, can only understand the language of tenderness.

In situations where the child is sexually abused, the defense mechanism elaborated by Anna Freud and Otto Fenichel and known as "identification with the aggressor" may arise, with all its complications: excusing the adult for what happened, the child feels it is her or his own fault and therefore identifies with the adult and justifies the adult's behavior. Some deeply ill adults misinterpret children's behavior and actions to mean that they are ready for sexual activity, but the child is not yet psychologically in a position to consent to sexual relations.

A deeply moving view of this painful subject, Pedro Almodóvar's complicated, riveting film *Bad Education* (2004) is full of the reverberations and repercussions of childhood abuse, which vibrate startlingly through the contemporary and flashback scenes. The film also concerns the thorny issues of gender identification and the effects of dishonesty and lying. See as well the explosive, award-winning Belgian film *Transfixed* (*Mauvais Genres*, 2004) by Francis Girod for a story that deals in part with the results of the incestuous abuse of a son by his father. And for accounts of real-life stories, there are Alice Miller's books and the important documentaries *The Jaundiced Eye* (1999) and *Capturing the Friedmans* (2003). Both are heartwrenching, distressing films, well worth seeing, although deeply upsetting and disturbing. The dreadful dysfunctionality of the families in these films is simply heartbreaking. Among other things, the way the legal system catches innocent people in its toils and fails them is graphically, upsettingly demonstrated. Another aspect of both these films is the dreadful part that homophobia, both external and internalized, assumes in the lives of individuals, where its consequences even lead to the possibility of suicide.

Oscar Wilde, Lord Alfred Douglas, and The Marquis of Queensberry in Moisés Kaufman's "Gross Indecency: The Three Trials of Oscar Wilde"

*I*n 1997 I was cast to create the role of the Marquis of Queensberry in act 1 and two prosecuting attorneys in act 2 in Moisés Kaufman's *Gross Indecency: The Three Trials of Oscar Wilde*, which Moisés wrote, staged, and directed superbly. I was also the production's dialect coach. The success of the piece depended largely on the ensemble work of the cast of highly motivated, excellent actors. *Gross Indecency* was one of those rare productions that went from being a showcase to being an off-Broadway hit, and it ran for a year and eight months. I did 561 performances and loved doing it. Michael Emerson created the leading role of Oscar Wilde, to great acclaim. Bill Dawes created the role of my son, Lord Alfred Douglas. John McAdams was Queensberry's lawyer, Edward, later Sir Edward Carson, Wilde's old acquaintance from Trinity in Dublin; and Trevor Anthony was Wilde's lawyer, Sir Edward Clarke.

Playing eighteen roles — including rent boys, newspaper reporters, and Queen Victoria — Gregory Steinbruner was one of four narrators, seated just below the stage throughout the play. The other narrators were Andrew Paris, Troy Sostillio (Frank Harris was one of his roles), and Greg Pierotti. Their function was to tell the story playing multiple roles, as indeed all the actors except for Emerson and Dawes did, and to move the play along energetically. The play itself has a dreamlike quality and abstract, nightmarish scenes at times. It is not a realistic play, although there are long realistic, chronological sequences in it. The psychology of the characters, however, is eminently real, and part of Kaufman's brilliance was to have told the story theatrically by putting it together from words spoken or written by the protagonists themselves. At the beginning of act 2, there is an interview between the playwright and a professor that takes us to our own times and points up the continuing relevance for us of what happened to Wilde.

As Gregory told me, the narrators dealt with the psychology of their roles in the following way: The play takes place in the context of a highly stratified society, so social class with its status, inculcated feelings of superiority and inferiority, and associated accents were the first things to be dealt with. This was the "fundamental point of departure." For Gregory's characterization of Queen Victoria, for instance, the idea of using the slight German accent she is said to have had was discussed but discarded as too confusing. He used a very posh upper-class English accent instead.

Playing various newspaper reporters among many other roles, the narrators read from articles written for sexually repressed readers and "from a stodgy, middle-class point of view." There was less than a minute in which to create the character of the reporter for the audience. Under Kaufman's expert direction and orchestration of the reporters' lines, the audience got the impression of the entire social background of the play as seen through individual members of society. As Gregory says, "By creating living persons out of these newspapers we were already underlining right from the beginning that what gets represented as reality is the point of view of a particular individual." In other words, the narrators played these representative Victorians as specific people very much immersed in their society and sharing its values. As Gregory says: "Being a man of his time and place is a critical element in interpreting a role." The actor has to ask "how someone living in a particular time and place pursues his or her objectives." Emotions and desires may be the same as they are for us today, but social conditions, customs, attitudes, habits, and behaviors are different.

John Sholto Douglas, Eighth Marquis of Queensberry (1844–1900), had a stormy life and a terrible childhood. His severe reactions to his early conditioning led this insecure, deeply frightened man to adult behavior that was bullying, sadistic, and abusive in the extreme. He had repressed and pushed down his basic fear of life and his deep-seated fear of punishment into the innermost depths of his unconscious.

His mother had died when he was a child, and his father committed suicide. The Marquis was thus heir to an ancient name and a vast fortune when still very young. His guardians sent him away from the family estate in Scotland to the Naval Academy in Portsmouth, a particularly rough school where early-morning cold showers and regular canings by teachers were common. The frail boy with the strong aggressive drive that he had to control because of his physical weakness was the object of brutal treatment by his fellow students as well, and he was miserable. Later, his guardians insisted he go to Cambridge, where he learned nothing and was horribly bored by academia.

The Marquis was always in a state of denial about his childhood. He justified the early training that brutalized him as a punishment he deserved, because unconsciously he felt guilt and responsibility for his parents' deaths. The Marquis displaced and projected his feelings of weakness, humiliation, inferiority, and vulnerability aroused by the horrible training he received at the Naval Academy onto his children. "Learn to be a man!" was his attitude, by which he meant, "Be a macho male like me, not a puny coward! Never let people know how you feel! They will only despise you for your weakness!"

He was particularly hard on his younger son, Alfred, Lord Douglas, who was not a very strong child. Alfred's weakness unconsciously reminded him of his own when a boy. He had rejected that threatening weakness as unworthy and unmanly and inured himself against his feelings of humiliation. Seeing weakness and frailty in his son unconsciously aroused his fears and repressions, with the concomitant necessity of keeping those repressions active. His unconscious, deeply repressed rage at himself was constantly seeping through (the return of the repressed) and had to be defended against by displacing it and directing it at others. The Marquis' ego ideal did not allow him to acknowledge or feel rage directed at the self, because the ego ideal defended him against the idea that he deserved punishment. And it did not permit feelings of weakness.

In addition, Alfred's willowy blond good looks made him the apple of his doting mother's eye and undoubtedly aroused the Marquis's unconscious Oedipal jealousy as well. She was an artistic beauty who passed her looks and sensitivity on to her son and brought him up to love the arts, while her husband, a womanizer who did not believe in marriage, was a well-known figure in the sporting world and not in the least interested in anything artistic. He and a friend devised the famous Marquis of Queensberry boxing rules by which the Marquis' name is still remembered, in an attempt to make the sport less brutal—ironically enough. He was a household terror and behaved like a fascistic tyrant: he could fly off the handle and become physically abusive at the drop of a hat, so paranoiacally touchy and overly sensitive was he to anything he considered a slight or the least manifestation of disobedience to his iron, inflexible will.

There were actually people who liked the Marquis. His father-in-law admired him, until the Marquis accused him of being homosexual. He had friends, especially among athletes and the sporting crowd. And there were many in the public who applauded his "moral" stance against Wilde, especially when he posed (which is what he accused Wilde of doing), no doubt to himself as well, as a father trying to "save" his son from an evil, decadent, profligate homosexual villain. He was viewed in some circles as a hero, and his self-justification was widely accepted in the repressive atmosphere of the day. Most people thought he was quite justified in pursuing the course he did.

To begin my preparation, I read everything I could get hold of about Oscar Wilde, Alfred Douglas, and of course, the Marquis of Queensberry, and everyone associated with them. I read biographies, Wilde's correspondence, the complete trial transcripts, and a volume of the Marquis' letters (a rare book that I found through the Internet), and much general history besides on life in Victorian England. In many instances, I was simply refreshing my memory and rereading such books as Richard Ellman's magisterial biography *Oscar Wilde* (1988) and the many books about Wilde by the prolific H. Montgomery Hyde, who was also the first editor of the trial transcripts.

All this reading led me to an understanding of the bases of the Marquis' violent character, and I began to realize that what underlay this warped, twisted, troubled man's virulent homophobia was deeply repressed homosexuality. He had a strong paranoid streak. As I have had occasion to remark, Freud tells us that this includes the unconscious fear of homosexuality. The very notion of such a thing would have enraged the Marquis to the point of homicidal madness, so defensive was he on the subject. Yet he surrounded himself with sportsmen and male companions and friends, and was always more comfortable in their presence, as he was in the company of his horses, than in that of the women he pursued sexually.

The Marquis projected his deeply held, unconscious fear onto his sons, two of whom were indeed homosexual. Alfred's brother Drumlanrig, Prime Minister Lord Roseberry's private secretary, had committed suicide. Alfred was crushed and devastated, and the despairing Marquis was inevitably reminded of his father's suicide. In fact, he refused to admit that Drumlanrig had killed himself, and maintained that his son had died in a hunting accident.

The Marquis's atheism and even his attitudes about marriage were both irrelevant to the play, except as background, which it was good to know for the sake of thoroughness and adding to the texture of the character. Equally irrelevant was the fact that his second wife was planning to divorce him on the grounds that the marriage had not been consummated. More relevant was that the Marquis had a problem with impotence, which is a great "actor's secret." It helped explain his furious rages and his projections onto everyone in his vicinity of his need to control them, a sort of overcompensation for his incapacity.

I went back to Reich's *Character Analysis,* because I remembered his talking about sadomasochism and the phallic-narcissistic character, and I thought these might be the bases of the Marquis's personality, along with his streak of paranoia and psychopathic traits. Not being a clinician but a thorough layman, I thought there might be no necessary mutual exclusivity between the character types, and that a phallic-narcissistic character could also be masochistic and psychopathic.

I also wanted to see what Reich had to say about how such characters' armoring works. The more I reread Reich, the more I thought I had possibly been right in my assessment of the Marquis as having all the Reichian sadomasochistic character traits. His masochistic side was indeed based on a deep fear of abandonment because of the abandonment he had experienced as a child. The self-depreciation Reich mentions would seem at first to be the missing trait that would identify him as a completely masochistic personality type, except that I discovered that he did indeed express self-depreciation satirically in some of his more sarcastic letters.

His masochism received overcompensation in a superiority complex (here, I could consult Alfred Adler's writings), in part because his aristocratic class background played a major role in shaping his social attitudes of superiority in the context of Victorian society. Although viewed as an eccentric bad boy, as an aristocrat he could make public his controversial views on religion and marriage, which he did in order to be provocative—more sadomasochism, since his provocation led to his being despised, and this was punishment. Such views got him cordially disliked in upper-class circles, which viewed him as the typical scion of the "mad, bad Douglases."

The Marquis' psychopathic traits included the inability to give or receive love. He was incapable of sustaining a relationship based on equality between partners, with the give-and-take compromises relationships require. He was also incapable of accepting responsibility for his actions, and blamed everyone around him for his misfortunes. In his letters, he constantly complains masochistically and paranoiacally about everyone, and about being misunderstood and unappreciated. We can also see in his letters a tendency to self-aggrandizement.

What would the audience ever see of all this analysis of the Marquis' character? They would see the external surface manifestations of his illness in the form of his behavior and feel how deep it ran, but they could never really know the nature or extent of the Marquis' unconscious conflicts unless they had done the same reading I had done. And that was exactly as it should be. The audience would be able to have its own visceral reactions and responses, and to leave the theater with a sense of the injustice done not only to Wilde in particular but, by extension, to gay people in general, by the vicious homophobia that deprives a large percentage of the population of its rights.

What did I actually do with all this information after I had completed my analysis of the Marquis? I forgot it! That is, having absorbed it and kept it in my unconscious, I went back to the script and began to play the actions that would lead me to the character's objectives and to find the relevant substitutions from my own life.

The psychological information conditioned the way I played the actions. Anger, for instance, can be expressed in many ways. And in playing the Marquis' angry tirades, I would act them with a cold, controlled fury and sometimes with a quietness that would be the opposite of their actual verbal expression. I could be horribly threatening in a concentrated, quiet manner, which would be all the more frightening, both for the characters on stage with me (the confrontation of Wilde in his library, for instance) and for the audience.

And what of Oscar Wilde? The question that many people have asked is, "Why did he stay in England, instead of fleeing to the continent, especially once it was apparent that he would be prosecuted and convicted?" Because it *was* quite clear that this would happen from the moment Wilde was forced by mounting evidence against him to withdraw from his libel case against the Marquis of Queensberry without having won a verdict. Wilde's hubris and his flippant testimony, during which he tripped himself up as much as he was tripped up, and his open, flagrant contempt for the Marquis' attorney Edward Carson, an old school acquaintance of Wilde's from Trinity College in Dublin, was another disservice to himself during his cross examination.

The charge against the Marquis was that he had libeled Wilde by publicly leaving a business card with the words "For Oscar Wilde, posing as a Somdomite [sic]." The misspelling was probably a result of the Marquis' having written it in furious haste; he had hoped to provoke Wilde into doing exactly what he did. It was clear from the beginning that the great writer would lose and that he should never have brought the case to begin with. He found out very quickly that the Marquis had hired a private detective who had unearthed the secrets of Wilde's private life and found witnesses with whom Wilde had been sexually involved. And Wilde knew the other evidence against him, such as his perfervid letters to Alfred, which the jury would view as damning, despite the literary, poetic construction Wilde could try to put on them. Wilde would not have pursued the case had he not been egged on by Alfred Douglas, who thought not only of the insult to Wilde and of possible future dangerous actions by the Marquis, but also—quite naturally—of himself and his long-desired revenge against the father who had so mistreated him and his mother (all very Oedipal) in his dysfunctional family setting. And Wilde was not merely enamored but besotted by his passion for Douglas, so he gave in. As Michael Emerson says, Wilde loved Douglas "in his own way, but he may not have understood love in the way you and I do. It was all mixed up with his obsession with aesthetics and his passion for the concept of the Greco-Roman male bond. Perhaps he misunderstood a kind of abstracted worship for love. He was rather an Alpha-male and turned his love into an object."

He genuinely wanted to help Douglas, with whose suffering at Queensberry's hands he sympathized. Wilde's friend Robbie Ross advised him to rip up the card and forget it; another friend, the obtuse Frank Harris, advised him to pursue it, but Harris knew nothing of the evidence against Wilde at the time, so he claimed (he was a notorious liar; in Kaufman's play, Harris is portrayed as more noble and unselfish than he was in reality). He was also arrogant, and in his hubris, he thought that because he was so successful and well known, with two highly acclaimed plays running in the West End simultaneously, he was above the law. And then his mother, an Irish nationalist, had told him that it was practically his duty as an Irishman to fight the English philistines. His honor was at stake! And he remembered the shame of his youth, when his father, a physician, had been accused of molestation and brought an action for libel. He won the case, but his reputation was ruined.

A notable aspect of the trial was that almost all the people involved in prosecuting the Irishman Wilde were Irish themselves. Queensberry's lawyer, Edward (later, Sir Edward) Carson was a Unionist, wanting to maintain the union of England and Ireland, and he had known Wilde very slightly at Trinity in Dublin. Unlike Wilde, who learned to speak with an impeccable upper-class English accent, Carson never lost his Irish brogue. The prosecutors, Gill, and Lockwood, who was Attorney General (both of whom I also played in act 2 of *Gross Indecency*) were of Irish background as well. I did not play them with Irish accents, however, since they had probably lost their accents by that time, although it is possible that Gill spoke with an Irish accent as heavy as Carson's is supposed to have been.

In the Wilde trials, so the popular defensive idea ran, there was no question of Irish politics, and Wilde was being tried simply for the crime of gross indecency. But of course politics was involved: the English establishment saw this case as an opportunity to assert its hegemony over Irish people once again. The prosecutors were even harder on Wilde precisely because he was "one of their own." It is possible that they were unconscious that they were being crueler to Wilde than they would have been to a non-Irishman. In other words, they were in a state of denial.

All Wilde's conscious reasons for staying in England instead of fleeing are real, but they are superficial compared to what was happening deep in his unconscious. Wilde could use all of them, and did, to convince himself that he had to stay and face the music. However, the principle psychological reason that Wilde behaved in such a self-destructive fashion was his underlying guilt and shame: he was ashamed on an unconscious level of his homosexuality, and he felt guilty about his sexual activities and, on a conscious level, about lying to his wife—whom he held in secret, unconscious contempt but whom he knew he had betrayed, as he felt he had the two sons he adored. Therefore, he felt unconsciously that he ought to be punished.

On the surface, Wilde, who was late in coming to a realization about his sexuality that others had come to long before he had, certainly took pleasure in his sexual activities and did not appear to feel guilty about them. In betraying his wife, he was able to tell himself that he felt he was doing what his nature dictated. He simply had to act as he had, because anything less would have been a betrayal of himself and who he was. His unconscious conflicts together with the conscious reasons led him to stay put and, indeed, induced him to drink himself into a kind of inertia. He could hardly move from his seat in the Cadogan Hotel bedroom and awaited patiently the arrival of the arresting officers.

The Marquis of Queensberry, who sat and gloated at Wilde's trials as he had at his own libel trial, was the perfect satanic instrument to destroy Wilde: he could punish Wilde for the sin of loving the Marquis' own son. The Marquis had been publicly humiliated by having his son branded as a homosexual. And his fury was based also on his unconscious jealousy of the love Alfred displayed for Wilde, while publicly loathing the Marquis. It was therefore almost with relief that Wilde—the target of public and private opprobrium, jealousy, contempt, and spite, enmeshed and embroiled in the bitter Douglas family battle royal—went to jail, there to serve out his punishment of two years at hard labor and to expiate the sin of being the person he was. After his release and his exile on the continent, the unconscious guilt over his homosexuality, for which he had paid so dearly, must have dissipated to some extent, and he now gloried in a lifestyle that he felt to be both natural and desirable. At the same time, his guilt had not completely disappeared, and he drank heavily, to punish himself unconsciously, as well as for the pleasure of being intoxicated. He was ruining his health—a terrible self-inflicted punishment.

His deathbed conversion to Roman Catholicism is further evidence of his unconscious guilt: he wanted God to forgive his sins. His wife had refused to forgive him, and he never again saw his two sons, whom he loved dearly. She would have pardoned him had he agreed to have nothing more to do with Alfred, but that was an impossible condition for him to agree to. As filled with ups and downs, with bitter quarrels and reproaches, with passionate love and longing as their relationship was, it was as necessary to him as the air he breathed.

And Wilde loved drama and being a star. He had a hysterical side to his personality, and as Michael Emerson says, he had created "a satisfying romance in which he played the role of a man brought low by love. He made the ultimate sacrifice." This is further evidence of his guilt complex, because the real-life drama he had "stage-managed," to use Michael's word, was one in which he was punished. All played perfectly the roles Wilde had unconsciously assigned to them. Talking of Wilde's immaturity, Michael Emerson says, "The whole trial business seems more properly to belong to him as a college student than as a grown man."

Alfred apparently felt the same way about Wilde as Wilde did about him, despite his later renunciation and betrayal of Wilde, long after Wilde's death. In fact, he turned out to be despicable, because of his own guilt over his homosexuality, against which he ultimately felt he had to fight and which he condemned in himself as sinful; he too had converted to Roman Catholicism. It is most unfortunate that the charming, handsome, unhappy young man, who aspired to be a poet and yearned for masculine love and affection, became a crabbed, nasty, homophobic crank devoted to propagating the most absurd, delusional anti-Semitic conspiracy theories. He was haunted all his life by his relationship with Wilde, and in the course of a libel trial that echoed his father's suit against Wilde — except that Douglas was found guilty — practically made a fetish of denying that they had ever had homosexual relations, as he also did when appearing as a witness in other trials. This was a stunning betrayal and a barefaced lie, which disgusted Wilde's other friends. Temperamentally and behaviorally, the warped Douglas of later years came very much to resemble the father he reviled and despised. Even earlier, many of Wilde's friends continually warned him against Douglas, whom they considered dangerous to Wilde's welfare, but Wilde was deeply in love and would hear none of it.

How much did Douglas love Wilde? Bill Dawes, who did extensive research when preparing the role, says, "He admired Wilde as a personality, and as an artist. I think that, lacking a compassionate father," he wanted and allowed Oscar Wilde to "take his place. He became a father figure. But Douglas was not particularly attracted to him sexually. He entertained Wilde's sexual overtures to him because he was in desperate need of love and affection." The unconscious identification of Wilde with Douglas's father, as he wanted that father to be, probably explains why Douglas reacted badly any time Wilde did not behave exactly as Douglas wished him to and why Douglas, who wanted Wilde to take care of him, was less than sympathetic when Wilde needed to be taken care of, as when he was ill, for instance. Bill, who is a humorous and charming person, introduced me to his own father one evening after a performance: "This is my *good* father," he said, with a broad smile.

In working on the role, aside from studying the character's psychology, Bill "also wrote poetry almost daily, because the character was obsessed with poetry — a mediocre poet trying to make his mark. My own writing helped me fall in love with Wilde's writing."

"The gray area in Douglas is intriguing," he continues. "One thing I found in my research was a lot of material that said he was manic-depressive, and he was also clearly bisexual, or at least experimented with different aspects of his sexuality. What is interesting about him is his 'poles' — a lot of opposites at work in him simultaneously. He was upper class, but hung out with lower-class rent boys. From being an agnostic, he became a devout Roman Catholic" — in other words, the inconsistencies, ambivalences, and contradictions in his character represented the key to playing the scenes. We would now call Lord Alfred's affliction a *bipolar affective disorder*, a term for a range of syndromes, from more to less severe, including simple melancholia and compulsive manias. The condition is now treated with lithium salts, because it is partly biophysical in origin, but in Douglas's day, that treatment did not exist. Manic-depressives can be mildly psychotic—that is, they are able to relate to reality, but they have periodic bouts of irrationality, dissociation, and disorientation, as they enter one or the other of their severest moods; hence, the value in studying the specific symptoms when interpreting a character and avoiding broad categories that are sometimes too general.

What the bipolar emotional disturbance meant in Douglas's case is that he was subject to severe mood swings: at one pole was a massively energetic, almost frenetic mood of elation and compulsion, in which he seemed deliriously happy; at the other pole was the opposite—namely, a severe depression verging on despair and extreme lethargy and lassitude, resulting from the amount of furious energy expended in the manic phase. Most of the time, Douglas was simply in a more neutral, reasonable, self-controlled mood, but anything could provoke his anxiety and set off the cycle of moods, especially something having to do with his father or when he experienced any kind of frustration. He was very reactive and his depression was situational and unpredictable. And he was easily agitated and volatile.

Bill Dawes says he came to the conclusion that Douglas "was unfairly blamed for Wilde's demise, but Douglas acted from the point of view of what he thought was best for himself, and what he thought was best for Wilde. The idea that he used Wilde to exact revenge is absurd." It is true that people do not generally act out of villainous motives, even if they turn out in the end to have been villainous. Bill was right, because Douglas never hid the fact from Wilde or anyone else who would listen that he wanted to get back at his father, and he also thought that Wilde was entirely justified in bringing his libel suit against the Marquis and that it would have been cowardly not to do so. Both Douglas and Wilde felt that if Wilde did not sue Queensberry, the door would be opened to further reprehensible and frightening behavior by the Marquis. Who knew what he might do next? It was actually imperative for Wilde either to fight him or to leave the country for a life of exile. In any case, Wilde needed nobody to lead him to his destruction: he was a willing if unconscious partner in his own demise.

ROBERT AND ELIZABETH BARRETT BROWNING
IN RUDOLPH BESIER'S "THE BARRETTS OF WIMPOLE STREET"

In 1850 Elizabeth Barrett Browning (1806–61) published her most famous book of poems, *Sonnets from the Portuguese*, but they are not translations; the title is a conceit. The sonnets are meant to resemble Renaissance love poetry, which they do. They are heartfelt love poems, full of yearning. Even a brief parting from the beloved is painful and a long one almost unthinkable, so much are their hearts and minds entwined. The poems are also meant to tell the story of her deep love for Robert Browning, whom she adored and idolized. He gave her love and was the opposite in his attitudes, feelings, and behavior of her tyrannical, despotic father, who kept his daughter isolated, using her illness as an excuse because he had incestuous longings for her.

Robert Browning (1812–59) was known for his passionate lyrics and, perhaps above all, for such narrative dramatic poems and monologues in verse as "My Last Duchess," "Rabbi Ben Ezra," and "Fra Lippo Lippi" and stirring lyrics such as "How They Brought the Good News from Ghent to Aix."

One of his most famous lyric poems, full of music and rhapsodic longing and evocative of spring, from "Home-Thoughts from Abroad" from *Dramatic Romances and Lyrics* (1845), begins: "Oh, to be in England / Now that April's there..." In his cynical pessimism, the bitter and acerbic T. S. Eliot was to mock the first two lines of this poem with his own gloss on them in "The Waste-Land" (1922): "April is the cruelest month / Breeding lilacs out of the dead land..." But Browning is nostalgic for the England he has left behind, and the images are gloriously romantic. One senses the love for the land and also for people who live there that lies behind this poem, particularly when he writes of buttercups as the "little children's dower," implicitly comparing the spring to the childhood phase of life, when all should ideally be enjoyment and enchantment. Browning embraces not only the landscape but also those who dwell therein.

The romantic love story of Robert and Elizabeth Barrett Browning is engrossingly told in Rudolph Besier's 1931 Broadway play *The Barrets of Wimpole Street* and in two movies made from it in 1934 and 1957. The oldest of twelve children (of whom nine survived), at the age of fifteen, Elizabeth became a bedridden invalid because of a spinal injury due to a fall from a horse. Her lungs were also severely impaired as a result of the accident, and she had difficulty breathing. But she began to write poetry, all the while remaining a recluse, immured within her perpetually dark, stuffy bedroom, a prey to laudanum and morphine, which she needed to ease her pain. Despite the medications, she suffered terribly from insomnia and had fainting spells and fevers. And she sometimes lost her voice. Nevertheless, she continued to write and publish, and developed a reputation as a brilliant poet. She lavished her affection on a spaniel name Flush and enjoyed the company of her siblings when her father allowed them to visit "Ba," as she was nicknamed.

The relationships with her family members and Robert are quite clearly laid out in the play. Her manner of behaving with her father is to seem accommodating and acquiescent while seething with fury underneath—an example of the playing of opposites and of the style of compliance while actually being detached, as Karen Horney describes it. She wanted to love her father and felt guilty because she could not.

Robert wrote to her because he loved her poetry and wanted to meet her, and he was introduced to her by a mutual friend. He himself was not yet well known, although he had already published some poetry. Elizabeth was perpetually tired and in need of constant rest, and only agreed to meet Robert reluctantly. But when she did, she fell head over heels in love with him.

Robert Browning was the son of a bank clerk who was an unusually erudite man. He amassed a library of more than six thousand volumes, and it was there that Robert received his early education, going on to the newly formed University of London, known for its nonconformity, especially in matters of religion and philosophy, no doubt much to his religious mother's disgust. His father had been sent to work on a plantation in the West Indies, to gain experience and a measure of independence. He was so horrified by the slavery that he observed there in all its evil that he fled back to England, and he would communicate this horror to his sensitive son.

Robert's mother was a fanatic evangelical Christian, but Robert did not follow in her footsteps, although he was a believer, having first investigated atheism. Interestingly enough, while it was his mother who was the unforgiving, rigid formalist and tyrant in the family, it was Elizabeth's father who was the religious fanatic in hers. The fact that Edward Barrett had inherited his fortune through the exploitation of his family's slave plantations in the Caribbean is an interesting point as well. Elizabeth must have seen in Robert the opposite attitude to her father's and shared Robert's horror of the institution. Also like Robert, she did not share her parent's perfervid brand of religion. And he saw the opposite of his mother in her, a sweet and accommodating beauty who needed to be taken care of.

Elizabeth was constantly watched over and spied on by her tyrannical father, played with all the cruelty, sadism, and coldness of the man by Charles Laughton in the 1934 version (the Brownings were played by Norma Shearer and Frederic March) and by John Gielgud, miscast in the 1957 film, with Jennifer Jones and Bill Travers equally unmemorable as the two poets. Edward Barett was a widower, and he had forbidden his daughters to marry. Naturally, he was deeply worried about his daughter's health, but he used her condition to tyrannize, control, and manipulate her, bending her perpetually to his will, decreeing whom she might and might not see and when, even convincing her she was far sicker than she was, and preventing her from gaining strength and curing such of her ailments as she could. Possessive and selfish, he wanted her all to himself for eternity. This was clearly an Oedipal transfer of the repressed infantile feelings he had had for his mother. No doubt he told himself on a conscious level that everything he was doing was for her good. He denied that he had any ulterior motives and repressed all knowledge of what Jungians would call his shadow, of which he did not wish to be aware. He would have said he was being protective of her, as he had to be out of necessity and both by duty and by right, and was not in the least taking care of her for possessive or jealous motives or trying to make her eternally dependent on him.

The character of Mr. Barrett is reminiscent of the father in Henry James's *Washington Square,* dramatized for Broadway by Ruth and Augustus Goetz as *The Heiress* (1947), and the character in James's novel may even be based on him. Basil Rathbone played the tyrannical father on Broadway, and Ralph Richardson was notably repugnant and understandable at the same time in the 1949 film, with a screenplay by the Goetzes, and Olivia de Havilland and Montgomery Clift as the two young lovers. The concerned, cynical father thinks consciously that in keeping his daughter away from the social climber Morris Townsend, he is merely acting for her own good. He has no consciousness of how his oppressive tyranny has cowed his daughter and made her rebellious. But her revolt against his authority is masochistic and takes the form described by Karen Horney as inner rebellion. She takes no action that would help her deal with her problems, and she does not dare to confront her father. Eventually, identifying with the aggressor, she comes to believe he is right after all and drives Townsend away.

Blindly, compulsively conscientious (in their own eyes), the fathers in *The Heiress* and *The Barretts of Wimpole Street* have certainly substituted their obsessive, paranoid approach to their relationships with their daughters for a judgment of reality. Therefore, any suitor, let alone the suspect Morris Townsend in *The Heiress* or the poetic Robert Browning in *The Barretts of Wimpole Street,* would be unacceptable and threatening to these men, who are incapable of seeing them as anything other than a threat to their authority. They have constructed their worlds as they wish them to be, and anything that does not conform to their expectations is simply dismissed as unacceptable.

When Robert Browning (a poet much appreciated for his psychological insight by Ernest Jones, according to his son Mervyn Jones) courted Elizabeth, she eventually worked up the courage to leave her miserable situation and elope with him. They had been obliged to keep their courtship secret because of her father's suspicious, paranoid attitude, although he had allowed Robert's visits because he assumed they involved only literary conversations and discussions of poetry. Robert and Elizabeth married in 1846, leaving for Italy a year afterwards, despite Elizabeth's physical pain and suffering. They spent much of their life in Venice and in Florence, where she died, leaving him bereft, although he survived her by twenty-eight years. It was actually after her death that he earned his reputation as one of the greatest English poets, so much so that he actually eclipsed his wife's reputation, which had been much more appreciated than his. In 1881 he was pleased to witness the founding of the Browning Society, devoted to his poetry. He died crowned with glory, one of the grand old men of Victorian English letters.

Emily Dickinson in William Luce's "The Belle of Amherst"

Emily Dickinson (1830–86) is known for her deeply symbolic, passionately evocative, cryptic, and elliptical poems. In one of them, written in 1861, which begins "Wild nights!—wild nights! / Were I with thee / Wild nights should be / Our luxury!" and ends "Might I moor, tonight, In thee!" we have an immediate sense that Dickinson must have had something or someone specific in mind. Her poetry is a way into her mind, and this poem in particular is a way into the role in *The Belle of Amherst,* because its subtext is so personal. Here she is, living alone and yet writing about spending a wild night of passionate lovemaking with someone. Would she ever have gone beyond that dream and into the reality of doing it, one wonders? Did she ever do so? At any rate, a secret love that underlies every word the character says is a fine actor's secret as well. The images in the complete poem are highly charged; the longing and loneliness run very deep in this simple lyric. At one point the poet exclaims, "Ah, the sea!" and this cry from the heart is born of primordial longing and desire.

Aside from being one of America's most famous poets, Emily Dickinson is known for living reclusively and seeing almost no one aside from family members, although she did have a number of important correspondents. She was from a prosperous, well-known family, and her father was a lawyer and the treasurer of Amherst College. He was also a strict, very religious orthodox Congregationalist and brought his family of three children up to respect puritanical principles of restraint and sobriety. They were quiet, retiring, staid, and respectable. Although he believed in education for women and sent her to the leading women's schools in Massachusetts, he dictated what books his daughter was allowed to read—nothing that might tend to bring religion into disrepute, certainly. But it was not he who decreed that she should be a recluse. She withdrew from the world of her own volition, without any prodding from him.

Emily's mother was remote and distant, unemotional and unaffectionate. As a young girl, Emily must have learned to distrust people. If the example of her parents showed how people behaved with each other, why have much to do with them? Why not withdraw and live alone? Who would ever be loving and affectionate if her parents weren't? "Heaven is what I cannot reach," she wrote in one of her poems.

Despite her self-imposed withdrawal from the world, she remained passionately interested in the nature of human relationships. Many of her poems seem very simple on the surface, but they are like a stone tossed into a pond: the ripples never seem to stop and awaken echoes in anyone who reads them. Her loneliness and longing for love come through very clearly. Deprived by her own actions and behavior of a loving relationship, she appears to have become even more sensitive to the nuances of love and relationships, seen from afar. And her ambivalence is equally apparent. Had she made the right choices in life? Was she really happier to be alone? Had she not been led down the wrong path? And was it too late to change now that she was growing older?

William Luce's *The Belle of Amherst*—starring Julie Harris, who won an unprecedented fifth Tony for her performance—is a heartwarming one-person play, very informative about her and about her poetry. It was also broadcast on television and is available in VHS and DVD formats. Harris portrays Dickinson as a terribly sweet, shy, and energetic person, agoraphobic but brimming with delightful humor, and avoiding contact with many of her neighbors, about whom she is quite judgmental. Her sunny personality and shyness make her very appealing, and we wonder why such a good person remains alone and unattached. Bowlby's style of avoidance applies to this character, and so does Karen Horney's style of shallow living: as the character in the play, Dickinson dwells often on the trivial and the banal. Her masochism is also apparent. If the fear of being abandoned is at the basis of the masochistic personality, as Reich maintained, then Dickinson, succumbing to unconscious terror, refused to allow it to dominate her by refusing to become involved with someone who might hurt her. Nobody could abandon her, because she was with nobody. Did this bring her peace of mind?

A. E. HOUSMAN IN TOM STOPPARD'S "THE INVENTION OF LOVE"

*A*lfred Edward Housman (1859–1936) was a lyric poet of immense charm and doleful melancholy. He never fails to arouse the reader's emotions, as he does in this pensive 1896 lyric "Loveliest of trees, the cherry now" from his collection *A Shropshire Lad,* one of the most popular books of poems in the English language:

> Loveliest of trees, the cherry now
> Is hung with bloom along the bough,
> And stands about the woodland ride
> Wearing white for Eastertide.
>
> Now, of my threescore years and ten,
> Twenty will not come again,
> And take from seventy springs a score,
> It only leaves me fifty more.
>
> And since to look at things in bloom
> Fifty springs are little room,
> About the woodlands I will go
> To see the cherry hung with snow.

The poem is full of symbolism and evocations. It would seem that the tree is personified as if it (she) were a bride, wearing white for Easter, the Christian holy day that celebrates the resurrection of Christ, as spring represents the resurrection of nature. We arrive at that image because we remember unconsciously that "ride" and "Eastertide" rhyme with "bride." Perhaps the image is that of a man dressed in white. The metaphor is ambiguous and possibly androgynous. "The cherry hung with snow" is (possibly) a highly charged sexual metaphor, susceptible of various interpretations. Seen in an erotic light and in a homoerotic light (the tree is a well known phallic symbol), the poem becomes frolicsome and playful, as well as philosophical.

Nevertheless, this poem evokes a peaceful landscape of open woodland, with cherry trees in spring blossom. Housman is calmer and more restrained than Browning, who waxes romantic over the spring. Cherries need light to grow, and the "woodland ride," or open space where one can ride, provides light enough. The poet regrets the passage of time, however, so there is a tinge of sadness that underlies the poem, which tells us that since time passes so rapidly and youth will not come again, we should take advantage of what time we have to really enjoy the beauty life has to offer—something of which Housman was not always capable himself. But Housman tells us that we can always continue to enjoy beauty and that we need not succumb to the sadness that the knowledge of the passage of time in our own lives and our growing older might bring, and there is a jocose sexuality in this poem that helps overcome the underlying atmosphere of melancholy.

But all is not paradisiacal and merry or even merely melancholy in the lonely land of Shropshire, for "Into my heart an air that kills / From yon far country blows," and lads and lasses, loved and mourned, die before their time—almost prophetically, for they would die in the trenches and battles of World War I eighteen years later. The landscape can be grim and gray. One must meet one's fate with determination and stoicism.

This attitude is only to be expected from a man who restrained and suppressed his emotions all his life because he found them unacceptable and anxiety provoking. He dared not reveal what he felt for fear of being reviled and ostracized, so he lived out his life in what Thoreau calls "quiet desperation." He limited himself, and this may explain why his sweetly evocative and sad poems also have a limited range of subject matter and emotion. But his sense of language and yearning are powerful, and our own longings are awakened when we read them. There is something in his striving that is common to us all.

Housman's poems have an unusual, touching lyricism. In all his poems underneath the beautiful abstractions there lurk sadness, regret, and longing for happiness and peace. They seem to evoke an era, just before World War I changed the world forever and shattered a way of life that insulated many people in Europe from the knowledge of what had been done to secure their comfortable manner of living—namely, the exploitation and brutality inflicted on the African and Asian colonies. The innocence and sweet naïveté, even with melancholy underlying it, comes at a price: the price of having blinders on or, even worse, of believing in the moral rectitude of the imperialists.

The eldest of seven children, Housman grew up in a staid, solidly bourgeois atmosphere of stifling respectability. Like Alfred, Lord Douglas, he was the son of a sporting man who was bluff, blunt, and hardy, where his son was small, frail, weak, and sensitive. The boy was deeply attached to his mother in a symbiotic relationship that aroused his father's jealousy in a classic Oedipal reaction. His father remained distant and withheld his affection—"Into my heart a wind that kills." The boy must have felt desolate and desperately unhappy. Then, when Housman was twelve, his mother died, and this worst of tragedies left him permanently scarred and devastated—"From yon far country blows." As an adult he remained extremely sensitive and was often quickly attuned to the nuances of his friends and associates, but at the same time quite unapproachable when he wished to be. He missed the "land of lost content" where he could not go again—his mother's love and the closeness of their relationship. As Proust said, "The true paradises are the paradises one has lost."

Much had been expected of him as a promising young scholar, but in 1881 he failed to get an honors degree and had to take a job in the Patent Office, which must have been stultifying for him. He was acutely ashamed, angry, and disappointed over his failure, and his repressed anger engendered a shy persona and a great sweetness that covered over and masked his threatening rage even from himself. Despite this setback, he wrote and published articles on the classics, and as a result, he was invited in 1892 to teach at University College, London, as a Professor of Latin.

In the course of a long and distinguished career spent mostly at Cambridge University, where he began teaching in 1911, Housman became the greatest English classics scholar of his day, throwing himself almost obsessively into his work. As a teacher, he had a reputation for remoteness and reticence, and his students tended to find him forbidding, almost as if he were acting out the role his stern father had played with him. And he could be scathing and insensitive in his critiques of his colleagues' work—again, much as his father had been with him.

He had to hide his homosexuality, and this forced concealment exacerbated the sadomasochistic element in his character. This necessity to hide who he really was may have contributed to his original failure at the exams, since his unrequited love for his fellow student, Moses Jackson, was making him miserable at the time. He was in love with Jackson, who was heterosexual, all his life. They remained always the best of friends, and Housman felt abandoned and bereft when Jackson married and moved to India—"Into my heart a wind that kills."

This is the character so compassionately portrayed in Tom Stoppard's play *The Invention of Love,* which looks insightfully into the life of this troubled, painfully sensitive, conflicted man. Like the Housman poem reprinted above, Stoppard's play evokes the dichotomy between the older and the younger man. Richard Easton's Tony Award–winning performance was suffused with genius and melancholy, with sweetness and vigor. Robert Sean Leonard as the younger Housman was equally sensitive and moving. The play goes back and forth in time. The contrast between respectable Victorian convention, with its repression of sexual desire and the destruction that repression wreaks, and the attitude of the hedonistic poets in *Total Eclipse* could not be clearer.

RIMBAUD AND VERLAINE
IN CHRISTOPHER HAMPTON'S "TOTAL ECLIPSE"

"Chanson d'automne" from *Poèmes saturniens* (1866) by Paul Verlaine is probably his most famous poem. Its first verse is the most famous of all:

> Les sanglots longs
> Des violins
> De l'automne
> Blessent mon Coeur
> D'une langueur
> Monotone.

My literal translation: The long sobs / Of the violins / Of autumn / Wound my heart / With a monotonous languor.

This gorgeously beautiful poem is notable for its sonority and its combination of sound and sense working together. The assonance, particularly in the first verse, suggests cold and misery, as the sobbing of the violins is likened to the sobbing of the autumn wind. As the poem continues, the despair of the poet and his feeling of futility—of being carried along by the wind, whirled now here now there like a dead leaf—are conveyed not only by the actual words but also by the compelling rhythm and the sounds of the rhymes. It would seem that Verlaine is attempting to exorcise his demons of unhappiness through the music of his poetry, but the attempt only gives rise to the mournful melancholy of sobbing wind and violins, which echo the poet's own sobs. He feels abandoned and at the mercy of fate, prey to a nostalgic vision of the happier past. The indication is that the poet himself is responsible for having ruined his own happiness. There is no clearer illustration of Verlaine's masochism and his creative ability to turn it into art than this poem.

Rimbaud's contribution to French poetry in such famous poems and books as "Le bateau ivre" (The Drunken Boat, 1871) and *Une saison en enfer* (A Season in Hell, 1873) is a combination of the most striking sonorities, images, and cryptic symbols expressing the most iconoclastic and fiercely opinionated view of life. In his prose poem "Number XXXVII, 'Démocratie,'" for example, which is from a volume called *Illuminations* (1872), he writes:

Le drapeau va au paysage immonde et notre patois étouffe le tambour.
Au centre nous alimenterons la plus cynique prostitution. Nous
    massacrerons les révoltes logiques.
Aux pays poivrés et détrempés! — au services des plus monstrueuses
    exploitations industrielles ou militaires.
Au revoir ici, n'importe où. Conscrits du bon vouloir, nous aurons la
    philosophie féroce; ignorants pour la science, roués pour le confort;
    la crevaison pour le monde qui va. C'est la vraie marche. En avant,
    route!

My literal translation: "The flag goes with the foul landscape and our patois stifles the drum. / At the center [in the interior of the country] we will nourish the most cynical prostitution. We will massacre [all] the logical revolts. / [Let's on] to the countries peppered and soaked! — in the service of the most monstrous industrial or military exploitations. / Goodbye here, no matter where [here is]. Conscripts of good will, we will have a ferocious philosophy; ignorant as to science, corrupted as to comfort; death [the somewhat vulgar, shocking word *crevaison* means an abject, horrible death, bursting open, collapsing, dropping dead] for the world as it goes. It's the real march. Forward, en route!

Some would see this poem as cynical, but others would see it as simply realistic and remarkably applicable to today's world, unfortunately. Rimbaud remains modern and even contemporary in many ways. He sums up succinctly and precisely the truth behind the patriotic exhortations of the imperialists, and the poem is a parody, a reversal of a patriotic speech given by a general to his troops before their departure to a distant, unknown country with a fierce, difficult climate. This poem is unusual in Rimbaud's oeuvre and atypical in being so outspokenly political, but typical in its rage at hypocrisy and its striking juxtaposition of images, as well as in the precision and savagery of its language.

In Henri Fantin-Latour's 1871 painting, now in the musée d'Orsay, *Le coin de table* (The Corner of the Table), a group portrait of poets well known at the time, Arthur Rimbaud (1854–91) sits demurely and pensively at a table in the painting's lower left next to his lover, Paul Verlaine (1844–96), who does not look at anyone in the picture but appears to be gazing into the distance to the right. The painting shocked the bourgeois public of its day because it showed some of the most notorious decadents of the age in a very bourgeois setting and depicted them as if they were respectable citizens.

Rimbaud was anything but demure or respectable. He had a reputation as someone who rarely if ever washed and raised hell whenever he could. He was an anarchistic rebel against bourgeois conventional morality in all its hypocritical aspects, as he perceived them to be. From infancy on, he had suffered from his fanatical religious mother's withholding of her love and constant disapproval, so that from an early age he had felt unwanted and was full of rage, which overflowed into an iconoclastic revolt against her manipulation and control. No doubt in behaving so punishingly towards her son, she was punishing herself for the "sin" of conceiving him, and was deeply guilty about any pleasure she might have felt in the sexual act. His father was absent, having deserted the family, but had behaved brutally.

Verlaine had married a woman from a wealthy middle-class family with pretensions, and the marriage was a mistake. The moment he saw the handsome but unwashed country boy who admired his poetry and showed up alarmingly one day on his doorstep in the Montmartre section of Paris, he fell madly in love with him.

Rimbaud wanted to liberate himself, to smash through the taboos surrounding sexuality, to live fully. Their relationship was stormy, to say the least, and mad, obsessional, and passionate. They lived their passion to the full, and it spilled over into violence sometimes. Hard drinking, hard living, and drugs killed them both at early ages, but they lived in exhilaration and excitement that is given to few to experience. They embraced everything and threw themselves with mad abandon into all that life had to offer, living in poverty but throwing off the restraints of the constricted bourgeois life as much as they could, and shocking their families as well as society at large. They seem, in fact, to have been larger than life. We are now no longer shocked by most of their antics and practical jokes, and no longer look on them as an abomination but rather as pioneers of a new, less fettered morality. They were fundamentally amoral, rather than immoral, if morality meant wearing the shackles of religion, kowtowing to capitalism, and observing the niceties of social conventions and politeness. Ultimately, Verlaine—and this is reflected even in his poetry, great as he was—was more conventional than Rimbaud, whom he followed into adventures and who tended to lead him around and do as he liked with him, all the time refusing to admit that they were tied together, even though they obviously were.

In one of the strangest reverses in literary history, Rimbaud simply gave up everything at the age of twenty-one, refused ever again to acknowledge his own brilliant artistic achievements, and went to Africa, where he became a trader and a gunrunner. He never wrote another line of poetry or saw Verlaine again, and returned to France only to die, cared for at the end by his sister, who wanted to burn all his manuscripts, a crime that was happily prevented by Verlaine.

Speculation regarding this seemingly sudden change in his attitude and lifestyle has always been rife. But then Rimbaud was one of the stranger poets ever to have been around: very erratic, independent, and individual; a genius, a visionary poet who invented perceptions and transformed language. Truly striking in its imagery and ideas, his poetry is a hallmark of originality. Verlaine's poetry, too, is a landmark in literary history, and the two of them are considered among France's greatest nineteenth-century poets.

Christopher Hampton begins his play with the arrival of Rimbaud in Verlaine's Paris apartment, which actually belongs to his ultraconservative, staid bourgeois in-laws, who represent all that is stultifying and disapprovingly moralistic. Rimbaud is so seductive that Verlaine leaves his wife to be with him. The Oedipal connotations in the fatherless Rimbaud's motivations are quite clear. They fit perfectly with Verlaine's frustrated, addictive personality, and he attaches himself to Rimbaud in a masochistic way that John Bowlby might have described as anxious/ambivalent and Martha Welch as avoidant and disorganized. In fact, the way they were attached to each other was very complicated. The core of Hampton's play revolves around the portrayal of their style of attachment and the sadomasochistic relationship of the two men, and includes the mutual fear of abandonment that Reich says is at the heart of masochism.

Verlaine's long-suffering wife is also masochistic, as Hampton's writing makes clear. She is very much under the thumb or her autocratic, conventional, respectable parents, who belong to that category of people who dread what other people think of them. Even some of the other bohemian poets in Verlaine's circle are quite conventional, despite their seeming iconoclasm and flouting of middle-class values. This attitude is contrasted with that of Rimbaud in particular, who professes not to care at all and even to despise the opinions of the bourgeoisie, a social class from which he himself sprang, and who really is a breaker of images and an intellectual revolutionary until his change of heart. In the play, we do not see him after he has gone to take up a new life, and we are left with the impression, which may be historically accurate, that he has not really changed his attitudes, only his life. In any case, aside from his writing, he was not an active revolutionary advocating armed rebellion against the existing order.

The behavior of the two poets includes sadistic acting out, as when Verlaine shoots Rimbaud in the hand, mirroring the scene where Rimbaud, asking Verlaine to trust him, had stabbed Verlaine in both of his hands. These two men are violent, full of seemingly boundless rage. Rimbaud and Verlaine also have a histrionic side to their personalities based on a deep fear of sexuality, despite the fact that they act out their sexuality. But they feel so guilty about it that they have to punish themselves and each other. Verlaine remains intensely loyal to Rimbaud and to his feelings for him even after their final meeting in 1875 in Stuttgart, when Rimbaud, in order to escape from Verlaine, beats him up. In the final moments of the play, Verlaine rips up the visiting card that Rimbaud's religious, puritanical, repressed sister has given him. The card contains the address to which Verlaine has promised to send Rimbaud's manuscripts so that the sister and Rimbaud's mother can select those they deem suitable for publication. In Verlaine's gesture, we see that he intends to save and publish all the manuscripts, which he did.

The 1995 film with Leonardo DiCaprio particularly well cast as the bratty, hauntingly attractive boy genius Rimbaud—in certain shots he strikingly resembles the photographs of Rimbaud—and David Thewlis as Verlaine did not have a screenplay as good as the stage script. But the screen opens up the play to different locations and actions that are impossible in a stage production. They run through fields, get drunk in cafés, fight in the woods, or walk through the garden of the Palais Royal, near the Paris train stations, or through the streets of Montmartre. And we see Rimbaud in Africa. He is ill and being carried to the coast in a litter. The story of human suffering and guilt and of the eternal search for love and forgiveness is almost a modern myth, and remains powerfully moving on the screen, as it does on the stage.

Selected Bibliography

Acting and Theater

Adler, Stella. *The Technique of Acting.* With a foreword by Marlon Brando. New York: Bantam Books, 1988.

Blumenfeld, Robert. *Accents: A Manual for Actors.* Rev. and exp. ed. New York: Limelight, 2002.

———. *Acting with the Voice: The Art of Recording Books.* New York: Limelight, 2004.

Caine, Michael. *Acting in Film: An Actor's Take on Movie Making.* New York: Applause Theatre Books, 1990.

Carnovsky, Morris, with Peter Sander. *The Actor's Eye.* With a foreword by John Houseman. New York: Performing Arts Journal Publications, 1984.

Chekhov, Michael. *To the Actor on the Technique of Acting.* With a preface by Yul Brynner. New York: Harper & Row, 1953.

Funke, Lewis and John E. Booth. *Actors Talk About Acting.* 2 vols. New York: Avon Books, 1961. [Interviews with John Gielgud, Helen Hayes, Vivien Leigh, Morris Carnovsky, Shelley Winters, Bert Lahr, Sidney Poitier, Alfred Lunt, Lynn Fontanne, José Ferrer, Maureen Stapleton, Katherine Cornell, Paul Muni, Anne Bancroft.]

Garfield, David. *The Actors Studio: A Player's Place.* With a preface by Ellen Burstyn. New York: Macmillan Collier Books, 1984.

Hagen, Uta. *A Challenge for the Actor.* New York: Charles Scribner's Sons, 1991.

Hagen, Uta with Haskell Frankel. *Respect for Acting.* New York: Macmillan, 1973.

Joseph, B. L. *Elizabethan Acting.* 2nd ed. London: Oxford University Press, 1964.

Meisner, Sanford, and Dennis Longwell. *On Acting.* New York: Random House / Vintage Books, 1987.

Moore, Sonia. *Training an Actor: The Stanislavsky System in Class.* New York: Penguin Books, 1979.

Morris, Eric. *Being and Doing: A Workbook for Actors.* Los Angeles: Ermor Enterprises, 1998.

Sonenberg, Janet. *Dreamwork for Actors.* New York: Routledge, 2003.

Stanislavsky, Constantin. *An Actor Prepares.* Translated by Elizabeth Reynolds Hapgood. New York: Theatre Arts Books, 1969.

———. *My Life in Art.* Translated by J. J. Robbins. New York: World Publishing Co. / Meridian Books, 1966.

Strasberg, Lee. *A Dream of Passion.* New York: Penguin Plume Books, 1987.

Strasberg at the Actors Studio: Tape-Recorded Sessions. Edited and with an introduction by Robert H. Hethmon; preface by Burgess Meredith. New York: Theatre Communications Group, 1991.

Plays and Playwrights

Bloom, Harold. *Shakespeare: The Invention of the Human.* New York: Penguin Putnam, 1998.

Chekhov, Anton. *The Portable Chekhov.* Edited and with an introduction by Avrahm Yarmolimsky. New York: Penguin Books, 1947.

Ellmann, Richard. *Oscar Wilde.* New York: Alfred A. Knopf, 1988.

Faber, M. D. *The Design Within: Psychoanalytic Approaches to Shakespeare.* New York: Science House, 1970.

Holland, Merlin. *Irish Peacock and Scarlet Marquis: The Real Trial of Oscar Wilde.* New York: HarperCollins, 2003.

Ibsen, Henrik. *Eleven Plays.* With an introduction by H. L. Mencken. New York: Modern Library, 1948.

Jones, Ernest. *Hamlet and Oedipus.* New York: Doubleday & Co., 1949.

Kataev, Vladimir. *If Only We Could Know! An Interpretation of Chekhov.* Translated from the Russian and edited by Harvey Pitcher. Chicago: Ivan R. Dee, 2002.

Lelyveld, Toby. *Shylock on the Stage.* London: Routledge / Kegan Paul, 1961.

Rayfield, Donald. *Anton Chekhov: A Life.* New York: Henry Holt, 1997.

Senelick, Laurence. *The Chekhov Theatre: A Century of the Plays in Performance.* Cambridge: Cambridge University Press, 1997.

Shakespeare, William. *Hamlet,* A New Variorum Edition of Shakespeare. 2 vols. Edited by Horace Howard Furness. New York: Dover Publications, 1963.

———. *The Merchant of Venice,* A New Variorum Edition of Shakespeare. Edited by Horace Howard Furness. New York: Dover Publications, 1964.

Simmons, Ernest J. *Chekhov: A Biography.* Boston: Little, Brown & Co., 1962.

Sinsheimer, Hermann. *Shylock: The History of a Character.* New York: Citadel Press, 1964.

Stanislavsky, Constantin. *Stanislavsky Produces Othello.* Translated from the Russian by Dr. Helen Nowak. London: Godfrey Bles, 1948.

Strindberg, August. *Five Plays.* Translated and with an introduction by Harry G. Carlson. Berkeley: University of California Press, 1983.

Tucker, Kenneth. *Shakespeare and Jungian Typology: A Reading of the Plays*. London: McFarland and Company, 2003.

PSYCHOLOGY AND PSYCHOANALYSIS

Abraham, Karl. *Clinical Papers and Essays on Psycho-Analysis*. New York: Karnac Books, 1997.

Adler, Alfred. *Individual Psychology*. Paterson, NJ: Littlefield, Adams, 1963.

————. *The Individual Psychology of Alfred Adler: A Systematic Presentation in Selections from His Writings*. Edited by Heinz L. Ansbcher and Rowena R. Ansbacher. New York: Harper & Row, 1956.

Alexander, Franz, Thomas Morton French, et al. *Psychoanalytic Therapy*. New York: Ronald Press Company, 1946.

American Psychiatric Association. *Diagnostic and Statistical Manual of Mental Disorders*. Fourth Edition, Text Revision (*DSM-IV-TR*). Washington, DC: American Psychiatric Association, 2000.

Bateman, Anthony and Jeremy Holmes. *Introduction to Psychoanalysis: Contemporary Theory and Practice*. New York: Brunner-Routledge, 1995.

Benjamin, Jessica. *The Bonds of Love: Psychoanalysis, Feminism, and the Problem of Domination*. New York: Pantheon Books, 1988.

Bertin, Celia. *Marie Bonaparte*. Paris: Plon, 1999.

Bettelheim, Bruno. *Freud and Man's Soul*. New York: Random House, 1982.

————. *Freud's Vienna and Other Essays*. New York: Alfred A. Knopf, 1990.

Billig, Michael. *Freudian Repression: Conversation Creating the Unconscious*. Cambridge: Cambridge University Press, 1999.

Binswanger, Ludwig. *Being-in-the-World: Selected Papers of Ludwig Binswanger*. Translated and with a critical introduction to his existential psychoanalysis by Jacob Needleman. New York: Basic Books, 1963.

Book, Howard E. *How to Practice Brief Psychodynamic Psychotherapy: The Core Conflictual Relationship Theme Method*. With a foreword by Lester Luborsky. Washington, DC: American Psychological Association, 1998.

Bowlby, John. *Attachment and Loss*. 3 vols. Vol. 1, *Attachment and Loss*, 1969. Vol. 2, *Separation: Anxiety and Anger*, 1973. Vol. 3, *Loss: Sadness and Depression*, 1980. New York: Basic Books, 1969–1980.

Brehm, J. W. *A Theory of Psychological Reactance*. New York: Academic Press, 1966.

Brenner, Charles. *An Elementary Textbook of Psychoanalysis*. New York: Random House, 1974.

Brome, Vincent. *Freud and His Early Circle*. New York: William Morrow, 1967.

Cavalli-Sforza, Luigi Luca. *Genes, Peoples, and Languages*. New York: Farrar, Straus and Giroux, 2000.

Chasseguet-Smirgel, Janine, and Béla Grunberger. *Freud or Reich? Psychoanalysis and Illusion*. Translated by Claire Pajaczkowska. New Haven: Yale University Press, 1986.

Claire, Thomas. *Body Work.* New York: William Morrow, 1995.

Cocks, Geoffrey. *Psychotherapy in the Third Reich: The Göring Institute.* New York: Oxford University Press, 1985.

Deutsch, Helene. *Neurosis and Character Types: Clinical Psychoanalytic Studies.* New York: International Universities Press, 1965.

————. *Psychoanalysis of the Sexual Functions of Women.* Edited by Paul Roazen. New York: Karnac Books, 1991.

Dewan, Mantosh J., Brett N. Steenbarger, and Roger P. Greenberg. *The Art and Science of Brief Psychotherapies: A Practitioner's Guide.* Washington, DC: American Psychiatric Publishing, 2004.

Erickson, Erik H. *Childhood and Society.* New York: W. W. Norton & Company, 1963.

Evans, Dylan. *An Introductory Dictionary of Lacanian Psychoanalysis.* New York: Brunner-Routledge, 1996.

Fagan, Joen and Irma Lee Shepherd, eds. *What Is Gestalt Therapy?* New York: Harper & Row, 1970.

Fairbairn, W. R. D. *Psychoanalytic Studies of the Personality.* London: Routledge, 1990.

Fenichel, Otto. *The Psychoanalytic Theory of Neurosis.* New York: W. W. Norton & Company, 1945.

Ferenczi, Sándor. *Thalassa: A Theory of Genitality.* Translated by Henry Alden Bunker. Albany, NY: The Psychoanalytic Quarterly, 1938.

Festinger, Leon. *A Theory of Cognitive Dissonance.* Evanston, IL: Row, Peterson, 1957.

Fisher, Seymour, and Roger P. Greenberg. *Freud Scientifically Reappraised: Testing the Theories and Therapy.* New York: John Wiley and Sons, 1996.

Frankl, Viktor E. *Man's Search for Meaning: An Introduction to Logotherapy.* 3rd ed. New York: Simon and Schuster, 1984.

Freud, Anna. *The Writings of Anna Freud.* 8 vols. Vol. 2, *The Ego and Its Mechanisms of Defense* (Orig. pub. 1936). Vol. 6, *Normality and Pathology in Childhood: Assessments of Development* (Orig. pub. 1965). Vol. 8, *Psychoanalytic Psychology of Normal Development* (Orig. pub. 1980). New York: International Universities Press, 1965–81.

Freud, Sigmund. *The Basic Writings of Sigmund Freud,* Translated and edited by A. A. Brill. *Psychopathology of Everyday Life; The Interpretation of Dreams; Three Contributions to the Theory of Sex; Wit and Its Relations to the Unconscious; Totem and Taboo; The History of the Psychoanalytic Movement.* New York: The Modern Library, 1995.

————. *Civilization and Its Discontents.* Translated from the German and edited by James Strachey. New York: W. W. Norton & Company, 1961.

————. *Collected Papers.* 5 vols. Edited by Ernest Jones. London: The Hogarth Press / Institute of Psycho-Analysis, 1950.

————. *The Future of an Illusion.* Translated by W. D. Robson Scott. New York: Doubleday, 1953.

————. *Leonardo da Vinci: A Study in Psychosexuality* (Orig. pub. 1910). Translated by Dr. A. A. Brill. New York: Random House, 1947.

————. *Moses and Monotheism.* Translated by Katherine Jones. New York: Vintage Books, 1939.

——. *The Standard Edition of the Complete Psychological Works of Sigmund Freud.* Translated under the general editorship of James Strachey in collaboration with Anna Freud, assisted by Alix Strachey and Alan Tyson. 24 vols. Vol. 20, *An Autobiographical Study* (Orig. pub. 1925). Vol. 18, *Beyond the Pleasure Principle* (Orig. pub.1920). Vol. 19, *The Ego and the Id* (Orig. pub. 1923). Vol. 18, *Group Psychology and the Analysis of the Ego* (Orig. pub. 1921). Vol. 20, *Inhibitions, Symptoms and Anxiety* (Orig. pub. 1926). Vols. 15, 16, *Introductory Lectures on Psycho-Analysis* (Orig. pub. 1917). Vol. 22, *New Introductory Lectures on Psycho-Analysis* (Orig. pub. 1933). Vol. 23, *An Outline of Psycho-Analysis* (Orig. pub. 1940). Vol. 20, *The Question of Lay Analysis* (Orig. pub. 1926). New York: W. W. Norton & Company, 1953–74.

——. *Three Case Histories: The "Wolf Man," The "Rat Man" and the Psychotic Doctor Schreber.* New York: Collier Books, 1973.

——. *Writings on Art and Literature.* In *The Standard Edition.* Edited by James Strachey. Stanford, CA: Stanford University Press, 1997.

Freud, Sigmund, and Ludwig Binswanger. *Correspondence, 1908–38.* Edited by Gerhard Fichtner. New York: Other Press, 2003.

Freud, Sigmund and Joseph Breuer. *Studies in Hysteria.* Translated by Nicola Luckhurst. New York: Penguin Books, 2004.

Freud, Sigmund and Ernest Jones. *The Complete Correspondence of Sigmund Freud and Ernest Jones: 1908–1939.* Cambridge, MA: Harvard University Press, 1993.

Friedman, Richard C., and Jennifer I. Downey. *Sexual Orientation and Psychoanalysis: Sexual Science and Clinical Practice.* New York: Columbia University Press, 2002.

Friedman, Susan Stanford, ed. *Analyzing Freud: Letters of H. D., Bryher, and Their Circle.* New York: New Directions, 2002.

Gabbard, Glen O. *Long-Term Psychodynamic Psychotherapy: A Basic Text.* Washington, DC: American Psychiatric Publishing, 2004.

Gay, Peter. *Freud: A Life for Our Time.* New York: W. W. Norton & Company, 1988.

Gilman, Sander. *Freud, Race and Gender.* Princeton, NJ: Princeton University Press, 1993.

Goffman, Erving. *Behavior in Public Places: Notes on the Social Organization of Gatherings.* New York: The Free Press, 1963.

——. *Forms of Talk.* Philadelphia: Pennsylvania University Press, 1981.

——. *Interaction Ritual: Essays on Face to Face Behavior.* New York: Pantheon Books, 1967.

——. *The Presentation of Self in Everyday Life.* New York: Anchor Books, Doubleday, 1959.

Greenacre, Phyllis. *Emotional Growth: Psychoanalytic Studies of the Gifted and a Great Variety of Other Individuals.* 2 vols. New York: International Universities Press, 1971.

Groddeck, Georg Walther. *The Book of the It.* Authorized translation by V. M. E. Collins. New York: Vintage Books, 1961.

——. *The Meaning of Illness: Selected Psychoanalytic Writings, Including His Correspondence with Sigmund Freud.* London: Maresfield Library, 1970.

Horney, Karen. *The Neurotic Personality of Our Time*. New York: W. W. Norton & Company, 1937.

Jacobson, Edith. *Depression: Comparative Studies of Normal, Neurotic and Psychotic Conditions*. New York: International Universities Press, 1971.

James, William. *The Principles of Psychology* (Orig. pub. 1900). New York: Dover, 1950.

Johnson, Stephen M. *Character Styles*. New York: W. W. Norton & Company, 1994.

Jones, Ernest. *Sigmund Freud: His Life and Work*. 3 vols. New York: Basic Books, 1953, 1955, 1957.

Jung, Carl Gustav. *The Collected Works of C. G. Jung*. 20 vols. Vol. 5, *Symbols of Transformation* (Orig. pub. 1952). Vol. 6, *Psychological Types* (Orig. pub. 1921). Vol. 9, Part 1, *The Archetypes and the Collective Unconscious* (Orig. pub. 1959). Princeton, NJ: Princeton University Press, 1953–79.

———. *Man and His Symbols*. New York: Dell, 1997.

———. *Memories, Dreams, Reflections*. New York: Pantheon, 1963; VintageBooks, 1989.

———. *Philosophical Reflections: An Anthology of the Writings of C. G. Jung*. Edited by Jolande Jacobi. New York: Harper & Row, 1961.

———. *Psychology of Dementia Praecox* (Orig. pub. 1907). Princeton, NJ: Bollingen / Princeton University Press, 1974.

Klein, Melanie. *The Selected Melanie Klein*. Edited by Juliet Mitchell. New York: The Free Press, 1986.

Kohut, Heinz. *The Analysis of the Self*. New York: International Universities Press, 1971.

Krafft-Ebing, Richard von. *Psychopathia Sexualis* (Orig. pub. 1886). New York: Bell Publishing Co., 1965.

Lacan, Jacques. *The Four Fundamental Concepts of Psycho-Analysis*. Translated from the French by Alan Sheridan. New York: W. W. Norton & Company, 1981.

Laing, R. D. *The Divided Self: An Existential Study in Sanity and Madness*. Baltimore: Penguin Books, 1965.

Lane, Christopher, ed. *The Psychoanalysis of Race*. New York: Columbia University Press, 1998.

Langer, Lawrence L. *Holocaust Testimonies: The Ruins of Memory*. New Haven, CT: Yale University Press, 1991.

Laplanche, Jean, and Jean-Bertand Pontalis. *The Language of Psycho-Analysis*. Translated by Donald Nicholson-Smith. New York: W. W. Norton & Company, 1973.

Lear, Jonathan. *Open Minded: Working Out the Logic of the Soul*. Cambridge, MA: Harvard University Press, 1998.

———. *Freud*. New York: Routledge, 2005.

Levi, Primo. *The Drowned and the Saved*, rep. ed.. New York: Vintage Books, 1989.

———. *Survival in Auschwitz*, rep. ed. New York: Touchstone, 1995.

Lewes, Kenneth. *The Psychoanalytic Theory of Male Homosexuality*. New York: Simon and Schuster, 1988.

Maidenbaum, Aryeh, ed. *Jung and the Shadow of Anti-Semitism: Collected Essays.* Berwick, ME: Nicolas-Hays, 2002.

Maslow, Abraham H. *Motivation and Personality.* New York: Harper and Brothers, 1954.

Masson, Jeffrey Mousaieff, ed. and trans. *The Complete Letters of Sigmund Freud to Wilhelm Fliess, 1887–1904.* Cambridge, MA: Harvard University Press, 1985.

May, Rollo. *The Discovery of Being.* New York: W. W. Norton & Company, 1983.

———. *Freedom and Destiny.* New York: W. W. Norton & Company, 1981.

———. *Love and Will.* New York: Delta, 1989.

McLynn, Frank. *Carl Gustav Jung.* New York: St. Martin's Press, 1996.

McWilliams, Nancy. *Psychoanalytic Case Formation.* New York: Guilford Press, 1999.

———. *Psychoanalytic Diagnosis.* New York: Guilford Press, 1994.

———. *Psychoanalytic Psychotherapy.* New York: Guilford Press, 2004.

Miale, Florence R., and Michael Selzer. *The Nuremberg Mind: The Psychology of the Nazi Leaders.* With an introduction by Gustave M. Gilbert. New York: Quadrangle / New York Times Book Company, 1975.

Miller, Alice. *The Drama of the Gifted Child* (formerly *Prisoners of Childhood*). Translated from the German by Ruth Ward. New York: Basic Books, 1981.

———. *Thou Shalt Not Be Aware: Society's Betrayal of the Child.* Translated by Hildegarde and Hunter Hannum. New York: Farrar, Straus, Giroux, 1984.

Mitchell, Stephen A., and Margaret Black. *Freud and Beyond: A History of Modern Psychoanalytic Thought.* New York: Basic Books, 1995.

Monte, Christopher F., and Robert N. Sollod. *Beneath the Mask: An Introduction to Theories of Personality,* 7th ed. New York: Wiley, 2003.

Moore, Burness E., and Bernard D. Fine, eds. *Psychoanalytic Terms and Concepts.* New Haven: The American Psychoanalytic Association / Yale University Press, 1990.

Perls, Fritz. *Gestalt Therapy Verbatim.* New York: Bantam Books, 1969.

Phillips, Adam. *Winnicott.* Cambridge, MA: Harvard University Press, 1988.

Pinker, Steven. *The Language Instinct: How the Mind Creates Language.* New York: HarperCollins, 1994.

Rachman, Arnold William. *Sándor Ferenczi: The Psychotherapist of Tenderness and Passion.* Northvale, NJ: Jason Aronson, 1997.

Rank, Otto. *Beyond Psychology.* New York: Dover, 1941.

Reber, Arthur S., and Emily S. *Penguin Dictionary of Psychology,* 3rd ed. New York: Penguin Books, 2001.

Reich, Ilse Ollendorf. *Wilhelm Reich: A Personal Biography.* New York: Avon, 1970.

Reich, Peter. *A Book of Dreams.* New York: Harper and Row, 1973.

Reich, Wilhelm. *Character Analysis,* 3rd ed. New York: Farrar, Straus and Cudahy, 1949.

———. *The Impulsive Character and Other Writings.* Translated by Barbara G. Koopman. New York: New American Library, 1974.

———. *The Mass Psychology of Fascism.* Translated by Vincent R. Carfagno. New York: Farrar, Straus and Giroux, 1970.

———. *Reich Speaks of Freud.* New York: Farrar, Straus and Giroux, 1967.

———. *The Sexual Revolution: Toward a Self-Governing Character Structure.* New York: Farrar, Straus and Giroux, 1962.

Reik, Theodor. *From Thirty Years with Freud.* Translated by Richard Winston. New York: International Universities Press, 1949.

———. *Listening with the Third Ear.* New York: Farrar, Straus and Company, 1948.

———. *The Secret Self: Psychoanalytic Experiences in Life and Literature.* New York: Farrar, Straus and Young, 1953.

Ridley, Matt. *Genome: The Autobiography of a Species in Twenty-three Chapters.* New York: HarperCollins, 2000.

Robb, Graham. *Strangers: Homosexuality in the Nineteenth Century.* New York: W. W. Norton & Company, 2004.

Róheim, Géza. *Psychoanalysis and Anthropology.* New York: International Universities Press, 1950.

Roland, Alan. *Cultural Pluralism and Psychoanalysis: The Asian and North American Experience.* New York: Routledge, 1996.

Rubenfeld, Ilana. *The Listening Hand: Self-Healing Through the Rubenfeld Synergy Method of Talk and Touch.* New York: Bantam Books, 2000.

Sandler, Joseph, Alex Holder, Christopher Dare, and Anna Ursula Dreher. *Freud's Models of the Mind: An Introduction.* Madison, CT: International Universities Press, 1997.

Sartre, Jean-Paul. *Being and Nothingness: An Essay on Phenomenological Ontology.* Translated and with an introduction by Hazel E. Barnes. New York: Philosophical Library, 1956.

Sayers, Janet. *Mothers of Psychoanalysis: Helene Deutsch, Karen Horney, Anna Freud, Melanie Klein.* New York: W. W. Norton & Company, 1991.

Schur, Max. *Freud: Living and Dying.* Madison, CT: International Universities Press, 1972.

Shapiro, David. *Autonomy and Rigid Character.* New York: Basic Books, 1981.

———. *Dynamics of Character: Self-Regulation in Psychopathology.* New York: Basic Books, 2000.

———. *Neurotic Styles.* New York: Basic Books, 1999.

———. *Psychotherapy of Neurotic Character.* New York: Basic Books, 1999.

Sharp, Daryl. *Personality Types: Jung's Model of Typology.* Toronto: Inner City Books, 1987.

Sullivan, Harry Stack. *Clinical Studies in Psychiatry.* New York: W. W. Norton & Company, 1956.

———. *The Interpersonal Theory of Psychiatry.* New York: W. W. Norton & Company, 1953.

———. *The Psychiatric Interview.* New York: W. W. Norton & Company, 1970.

Tomkins, Silvan S. *Affect Imagery Consciousness.* 4 vols. Vol. 1, *The Positive Affects* (Orig. pub. 1962). Vol. 2, *The Negative Affects* (Orig. pub. 1963). Vol. 3, *The Negative Affects: Anger and Fear* (Orig. pub. 1991). Vol. 4, *Cognition* (Orig. pub. 1992). New York: Springer Publishing Company, 1962–92.

Wehr, Gerhard. *Jung: A Biography.* Translated from the German by David M. Weeks. Boston: Shambhala, 1987.

Winnicott, D. W. *Playing and Reality.* London: Tavistock, 1971.

———. *Psycho-Analytic Explorations.* Edited by Clare Winnicott, Ray Shepherd, and Madeleine Davis. Cambridge, MA: Harvard University Press, 1989.

Yalom, Irvin D. *Existential Psychotherapy.* New York: Basic Books, 1980.

Young-Bruehl, Elizabeth. *The Anatomy of Prejudices.* Cambridge, MA: Harvard University Press, 1996.

———. *Anna Freud: A Biography.* New York: Summit Books, 1988.

Literary Works, Literary Biographies, and Criticism

Bonaparte, Marie. *The Life and Works of Edgar Allan Poe: A Psycho-Analytic Interpretation.* With a foreword by Sigmund Freud. London: Imago, 1949.

Carter, William. *Marcel Proust: A Life.* New Haven: Yale University Press, 2000.

Fuss, Diana. *The Sense of an Interior: Four Writers and the Rooms That Shaped Them.* New York: Routledge, 2004. [What the rooms where they lived and wrote meant for Sigmund Freud, Marcel Proust, Helen Keller, and Emily Dickinson.]

Haddon, Mark. *The Curious Incident of the Dog in the Night-Time.* New York: Doubleday, 2003.

Hamilton, Edith. *Mythology.* New York: Little, Brown & Company, 1940.

Lever, Maurice. *Sade: A Biography.* New York: Harvest Books, 1994.

Moran, Martin. *The Tricky Part: One Boy's Fall from Trespass into Grace.* Boston: Beacon Press, 2005.

Proust, Marcel. *In Search of Lost Time.* Translation of *A la recherche du temps perdu* by C. K. Scott Moncrieff and Terence Kilmartin, revised by D. J. Enright. 6 vols. New York: The Modern Library, 1992.

———. *Swann's Way.* Translated and with an introduction and notes by Lydia Davis. New York: Viking, 2002.

Robb, Graham. *Rimbaud: A Biography.* New York: W. W. Norton & Company, 2000.

Sedgewick, Eve Kossofsky. *The Epistemology of the Closet.* Berkeley: University of California Press, 1990.

List of Films and Television Series

List of Plays

ABOUT THE AUTHOR

*R*obert Blumenfeld, author of *Accents: A Manual for Actors* (Limelight, revised and expanded edition, 2002) and *Acting with the Voice: The Art of Recording Books* (Limelight, 2004) lives and works as an actor, dialect coach, and writer in New York City. He studied acting with Alice Spivak and, more briefly, with Uta Hagen. Mr. Blumenfeld has recorded more than 290 talking books for the American Foundation for the Blind. As an actor, he has worked in numerous regional and New York theaters. He created the roles of the Marquis of Queensberry and two prosecuting attorneys in Moisés Kaufman's off-Broadway hit play *Gross Indecency: The Three Trials of Oscar Wilde* and was also the production's dialect coach. Among his favorite roles are the Lord Chancellor in Gilbert and Sullivan's *Iolanthe* and Sir Joseph Porter in *H.M.S. Pinafore* for Dorothy Raedler's American Savoyards; Norman in Ronald Harwood's *The Dresser* at ACT Seattle; and in Chekhov's plays: Kulygin in *Three Sisters,* Waffles in *Uncle Vanya,* the Old Actor in *Swan Song,* Smirnov in *The Boor,* and Nyoukhin in *On the Harmfulness of Tobacco.* Mr. Blumenfeld received the 1997 Canadian National Institute for the Blind's Torgi Award for the Talking Book of the Year in the fiction category, for his recording of Pat Conroy's *Beach Music;* and the 1999 Alexander Scourby Talking Book Narrator of the Year Award in the fiction category. He holds a B.A. in French from Rutgers University and an M.A. in French Language and Literature from Columbia University. At Rutgers he completed his Ph.D. courses in Comparative Literature. He also speaks Italian and German, and has a smattering of Yiddish, Spanish, and Russian.